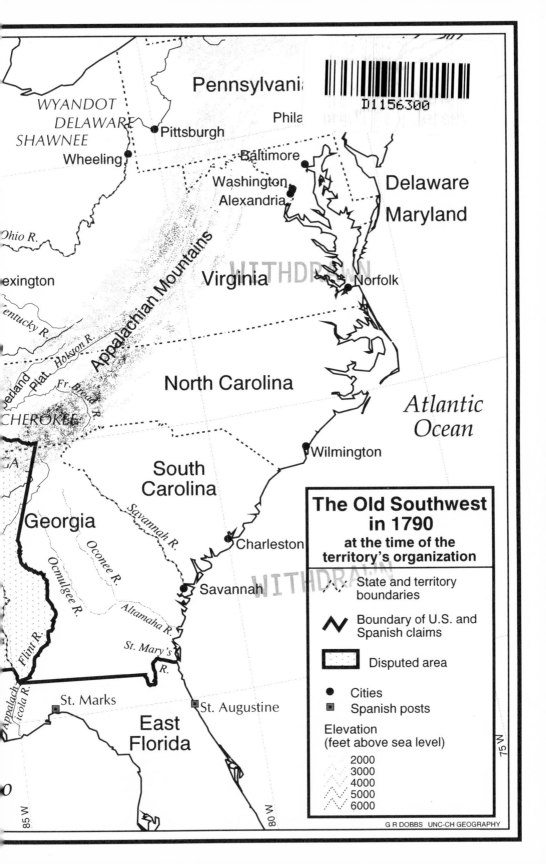

Pennsylvania

D1156300

WYANDOT
DELAWARE
SHAWNEE
● Pittsburgh

Phila

● Baltimore
Washington
Alexandria

Delaware

Maryland

● Wheeling

Ohio R.

exington

Virginia

Norfolk

entucky R.

Holston R.

Appalachian Mountains

North Carolina

Atlantic
Ocean

Plat.
erland

Fr. Broad R.

CHEROKEE

A

Wilmington

South
Carolina

Georgia

Savannah R.

Oconee R.

Ocmulgee R.

Charleston

Savannah

The Old Southwest
in 1790
**at the time of the
territory's organization**

State and territory
boundaries

Boundary of U.S. and
Spanish claims

Disputed area

Altamaha R.

Flint R.

*St. Mary's
R.*

*Appalach
icola R.*

St. Marks

St. Augustine

East
Florida

● Cities

▣ Spanish posts

Elevation
(feet above sea level)

2000
3000
4000
5000
6000

75 W

85 W

80 W

G R DOBBS   UNC-CH GEOGRAPHY

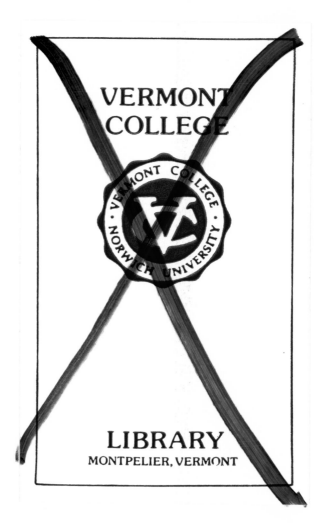

The First Impeachment:
The Constitution's Framers
and the Case of
Senator William Blount

William Blount

The First Impeachment:
The Constitution's Framers
and the Case of
Senator William Blount

Buckner F. Melton, Jr.

Mercer University Press
Macon, Georgia
1998

ISBN 0-86554-597-9
MUP/ H449

Mercer University Press
6316 Peake Road
Macon, Georgia 31210-3960
1998

Second printing February 1999

The paper used in this publication meets the minimum
requirements of American National Standard for
Permanence of Paper for Printed Library Materials.

The quotation on p. 263 is from
John Milton, *Paradise Lost*, Book XII.

Book design by Marc A. Jolley
Printed by McNaughton & Gunn, Inc.
Jacket design by Jim Burt
Jacket produced by Phoenix Color

Library of Congress Cataloging-in-Publication Data

Melton, Buckner F.
The first impeachment: the constitution's framers
and the case of senator William Blount
p. cm.
Includes bibliographical references and index.
ISBN 0-86554-597-9 (alk. paper)
1. Blount, William, 1749-1800—Impeachment.
2. Impeachments—United States—18th century.
3. Constitutional history—United States.
4. United States—Politics and government—1783-1809.
I. Title.
KF4961.B58M45 1998
342.73'068—dc21
98-9236
CIP

Table of Contents

Illustrations

Frontispiece: William Blount.

Illustrations, following p. xiv.

Hugh Williamson, William Blount, William Richardson Davie, Richard Dobbs Spaight, and Alexander Martin (center).

Alexander James Dallas. Courtesy of The Historical Society of Pennsylvania.

Timothy Pickering. Courtesy of The National Portrait Gallery, Smithsonian Instituition.

Aaron Burr. Courtsey of The Historical Society of Pennsylvania.

Carlos Martinex de Yrujo. The Historical Society of Pennsylvania.

William Eaton. The Historical Society of Pennsylvania.

Samuel Sitgreaves. The Historical Society of Pennsylvania.

James A. Bayard. The Historical Society of Pennsylvania.

Robert Goodloe Harper. The Historical Society of Pennsylvania.

Jared Ingersoll. The Historical Society of Pennsylvania.

Preface

What follows is a twofold tale of discovery: the first, a story of ventures on the old frontier; the second, a chronicle of the nation's foray, spawned by these events, into new constitutional territory.

I first learned of Mercer University Press's intention to publish this book exactly two centuries, almost to the day, after the House of Representatives voted to impeach Senator William Blount. I experienced the usual satisfaction that a writer feels at hearing such news, having worked on this project on and off for a decade, but I was also particularly pleased that at last, after two hundred years, a relatively full account of that vote of impeachment and its results was about to come to light.

For these two centuries, historians have ignored the story of how Congress handled this episode. The tale of the Blount Conspiracy, the strange plot that prompted the impeachment, is notorious in the annals of American frontier history, though it has never ranked in importance with such national political developments as Jay's Treaty, the XYZ affair, and the Alien and Sedition Acts. But the impeachment itself has languished, a prisoner of the archives and the manuscript rooms, despite the ready availability of many of its key sources. When frontier historians mention it, they usually do so as an aside, for their concern is with the conspiracy and the West, that mysterious land lying beyond the Smoky Mountains; when political and constitutional historians address it, they are perfunctory in their treatment. The reader can find books on the impeachments of Samuel Chase and Andrew Johnson, as well as upon the near-impeachment of Richard M. Nixon, but only pages about other impeachments, including Blount's. No one has seemed to realize that as Blount and other frontiersmen explored and advanced into the West, they also occasioned the federal government's similar exploration of new consitutional issues, both dangers and possibilities alike.

Even when researchers do pull forth the records of the Blount affair into the light of day, to examine them briefly before thrusting them back into their musty tombs, something about the episode misleads them in ways at once both elementary and essential. One scholar, for instance, recently declared that Representative John Adams brought the impeachment against Blount, when in fact Adams, never a representative, was President at the time. Another has stated that the Senate failed to decide the issue of the Sixth Amendment's applicability to the impeachment process; this, too, is wrong. Others variously identify Blount as a senator from Ohio, or Georgia, when in fact he was a native of North Carolina who served as a senator from the state of Tennessee. Even as the impeachment was underway it worked its strange enchantment; Rufus King, American Minister to the Court of St. James, wrote to English Foreign Minister William, Lord Grenville in 1797 identifying the reprobate not as William Blount but instead as his brother Thomas Blount, a North Carolina representative.[1] This list could go on until it reached a surprising length, but by now the point should be clear.

The obscurity of Blount's tale is puzzling, especially when one realizes the striking similarities it bears to the Chase impeachment and especially to the Burr Conspiracy and treason trial, each of which has a more prominent place in the annals of American constitutional and political history than its 1790s forerunner. In view of these similarities, the question becomes compelling: Why has this impeachment drawn so little attention, especially when the events surrounding it are as dramatic as the Chase and Johnson episodes, and more so than any other impeachments that we have yet witnessed? A possible answer lies in the perceived importance of the impeachment process itself. Rather than becoming the national inquest, as Alexander Hamilton wrote in the sixty-fifth number of *The Federalist*, into the conduct of public men, impeachment has developed into a pedestrian device for removing a handful of the throng of federal judges to have occupied the nation's benches when their conduct has gone beyond the pale. Individual impeachments, such as that of a president or a Supreme Court justice, spark some attention, but the overall triviality of the process has for the most part tended to infect scholars' assessment of individual episodes, blinding them to the importance that impeachment sometimes assumes and drawing the record of those earlier impeachments into obscurity.

This is a strange, and possibly a dangerous, development. Anyone with personal memories of Watergate can recall something of the

---

[1] Rufus King to Lord Grenville, 28 August 1797, *in* 2 Charles R. King, *The Life and Correspondence of Rufus King* (New York: G.P. Putnam's Sons, 1895) 216.

gravity that impeachment may entail, though it seems mundane enough—mercifully—most of the time. Both historians and common law legists should realize that a key premise of their respective disciplines is that theory is born of experience, that action precedes idea. As John Adams and others before him noted, "Facts are stubborn things." To ignore or overlook an impeachment because of a sense that impeachments by definition lack importance is to enslave facts to theory. In scientific terms, it amounts to drawing a line on the graph, and then plotting the data points; in Macaulay's, it casts facts in the mold of the hypothesis.[2]

Impeachment's drab reputation is not the only reason, however, why scholars have neglected the eastern half of the Blount story, though they have sometimes written of the western half. Perhaps, one might argue, the Blount impeachment accomplished nothing. Perhaps, together with the ensuing impeachment of the insane judge John Pickering and the abortive attempt to neutralize the vitriolic justice Samuel Chase, it even gave birth to the notion that the process was trivial. The latter point is just another case of drawing the line before plotting the points, since no one has examined the Blount impeachment closely enough to decide one way or another how trivial it was, either for the individuals involved or for succeeding generations.

As for accomplishing nothing, quite the contrary is true. Besides what befell Blount and his designs, the constitutional developments that resulted from the episode remain with us today, although we would benefit from a more thorough knowledge of them. Some of these developments were positive, in the sense of helping to shape what powers the Congress could and would exercise; others were negative, in the sense of determining what powers it either could not or would not exercise. The latter developments are just as important as the former, if only to help us to contemplate how our government might otherwise have evolved, and thus to understand more thoroughly the governmental system that did result. Whatever the outcome, the Blount impeachment often raised fundamental questions, and sometimes provided dispositive answers to those constitutional questions. Among these are the relationship between

---

[2]Thomas Babington Macaulay, Review, "The Romance of History," 47 *Edinburgh Rev.* 331, 331 (1828).

the impeachment and the expulsion powers; the nature of civil–military relations; the extent of the unwritten congressional investigatory power; the relationship between House and Senate; the nature of the "office" of senator, and by implication that of a representative; the possibility of the existence not only of a federal common law of crimes, but of an American *lex Parliamenti*, a supreme judicial law of Congress that lay beyond the cognizance of both state and federal courts; and the incorporation of the principles of the law of nations into the American constitutional system. This is quite a list, and all the more impressive when one realizes that many of the men who spoke or wrote about them during the course of Blount's impeachment had served in the Philadelphia Convention or one of the state ratifying conventions.

The impeachment, of course, settled some constitutional issues, but on the whole it spawned at least as many questions as it answered, and as the above list shows, many of them are of the speculative sort. Such questions are important; asking them, indulging in the game of "What would have happened if ...." is a useful process for historians, but playing it should not become their sole preoccupation. As for what did happen to the Constitution and to the development of the federal government as a result of the Blount Conspiracy, the reader will find that story in the following chapters.[3] It is not quite a tale of lost innocence: Blount himself certainly knew that he was playing with fire, and what might happen if the wrong people learned of his plans. By 1797 too the generation of the founders had learned (as it had probably expected anyway) that the brief document that had come out of Philadelphia a decade earlier would assume a life of its own and lead the American governmental system in directions that its authors might not have foreseen. But few, if any, of the preceding constitutional developments grew out of quite the same sense of gravity that accompanied Blount's exposure. In that sense, the Blount impeachment was one of the first major tests of how the Constitution would evolve in moments of crisis and under great political pressures. Far greater crises awaited in the future; but Blount's was one of the

---

[3]The Prologue and Chapter 1 comprise a theoretical discussion of constitutional interpretation and the underpinnings of Congress's impeachment power; the reader who wishes to proceed directly to the narrative of the Blount Conspiracy and impeachment should begin reading at Chapter 2.

first, if not the first, of them all.

When I began to study the Blount impeachment, I approached it from the perspective of a constitutional historian. Supposing constitutional history to consist of theory and doctrine, I eventually learned the full truth of Holmes's statement that "The life of the law has not been logic; it has been experience." The Blount impeachment, and its effects, resulted from circumstances far removed from what one may have heard in the inns of court in the 1700s, or what one may read to this day in the pages of Blackstone. To understand the full meaning of those effects I had to study their causes, and the context from which they emerged; to do this I had to move beyond the confines of constitutional abstraction and into the realms of frontier, political, and diplomatic history, going so far as to teach courses in the latter two subjects as well as in my own field. (I also married a military historian, who came equipped with an expert's knowledge of grand strategy and the Napoleonic era, not to mention an excellent personal library.) While I would be exaggerating were I to write that I thereby became a specialist in these other areas of history, or that I pursued any of these objects merely to produce this book, all of the above measures proved helpful. Of equal importance, however, have been the many individuals I have encountered in the course of this project who have been willing to help. I wish to express my particular thanks to Professors Clark R. Cahow, Robert F. Durden, I.B. Holley, Jr., and Charles R. Young of the Department of History of Duke University; Professor Peter G. Fish of Duke's Political Science Department and Law School; Stuart Basefsky of Cornell University; Dean Judith W. Wegner and Professors John V. Orth and A.M. Weisburd of the School of Law of The University of North Carolina at Chapel Hill; Justice Willis P. Whichard of the Supreme Court of North Carolina; Vicki Arnold, Amie Barto, Griffin Bell, Renée Gordon, Kathryn Sherer Hart, R. Kent Newmyer, Zachary Perryman, Charles Singleton, Leigh M. Singleton, James Summerville; and, by no means least, Steven J. Melamut.

To all of these people, and to the many others who assisted me, I offer my thanks, while simultaneously acquitting them of all responsibility for any errors or omissions that appear in these pages. That responsibility is mine alone.

Finally, I wish to thank my parents and my wife, without whose love, patience, and support I could never have begun, much less completed, this project. To them I dedicate this book.

Buckner F. Melton, Jr.
1 October 1997

As I note in the main preface, I began work on this book over a decade ago. The manuscript was well into the galley stage last year when Monica Lewinsky's name first came to public attention, beginning what eventually became the first impeachment of an elected American president. This timing was either chance or fate; it certainly was not prescience on my part. I have often said, though only half in earnest, that historians should never try to predict the future. I certainly could never have foretold the events of the previous year, events that are still unfolding as I write this new foreword.

But though I can take neither blame nor credit for the timing of the book, I have become the beneficiary of that timing. Largely because of what I have written here, I have found myself a player, if only a very minor one, in the current proceedings. Since early 1998 I have consulted often with several members of the House Judiciary Committee on both sides of the aisle; other members of both House and Senate; a few of the House managers and their staffs; and a great many members of local and national news agencies.

I wish here to thank all who, in Washington and elsewhere, have taken an interest in what I have written, particularly those in government and media circles who have lately given me an invaluable education in the ways of Congress and the news business, particularly Bill Johnstone, Ted Kalo, Mike Platt, Richard Ray, Robert L. Steed, Tom Swanson, and Christian Walters. I renew my thanks to Judge Griffin B. Bell, Professor R. Kent Newmyer, and Dr. James Summerville. I am also happy to have the opportunity to thank the faculty and staff members of the School of Law at the University of North Carolina at Chapel Hill for the valuable time and counsel that they have so freely shared with me in the last half-year. Finally I give my thanks to Mercer University, to Mercer University Press, and, as always, to my wife and parents for their support.

Buckner F. Melton, Jr.

27 January 1998

Seest thou yon dreary Plain, forlorn and wilde,
The seat of desolation, voyd of light,
Save what the glimmering of these livid flames
Casts pale and dreadful? Thither let us tend
From off the tossing of these fiery waves,
There rest, if any rest can harbour there,
And reassembling our afflicted Powers,
Consult how we may henceforth most offend
Our Enemy, our own loss how repair,
How overcome this dire Calamity,
What reinforcement we may gain from Hope,
If not what resolution from despare.

Paradise Lost, Book 1

[T]he Defendant demurred, supposing the new act had barred this suit; but I overruled the demurrer; for . . . I had some reason to know the meaning of this law; for it had its first rise from me, who brought in the bill into the Lord's House, though it afterwards received some additions and improvements from the Judges and the civilians.

Lord Nottingham
Ash v. Abdy, 3 Swan's App. 664, 36 Eng. Rep. 1014 (Chancery 1678)

It will be remembered, the subject was new, this being the first impeachment under the Constitution, and a diversity of opinion, on the form of proceedings was to be expected . . . .

Connecticut Courant
21 August 1797

Clockwise from upper left: Hugh Williamson, William Blount, William Richardson Davie, Richard Dobbs Spaight, and Alexander Martin (center).

Alexander James Dallas

Timothy Pickering

Aaron Burr

Carlos Martinez de Yrujo

William Eaton

Samuel Sitgreaves

James A. Bayard

Robert Goodloe Harper

Jared Ingersoll

Prologue

Impeachment,
The Constitution,
and Original Intent

ॐ

In broad terms, what happened to Senator William Blount in 1797 was not the first impeachment. Even in the eighteenth century impeachment was an ancient part of English and American law, a process born bloodily in a day long before the dawn of modern times.

Perhaps the first impeachment may be said to have occurred in November 1330, early in the reign of Edward III, a young, and at first a powerless, monarch. In the preceding years, as civil war rocked English society, one Roger Mortimer, eighth Baron of Wigmore and first Earl of March, had involved himself in myriad intrigues. Imprisoned for treason in 1322 during the rule of Edward's father, that weak Plantagenet king Edward II, Mortimer escaped the Tower the following year, quit the realm, and found his way to France. There, taking the English king's wife Isabella as his own mistress, Mortimer helped her to raise an army, with which they returned to England in 1326.[1] Together the couple hunted down Edward and his two violent, acquisitive supporters the Despensers, Hugh the Elder and Hugh the Younger. The subsequent trial and execution of the elder Despenser, an "example of judicial murder," was not the last time that Mortimer arranged an enemy's death.[2] The Younger

---

[1]. May McKisack, *The Fourteenth Century 1307-1399* (Oxford: The Clarendon Press, 1959) 73, 81-83; 13 *Dictionary of National Biography* 1036-37.

[2]McKisack, *The Fourteenth Century* 82-86; 13 *Dictionary of National Biography* 1037. "The execution of Lancaster and of the rest of the Contrariants [in 1322] had made political murder or execution for treason (whichever way you

Despenser soon followed, and shortly thereafter Edward abdicated in favor of his son Edward III, spurred on by veiled threats that if he tried to retain the throne, the result might be a Plantagenet forfeiture and Mortimer's own assumption of the crown.[3] But even this concession was not enough, and some evidence suggests that Mortimer subsequently ordered the death of the monarch that he had helped to depose. The official announcement stated that natural causes had claimed the former king's life, but Edward II was young and robust, and according to legend, horrible screams came from the castle on the night he died. Whatever Mortimer's involvement in that affair, he continued to gain ever more titles, riches, power, and prestige, piling estate on estate and office on office, completely overshadowing the young new king, Edward III.[4]

For three years this state of things continued, but by 1330 Edward, together with Mortimer's enemies, had had enough of his errant nobleman. On the evening of October 19 he joined an armed party that had entered Nottingham Castle through a secret passage. The group progressed to the miscreant's chamber and proceeded to arrest Mortimer, who slew at least one of his assailants before he was taken.[5] "Fair son," Isabella cried, rushing into the room, "have mercy on the gentle Mortimer!" Edward, however, was in no mood to show mercy. He quickly summoned Parliament, proclaimed that he was taking control of the government, and ordered the Peers to do justice. The lords promptly examined the fourteen charges against the earl, and as promptly they found him guilty of treason, as the York Parliament had eight years earlier.[6] This time, however, the sentence

---

happen to view it) into one of the most terrifying and, for many notables, inadmissible recent innovations." Natalie Fryde, *The Tyranny and Fall of Edward II, 1321-1326* (Cambridge: Cambridge University Press, 1979) 195; *see also* McKisack, *The Fourteenth Century* 67, 73.

[3]McKisack, *The Fourteenth Century* 90.

[4]Ibid., 85-91; Fryde, *Tyranny*, 192-200; Bryce Lyon, *A Constitutional and Legal History of Medieval England* (New York: Harper & Brothers, 1960) 486. McKisack concludes that Mortimer ordered Edward's murder, but Fryde is less certain. McKisack, *The Fourteenth Century* 96-100; Fryde, *Tyranny*, 207-09.

[5]13 *Dictionary of National Biography* 1039-40; McKisack, *The Fourteenth Century* 100-02.

[6]1 *Cobbett's Parliamentary History of England* (London: T. Curson Hansard, 1808-20) 84-87.

was to be more final.

On November 29 Mortimer, clad in black, was taken from the Tower to Tyburn Elms, the blood-soaked plot of ground where so many others before and after met their fates; there he was drawn, hanged, and quartered—the same punishment, according to some, that he himself had chosen for the younger Despenser. His body, such as it was, remained there for two days before the king magnanimously allowed a burial.[7] Thus ended an episode that some scholars have identified as the first impeachment.[8]

Within the context of American national government, however, Blount's was the earliest such event, for the chain of circumstances popularly known as the Blount Conspiracy resulted in Congress's first invocation of its impeachment power. In the fall of 1796 Blount secretly plotted with frontiersmen and Eastern speculators to wrest Louisiana from Spain in order to open the Mississippi Valley to settlers eager to purchase acres of his vast land holdings. To achieve this goal he sought help, through intermediaries, from English forces. But when news of these plans traveled from the savage wilderness of the West to the polished halls of government in Philadelphia, the House of Representatives impeached Blount, and the Senate convened as a tribunal to hear and decide the charges against him.

Few Americans, in the summer of 1797, would have debated Congress's collective wisdom in instituting these proceedings, or the makeup of Blount's own character. Here, exposed for all to see, was the deviltry of a man whom two states, and President George Washington himself, had entrusted with powers of both sword and purse; a man who had served as revolutionary militia paymaster in North Carolina, member of the Continental Congress, delegate to the Constitutional Convention, territorial governor, and United States

---

[7]13 *Dictionary of National Biography* 1040; McKisack, *The Fourteenth Century* 389-92; Fryde, *Tyranny*, 224-27. For a chronicle of Tyburn and the fifty thousand lives it supposedly claimed, together with a clinical description of the sentence in question, see Alfred Marks, *Tyburn Tree: Its History and Annals* (London: Brown, Langham & Co., 1908). We may never learn the exact number of those who died at this place, but we do know that Mortimer's death was not the first. *See id.* at 103.

[8]William R. Riddell, "Powers of a Colonial Legislature in Impeachment and Contempt," 21 *Proceedings and Transactions of the Royal Society of Canada* (3d Ser., § 2) 83, 83-84 (May 1927).

Senator from Tennessee. In attempting, as had Mortimer, to increase his own political power and business interests, Blount intrigued with a foreign power, and, again in the fashion of Mortimer, he suffered for it at the hands of the national legislature.

In retrospect Blount was, and is, an apt target for charges of maleficence, except to the citizens of his adopted state of Tennessee, who continued to revere him not only after his wrongdoing, but indeed after his death.[9] In Howard Chandler Christy's famous 1940 painting of the Constitutional Convention, Blount stands upon the podium, half turned towards Washington, the only other figure so standing. The impression is one of Blount, like Milton's Satan, presuming to equate himself with a man who, for that generation of Americans, had no peer.[10] In fact this is but a relatively recent example of the contempt that Blount's machinations earned him. In July 1797, as soon as evidence of his designs came to the attention of Congress, he found himself amid the eighteenth century equivalent of a media circus, and the subject of a process that has been called the most awe-inspiring, though least-used, congressional power.[11]

Within the course of a single week all of the branches of the national government simultaneously instituted various proceedings against him, and at least one of these processes hit its mark squarely. The public outcry against Blount and his conspiracy matched or exceeded any of the decade. The impeachment itself, though, was to

---

[9]Writing a century after the fact, Theodore Roosevelt recorded a summary of Blount's reputation that remains true today, when anyone bothers to remember Blount at all.

> The Tennesseeans . . . who cared little for the niceties of international law, and sympathized warmly with any act of territorial aggression against the Spaniards, were not in the least affected by his expulsion [from Congress]. They greeted him with enthusiasm, and elected him to high office, and he lived among them the remainder of his days, honored and respected. Nevertheless, his conduct in this instance was indefensible."

This last comment the expansionist Roosevelt penned despite his belief that Blount's was otherwise an "honorable and useful public career." 1 Theodore Roosevelt, *The Winning of the West* (New York: G.P. Putnam's Sons, 1910) 213.

[10]*See* illustration on book jacket.

[11]Congressional Quarterly, *Powers of Congress* (Washington: Congressional Quarterly, Inc., 1976) 127.

end a year and a half later, not with the bang of which the July furor seemed a portent, but instead with a whimper. Yet the impeachment stands as the first of its kind, and Blount's name still wears its shroud of infamy.

ॐ

Many similarities exist not only between the Blount and Mortimer episodes, but in the very nature of impeachment in their respective eras. In each case those who conducted the affair had few principles or precedents to guide them, for despite impeachment's four hundred-odd year history as of 1797, the express foundations of the American federal process were only a decade old. Unlike the common law, moreover, in which adjudication served to clarify and define general legislative statements and to further define the law, impeachment provided members of the Fifth Congress no national precedents for guidance in their efforts to deal with Blount.[12]

Such a comparison of impeachment to judicial proceedings is quite appropriate. Despite the debate on whether impeachment is a political or a judicial proceeding, impeachment and case law undeniably share many elements. Impeachment, as does a criminal case in regular courts, consists of an official charge or accusation of wrongdoing (to which the term "impeachment" technically refers) by representatives of the public—in this case the lower house of a legislature—against an individual who often is called a defendant. The defendant then undergoes an adversarial trial process before the upper house, which is sometimes styled a court of impeachment while it sits for this purpose.[13] The upper house decides the innocence or guilt of the defendant, and if it chooses the latter, it imposes judgment. In fact, some authorities see the impeachment itself, the official accusation, as a specialized indictment with origins traceable

---

[12]This book is concerned primarily with the issue of American federal, or national, impeachment, as opposed to state practices. When the term impeachment appears henceforth, therefore, the reader should assume American national impeachment to be the reference unless express statements to the contrary appear.

[13]Alexander Simpson, *A Treatise on Federal Impeachment* (Philadelphia: The Law Association of Philadelphia, 1916) 25-30.

directly to its better-known criminal law counterpart.[14] Others, while denying the existence of this direct connection, nevertheless view impeachment as a process born of other criminal law procedures.[15]

While debates over the origin and the criminal nature of impeachment are extensive, they form but a small portion of inquiries regarding the entire impeachment issue, and the scarcity of precedents remains a problem. Even today, two hundred years after the Constitution's adoption, fewer than a score of impeachments have taken place, compared to innumerable cases before the regular courts on other constitutional provisions. The number of regular court cases relating directly to impeachment is even smaller than the number of impeachments themselves.[16] While scholars, lawyers, and politicians have written much on the subject, almost no controlling authority on any question of impeachment exists—assuming impeachment is correctly spoken of as if it were a judicial proceeding like any other, defined by precedent and controlling authority. Thus a problem presents itself: how are we to understand the nature, the scope, the extent of the federal impeachment power, amid so much political and scholarly speculation, when we have so little authoritative information on the subject?

The most obvious and authoritative source is the text of the

---

[14]*See generally* M.V. Clarke, "The Origin of Impeachment," *in Oxford Essays in Medieval History Presented to Herbert Edward Salter* (Oxford: The Clarendon Press, 1934). Writers often erroneously use the word "impeachment" to mean the entire process of accusation, trial, and judgment.

[15]T.F.T. Plucknett, "The Origin of Impeachment," 24 *Transactions of the Royal Historical Society* (4th Ser.) 47, 50-51, 71 (1942); William R. Riddell, "Impeachment in England and the English Colonies," 7 *N.Y.U. L. Q. Rev.* 702, 702-04 (1930).

[16]The only cases relating directly to specific impeachments are *Ritter v. United States*, 84 Ct. Cl. 293 (1936), *cert. denied*, 300 U.S. 668 (1937); *Claiborne v. United States Senate*, No. 86-2780 (D.D.C. Oct. 8, 1986); *Hastings v. United States Senate, Impeachment Trial Committee*, 716 F. Supp. 38 (D.D.C.), *aff'd*, 887 F.2d 332, 1989 WL 122685 (D.C. Cir. 1989); *Nixon v. United States Senate*, 887 F.2d 332 (D.C. Cir.), *aff'g Hastings v. United States Senate, Impeachment Trial Committee*, 716 F. Supp. 38 (D.D.C. 1989); *Hastings v. United States*, 802 F. Supp. 490 (D.D.C. 1992), *vacated and remanded*, 988 F.2d 1280, 1993 WL 81273 (D.C. Cir.), *dismissed*, 837 F. Supp. 3 (D.D.C. 1993); *Nixon v. United States*, 506 U.S. 224 (1993), *aff'g* 938 F.2d 239 (D.C. Cir. 1991), *aff'g* 744 F. Supp. 9 (D.D.C. 1990). *See also* Epilogue, *infra*.

Constitution, which most writers tacitly agree is the origin of Congress's powers of impeachment.[17] The drawback to relying upon the constitutional text that bears upon impeachment is its brevity and occasional ambiguity. Only a few clauses concerning impeachment appear, and commentators have interpreted all of them in various ways over the years. We may thus regard very little, if anything, about the constitutional language as certain.

Article I, Section 3, for instance, gives to the Senate "the sole Power to try all Impeachments." Does this phrase mean that the Senate's judgment is unreviewable by any court or does it refer only to a trial on the merits—a trial on the facts—with an appellate court (presumably the Supreme Court) free to review issues of law? The next passage goes on to state that judgment "shall not extend further than to removal from Office, and disqualification to hold and enjoy any Office of honor, Trust or Profit under the United States."[18] Does this passage mean that a defendant, to be amenable to impeachment, must be a current officeholder? Does it imply that some lesser, though unnamed, penalty than removal, such as censure, may attach? If so, this leads to the question of exactly what penalties fall within this category. Article II, Section 4 requires that the "President, the Vice President and all civil Officers of the United States, shall be removed from office on Impeachment for, and Conviction of, Treason, Bribery, or other high Crimes and Misdemeanors." This last phrase is the source of perhaps the greatest question: what sort of act or failure to act qualifies as a high crime or misdemeanor? Does the term "high" modify the word "crimes" only, or "misdemeanors" as well? Does a difference exist between a misdemeanor and a high misdemeanor? The constitutional language itself contains little or no clue to the correct answer to these questions, and often it is clearly capable of multiple interpretations.[19]

---

[17]*See, e.g.,* Raoul Berger, *Impeachment: The Constitutional Problems* (New Haven: Yale University Press, 1973) 35 *et. seq.*; Philip B. Kurland, "Watergate, Impeachment, and the Constitution," 45 *Miss. L.J.* 531, 535 (1974). *But cf.* Joseph Isenbergh, "The Scope of the Power to Impeach," 84 *Yale L.J.* 1316 (1975), the best representative of a small number of articles taking a far broader view of the impeachment power.

[18]U.S. Const. art. I, § 3, cl. 7.

[19]See Appendix 1 for a digest of all impeachment and related clauses.

≈

Actually the Constitution is not unique in its paucity of information. Any positive, prescriptive rule that speaks to succeeding generations of society, such as a constitution or statute, is a general statement designed to cover a multiplicity of particular future events. Some entity must, when such events occur, interpret the general rule; that is, it must decide whether the statute or constitutional provision extends to cover the specific parties, controversies, and circumstances currently at issue. In fact, judicial interpretation of statutes (or constitutional phrases—they present similar problems) is nothing more than an attempt to define the limits of, to describe, the enactment that the lawmaker originally prescribed. The main difficulty of this task lies in the fact that the general language of statutes, even narrowly-drawn ones, is often capable of several different meanings, as the above problem with the word "misdemeanors" reveals.

Another, simpler example will serve to illuminate the complexity of the problem for those who may be new to the subject of legal interpretation. Suppose that a statute or constitutional provision, enacted in 1950, declares that "all school buses must stop at railroad crossings." What does this law mean? Does it contemplate only those buses owned by schools, or does it include any buses that schools use? What is the definition of school? Can the term reasonably include Sunday schools, for instance? If so, does it actually include Sunday schools in this particular law? May we consider any school vehicle carrying students, despite its size or design, to be a school bus? If we do, then we are assuming that the purpose of the law is to protect students, for the words of the law say nothing about students. Perhaps the residents of this jurisdiction value vehicles far more than they do student safety, in which case our assumption about students, and thus our reading of the law, may be incorrect. What does stopping "at" a railroad crossing mean—must a school bus stop just *before* it crosses railroad tracks, or may it stop immediately *after* it crosses the tracks—or must it stop on the tracks themselves? Having stopped, may the bus ever continue its journey? The statute is silent on this point. Suppose that in the twenty-first century a new sort of transport called a monotram comes into widespread use; it resembles railroads in some respects, but it is completely separate from the existing rail system. Does our statute require school buses to stop at monotram crossings? After all, it speaks only of railroads, not monotrams. The questions could go on for some time, but the point should now be clear. In answering each of these questions, none of which the statute expressly addresses, the interpreter must look to some authority besides the statute's words for the law's meaning, for the words alone are an insufficient guide.

To aid them in their efforts to determine which interpretation of a statute or other enactment is the correct one, insofar as any particular interpretation may be called "correct," courts through the centuries have developed a variety of rules by which to construe the words of the enactment. As a court's appeal to any one, or any combination, of these rules may determine the outcome of the matter in question, each rule has often been the center of controversy, political and scholarly as well as legal.

While many interpretive theories have cropped up over the years, especially in quite recent times, courts have historically resorted to rules that fall into two favorite categories. The first focuses upon the language of the enactment itself. Based upon the premise that the function of the lawmaker (the legislature, the constitutional convention, or other sovereign drafter of prescriptive rules) is to enact words that contain the meaning or essence of the law, courts using this approach focus on those words thus enacted.

The sub-categories of the language approach differ from each other only in terms of degree. The "plain meaning" or "literal" rule finds courts applying the strict wording of the statute in question to the issue at hand, regardless of the outcome. A more moderate approach is the so-called "golden rule"; courts employing this maxim of construction follow the meaning of a statute's words up to the point at which an absurdity would result if the court continued to adhere to the words. At this point the court deviates from the enactment's language in order to produce a sensible outcome. Within this golden rule lies a broad range of choice, depending primarily on what the judge or judges regard as absurd. In our railroad example, we probably reach this point when we realize that the text of the statute makes no provision for the school bus ever resuming its trip. To avoid the absurdity of a permanent stop, we could read into the statute an implied provision allowing the bus to proceed once the driver had made sure that no trains were coming.

In contrast to the language approach stands the second broad rule, which treats statutory language as symbols (as indeed all words are) that the lawmaker uses to convey his intent. To the judge using this approach, the thing of greatest importance is not the language of the enactment, but the lawmaker's intended will or policy. While the words of the statute are usually the primary means of discovering this intent, they may not clearly provide the definitive statement required because of their capacity for several different meanings. The court may thus turn to other aids to discover the will of the lawmaker, or the meaning that the lawmaker attributed to the words.[20]

Perhaps the best, and earliest, explicit statement of this rule is to be found in *Heydon's Case*.[21] In that English decision the court set out a four-part rule designed to determine the purpose for which a statute was enacted. The judge who follows the *Heydon* rule examines the state of the law before the passage of the statute in question, the mischief for which the law did not provide a remedy, and the remedy for this mischief that the new statute intended. The judge then gives the statute an interpretation that effects the intended remedy.[22]

For the judge who follows this rule or one of its variants, the question becomes that of *how* to know, other than through the enactment's own words, the lawmaker's intent. One popular and controversial manner is by an appeal to the legislative history of a statute or constitutional clause, such as the record of committee or floor debates relating to the enactment, its words, and the conditions of its adoption. When we turn, for instance, to James Madison's notes on the Constitutional Convention, we are pursuing an intent or purpose approach based on the legislative history of the Constitution's drafting.[23]

---

[20]See generally John Willis, "Statutory Interpretation in a Nutshell," 16 *Canadian B. Rev.* 1 (1938), for an extended discussion of these rules and their variants. A more recent survey appears in Carlos E. González, "Reinterpreting Statutory Interpretation," 74 *N.C. L. Rev.* 585, 594-633 (1996).

[21]3 Co. Rep. 7a, 76 Eng. Rep. 637 (Exchequer, 1584).

[22]Ibid. at 7b, 638.

[23]For an example of the intent approach, see *Church of the Holy Trinity v. United States*, 143 U.S. 457 (1892), in which the court refused to apply a congressional act to a case clearly falling within the letter of the law, on the grounds

Another tool for determining the lawmaker's intent, and perhaps the earliest to appear in the Anglo-American legal tradition, was born in the same century as impeachment itself. In an age when the size of government was far smaller than that of the present day, and the lines between the various governmental branches were blurred when they existed at all, often those who were in a position to interpret statutes had had a hand in drafting them to begin with.[24] Probably the most celebrated legislator-*cum*-judge was King's Bench Chief Justice Ralph Hengham. In one famous case before his court, when an attorney pontificated upon a law's meaning, Hengham reproached him. "Do not gloss the statute," he told the counselor, "for we know better than you; we made it."[25]

Eventually, however, many judges and commentators came to attack this view. For them an inside knowledge of the statute's origins was a liability rather than an asset. The most famous expression of this view came from the pen of the Earl of Halsbury in 1902. "My Lords," he wrote,

> I have more than once had occasion to say that in construing a statute I believe that the worst person to construe it is the person who is responsible for its drafting. He is very much disposed to confuse what he intended to do with the effect of the language which in fact has been employed. At the time he drafted the statute, at all events, he may have been under the impression that he had given full effect to what was intended, but he may be mistaken in construing it afterwards just because what was in his mind was what was intended, though, perhaps, it was not done.[26]

Legists and jurists who agree with this statement often declare that the question of *whose* intent mattered is a difficult one to answer,

---

that the legislative history of the act revealed a legislative purpose that excluded such circumstances.

[24]T.F.T. Plucknett, *Statutes and Their Interpretation in the First Half of the Fourteenth Century* (Cambridge: Cambridge University Press, 1922) 55.

[25]*Aumeye v. Anon.*, Y.B. 33 & 35 Edw. I (Rolls Series) 82; T.F.T. Plucknett, *A Concise History of the Common Law*, 5th ed. (Boston: Little, Brown, and Company, 1956) 331.

[26]*Hilder v. Dexter*, [1902] A.C. 474, 477.

and some even allege that the courts can never hope to discover the relevant intent. Does the intent of those legislators alone who voted for the statute matter, or should we consider that of the bill's opponents as well? What if different supporters had different reasons for agreeing to a statute? What if they themselves held a variety of views about the meaning of the statute's words? What if the minutes of the legislative debates were incomplete or misleading? Finally came the accusation that judges invoking an intent rule may do so in order to give an enactment an interpretation that the judges themselves wish to impose upon it, although the words of the enactment alone could never support such an interpretation. According to these critiques, an intent approach provides at best a vague standard of construction and at worst a means for judicial usurpation of legislative powers.[27] The position gains force when one realizes that resorting to archives, manuscript collections, and decades- or centuries-old legislative and convention debates is a task with which most legal scholars, to say nothing of judges and attorneys, are unfamiliar, and for which they have no training. Justice Robert Jackson once observed that "Judges often are not thorough or objective historians," and more recently Justice Antonin Scalia has noted that this sort of investigation is often "better suited to the historian than the lawyer."[28]

The language-based approach, however, is not without its own critics and difficulties.[29] Language is composed of symbols—letters, numbers, words—that in themselves have no meaning. As the famous historian Carl L. Becker once noted, words are nothing more than ink spread across a page in certain patterns.[30] The patterns are fixed, moreover, while the facts to which the judge must apply them are potentially infinite in their possible variations. A jurist who deals with

---

[27]*See* Max Radin, "Statutory Interpretation," 43 *Harv. L. Rev.* 863, 870 (1930).

[28]Robert Jackson, "Full Faith and Credit—The Lawyer's Clause of the Constitution," 45 *Colum. L. Rev.* 1, 6 (1945); Antonin Scalia, "Originalism: The Lesser Evil," 57 *U. Cin. L. Rev.* 849, 856-57 (1989).

[29]See generally James M. Landis, "A Note on 'Statutory Interpretation,'" 43 *Harv. L. Rev.* 886 (1930) for a rebuttal of Radin; for a critique and recent history of the plain meaning rule, see generally Arthur W. Murphy, "Old Maxims Never Die: The 'Plain-Meaning Rule' and Statutory Interpretation in the 'Modern' Federal Courts," 75 *Colum. L. Rev.* 1299 (1975).

[30]Carl L. Becker, "What are Historical Facts?," 8 *W. Pol. Q.* 327, 331 (1955).

an enactment in any way, using any rule of construction, thus engages in some legislative second-guessing; this fact helps explain Charles Evans Hughes's well-known statement that "the Constitution is what the judges say it is."[31] So long as the enactment's words are capable of two or more meanings, as is almost always the case at least in theory, then no "plain meaning" exists, and the judge inevitability exercises some discretion in applying the enactment.

If we accept Becker's comment as true, however, we must also admit the truth of other things. Judge Learned Hand once wrote that "statutes always have some purpose or object to accomplish, whose sympathetic and imaginative discovery is the surest guide to their meaning."[32] If words are nothing more then ink on a page, however, then that ink has no self-awareness or will of its own, much less any purposes or objects that it wishes to accomplish. But as Becker also noted, that ink appears in certain patterns, and whoever caused the ink to flow across the page chose those patterns. We may see different meanings in them than did their creator; we could easily dispense with the creator's meaning and adopt our own perceived meanings as the ones that should govern our society from now on. If we go this far, then ignoring the words of the statute themselves is but a short step away, for once we look to our own values and experiences for meaning, then why look at patterns of ink at all? If we do choose to look at such patterns, why not let the patterns be ones of our own choosing, such as books of sociology, literature, or philosophy? Why bind ourselves to the ancient words of a long-dead legislature or convention and give those particular words, and that body's understanding, a place of particular authority?

Whether or not we should take this approach to law, and although we probably do take it to some degree, we do not do so completely. Our legal system, in refusing to divorce the meanings we see in the patterns from the patterns themselves, implicitly accepts at some level the authority of the meaning that the creator attributed to them. To do otherwise would be to dispense with the need for the patterns at all, and we have for the most part refused to take this step. Judicial systems, after all, do not need statutes and written

---

[31]1 Merlo J. Pusey, *Charles Evans Hughes* (New York: The MacMillan Company, 1951) 204.

[32]*Cabell v. Markham*, 148 F.2d 737, 739 (2d Cir.), *aff'd*, 326 U.S. 404 (1945).

constitutions to go about their business; common law and equity courts, especially in their formative years, demonstrate this fact. Our written constitutions, however, together with the ever-increasing volume of statutes and even administrative regulations, force us to look not only around us, or within ourselves, but backwards across time to the day when the patterns of ink first took shape. The interpretation of constitutional and statutory language, in short, is not only an inherent part of our constitutional system; it is also inherently an exercise in historical thinking, at least to some degree.

We must, then, be willing to try to understand what the language of such provisions meant to those who wrote them, and confining ourselves to the language itself makes this difficult. While the chance exists that we can find some guidance as to its understanding of an enactment's meaning through extrinsic materials that serve to narrow the range of potentially correct interpretations, we should be bound to seek such evidence, much the principles of precedent and *stare decisis* bind judges.

Of course, the process may be difficult, and all too often the result may prove of little value. Documents may disappear; handwriting may be indecipherable; secret opinions and motivations may never have found their way onto paper at all. One historian's remark that historical records comprise only "the recorded part of the remembered part of the observed part of what happened" has considerable merit.[33] At the end of the inquiry, our constitutional provision may confuse us even more than it did at the beginning, and even if it seems clearer, the clarity might be deceptive.

These dangers of viewing law as history no doubt form some of the basis for the denunciations of intent-based approaches that have grown more strident in the late twentieth century. Discussions of the merits of originalism, as we now call intent-based theories of interpretation, erupted into a high-profile running debate in the middle years of the 1980s. Then-Attorney General Edwin Meese, speaking out in support of originalism, and Supreme Court Justice William J. Brennan, attacking Meese's position a few weeks later, fired

---

[33]Willis P. Whichard, "A Place for Walter Clark in the American Judicial Tradition," 63 *N.C. L. Rev.* 287, 288 (1984) (quoting Dr. George V. Taylor, Professor of History at the University of North Carolina at Chapel Hill).

the opening salvos in 1985.[34] The overtly political nature of this new debate has contributed to both its ferocity and its longevity, and has caused it to produce heat as well as light. The best-known popular statement of originalism appeared in former federal judge and failed Supreme Court nominee Robert Bork's best-selling *The Tempting of America* in 1990.[35] This work drew heavy fire from many quarters, with one critic calling it "the most widely and most unfavorably reviewed book in law review history."[36] Though some still speak out in favor of originalism, the doctrine for the most part has taken quite a pounding in the closing years of the twentieth century.

The Reagan Administration's championing of originalism no doubt stemmed from concern over judicial activism and the new schools of interpretation that had promoted it.[37] Some of these theories deny not only that we can ever know the original intent of the framers of a statute or constitutional provision, but that we cannot even be sure of the meaning of the provision's words themselves. This interpretive development, resembling and even related to that attack on the stability of language known as Deconstructionism, has emphasized theories of interpretation that center not upon the originator of constitutional or statutory language, nor upon the medium of constitutional or statutory language, but upon the receiver of the message that the language presumes to convey. One may find many varieties of this argument, from Stanley Fish's interpretive community to William N. Eskridge, Jr.'s dynamic principles of statutory interpretation to Judge Guido Calabresi's concept of the activist judiciary.[38]

---

[34]Jack N. Rakove ed., *Interpreting the Constitution: The Debate Over Original Intent* 3 (Boston: Northeastern University Press, 1990).

[35]Robert Bork, *The Tempting of America: The Political Seduction of the Law* (New York: The Free Press, 1990).

[36]Lino A. Graglia, " 'Interpreting' the Constitution: Posner on Bork," 44 *Stan. L. Rev.* 1019, 1019 (1992).

[37]This development caused consternation in the administration. For an example of its response, and its view of some of the schools of interpretation that most concerned it, see *Statement of Stephen J. Markman, Assistant Attorney General, Office of Legal Policy, Before the Committee on the Judiciary, United States Senate, Concerning the Judicial Selection Process in the Reagan Administration, February 2, 1988*, at 8 (Department of Justice, 1988), which lists a number of standards of interpretation proposed within the last 30 years.

[38]See Stanley Fish, *Is There a Text in This Class? The Authority of Interpretive*

Since the rise of Legal Realism in the first part of the twentieth century, legal scholars, as have scholars in other fields ranging from history to theoretical physics, have come more and more to proclaim that objective reality (in the case of the former, objective legal truth) either is not readily discernible or does not exist. According to these views truth, like beauty, lies in the beholder's eye. The natural result is a subjectification of legal authority, along with an obvious diversity in schools of legal thought ranging from the Law and Economics School on the one hand to Critical Legal Studies on the other. In an era such as this, when enough cases are on the books to allow any advocate or jurist to find a precedent for nearly anything,[39] and when law has largely ceased to prevent a determined judge from applying his own values more or less plainly, a smorgasbord of interpretive theories is a boon to one who would denounce authority. Critics might respond that that authority was a chimera to begin with, but the ideal of an objective standard has no doubt exercised a considerable influence over development of constitutional and legal doctrine for generations, if not centuries. As any inferior court judge striving to avoid reversal on appeal, or any attorney whose case depended on arguing the plain or original meaning of an authority would remind us, it still does, for better or for worse. The values that restrain judicial authority in such a system might not be ideal ones, and may on occasion be quite objectionable. If the goal, however, is to ascertain the rights and duties of society's members with regularity and predictability, then an objective, authoritative rule, even if it is a fiction, is necessary.

This is not to say that rules of law are, or should be, set in stone, or that laws and constitutions should not adapt. Indeed, one secret to the federal Constitution's longevity is that it can, and does, change to meet new circumstances. As the words of the hymn go, "Time makes ancient good uncouth," or, in legal parlance, "*Cessante ratione legis,*

Communities (Cambridge: Harvard University Press, 1980); William N. Eskridge, Jr., "Dynamic Statutory Interpretation," 135 *U. Pa. L. Rev.* 1479 (1987); Guido Calabresi, *A Common Law for the Age of Statutes* (Cambridge: Harvard University Press, 1982). For a summary of some of these theories, see González, "Statutory Interpretation," 594-633.

[39]See generally Susan W. Brenner, *Precedent Inflation* (New Brunswick: Transaction Publishers, 1992).

cessat et ipsa lex."[40] This being the case, then, what is originalism's proper role? Its best function, perhaps, is to provide a point of departure.[41] It is a benchmark by which to measure modern understanding of an ancient document, so that we may know when we are changing it, as well as knowing when and how that rule needs changing. Law is inherently a specialized sort of historical study, not merely in its privileging of ancient constitutional and statutory texts, but in its insistence on the authority of precedent, looking to what occurred in the past. Until we adopt a system of perfect justice in its place, concerned not with the rules but only the substance of equity—until attorneys and judges everywhere in the United States stop citing prior cases as precedent, and focus purely on the particulars of the case at bar instead of the idea of general legal rules—law will remain at least partly historical in method. When we view the law in this light, judicious use of originalism becomes simply more comprehensible, and perhaps more palatable, to the legal community, which is largely accustomed to finding its highly-organized sources appearing in their proper places in the casebooks or annotated codes resting close at hand. Thus, whatever uncertainty awaits us in the archives, we should be loath to say "The first thing we do, let's kill all the historians." In fact, until legists and jurists are uniformly willing to undergo some historical training, they may, or at any rate should, find historians and their work useful on occasion.

Even for those who are inclined to denounce originalism entirely, however, a few reasons yet remain to consider its continued application. One is the self-contradiction inherent in some recent critiques of originalism, notably Jack N. Rakove's and H. Jefferson Powell's. These writers seek to turn originalist arguments upon the originalists by showing that the framers themselves eschewed originalism in favor of what Rakove calls "a closely reasoned analysis of the text emphasizing manifest language, internal consistency, and fidelity to general principles."[42] At first glance the argument is a

---

[40] Herbert Broom, *A Selection of Legal Maxims, Classified and Illustrated* (London: Sweet & Maxwell, Ltd., 9th ed. 1924) 110-12; *see* 2 William Blackstone, *Commentaries on the Laws of England* (Oxford: Clarendon Press, 1766) *390-91.

[41] See Jack N. Rakove, *Original Meanings: Politics and Ideas in the Making of the Constitution* (New York: Alfred A. Knopf, 1996) 8-9.

[42] Ibid,, 349; *see also* H. Jefferson Powell, "The Original Understanding of Original

powerful one, but at second glance we see the paradox. One who invokes the framers' intent to challenge the validity of originalism thus adopts an originalist position. If we pursue this course, we may remove the framers from their interpretive pedestal by revealing how they implicitly refused to accept a position of special authority upon, or knowledge of, constitutional interpretation, but we have also shown that originalism retains a standing no less illustrious than other canons of interpretation, though no longer a preferred position. When we use originalism to illuminate the problem of interpretation, we thereby validate it in the process, whether the framers would have us do so or no.

This eristic use of interpretive theory—both that of the above-named critics of originalism and that of this author—brings us to the final, and perhaps most persuasive, argument in favor of originalism. One who takes a utilitarian view of legal matters, as most attorneys and judges probably do, must concede that whatever the doctrine's shortcomings as we may see them with a scholar's eye, the bench yet has its share of judges who accept originalism as either a valid theory, or even the only valid theory. For advocates who face such judges, originalism may become a necessary, though perhaps not the exclusive, weapon. The advocate who is willing to wield that particular weapon, and who wields it well, may find that it helps her win the day. Scholarly merits aside, then, the final argument is one of utility. In our legal system, the advocate who chooses to stand on principle and discount some particular rule of construction, whether originalism or another, does so at her peril. Originalism, in short, is very much alive.

The Supreme Court has said as much, though the most explicit statement is quite dated. "This court," wrote Chief Justice William Howard Taft for the court in 1926, "has repeatedly laid down the principle that a contemporaneous legislative exposition of the Constitution, when the founders of our government and framers of our Constitution were actively participating in public affairs, acquiesced in for a long term of years, fixes the construction to be given its provisions."[43] Despite its age, the holding presumably

---

Intent," 98 *Harv. L. Rev.* 885 (1985).

[43]*Myers v. United States*, 272 U.S. 52 (1926). In support of this conclusion, the Court cited a line of venerable cases, some of which dated from the framers'

remains in force. But this rule, as are the other variations of originalism as well as the other interpretive theories discussed above, is principally a rule of construction that courts have thrashed out, or that scholars have put forth for judicial consumption. Whether these rules are applicable to impeachment is still an open question.

If impeachments were subject to judicial review, the answer, at least in the judicial review phase of the process, would undoubtedly be yes. In 1936, however, the United States Court of Claims refused to hear the complaint of a former federal judge who sought to challenge his impeachment proceedings' validity. In refusing to take jurisdiction in the case, the court emphasized the Constitution's mandate that "The Senate shall have the sole Power to try all Impeachments" as well as historical and policy arguments against judicial intervention in the process. Following this analysis, the court concluded unequivocally that the Senate's decision was beyond review.[44] Halsted L. Ritter's case was the first, and for another half-century the last, judicial challenge to the regularity of the impeachment process. In 1986, however, a spate of similar cases sprang up, culminating in 1993 with the Supreme Court's decision in *Nixon v. United States*.[45] In this case the Court finally, or at least for the time being, resolved the running scholarly debate as to whether impeachments were legitimate subjects for judicial review. The Court unanimously held that they are not; none of the justices, however, did so as categorically as the *Ritter* court had done in 1936. Instead, the Supreme Court took jurisdiction, thus letting impeached officials clear the first and highest hurdle that they faced in their effort to achieve judicial review of their impeachment proceedings. The stumbling block that the Court interposed instead was the prudential obstacle of nonjusticiability, which it based on the political question doctrine. Some of the justices, moreover, equivocated on this point, thus leaving open the possibility that the Court might some day

---

generation or shortly thereafter. The statement came within the context of a discussion of the proper interpretation of the president's power to remove executive officers. Ironically for our purposes, an earlier, highly politicized dispute between president and Congress on this point, as the Court noted in *Myers*, precipitated the impeachment, trial, and near-conviction of President Andrew Johnson in 1868.

[44]*Ritter v. United States*, 84 Ct. Cl. 293, 296-300 (1936), *cert. denied*, 300 U.S. 668 (1937) (quoting U.S. Const. art. I, § 3, cl. 6).

[45] 506 U.S. 224 (1993).

throw open the door that it left ajar in *Nixon*.[46]

But for now the question of interpretation seems to be up to Congress, serving as it does as a court of last resort in the impeachment process. A legislative body by nature knows at least something of arbitry, with will trumping reason,[47] and though impeachment has some judicial elements, it is also at least partly political. As the author has argued elsewhere, then, Congress has discretion, not only because of the nature of the process but because no one is in a position deny it that discretion.[48] In such a grave matter as impeachment, however, and especially in such partisan times as our own, Congress would do well to look to history, if not for definitive answers, then at least for guidance. As is the case in a related area of law, if the targets of impeachment have no recourse to the regular courts, then Congress should provide for some degree of procedural and substantive protections in the impeachment process itself; an expectation of consistency and predictability would seem to be one good way of doing so. A premise of the present work is that guidance such as this is at least useful, at most necessary, and at best—without the aid of serious scholarly historical research—difficult.

Thus we return to the original question of how we are better to understand impeachment. Precisely because information is so scarce, we cannot afford to leave any avenue uninvestigated which holds the possibility of bringing further light to bear upon the subject. From a historical, as opposed to a legal, point of view, evidence extrinsic to a statute's words is even more important, for history, as an effort to

---

[46] See ibid. at 239-52 (White, J., concurring in the judgment); *id.* at 252-54 (Souter, J., concurring in the judgment).

[47] Blackstone, at any rate, suggested thus: "I know it is generally laid down more largely," he wrote, "that acts of parliament contrary to reason are void. But if the parliament will positively enact a thing to be done which is unreasonable, I know of no power that can controul it . . . ." 1 William Blackstone, *Commentaries* *91. Of course, Blackstone was writing not of legislatures in general but of the Parliament of the eighteenth century. The relationship of reason to will in the legislature, however, is an interesting one for contemplation.

[48] See Buckner F. Melton, Jr., "Federal Impeachment and Criminal Procedure: The Framers' Intent," 52 *Md. L. Rev.* 437, 456-57 (1993).

reconstruct the past, and particularly past states of mind, can afford to ignore no piece of evidence, as scant as the evidence often is. And of the devices listed above, as regards the Blount impeachment, one method stands out. This method is an originalist approach, by which we can seek to gain a better understanding of the ideas of those who drafted, debated, and ratified the Constitution's impeachment clauses.

In 1797 most of the generation of men involved in the creation of the Constitution were still alive. Many of the framers themselves in fact not only continued to walk the earth, but even to stroll the halls of political power in Philadelphia. Who would be in a better position to know the original meaning of the basic law's broadly-worded provisions than those who had been present at their writing, and those who had kept counsel with them during the first decade of the new system of government? William Blount himself attended the Philadelphia Convention, albeit rarely, and a few of his fellow senators and representatives as of the late 1790s shared this distinction. If we also consider the close associates of these individuals, then the circle of primary or secondary participants involved in drafting or ratification widens considerably. In the events of 1797-1799, then, we have a rare opportunity to observe how the framers and their generation applied the impeachment process; what precedents they relied upon, and what precedents they established; what limits they placed on the power; and in what general light they viewed the subject. The general question, then, that leaps forth from the Blount episode is this: what does the record of that impeachment reveal about the framers' early ideas of the impeachment power and other aspects of congressional and constitutional authority?

Some may take issue with the practice of appealing to a group of men nearly two centuries dead in order to understand a process that has only lately experienced a renaissance.[49] But although particular circumstances may have changed, and may continue to change, broad issues of republican government, and of the use and abuse of power, remain. No reason exists whereby a 1790s impeachment should not serve as precedent, or at least persuasive authority, if at present or at some point in the future we find the same circumstances and issues arising that arose then.

---

[49]For a discussion of recent impeachments, see Epilogue, *infra*.

Although we can never reconstruct the whole truth, even the truth about a single facet of history, and we have not determined that general empirical laws of human conduct exist, historians nevertheless continue to gather facts about the past, setting them within causal relationships to one another. In this regard historians proceed upon a leap of faith—the unprovable assumption that their histories can reflect, with some accuracy, the past about which they write. And just as researchers in the natural sciences advance upon faith, assuming their descriptive laws of nature will hold true in a future yet to be experienced, historians strive to infer general rules from their incomplete records of past actions. The justification for history study is that these general rules will accurately describe future circumstances. By turning to these rules for guidance, those involved in new impeachments can help the power to evolve consistently, with predictability and stability.

Legists opposed to theories of originalism, and historians who disavow the possibility of reconstructing an accurate picture of the past, may object to the use of history to guide Congress's modern proceedings. But in the final analysis, Congress alone will decide if some issue to be found in the Blount case is analogous to, or distinct from, a new impeachment question. Although the chances of an exact similarity are remote, the probability of a general resemblance remains, and thus we must attempt to uncover the resources that comprise the legacy of the first impeachment.

Impeachment did not, however, spring into existence spontaneously in 1797, or even at the convention that met in Philadelphia ten years before. Its history stretches back beyond that point by nearly half a millennium. From this context the framers drew the principles that they used to fashion the national impeachment power, and so with impeachment's medieval genesis, in a sense, Blount's story properly begins.

Chapter 1

The Heritage of the Blount Impeachment

𝔢

Forty-seven years before Roger Mortimer's downfall, in the autumn of 1283, his kinsman David ap Gruffydd, the last Cymric Prince of Wales, suffered the penalty of death at Parliament's behest. David's offense was that of levying war against his English masters. On the eve of Palm Sunday the previous year he had staged an uprising and begun the seizure of English strongholds in Wales. The rebellion continued for a year and a half, entailed many campaigns, and saw the demise of Llywelyn ap Gruffydd, David's brother and predecessor. Finally the forces of King Edward I captured David and crushed the last resistance. The Prince's execution, and the placement of his severed head upon the Tower alongside Llywelyn's, symbolized the end of Wales's existence as an independent power.[1]

At least one author has seen in this episode the earliest indications of a parliamentary impeachment power.[2] Most writers, however, put impeachment's genesis somewhat later. The most popular date is 1376, when Parliament tried Lord William Latimer and Richard Lyons for lining their pockets with royal funds.[3] Others find antecedents for the process in early Norman times, when William the Conqueror first

---

[1]Maurice Powicke, *The Thirteenth Century 1216-1307* (Oxford: The Clarendon Press, 1953) 419-29; T. F. Tout, *The History of England from the Accession of Henry III to the Death of Edward III* (London: Longmans, Green, and Co., 1905) 160-65.

[2]1 James Fitzjames Stephen, *History of the Criminal Law of England* (London: Macmillan and Company, 1883) 146.

[3]T.F.T. Plucknett, "The Impeachments of 1376," 1 *Transactions of the Royal Historical Society* (5th Ser.) 153, 161-62 (1951).

established the *Aula Regis*, a court composed of his high officers,[4] or even far earlier, in legal processes of the city-states of ancient Greece.[5]

To solve the riddle of when impeachments began, one should first seek to establish some sort of definition, some general principles with which one can identify an impeachment. We might best begin with the term itself. According to the *Oxford English Dictionary* its origins are fairly simple; its earliest form, *empeschement*, is born of words meaning to hinder or to impede (literally, to fetter the foot).[6] The term apparently first acquired a technical meaning, first became a term of art, some time in the 1320s.[7] The medieval scholar Gabrielle Lambrick, however, looking more deeply into the question, has shown that the word's etymology, at least in legal usage, is rather more complex, and this complexity lies at the heart of a great deal of confusion over impeachment's exact legal nature. Noting the use of three types of Latin words relating to the modern term impeachment, "the *impech-* type of word . . . words which had *imped-* as their prefix and root; and . . . the *impet-* group," she observes that sometimes legists appeared to use the words interchangeably, but at other points used them in distinct ways, often within the same legal phrase. "For our purpose," she continues,

> *impetitio* is the most important of the words used for impeachment, not only because the verbal *impetitus* came to be almost universally adopted for "impeached" in its specialized meaning, but also because it expressed two different ideas; on the one hand it might mean a charge or accusation of a crime or offense, and it is to this set of meanings that its translation as "impeachment" is usually assumed to belong; on the other hand it might imply an

---

[4]Wrisley Brown, "The Impeachment of the Federal Judiciary," 26 *Harv. L. Rev.* 684, 685 (1913).

[5]John Feerick, "Impeaching Federal Judges: A Study of the Constitutional Provisions," 39 *Fordham L. Rev.* 1, 5 n.15 (1970). For a brief survey of English impeachment, which synthesizes many of the sources appearing in this section, see 1 William Holdsworth, *A History of English Law* (London: Methuen & Co. Ltd, 7th ed. 1956) 379-85.

[6]7 *Oxford English Dictionary* (2d ed. 1989) 703.

[7]M.V. Clarke, "The Origin of Impeachment," *Oxford Essays in Medieval History Presented to Edward Salter* (Oxford: The Clarendon Press, 1934) 164.

impediment, a let or hindrance in the lawyers' sense and hence a claim to property or rights, a demand, or a suing. It may well be that the word expressed both types of meaning simultaneously, on some occasions, to the fourteenth-century mind.[8]

This conceptual difficulty has divided scholars as to impeachment's essence. Consensus does exist upon one or two points. Practically all who have written on the subject agree that impeachment involves a protection of a public interest, incorporating a public law element, much like a criminal proceeding. Unlike private litigation, impeachment is a process instigated by the government, or some branch thereof, against a person who has somehow harmed the government or the community. The process, moreover, is adversarial in nature and resembles, to that extent, a judicial trial.[9] Most researchers also point out impeachment's procedural flexibility, in which some of them find the main reason for the doctrine's emergence.[10] But here consensus ends.

The main point of contention in the debate over impeachment's appearance relates to its structural characteristics: What branches of government are involved in impeachment, and what roles do they play? In American national impeachment, these questions are of little concern, for the Constitution expressly vests the power to prefer and the power to try impeachments in the House of Representatives and the Senate, respectively. But even the American experience contains warnings that the issue was at first not so clear. During the 1787 convention, delegates proposed several structural models of impeachment before settling on the one finally adopted.[11]

---

[8]Gabrielle Lambrick, "The Impeachment of the Abbot of Abingdon in 1368," 82 *Eng. Hist. Rev.* 250, 263-64 (1967).

[9]Ibid. at 275-76; Peter C. Hoffer & N.E.H. Hull, *Impeachment in America, 1635-1805* (New Haven: Yale University Press, 1984) 3; T.F.T Plucknett, "The Rise of the English State Trial," 2 *Politica* 542, 555 (1937).

[10]Lambrick, "Abington," 276; Plucknett, "State Trial," 557; Clarke, "Origin," 172-74; Colin G.C. Tite, *Impeachment and Parliamentary Judicature in Early Stuart England* (London: Athlone Press, 1974) 23.

[11]1 Max Farrand, ed., *The Records of the Federal Convention* (Revised ed.: New Haven: Yale University Press, 1937) 223-24, 244, 292. The main question of structure at issue in recent years is whether impeachment is subject to judicial

Scholars have proposed several standards for determining when impeachment first appeared; most of them involve a structural rather than a functional approach to the process. One source argues that we may find its genesis on that occasion when the Lords, although not yet a separate house of Parliament, first rendered judgment without similar participation by the Commons.[12] Another view holds that the key is to be found in Parliament's appropriation of indictment, a criminal law device, to initiate proceedings against those individuals whom regular indictments would not reach.[13] Still another author, while rejecting the notion that impeachment was a form of indictment, nevertheless finds its peculiar nature in Commons's prosecution of the case before the Lords.[14] Finally, Lambrick has suggested that impeachment in some sense was a procedure that had some existence independent of Parliament; members of the community of Abington used it against the abbot of the abbey there in 1368 after common law procedures had failed them.[15]

Whatever the criteria used, all sources agree that by the end of 1376 impeachment existed in more-or-less the form that it would hold throughout the following centuries. Under this process the House of Commons brought charges of wrongdoing against the defendant, and the Lords heard the case as presented by Commons, with the accused having an opportunity to defend himself. The process in these respects resembles an adversarial judicial trial, whether or not its origins may be traced to England's criminal law. Impeachments thus defined are rather common in the records from 1376 down to the middle of the following century.[16]

What of impeachment's function? What, and whose, purpose did it serve during this medieval period? Once again we find some general agreement among authorities. The main targets of the process were

---

review; see Epilogue, *infra*, and Berger, *Impeachment* 103-21 for arguments on this point. A similar question is that of the Senate's use of committees to take evidence; See Epilogue, *infra*, for a discussion of this issue.

[12]Riddell, "Powers," 83.

[13]Clarke, "Origin," 184.

[14]T.F.T. Plucknett, "The Origin of Impeachment," 24 *Transactions of the Royal Historical Society* (4th Ser.) 47, 55 (1942); Plucknett, "1376," 160-62.

[15]Lambrick, "Abington," 257-63.

[16]4 John Hatsell, *Precedents of Proceedings in the House of Commons* (London: Luke Hansard and Sons, 1818) 56-84.

royal officials, often corrupt ones, whom parliamentary opposition could not check in any other way.[17]

In many respects this use of impeachment reflects a power struggle between the executive and legislative branches of government, a struggle between relative equals, at least in comparison to the Continental experiences.[18] Impeachment appeared when it did, some argue, because at the time Parliament had the upper hand, and the king had no choice but to allow the process to continue.[19] Perhaps we may trace Parliament's new position of power to its role of grantor of supply, or the fact that by the mid 1300s it had come to represent a broader range of the estates or classes of English society than before, gaining power in the process.[20] Meanwhile, as Parliament's power had grown the king's had declined. By 1376 Edward III, who had so energetically seized the reins of government from Mortimer forty-six years earlier, was old and occupied with foreign affairs. He refused to deal with the corrupt chamberlain Latimer or the scheming merchant Lyons, but he was either unable or unwilling to oppose Parliament's desire to call these men to answer for their deeds.[21] The Commons thus resolved to take the initiative, for it considered Latimer and Lyons, by their misappropriation of funds, to be responsible in part for the great tax burden.

Upon hearing the Commons's accusation, Latimer demanded a formal trial, and Parliament complied. Here, then, impeachment as an adversarial trial process becomes clearly discernible. In the end

---

[17]T.F.T Plucknett, "Impeachment and Attainder," 3 *Transactions of the Royal Historical Society* (5th Ser.) 145, 148; Clarke, "Origin," 165; Berger, *Impeachment* 3.

[18]Bryce Lyon, *A Constitutional and Legal History of Medieval England* (New York: Harper & Brothers, 1960) 642-49.

[19]Some authorities maintain that impeachment, unlike indictments, were brought not in the king's name but instead the name of the Commons, thus indicating the presence of a sovereign power having nothing to do with the executive, and thus not being subject to a royal check. William R. Riddell, "Impeachment in England and English Colonies," 7 *N.Y.U. L. Q. Rev.* 702, 704 (1930); Plucknett, "Attainder," 146. But see Lambrick, "Abington," 268; Plucknett, "1376," 156.

[20]Clarke, "Origin," 176-178. Bryce Lyon maintains that the major constitutional theme of the fourteenth century was "the maturing of parliamentary institutions," and that a major aspect of this development was the growing importance of the representative element. Lyon, *Medieval England*, 535.

[21]Plucknett, "1376," 161-62; Lambrick, "Abington," 373.

Latimer's efforts to save himself proved futile, and Parliament eventually consigned both men to prison.[22] With these episodes impeachment assumed its function as a parliamentary tool for trimming royal excesses of power.

Although some exceptions are to be found, most of the individuals against whom Parliament proceeded in the medieval period were royal officers.[23] On occasion royal judges were the target. In one interesting group of impeachments occurring in 1388, the defendants were jurists from whom Richard II had solicited opinions on the question of whether Parliament could prefer impeachments without royal consent. The judges stated that Parliament could not, whereupon Parliament, in an ironic twist, impeached, tried, and convicted them.[24]

When the executive was strong enough to threaten Parliament's power, although not strong enough to subdue it completely, impeachment saw its most frequent use. Conversely, Parliament did not use the process (at least not successfully) when the match was unequal. Henry IV, for instance, was too weak a monarch for Parliament to concern itself with; Henry V proved too strong.[25] This pattern continued for three-quarters of a century following the 1376 impeachments before the process began its decline.

Some authorities have claimed that the last true medieval impeachment took place in 1449. Thereafter Parliament turned increasingly to attainders, statutes declaring certain individuals to be guilty of capital offenses, as a more convenient and effective means of dealing with its opponents. Then in 1485 came the accession of Henry VII and the beginning of the powerful Tudor monarchy, and as Parliament's power dwindled the impeachment process disappeared altogether for a century and a half.[26]

ॐ

In 1621, in the eighteenth year of the reign of first Stuart king, James

---

[22]Plucknett, "1376," 158-62; McKisack, *Fourteenth Century* 389-92.

[23]Clarke, "Origin," 165, 168, 175.

[24]4 Hatsell, *Precedents* 59-61; Plucknett, "Attainder," 145-47.

[25]Clarke, "Origin," 184.

[26]Riddell, "England," 705; Tite, *Judicature* 1; Clarke, "Origin," 184-85.

I, Parliament found itself in circumstances similar to those of the mid-1300s. Since Elizabeth's death in 1603, the monarchy had grown less effective, and James's extreme assertions of royal prerogative compounded the problem. The time was ripe for renewed parliamentary attacks upon the Crown, and to reach the king's agents Commons turned once again to impeachment, by now all but forgotten.[27]

Parliament had not waited until 1621 to oppose the king, but having met with failure up to that point, its members began to look for other means of checking royal power. Having re-instituted impeachments in that year, the Commons continued to experiment, and impeachment became, as it had been in the 1300s, a device of considerable procedural flexibility. Sometimes the lower house went so far as to impose a punishment upon the accused, merely asking the Lords to ratify its actions. In other cases it would turn the matter over to the Lords, taking varying degrees of interest in the subsequent proceedings.[28] Relying upon the commentaries of John Selden, Sir Edward Coke, and others to furnish it with a weapon against executive abuses, Parliament used precedent but did not become a slave to it. On the whole, its approach to impeachments was, as it had always been, a pragmatic one.[29]

The mid-seventeenth century saw the high tide of English impeachments. Francis Bacon, probably the most famous Englishman to find himself the target of this process, was one of its first modern victims, suffering conviction in 1621. In the following three decades impeachments and related procedures grew in number as the power struggles between Crown and Commons increased in magnitude. One source records that after 1621 Parliament voted over fifty impeachments, although not all of these cases went to trial.[30]

During this period the idea of a public interest as an element in

---

[27]Tite, *Judicature* 1-2.

[28]Ibid. at 141.

[29]Ibid. at 23, 31-53. Selden and others, in fact, divided the proceedings of the 1620s into several categories, only one of which included impeachments. Ibid. at 145. *Cf.* Clarke, "Origin," which finds impeachment to be growing clearer and more regularized by the 1640s.

[30]1 Stephen, *Criminal Law* 158-59; *cf.* Clayton Roberts, "The Law of Impeachment in Stuart England—A Reply to Raoul Berger," 84 *Yale L. J.* 1419, 1433-34 (1975).

impeachment continued as well. One author has attempted, with some success, to demonstrate a concept of public office emerging in England in the 1600s that held such offices to be a trust—a vesting of title to property (in this case the office) in one party (the officeholder) and the benefit or enjoyment of the property in another party (in this case the public). When the officeholder, the trustee, breached his trust, removal was the remedy. Along the same lines, we may also view impeachment as a sort of property action, preferred in consequence of the officeholder's breach of a condition on the property's use, the result of which is the reversion of title to the office to the grantor.[31] Forfeiture of office was, however, only one of many penalties that defendants faced.[32]

Opposed to this theory stands the view that reiterates the widespread opinion that impeachment was a criminal process aimed at the wrongdoer rather than the office, with the goal of punishing the miscreant rather than merely divesting him of his property interest. This interpretation is the dominant one, supported as it is by the fact that several defendants received sentences of imprisonment and death.[33] (This would seem a rather extreme means of recovering title to property.) In either case, however, a public interest element is present.

Impeachment remained a much-used practice until the late 1600s. As royal ministers eventually came to be directly responsible to Parliament, however, the use of impeachment as a check upon executive abuse of power became less necessary, and the practice began to decline once again, although Parliament continued to use the process for this purpose through the reign of George I. Impeachments of corrupt officials such as royal governors occurred on occasion thereafter.[34] But by 1800, with the Commons having

---

[31]E. Mabry Rogers & Stephen B. Young, "Public Office as a Public Trust: A Suggestion that Impeachment for High Crimes and Misdemeanors Implies a Fiduciary Standard," 63 *Geo. L.J.* 1025, 1028, 1040 (1975); *cf.* Edwin Brown Firmage, "The Law of Presidential Impeachment," 1973 *Utah L. Rev.* 681, 684 (1973); Roberts, "Reply," 1428; Berger, *Impeachment* 133. See Chapter 5, *infra*, for a discussion of this theory as it appeared in debates during the Blount affair.

[32]See note 33, *infra*.

[33]Tite, *Judicature* 1; Hoffer & Hull, *Impeachment* 3; 4 Blackstone, *Commentaries* *256.

[34]Berger, *Impeachment* 2-3.

established itself as the supreme governing branch, impeachment in England had practically disappeared, and no one in that country since 1805 has found himself the subject of an impeachment attempt.[35]

ᴣᴥ

Even as impeachment was being reborn in its native land during the early Stuart years, it was also finding its way into British North America. In 1635, fourteen years after Commons voted its first modern impeachment, the Virginia Burgesses brought charges against Governor James Harvey and tried him before his council. This event perhaps qualifies as the first impeachment to take place in the New World, although the process was not called by that name. Whatever the colonists called it, however, it mattered little to Harvey, whom the assembly removed from office and sent back to England for sentencing.[36] In 1657 we first find the term impeachment being used in America, with Roger Williams asking the bicameral Rhode Island legislature to impeach one William Harris on grounds of heresy and treason, which the legislature did. Harris, as had Harvey, consequently found himself bound for England. Following this episode came a smattering of other impeachments or impeachment-like proceedings.[37]

In addition to imitating the structural lines of established English impeachment—specifically, the bicameral division of impeachment powers—these colonial impeachments shared other traits with the English process. Just as the elements of medieval impeachment fell into place gradually, so too did American colonial impeachment evolve over time. Another similarity is the purpose that the seventeenth century colonial processes served. Although most cases targeted government officers' private wrongdoing, the public interest standard is still discernible as a motivation in these cases.[38] Finally,

---

[35]1 Holdsworth, *A History of English Law* 379-85; Riddell, "England," 706; Roberts, "Reply," 1428; Hoffer & Hull, *Impeachment* 7, 8, 39.

[36]Hoffer & Hull, *Impeachment* 16.

[37]Ibid. at 17.

[38]Hoffer and Hull argue that evidence of illegal acts injurious to the public proved necessary to justify impeachments, even when impeachment efforts arose from private motives. Ibid. at 25.

impeachment served in seventeenth century America, as it did in medieval and modern England, as a device whereby the representative assembly—usually the weakest branch of government—sought to gain more political power.[39]

Despite all of these similarities, some major differences emerged between parliamentary and American colonial impeachment even as early as the 1600s. The most striking distinction is probably the absence, in colonial impeachments, of penalties other than removal from office. The best authority on colonial impeachment argues that this limitation arose because those who brought the impeachments wished to avoid offending the officeholders' patrons in England.[40] This point reveals another difference. While impeachment arose in Parliament under a claim of right, in the colonial assemblies no such right existed.[41] Virginia, for example, was part of the royal domain, and the burgesses, in impeaching Harvey and others, did so without any grant of power from the Commons. The Crown, as grantor of the Virginia estate, was consequently in a position to review the colonial proceedings and protect its royal servants from undue punishment, as was not the case with parliamentary impeachments.[42] This avenue of appeal, moreover, was in itself another difference, for in England the Crown could not even pardon impeachment convictions, much less review or reverse them.[43]

In general, however, impeachment in the colonies was born of the same need for practicality and flexibility that had given rise to English impeachments. This practical approach, in fact, is what led to procedural vagaries in colonial impeachment practice, for colonial assemblies, though aware of the doctrine of impeachment, were not well acquainted with particular precedents. At any rate they applied the impeachment power in ways consistent with their needs, precedent notwithstanding.[44]

In the 1700s impeachments, even after beginning to decline in England, became more frequent in the colonies. In light of the

---

[39]Ibid. at xi.

[40]Ibid. at 25.

[41]Clarke, "Origin," 184; Hoffer & Hull, *Impeachment* 9, 27.

[42]Hoffer & Hull, *Impeachment* 16-17.

[43]Riddell, "Colonies," 704.

[44]Hoffer & Hull, *Impeachment* 26.

continuing power struggles between the Commons and the councilors of William and Mary, Anne, and George I, the colonists became increasingly aware of impeachment's potential as a political weapon, and they finally began to use it as such. While in the 1600s colonial assemblies aimed impeachments at individual wrongdoers in response to corruption or mismanagement, in the 1700s they often did so in order to attack the power of other branches of government.[45] This trend culminated in the Revolutionary era as Whig assemblies began to use the process to attack royal officials, and through them the very concept of English rule.[46] When Parliament finally began to deny the existence of a colonial impeaching power, Whig partisans then began to set forth legal justifications for a power that they had hitherto exercised as a matter of course.[47] One of the more famous episodes involving such arguments was the last colonial impeachment, occurring in 1773, which pitted Massachusetts Whigs against Chief Justice Peter Oliver and his supporter, Governor Thomas Hutchinson. While Oliver escaped trial and conviction, the affair greatly reduced the sway of these men over the colony, and thus it stands as a victory of revolutionary theory over English rule.[48]

By 1776, then, impeachment was a recognized and not infrequently-used device in North America; and just as revolutionaries before 1776 used this process to attack the power of those government branches under royal control, in the new era of statehood they incorporated it into their new systems of government as an instrument whereby the people, acting through legislatures, could continue to control abuses of executive authority. Indeed, in the new state constitutions we find the first prescriptive enactments or codifications of the impeachment power.[49]

Various models of impeachment came to exist in these constitutions. Pennsylvania and Vermont delegated the power to the supreme executive council. While several constitutions specified the upper house of the legislature as the place of impeachment trials, New York's provided for a special court composed of both legislative and

---

[45]Ibid. at 27, 28, 38.
[46]Ibid. at 41.
[47]Ibid. at 55-56.
[48]Ibid. at 10-14, 49-56.
[49]Ibid. at 68.

judicial officers. The Virginia Constitution took the process in a different direction, establishing the state supreme court as the place of trial.[50] The degree of emphasis that the Virginia Constitution placed on impeachment's judicial aspects is interesting, and it would have an effect on the first federal impeachment some years later.[51]

Generally, the new state impeachment provisions extended only to state officials. In this respect, while the constitutions followed colonial traditions (colonial impeachments being aimed exclusively at officeholders),[52] the new impeachment provisions raise an important question. Now that all branches of government were theoretically in the hands of the people, and were not under the control of different social interests or classes, what function would impeachment, thus restricted, serve?[53] In fact one immediate use soon became apparent. States promptly came to avail themselves of the process's flexibility to control officeholders' corruption, incompetence, and other sorts of wrongdoing for which no remedies lay in the criminal or common law. A number of these sorts of cases took place from the mid-1770s to the close of the following decade.[54]

As of the 1780s, then, impeachment was an old and well established practice in a number of the states, and although it had undergone some structural and functional changes, it continued to play a role in state politics before the adoption of the federal Constitution. This was the heritage that the delegates to the Constitutional Convention brought with them to Philadelphia in 1787.

---

[50]Pa. Const. of 1776, § 20, *in* 8 William F. Swindler, ed., *Sources and Documents of United States Constitutions* (Dobbs Ferry, New York: Oceana Publications, 1979) 282; Vt. Const. of 1777, § 18, *in* 9 Swindler, *Sources* 493; N.Y. Const. of 1777 §§ 32-34, *in* 7 Swindler, *Sources* 177; Va. Const of 1776, *in* 10 Swindler, *Sources* 55.

[51]See Chapters 4 and 5, *infra.*

[52]Hoffer and Hull, the best authorities on early American impeachments, assert that officers were the sole targets of the process because of the absence of an aristocracy, leaving officers the only obvious source of concentrated power. Hoffer & Hull, *Impeachment* 25-26.

[53]Hoffer and Hull (p. 60) stress this problem unduly; struggles between branches of government may involve the interests of the particular officers as much as those of the classes of whom they are representative.

[54]Ibid. at 78-95.

୬

The framers, for the most part, were probably very familiar with the concept of impeachment. The process was not only an important aspect of Whig political theory and practice upon which the revolutionaries drew, but also a process of which a number of delegates to the Philadelphia Convention had direct experience.[55]

Yet some controversy surrounds the question of the background out of which the constitutional version of the process emerged. The English tradition is the most frequently cited source. Common sense would suggest that English precedent played a major role in the framers' thought; one author notes, for instance, that a fair number of delegates had studied law in England,[56] and those who had simply read law in America gained exposure to the doctrine in the pages of Blackstone.[57] Even as the convention met, moreover, a celebrated impeachment, one of the last in England, was taking place in Parliament, as Edmund Burke and others sought to charge Warren Hastings, late Governor General of India, with corruption in office. This event did not escape the framers' notice.[58]

The framers, however, no doubt felt influences from other quarters as well. At least one writer has stressed the impact of Continental legal tradition upon the American concept, although his conclusions are questionable.[59] Another source of doctrinal influence was impeachment's colonial and early state history. Surprisingly, only a few scholars have paid any attention to the pre-1787 American experience; by far the best and most extensive work, by Peter C. Hoffer and N.E.H. Hull, contains substantial evidence that colonial

---

[55]Among those framers who had been involved in some way with impeachments or impeachment law prior to 1787 were Abraham Baldwin, William Richardson Davie, Jared Ingersoll, James Iredell, and Richard Dobbs Spaight. Hoffer & Hull, *Impeachment* 81, 88, 91; 20 Walter Clark, ed., *The State Records of North Carolina* (Goldsboro, N.C.: Nash Brothers, 1902) 205, 230.

[56]Firmage, "Law," 682.

[57]4 William Blackstone, *Commentaries* *256-58.

[58]Hoffer & Hull, *Impeachment* 113-15.

[59]Mitchell Franklin, "Romanist Infamy and the American Constitutional Conception of Impeachment," 23 *Buffalo L. Rev.* 313 (1974); Mitchell Franklin, "Further Considerations Relating to Romanist Infamy and the American Constitutional Conception of Impeachment," 24 *Buffalo L. Rev.* 29 (1974).

and early state antecedents exercised a profound influence in the framers' shaping of the national power.[60] This conclusion, in retrospect, seems obvious.[61]

The records of the convention reveal clearly that the framers' main goal in adopting the impeachment process was to provide a check upon the executive branch's abuse of power, which was of course the main function that impeachment had served in England. Most of the early proposals usually mentioned impeachment in connection with the executive officer, as indeed two clauses do today.[62] Many delegates sought to make the executive removable for such offenses as "mal-practice or neglect of duty,"[63] and even those who opposed impeachment did so on the grounds that it would make the executive the pawn of the legislature.[64] When two delegates moved to strike the clause that rendered the executive impeachable, George Mason replied in outrage, "Shall any man be above Justice? Above all shall that man be above it, who can commit the most extensive injustice?" Benjamin Franklin followed this comment with the wry observation that removal of an executive by impeachment was preferable to removal by assassination.[65] Thus, the primary function for impeachments, as intended by the framers, seems clear.

Some indications that the framers intended federal judges to be impeachable also exist, but compared to the clauses relating impeachment to the executive they are few in number and appear almost as an afterthought. August 22 found a committee recommending that the Constitution include provisions for the impeachment of Supreme Court judges. A few days later appear discussions of the standard for judicial removal, with Gouverneur Morris arguing that if judges were removable for misbehavior (good behavior being the constitutionally mandated condition for their continuance in office) some sort of trial procedure should be available

---

[60]Hoffer & Hull, *Impeachment* 268-69.

[61]The debates surrounding the drafting of the Constitution's impeachment provisions have been the subject of numerous inquiries. Because some cover the affair far more thoroughly than is necessary or appropriate here, we will confine our study of the convention to a few of the most relevant issues.

[62]U.S. Const. art. I, § 3, cl. 6; U.S. Const. art. II, § 4.

[63]1 Farrand, *Records* 78.

[64]Ibid. at 86; 2 Farrand, *Records* 53.

[65]2 Farrand, *Records* 65.

to determine when breach of this condition had occurred. During this same discussion John Dickinson moved to make judges removable by legislative address, an English device which does not appear expressly in the finished Constitution.[66]

The convention's rejection of address has led to considerable debate as to whether judges are removable by impeachment—the only removal process the Constitution expressly mentions—and if so, the appropriate standard for removal. Article III, Section 1 provides that judges shall hold office "during good Behaviour," yet the only express standard for removal by impeachment, found in Article II, Section 4, is "Treason, Bribery, or other high Crimes and Misdemeanors."[67] The difficulty of reconciling these clauses with respect to judicial removal continues to plague scholars, politicians, and judges today, and judicial removal itself is perhaps the most prominent issue to be found within recent impeachment debates.[68] The question of the framers' intent regarding judges' impeachment thus remains an open one.

Whether the framers considered legislators to be subject to the impeachment process is an interesting question. Although the issue received considerable attention during the ratification debates, not to mention the Blount impeachment, little mention of the issue appears in the records of the convention itself. The only such comments appear in the records for July 20th; the first is an observation by James Madison, which (like so many other impeachment debates) relates primarily to the need for executive accountability.

---

[66]Ibid. at 367, 428.

[67]See 40-46, *infra*, for a discussion of the meaning of the term "high Crimes and Misdemeanors."

[68]For a small sampling of these debates, See Feerick, "Judges," *passim.*; Warren S. Grimes, "Hundred-Ton-Gun Control: Preserving Impeachment as the Exclusive Removal Mechanism For Federal Judges." 38 *UCLA L. Rev.* 1209 (1991); Howell T. Heflin, "The Impeachment Process: Modernizing an Archaic System," 71 *Judicature* 123 (August/September 1987); Philip B. Kurland, "The Constitution and the Tenure of Federal Judges: Some Notes From History," 36 *U. Chi. L. Rev.* 665 (1969); W.G. McAdoo, "Alternative Method to Impeachment for Trial of Inferior Court Judges," 42 *Case & Com.* 9 (1936); Mitch McConnell, "Reflections on the Senate's Role in the Judicial Impeachment Process and Proposals for Change," 76 *Ky. L.J.* 739 (1987-88); Melissa H. Maxman, "In Defense of the Constitution's Judicial Impeachment Standard," 86 *Mich. L. Rev.* 420 (1987). In practice impeachment has proven to be the only means for removal of Article III judges.

The case of the Executive Magistracy [argued Madison] was very distinguishable from that of the Legislative or of any other public body, holding offices of limited duration. It could not be presumed that all or even a majority of the members of an Assembly would either lose their capacity for discharging, or be bribed to betray, their trust. Besides the restraints of their personal integrity & honor, the difficulty of acting in concert for purposes of corruption was a security to the public. And if one or a few members only should be seduced, the soundness of the remaining members, would maintain the integrity and fidelity of the body.[69]

In the debate that followed, New York delegate Rufus King argued that the judiciary, but not the executive, should be subject to impeachment. The difference, he maintained, was that "the Judiciary hold their places not for a limited time, but during good behaviour. It is necessary therefore," he continued, "that a forum should be established for trying misbehaviour." In contrast, King pointed out, the executive was to hold office for a fixed term, as would the members of the Senate; like senators, he argued, the executive "would periodically be tried for his behaviour by his electors, who would continue or discontinue him in trust according to the manner in which he had discharged it." Therefore, King concluded, like senators the executive "ought to be subject to no intermediate trial, by impeachment." [70] To this James Wilson added his own comment that if the convention wished to make the executive subject to impeachment, then "the Senators who are to hold their places during the same term with the Executive ought to be subject to impeachment & removal."[71]

King's statements are the strongest ones against the impeachability of legislators, although Madison's suggest that he agreed; Wilson's declaration that senators should be amenable to the process was almost certainly rhetorical, and the lack of any recorded reply to his claim seems to demonstrate that this was how the other delegates

---

[69] 2 Farrand, *Records* 66.
[70] Ibid. at 66-67.
[71] Ibid. at 68.

viewed it as well. But the vote that took place at the end of this debate was expressly upon the question of whether the executive was to be subject to impeachment, so this brief, tangential discussion of senatorial susceptibility to impeachment is not an entirely satisfactory answer to the question, especially in light of issues that appeared in the ratification debates.

The constitutional text that resulted from these debates also fails to answer the question, as debates during the Blount impeachment reveal. Article II, Section 4 provides that "The President, Vice President and all civil Officers of the United States" are subject to removal by impeachment. As to members of other branches of government, or for that matter the definition of the term "civil Officers," neither the text nor the convention debates are very helpful. One thing, however, is clear: the framers, like Parliament before them, devised this power mainly with the executive branch in mind. As Raoul Berger has written,

> The Framers were steeped in English history; the shades of despotic kings and conniving ministers marched before them .... It was not developments in parliamentary government during the eighteenth century upon which the eyes of the Framers were fixed, but rather on the seventeenth century, the great period when Parliament struggled to curb ministers who were the tools of royal oppression. Familiarity with absolutist Stuart claims raised the specter of a President swollen with power and grown tyrannical; and fear of presidential abuses prevailed over frequent objections that impeachment threatened his independence.[72]

Despite these observations, the fact remains that of over a dozen impeachments in American national history, only two targeted executive officers—those of President Andrew Johnson in 1868 and Secretary of War William W. Belknap in 1876.[73] The Watergate

---

[72]Berger, *Impeachment* 4-5 (footnotes omitted).

[73]U.S., Congress, House, Committee on the Judiciary, *Constitutional Grounds for Presidential Impeachment* (Washington: Public Affairs Press, 1974) [SuDocs Y4.J89/1:Im7/3] 47, 49; Charles Morgan, Jr. et al., "Impeachment: An Historical Overview," 5 *Seton Hall L. Rev.* 689, 702-05 (1974).

proceedings raise this number to three. Congress directed the first impeachment at a senator, the second at an inferior court judge, and the third at a Supreme Court associate justice. Because the convention debates in themselves contain little indication as to whether such uses of the power were what the framers contemplated, we must look elsewhere, beginning with the ratification debates. But another issue remains regarding the convention's collective deliberations. This is the most controversial impeachment issue of all, an issue that, if effectively resolved, would decide the theoretical limits of Congress's impeachment powers.

ॐ

The debate over the meaning of the phrase "other high Crimes and Misdemeanors," while in itself of little importance in the Blount episode, nevertheless is representative of a conflict between general interpretations of the impeachment power that were first clearly enunciated, with significant theoretical repercussions, in that case. These conflicting views are the broad-construction and the strict-construction approaches, both of which attempt to fix the limits of Congress's impeachment jurisdiction. The question of what constitutes an impeachable offense, of what is included in the term "other high Crimes and Misdemeanors," is the leading one in this larger controversy. The phrase's English origins, and the history of its incorporation into the Constitution, have often been the subject of researchers' scrutiny, and diverse conclusions as to the term's definition may be found in the literature and in various congressional and convention debates.

The phrase, which appears frequently in the context of English impeachments, in fact has an uncertain history. Different scholars place the time of its first use as early as 1386 and as late as 1642.[74] The meaning of the term as used in English law is also in doubt. Sir William Blackstone, author of the famed commentaries that carried such authority in North America, asserted—at least according to Raoul Berger—that the phrase was merely solemn wording, having no

---

[74]Jerome S. Sloan & Ira E. Carr, "Treason, Bribery, or Other High Crimes and Misdemeanors—A Study of Impeachment," 47 *Temp. L.Q.* 413, 427 (1974); Roberts, "Reply," 1431.

substantive meaning.[75] Berger differs, holding the term to encompass political offenses, that is, crimes against the government.[76] Another author flatly contradicts this finding, attempting to demonstrate that the concept of crimes against the state did not exist in England in the period in question. (This same author, however, supports the idea of a public trust impeachment standard, with its notion of public or community interest which is similar in some ways to the idea of crimes against the state).[77] He goes on to argue that under the "high Crimes and Misdemeanors" formula, no one in England ever suffered conviction for acts that were not also regular criminal law offenses, thus asserting, in effect, that this phrase meant only indictable (not political) offenses.[78] A number of scholars have taken issue with this standard as well, arguing that the term also includes nonindictable acts.[79] Regarding the English usage, then, the only thing that is clear is that little or no agreement exists.

When we turn to secondary accounts of the term's incorporation into the Constitution, matters only grow worse. Although one author contends that "maladministration," rather than "high Crimes and Misdemeanors," was the phrase appearing in state constitutions before 1787,[80] for use in the federal document the framers chose the term that has ever since been the subject of so much scrutiny. The context of the term's adoption appears relevant, so the oft-reproduced account of the key debate appears yet again below. The date was September 8, and the convention's end was approaching. Most other impeachment provisions had taken a fairly complete form, but then George Mason, according to Madison's notes, made an

---

[75]Berger, *Impeachment* 59 (citing 4 Blackstone, *Commentaries* *5 [observing that crimes and misdemeanors are synonymous]). *But cf.* 4 Blackstone, *Commentaries* *121 (classifying a high misdemeanor as a misprision rather than a crime, and thus suggesting that "high Crimes and Misdemeanors" may have identify some particular offenses).

[76]Berger, *Impeachment* 59-60.

[77]Roberts, "Reply," 1427-28.

[78]Ibid. at 1432.

[79]Firmage, "Law," 687.

[80]Feerick, "Judges," 49; see, e.g., N.C. Const. of 1776, § 23, *in* 7 Swindler, *Sources* 406; Pa. Const. of 1776, § 22, *in* 8 Swindler, ed., *Sources* 282; Vt. Const. of 1777, § 20, *in* 9 Swindler, *Sources* 493; Va. Const. of 1776, *in* 10 Swindler, *Sources* 55.

objection.

> Col. Mason: Why is the provision restrained to Treason & bribery only? Treason as defined in the Constitution will not reach many great and dangerous offenses. Hastings is not guilty of Treason. Attempts to subvert the Constitution may not be Treason as above defined— As bills of attainder which have saved the British Constitution are forbidden, it is the more necessary to extend: the power of impeachments. He movd. to add after "bribery" "or maladministration". Mr. Gerry seconded him—
> Mr. Madison: So vague a term will be equivalent to a tenure during pleasure of the Senate.
> Mr. Govr Morris, it will not be put in force & can do no harm—An election of every four years will prevent maladministration.
> Col. Mason withdrew "maladministration" & substitutes "other high crimes & misdemeanors" <agst. the State">.[81]

On the face of this passage, the speakers' intent seems clear. Mason undoubtedly wished at the outset to enlarge the scope of impeachable offenses beyond that of treason and bribery. Madison objected to Mason's proposal of the term "maladministration" because he feared that it would be too broad. As to whether Mason intended the breadth to which Madison objected, or instead had unwittingly chosen a term that signified a broader power to Madison than it did to himself, we have no clue. Morris apparently concurred in Madison's understanding of the word, although he did not object to its use. Finally Mason withdrew the contested word and offered instead the English phrase, to which a majority of the convention agreed.

Because of the inclusion of words in addition to the original wording of treason and bribery, as well as Mason's first comments that show his desire to broaden the scope of impeachable offenses, no doubt exists that impeachable offenses finally came to include something more than treason and bribery. Since Mason apparently

---

[81]2 Farrand, *Records* 550. The bracketed words were taken from the convention journal and appear as they do above in Madison's account.

substituted "other high crimes & misdemeanors," with or without the "agst the State" qualification, in response to Madison's objection as to the breadth of "maladministration," and because no broader definition than tenure at pleasure exists, we may infer that Mason gave the English phrase a more restricted meaning than the standard of maladministration. On the face of the debate, then, we may conclude that the framers, in agreeing to Mason's change, endorsed an impeachment power that had certain limits—that they enjoined the Senate from constitutionally convicting impeachment defendants at whim, or in Madison's phrase, at pleasure. Unfortunately, in light of the key phrase's nebulous pre-1787 history, the 8 September debate reveals little else.

Some authors maintain that we cannot safely conclude even as much as this analysis would have us believe. Relying upon Blackstone's assertion that the English term "misdemeanor" includes, among other things, maladministration, Arthur Bestor has claimed that Madison and the other framers, in accepting Mason's second term, actually broadened the scope of impeachable offenses to include maladministration.[82] Certainly Bestor's view may justify a broad "tenure at pleasure" interpretation—depending on our (and Blackstone's) understanding of the term in question as used before 1787—if we ignore the framers' intent entirely and adopt a "plain meaning" approach. Bestor's conclusion, however, stands in sharp contrast to the framers' desire, as seen on the face of the 8 September debate, to restrict the definition of impeachable offenses and exclude maladministration from that definition.

Here arises a conflict between rules of construction that illustrate the problems in interpretive theory addressed above;[83] the controversy's outcome depends largely on the rule that the interpreter applies. Neither the plain meaning rule nor the original intent rule is inherently invalid; in this instance, however, the former is far less conclusive and therefore less suitable, for two reasons.

In the first place, as has been noted, the meaning of the term "high Crimes and Misdemeanors" as used in England is in doubt, and

---

[82]Arthur Bestor, "Book Review, Berger, Impeachment: The Constitutional Problems," 49 *Wash. L. Rev.* 255, 269-70 (1973) (citing 4 Blackstone, *Commentaries* *121).

[83]See Prologue, *supra*.

this statement was true even in 1787, if Bestor's assertion is to be believed. For if Mason knew of Blackstone's definition, and Madison did not, then a difference of understanding as to the term's meaning existed at that time. Even if this is so, however, the September 8 debate reveals a relatively clear intent on the part of the framers— Mason's understanding of the term notwithstanding—that the term be adopted as a more restricted definition than maladministration. This intent is much clearer than the pre-1787 meaning of the phrase in English law.

If, on the other hand, Mason did *not* know of Blackstone's definition, as Madison apparently did not, we have, once again, a clear intent—this time with Mason's concurrence—and the confused state of the English law remains unchanged. Even if the framers themselves were guided by what they believed to be a plain meaning of the term, upon which they agreed, then *that* "plain meaning," of all the possible "plain meanings" suggested by recent scholarship, becomes authoritative only because of the framers' adoption of it—and the record reveals that the meaning adopted on September 8 was a restricted one.

Only if Mason actually *intended* to deceive Madison (to take Bestor's argument to the extreme), and, moreover, a majority of the other delegates knew of, and agreed to, Mason's definition—leaving Madison and perhaps a few others in the position of unwittingly agreeing to the broad definition—only then does the record of this debate mislead us, thus making original intent rule an unsafe guide. The fact is, however, that a conspiracy of this sort seems unlikely, for the chance that everyone present who knew Blackstone's definition wished to deceive Madison is remote. Therefore the record of the September 8 debate almost certainly reveals accurately the framers' original intent. Those who are partial to the plain meaning rule may apply it with far greater certitude to that passage than to the pre-1787 history of the term "high Crimes and Misdemeanors."[84]

---

[84]On June 17, 1789, Madison described impeachable offenses as including maladministration, thus apparently contradicting his statement of 1787. 1 *Annals of Cong.* 515, 517 (J. Gales ed. 1789). Perhaps he had by the latter date acquainted himself with Blackstone's definition; but in any case his subsequent state of mind has no bearing on what he (and more importantly, what the other delegates) took the term to mean in September 1787. This sort of change of heart,

The second reason why the framers' intent, as found in the 1787 debates, should serve as the principal guideline is not one of clarity but sovereignty. As of 1787 English law no longer served as controlling authority in the United States. Even when English common law precedents appeared in state legal systems, they existed there only because the newly sovereign state governments had ratified or accepted them either through positive enactment or through consent by silence.[85] Although English authority could serve in a persuasive role—as it continues to do even today—some time before the acceptance of the 1783 Treaty of Paris it ceased to be the controlling law. The English experience with impeachment, at points on which it is clear, may furnish us with valuable guidelines, but in all circumstances the English experience is that of another jurisdiction, the law of which American constitutional institutions are not bound. The Philadelphia Convention is the focal point, the sieve through which English antecedents of the federal constitutional provisions were sifted and adapted. Whatever the meaning of the term in question before 1787, the relatively clear intent of the framers preempted it. And the nation at large ratified not English law, but the framers' handiwork. What this means in sum, then, is that if we discern a clear intent that the term be limited in American usage, then the term is one of limitation regardless of the state of English law as of 1787.

Thus we must conclude, based on the framers' intent as revealed in the account of the September 8th debate, that the category of impeachable offenses was restricted, and that the convention placed Congress under some degree of limitations in its exercising the impeachment power. The other debates of 1787 further reveal that the principal subject of the power was to be the President and his officers; judges were possibly amenable to the process, and the liability of legislators, while unlikely, was enough of a possibility to

---

intentional or inadvertent, is a prime reason to approach subsequent comments of the drafters with caution; but the dangers posed by misleading aberrations such as these diminish in direct proportion to the number of subsequent statements studied, especially if more than one delegate is involved.

[85]For a discussion of the common law's history in the early United States, including the reception statutes, see *Lawrence M. Friedman, A History of American Law* (New York: Simon & Schuster, 1985) 110-15.

warrant our attention. In the final analysis these are very few facts. While the Constitution is vague on impeachable offenses, moreover, it says almost nothing at all about procedural matters;[86] thus Congress, of necessity, is in a position to develop in actual practice both the substantive and procedural parameters of impeachment. But before such circumstances arose, the nation at large, through its representatives and commentators, would speak out on the provisions of the new Constitution. In doing so they would help to illumine the ratifiers' intent and understanding of the Constitution and its impeachment provisions.

৵

Undoubtedly the best-known commentary on the impeachment power to appear in the years immediately following the convention came from the quill of Alexander Hamilton, who devoted a good deal of space to the subject in his *Federalist* writings. Concerning the question of impeachable offenses, in the context of the Senate's role in the impeachment process, Hamilton wrote:

> The subjects of its [the Senate's] jurisdiction are those offenses which proceed from the misconduct of public men, or in other words from the abuse or violation of some public trust. They are of a nature which may with peculiar propriety be denominated POLITICAL, as they relate chiefly to injuries done immediately to the society itself.[87]

Despite Hamilton's identification of impeachment's political objectives, however, he furnished few guidelines for determining the extent of the power. Nor did he consider these political aspects—despite his emphasis on that word and his characterization of the process as a "NATIONAL INQUEST into the conduct of public men"[88]—to conflict with the process's judicial nature.[89] Perhaps in

---

[86]Napoleon B. Williams, Jr., "The Historical and Constitutional Bases for the Senate's Power to Use Masters or Committees to Receive Evidence in Impeachment Trials," 50 *N.Y.U. L. Rev.* 512, 520 (1975).

[87]*The Federalist* No. 65, at 439 (A. Hamilton) (Jacob E. Cooke ed., 1961).

[88]Ibid. at 440.

this age in which legislatures, in accordance with Blackstone's descriptions, sometimes acted arbitrarily, often with great power and usually with no check,[90] Hamilton considered judicial proceedings to be a more rational and detached means of exercising the impeachment power. In discussing impeachment's judicial nature he emphasized the Senate's independent and dignified character.[91]

Hamilton was by no means alone in understanding the process to be at least partly judicial rather than purely political. Within days of the convention's end, a Philadelphia commentator had described the Senate as a mature and detached group of judges, whom the Constitution required to sit under oath.[92] In December 1787 a Virginia Federalist also noted this judicial character, pointing out that because the Senate shared the impeachment powers with the House of Representatives, the process would not get out of hand.[93] Still another Virginian went so far as to call the Senate a court.[94]

This characterization appeared not only among Federalist writings, but in those of Antifederalists as well. A published dissent of a minority of the Pennsylvania legislature, answering a Federalist representative's arguments on this point, protested the vesting of judicial powers in the Senate. Because of its role in confirming presidential nominees, the dissent read, the Senate would be an interested party, judging officers whom the senators themselves had helped to appoint.[95] These same officers might have the duty of enforcing the provisions of Senate-approved treaties, complained a New York author. As a result of this blending of executive and judicial

---

[89]Ibid. at 439.

[90]1 Blackstone, *Commentaries* *46, *91.

[91]*The Federalist* No. 65, at 441 (A. Hamilton) (Jacob E. Cooke ed., 1961). Madison, in the pages of *The Federalist*, went at least as far as Hamilton toward viewing the power as judicial. See *The Federalist* No. 38, at 245 (J. Madison) (Jacob E. Cooke ed., 1961) (indicating his belief that impeachment is a judicial power despite its exercise by the legislative branch); *The Federalist* No.47, at 325 (J. Madison) (Jacob E. Cooke ed., 1961) (describing the Senate as "the sole depository of judicial power in cases of impeachment").

[92]13 Merrill Jensen, ed., *The Documentary History of the Ratification of the Constitution* (Madison: State Historical Society of Wisconsin, 1981) 265 (hereinafter *Documentary History*).

[93]8 Ibid. at 246.

[94]16 Ibid. at 168.

[95]15 Ibid. at 29.

authority in the upper house, the country might witness at some point the "monstrous absurdity" of the Senate sitting in judgment of officers charged with executing that to which the Senate itself had consented.[96] Many people thus viewed impeachment as a judicial function.

As these statements show, the Senate's role in the executive treaty-making power, and the relationship between Senate and president that many believed would evolve, caused some concern regarding the impeachment power's viability. In fact some of the debates on this point shed a good bit of light on issues that would surface again during the Blount affair.

Many citizens objected to the Constitution's impeachment provisions because of their belief that the Senate would serve as an executive council, or in Madison's words, as "a great constitutional council to the executive chief."[97] Their memories of colonial traditions are visibly at work here, for in many cases the "upper house" of a legislature was actually a quasi-legislative, cabinet-like body having more in common with the governor, in functional terms, than with the assembly or lower legislative house.[98] Even though the Senate, as established by the Constitution, was much more a part of the legislature than the colonial agencies, it still retained some non-legislative attributes, particularly the power to ratify treaties and to confirm presidential appointees, as Hamilton had noted in *The Federalist*.[99] Many members of the framers' generation perceived other such powers as well.

One constitutional clause that many individuals apparently feared was Article II, Section 2, Clause 2, which grants the president the power "by and with the Advice and Consent of the Senate, to make Treaties." This wording would seem to suggest, and in fact it did suggest to many people in the late 1780s, that the Senate would play an active role in negotiating and drafting treaties. President Washington, within the first months of his inauguration, attempted to confer with the Senate while preparing an Indian treaty, but the

---

[96]14 Ibid. at 184, 189.

[97]*The Federalist* No. 47, at 325 (J. Madison) (Jacob E. Cooke ed., 1961).

[98]See Gordon S. Wood, *The Creation of the American Republic 1776-1787* (Chapel Hill: The University of North Carolina Press, 1969) 210-11.

[99]*The Federalist* No. 65, at 439 (A. Hamilton) (Jacob E. Cooke ed., 1961).

Senate soon rebuffed him.[100] This episode probably helped the cabinet to acquire a more important position within the American system of government.

Washington was not alone in his thinking. Less than a month after the adjournment of the 1787 convention, Arthur Lee wrote John Adams a letter, protesting that under the new Constitution the president was to be tried by his own councillors, perhaps for acts that they themselves had advised.[101] The following summer, a delegate to the North Carolina ratifying convention echoed this concern.[102] Hamilton, in *The Federalist*, answered arguments such as these, but not by denying the link between Senate and executive. Instead he predicted that the Senate would certainly convict a president who failed to follow the Senate's instructions in treaty negotiations, since the senators would act out of pride, if not virtue.[103]

Commentators on the subject of impeachment discussed possibilities other than trials of presidents. A large amount of writing and debate on the issue of legislators' (or at least senators') amenability to impeachment also appears, including many comments that evince a widespread belief that senators were in fact subject to the impeachment process. Hamilton, for instance, adopted this position in *The Federalist*. The "American Cicero" was probably absent from the Convention on July 20, the day that what passed for a discussion of the impeachability of legislators took place,[104] but he no doubt had opportunities to know what the delegates—including his collaborator Madison—had said that day. Nevertheless, he took the position that senators were subject to the process.[105]

---

[100]1 *Annals of Cong.* 67-72 (J. Gales ed. 1789); William Maclay, *The Journal of William Maclay* (New York: Albert & Charles Boni, 1927) 124-30; Henry Barrett Learned, "The Origin and Creation of the President's Cabinet," 15 *Yale Rev.* 160 (1906).

[101]8 *Documentary History* 34.

[102]4 Jonathan Elliot, *The Debates in the Several State Conventions on the Adoption of the Federal Constitution* (Washington: Printed for the Editor, 1836) 124-25.

[103]*The Federalist* No. 66, at 450-51 (A. Hamilton) (Jacob E. Cooke ed., 1961).

[104]3 Farrand, *Records* 588; John C. Miller, *Alexander Hamilton: Portrait in Paradox* (New York: Harper & Brothers, 1959) 171, 178.

[105]One scholar has recently declared that in *The Federalist* Hamilton denied that senators were impeachable. Gerhardt, *Impeachment Process* 15, 183 (citing the Clinton Rossiter edition of *The Federalist*). A close reading of the passage in

Hamilton was by no means alone. Shortly after the convention's end, Virginia delegate Edmund Randolph penned his desire to have the states demand the creation of a tribunal other than the Senate for the purpose of trying the impeachment of senators. Unlike Hamilton, Randolph was unquestionably present during the 20 July debate on impeachment; indeed, he spoke that day on the subject, though none of his comments touched upon the question of the impeachability of legislators. As his latter comments show, whatever he heard that day failed to convince him that senators were were exempt from the process, although he obviously had reservations about this state of things.[106] About this same time Arthur Lee objected to the impeachment power because senators, being advisors on all great matters of state, would frequently be both judge and party.[107]

Richard Henry Lee was a vociferous opponent of the proposed Constitution, and he aimed one of his many criticisms at the impeachment process. Protesting that the president and the Senate between them would control all executive and most of the legislative power, he claimed that the House of Representatives would be able to exercise little authority over these agencies as the Senate was to try

---

question, however, shows this conclusion to be erroneous; Hamilton simply denied the impeachability of a large number of senators for acts that they committed in a collective capacity, for the practical reason that the requirement of a two-thirds vote for conviction would render the process impossible to complete. The framers, he wrote, might

> have had in view the punishment of a few leading individuals in the senate, who should have prostituted their influence in that body, as mercenary instruments of foreign corruption: But they could not with more or less equal propriety have contemplated the impeachment and punishment of two-thirds of the senate, consenting to an improper treaty, than of a majority of that or of the other branch of the national legislature, consenting to a pernicious or unconstitutional law: a principle which I believe has never been admitted into any government.

If, on the other hand, the leading members of the senate somehow convinced a majority to approve evil measures, "there would be commonly no defect of inclination in the body, to divert the public resentment from themselves, by a ready sacrifice of the authors of their mismanagement and disgrace." *The Federalist* No. 66, at 450-51 (A. Hamilton) (Jacob E. Cooke ed., 1961).

[106]15 *Documentary History* 134; 2 Farrand, *Debates* 67.
[107]13 *Documentary History* 510.

both its own members and executive officers as well. On another occasion Lee wrote to Randolph that the Senate's power to try its own members was an improper one, since this arrangement allowed the Senate to exercise both judicial and executive powers.[108] In this passage Lee does not suggest another interpretation of the impeachment provisions that would preclude the possible impeachment of senators. On the contrary, he patently accepts as a given the fact that senators were impeachable. Whether he adopted this belief sincerely or instead merely seized upon it as one of many weaknesses to exploit in his campaign against ratification is uncertain, but the statements themselves are unequivocal.

Federalists often agreed that senators were impeachable. Delegate James Wilson, speaking in the Pennsylvania ratifying convention, conceded that the combining of the treaty and impeachment powers in the same body would make the process of calling senators to account for their actions a difficult one. He dismissed the idea, however, that more than a few senators would behave wrongly at any given moment, the miscreants thus being answerable by virtue of their small numbers to their honest colleagues. Wilson then went on to point out that even if convictions in impeachment trials did not result, the errant senators would still be subject to regular criminal processes.[109]

Perhaps the most revealing episode on this point took place on June 14, 1788, as the Virginia ratifying convention debated the question of federal control of the state militia. As the delegates discussed the accountability of the national government, Patrick Henry suddenly turned upon James Madison, ridiculing his claim that the new government would responsibly exercise its limited powers. In opposition to this claim, Henry entreated his fellow delegates to consider "the American Parliament," a stinging comparison of the proposed government to that of England, from which the states had so recently wrested their independence. "Are the members of the Senate responsible?" he asked rhetorically. "They may try themselves, and, if found guilty on impeachment, are to be only removed from

---

[108]14 Ibid. at 367; 8 Ibid. at 61-62.

[109]2 Elliot, *Debates* 477. Wilson was referring to Article I, Section 3, Clause 7, which provides that a party convicted by impeachment is also liable to criminal proceedings in the regular courts.

office." In England, Henry went on, they would face execution instead. Congress, moreover, might shield its own wrongdoers by publishing its minutes rarely, thus keeping its proceedings private.[110]

Madison, in responding to Henry, noted that the Constitution forbade senators to hold offices while they remained in the legislature. He may have meant to reduce the fear of unchecked senatorial power by this comment. This passage, however, might also mean that senators, not being civil officers, are not subject to impeachment at all, in which case it might have had the opposite effect on the other delegates. At any rate, Randolph then spoke in support of Madison, maintaining that the Senate's abuse of its treaty power would be the source for many impeachments; and as treaties would be as public in the new nation as they were in England, he went on, potential wrongdoers would be quite visible.[111]

George Mason then joined the debate on Henry's side. After the Senate had secured a treaty "manifestly repugnant to the interests of the country," he asked, how would the country punish its members? What if the senators had supported the treaty because of bribery or corruption? How was the truth to come out? As senators were to try themselves, Mason asked, if a majority were guilty would they convict themselves? He dismissed the idea that either state or federal courts would try members of the government even for indictable offenses, and argued that impeachment would thus be the only process available for holding them accountable, all the worse because it would be one in which the accused would make their own rules. Mason scoffed at Madison's assertion that such devices would lead to a responsible government.[112]

Although Madison replied that Congress, more than Parliament, would be bound by law (in itself a significant remark revealing a belief in proscriptions upon impeachment), he had little else to say on the issue. Henry's and Mason's objections did not prove fatal, however, to the Virginia Federalists' ratification efforts, which succeeded soon

---

[110]3 Jonathan Elliot, ed., *The Debates in the Several State Conventions on the Adoption of the Federal Constitution*, 2d ed. (Philadelphia: J.B. Lippincott & Co., 1859) 397.

[111]Ibid. at 399-401.

[112]Ibid. at 402-03.

after this debate.[113] The exchange, however, failed to quell concerns about conflicts of senatorial interest during impeachment trials. Before adjourning, the convention proposed several amendments to the constitution. Among these appeared a requirement that "some tribunal other than the Senate be provided for trying impeachments of Senators." [114]

One fact is quite obvious from this and other episodes. When a discussion of the impeachment of senators arises in the ratification debates, as it frequently does, the speakers and writers usually connect senators' susceptibility to the process to their executive duties, particularly the treaty power. This coincidence indicates that the ratifiers, and some framers too, equated senators with the royal councillors who had so often been the target of earlier impeachments.

Still other evidence supports this conclusion. A few months before the Virginia convention met, the writer "Civis Rusticus" declared that the executive advisory power, because of the lack of an executive council proper, rested improperly in the Senate. These sentiments echoed even earlier comments issuing from a New Jersey commentator to the effect that the president should be able to choose his own advisors, a measure which would at once make him more responsible for their conduct and eliminate any conflict of interest that senators might face in being both members of an executive advisory body and judges at the president's impeachment. Finally came a critique from the outspoken Antifederalist Luther Martin of Maryland, who dismissed out of hand any thought that senators, as presidential advisors, would ever convict the chief executive even in the unlikely event that the House impeached him at all.[115]

Two statements in the Massachusetts ratifying convention also support this interpretation, though here some stretching is necessary.

---

[113]Ibid. at 409, 653-57.

[114]3 Jonathan Elliot, ed., *The Debates in the Several State Conventions, on the Adoption of the Federal Constitution, as Recommended by the General Convention at Philadelphia in 1787* (Philadelphia; J.B. Lippincott Company, 1836), 661. Likewise, a 1789 congressional draft of proposed constitutional amendments included a provision that incorporated the same language. See Helen E. Veit et al., eds., *Creating the Bill of Rights: The Documentary Record from the First Federal Congress* (Baltimore: The Johns Hopkins University Press, 1991) 45.

[115]8 *Documentary History* 333; 13 Ibid. at 561; 14 Ibid. at 292.

In January of 1788 General John Brooks, arguing in favor of ratification, attempted to show that the proposed Constitution provided the public with safeguards against the mischief of "bad men." "If there should be such in the Senate," he declared, "we ought to be cautious of giving power; but when that power is given, with proper checks, the danger is at an end." As an example of this dynamic, Brooks cited the circumstances of senators. "The Senate can frame no law but by the consent of the Representatives," he observed, "and is answerable to that house for its conduct. If that conduct excites suspicion," he continued, "they are to be impeached, punished, (or prevented from holding any office, which is great punishment.)"[116]

Why did Brooks single out the Senate? Obviously several things distinguished that chamber from the House, including its members' longer tenure and their indirect election. Brooks's characterization of the representatives as the defenders of the public highlights the tension that many citizens no doubt perceived between the two houses. Nevertheless, the Senate's executive functions, which also set it apart from the House, may well have been on his mind. Whether or not this was so, however, he undeniably considered senators to be impeachable.

The following month delegate Samuel Stillman made a similar remark, though in light of developments in the Blount impeachment his are a bit more intriguing. Stillman, like Brooks, supported ratification; like Brooks, he wanted to show that the Constitution provided for popular control of the central government. "Another check in favor of the people," he stated on February 6th, "is this—that the Constitution provides for impeachment, trial, and punishment of every officer in Congress, who shall be guilty of malconduct. With such a prospect," he asked rhetorically, "who will dare to abuse the powers vested in him by the people?"[117]

Though Stillman failed to explain what he meant by "officers," he obviously chose the word because the constitutional language provided that all "civil officers" were subject to impeachment. Stillman could just as easily have stated that all members of Congress were impeachable, had he believed that all members of Congress were civil officers, but he refrained from doing so. The logical conclusion is

---

[116]2 Elliott, *Debates* 44-45.
[117]Ibid. at 168-69.

that he believed only some members of Congress to be civil officers. The question then becomes one of who these officers were. Immediately following its mention of the Speaker of the House, the Constitution makes a vague reference to "other officers;" It similarly treats the Vice President, who of course serves as President of the Senate, though paradoxically it mentions the Senate's President *pro tempore* separately, raising the incongruous possibility that the holder of this position is not an officer.[118] These posts might together comprise the category of which Stillman spoke; on the other hand, the possibility that all senators were to be officers, by virtue of their executive duties, is not beyond the realm of plausibility.

Although many people thus apparently subscribed to the belief that senators, because of their executive powers and their relationship to the president, were to be amenable to the impeachment process, debates on this point as of the late 1780s were almost completely theoretical. The first few years under the Constitution saw the modification of the Senate's role in actual practice, including not only Washington's abortive attempt to secure treaty advice and instructions from that body,[119] but also the evolution of the president's cabinet, which was accompanied by further debates on the impeachment and removal of executive officers.[120] But though these events effectively altered the Senate's relation (as the framers and ratifiers had apparently contemplated it) to the presidency, the possibility that they had the effect of exempting senators from amenability to impeachment (if, indeed, the framers and ratifiers had collectively agreed that they were impeachable at all) remained unexplored, for no facts had emerged against which to test the theory. Not until nearly a decade later, when a senator actually stood impeached, did the issue of legislative amenability to the process—and many other procedural and substantive questions—demand authoritative resolution. At that time the Senate, in deciding whether to try one of its own members, would take the first step towards

---

[118]U.S. Const. art. I, § 2, cl. 5; Ibid. § 3, cls. 4-5.

[119]See note 100, *supra*.

[120]For an account of the debates surrounding the creation of the first executive departments see Learned, "President's Cabinet," 176-82; Louis Fisher, *The Constitution Between Friends: Congress, the President, and the Law* (New York: St. Martin's Press, 1978) 51-56.

effecting either a restricted or an unlimited impeachment power.

A year before Blount's affair came to light, however, Congress found itself confronting a concrete episode of wrongdoing. Thus began the first serious investigation into whether the House of Representatives should exercise its impeachment power.

※

In May 1796 the House received a petition from forty-nine inhabitants of St. Clair County in the Northwest Territory. This petition listed several complaints against George Turner, a territorial judge. Turner had long been a source of controversy. He was a second choice for his office, and three years before the petition's arrival, he had embarked upon a prolonged absence from the territory, which caused Washington to threaten him with legal action in order to induce him to go and assume his duties.[121] While serving as judge he acted arbitrarily and even dictatorially, such as when he refused to hold court sessions in two of the three towns Governor Arthur St. Clair had designated for the purpose.[122] These and other actions prompted the outraged citizens of the territory to appeal to the federal government. According to the petition, Turner had among other things held court at remote and inaccessible locations; he had imposed unreasonable fees upon litigants; and he had committed a number of offensive acts regarding property inheritance and conveyance, some of the more extreme ones being the conversion and appropriation of intestate estates to his own use. This charge apparently referred in part to Turner's seizure of goods on the Ohio River on the grounds that they might be bound illegally for the Indian

---

[121]1 U.S., Congress, Senate, *Journal of the Executive Proceedings of the Senate of the United States of America* (Washington: Duff Green, 1828) [SuDocs Y1.3:Ex3/1] (hereinafter cited as *Executive Journal*) 25 (1789); 2 Clarence Edwin Carter, ed., *The Territorial Papers of the United States* (Washington: Government Printing Office, 1934) 452.

[122]Beverley W. Bond, Jr., *The Civilization of the Old Northwest* (New York: The MacMillan Company, 1934) 81-84; 1 William Henry Smith, ed., *The St. Clair Papers: The Life and Public Services of Arthur St. Clair* (Cincinnati: Robert Clarke & Company, 1882) 195-96. For other controversies involving Turner see 2 Carter, *Territorial Papers* 511-18; 3 Ibid. at 406-07.

territories.[123] The territorial residents closed their petition by requesting the House of Representatives to provide some remedy.[124]

Why did the aggrieved citizens direct their complaints specifically at the House, in which they had no representation? On November 4, 1791 Arthur St. Clair and his troops, campaigning against the Indian peoples in the Northwest Territory, had suffered a shattering defeat at the headwaters of the Wabash; the debacle had sparked the first congressional investigation of the executive branch the following March. The House had been the chamber to conduct that investigation, and possibly the territory's inhabitants remembered that affair when contemplating what to do about Turner.[125] Possibly too, they identified themselves more closely with the representatives, who stood for election (and popular election at that, unlike senators or president) more often than any other branch. Perhaps, on the other hand, the petition's authors hoped that the House would consider invoking its impeachment power against Turner; but all this is conjecture. Whatever the petitioners' intent, the House chose for the moment to pass the question on to Attorney General Charles Lee. The representatives were not sidestepping the problem, however, for instead of washing their hands of the affair, they asked Lee, through a resolution, to report back to them the proper measures to take in the business.[126]

A few days later Lee communicated his opinion that the charges against Turner were serious enough to warrant a full and fair examination. He went on to describe the judge's tenure, however, as that of good behavior, which prevented his removal unless he had committed "malversation in office."[127] Lee then observed that a judge might be prosecuted for official crimes and misdemeanors by indictment, by information (a criminal accusation similar to indictment), or by impeachment. He went on to note that impeachment, being the most solemn of these proceedings, was

---

[123]2 Carter, *Territorial Papers* 544.

[124]1 *American State Papers, Misc.* 151-52.

[125]George C. Chalou, "St. Clair's Defeat, 1792," *in* 1 Arthur M. Schlesinger, Jr. & Roger Bruns, *Congress Investigates: A Documented History, 1792-1974* (New York: Chelsea House Publishers, 1975) 3, 4; 3 *Annals of Cong.* 490-94 (1792).

[126]1 *American State Papers, Misc.* 151.

[127]Ibid.

probably the most suitable process, albeit an impractical one in this case because of the distances involved.

Lee's discussion of the standards of good behavior and high crimes and misdemeanors in separate contexts is of no help to the scholar seeking to understand the relationship between the two concepts. Concerning the impeachment process in general, however, Lee had a fair amount to say, especially in light of the Constitution's silence on procedural matters. He suggested that Congress either follow rules of proceedings as were to be found in a regular court, or that it at least apply rules analogous to those of regular courts. Accordingly, he argued, a House committee should examine witnesses, in the manner of a grand jury, before it sent an impeachment to the Senate. The petition against Turner, Lee suggested, served as an adequate justification for such an investigation. Lee even went on to describe (albeit briefly) the trial process, holding that witnesses should be sworn and examined before the senators just as before a regular court, and that the defendant should be receive compensation for his costs if he were acquitted. The attorney general then closed his opinion by reiterating that proceedings in a territorial court would prove more practical than an impeachment in this case.[128]

Upon receiving Lee's communication, the House referred it to a select committee.[129] For the next nine months no record of the committee's deliberations, or any other information pertaining to Turner, appears in the congressional journals; then, abruptly, on February 16, 1797, the Speaker notified the representatives that Turner himself, hearing of the charges against him, had come to Philadelphia to offer a defense. The House, however, tabled the judge's request to be heard.[130]

Less than two weeks later the select committee made its report, which recommended the same course of action that Lee had suggested the previous summer, namely, the institution of proceedings in territorial court. As Lee had, at some point, informed the committee that he had alerted Washington to the Turner episode, and the president in turn had instructed his secretary of state to have Governor Arthur St. Clair bring Turner to trial, the committee

---

[128]Ibid.
[129]5 *Annals of Cong.* 1338 (1796).
[130]Ibid. at 2166 (1797).

recommended that the House refrain from further action until the results of the court proceedings were known.

The House promptly tabled the resolution, abruptly ending the first relatively serious impeachment investigation without voting an impeachment.[131] But by then, unknown to Congress or to any other agency of the Federal government, events were underway on the frontier that would usher in the impeachment question again, and in a far more spectacular fashion, within a matter of months.

---

[131]2 Carter, *Territorial Papers* 618, 622; 1 *Executive Journal* 261 (1798).

Chapter 2

Conspirators and Conspiracies: William Blount and The Old Southwest

Between the age when Roger Mortimer lived and died in England and the day that the southern expanse of British North America became a sovereign country, many things changed. Europeans discovered and settled (some would say invaded) this new continent upon which, and for which, nations would do battle. Spain would soar to then-unrivaled heights before seeing her fortunes begin a long, unstoppable decline into imperial dusk; meanwhile England would slowly, and sometimes violently, begin building an empire that would ultimately eclipse Spain's as well as all others', and a constitution that the Continental writer Montesquieu would describe in glowing terms, even as his own country imperceptibly started its long march toward the Bastille and what lay beyond. To this same unwritten constitution American Whigs would appeal when they perceived parliamentary abuses of their liberties. Crèvecoeur may not have been the first to sense the immensity of the changes that the new United States represented, but he best summarized it in 1782 in an utterance at once both question and answer: "What, then, is the American, this new man?" In expansive terms, Thomas Jefferson would announce the new states' credo of human equality and God-given rights; meanwhile, more cannily, John Adams would call for a government of laws and not of men. In the end, though, despite all of these sweeping changes that redrew the world's maps and revolutionized its governments, the essence of human nature remained the same. Humanity's grasp of this essence is innate and undeniable. It is what always prompts the audience to gentle but ironic laughter at awe-stricken Miranda's most famous, most heartfelt words: "O, wonder! / How many goodly creatures are there here! / How beauteous mankind is! O brave new world, / That has such people in 't!"

William Blount was born on Easter Sunday, March 26, 1749, in Bertie County, North Carolina. He was a descendant of a moderately successful English line; one of his ancestors was no doubt the same Thomas Blount who had broken the household staff of Edward II, signaling the end of that king's reign and Mortimer's rise to near-absolute power. His father Jacob was something of an entrepreneur, and William, according to his biographer, inherited this trait. Eventually he would come to exemplify the early American businessman, the self-interested mercantile class of citizens who lived in eighteenth century United States. Among other things in which Jacob Blount involved himself was the real property trade;[1] his sons, William, John Gray, Thomas, Willie, and Jacob Jr., were to find similar employment, although often on a much grander scale.[2]

Within a few years of William's birth, Jacob Blount moved the family south to Craven County near New Bern, where significant economic and political development was underway. As William and his younger siblings grew, they witnessed their father play several roles in that development. Jacob served as militia officer, local court justice, and assemblyman, even while remaining involved in the real property trade. These activities were not the only ones the family witnessed. The grandly-named Blount Hall incorporated aspects of "farm, mill, and shop," and the Blount children undoubtedly learned

---

[1]William H. Masterson, *William Blount* (Baton Rouge: Louisiana State University Press, 1954) vii., 3.

[2]McKisack, *The Fourteenth Century* 91; Willie (pronounced Wylie) and Jacob Jr. were in fact half brothers to the others, Jacob Sr. having re-married in 1763 after the death of his first wife. Masterson, *William Blount* 12; Kenneth McKellar, *Tennessee Senators as Seen by One of Their Successors* (Kingsport, Tennessee: Southern Publishers, 1942) 52. The proper pronunciation of the family surname, incidentally, rhymes with "blunt," especially in Southern descendants of the family; "Blunt" is in fact a variant spelling in some English branches of the line. *See* Sir Bernard Burke, *A Genealogical and Heraldic Dictionary of the Peerage and Baronetage of the British Empire* (London: Harrison, 20th ed. 1858) 96-97.

skills relating to the operation and management of these enterprises.[3] Another fact of life to which William and the others were exposed was their father's transactions, both personal and otherwise, with numbers of local citizens. William learned these business lessons in lieu of receiving any formal education during his early life, for the area had no regular schoolmaster until 1764.[4] In many ways these earliest lessons were to be the most influential.

Blount was, or at any rate became, a creature of the frontier, and he had an early taste of that world to the west. In the late 1760s and the early 1770s the Regulator uprising occurred in North Carolina; in this contest that was at once reminiscent of Bacon's Rebellion and a forerunner of Shays's and the Whiskey Rebellions, the colony's frontiersmen violently protested the policies and political power of the financially established Easterners. In response to Governor William Tryon's call for troops Blount, along with his brother John Gray and their father, rode with the militia for Alamance Creek in 1771 to put down the insurrection. They had good reason for doing so; Regulator demands for western equity threatened Jacob Blount's financial interests, and Blount Hall lay on a path between the western town of Hillsborough and New Bern, along which a Regulator invasion might come. This event never happened, however, for on May 16, 1771 the militia soundly defeated the Regulators at Alamance.[5] Although playing an insignificant role, William Blount first fought for his property interests, quite literally, on this occasion.[6]

By this time William and John Gray had begun to participate in their father's business concerns. While his brother possessed the cooler judgment, William had the quality of ingenuity. Both became speculators, and both were ambitious. But when Tryon's successor, Governor Josiah Martin, took office a few months after the Battle of Alamance, the new executive promptly began to follow policies that alienated the eastern speculator-merchant group. By 1774 the Blounts, in order to protect their economic interests, aligned

---

[3]Masterson, *William Blount* 8.

[4]Ibid. at 4-11.

[5]For a history of the Regulator uprising and the Battle of Alamance, see William S. Powell et al., eds., *The Regulators in North Carolina: A Documentary History 1759-1776* (Raleigh: State Department of Archives and History, 1971) xv-xxvii.

[6]Masterson, *William Blount* 16-17.

themselves against the British regime. Thus for the second time in his young life, William Blount's economic circumstances determined his politics.[7]

From 1775 to 1779, William Blount began to play roles of increasing prominence in both public and private financial concerns. As Jacob became more involved in political events, William and John Gray began to assume greater control of their father's business ventures, and in the economically unstable days of the Revolution the brothers quickly gained both experience and skill. In April of 1776, the day after Jacob's appointment as paymaster of all North Carolina troops, William took on a corresponding post in the New Bern District militia. Acting in this capacity, he traveled to Philadelphia in early 1777 to receive half a million dollars that the Continental Congress had voted to pay North Carolina soldiers. Blount made arrangements to get the money to Governor Richard Caswell, but not before telling John Gray of the sum's imminent arrival.[8] In giving his brother this opportunity to recoup funds due the Blounts before others put in their claims, William displayed a shrewdness and a degree of self-interest that would continue to rival his loyalty to the established political regime. These traits would grow even stronger with time.

Although Blount showed an interest in political office as early as 1779, when he ran against Richard Dobbs Spaight for a North Carolina assembly seat, the election was later declared illegal, and Blount did not gain a place in the legislature until 1781. In the meantime he occupied himself with business and militia affairs, and his family's holdings gave him considerable power in a time of rampant inflation. Buying goods at low prices and selling at high ones, Blount earned the enmity even of his cousin Thomas Hart, who insinuated that he was a usurer. Whatever glory Blount may have rightly achieved later in life, we can discern in him a hint of something less savory if we see him through Hart's not entirely inimical eyes.

What a Sett of Atheistical fellows must there be in Newbern that thinks there is neither God nor Devil to punish them in a

---

[7]Ibid., 19-25.
[8]Ibid., 29-40.

Nother World, for their usury to us in this, I must send down
Debow Once more to preach up the Doctrine of Regeneration
or the New Birth to you .... I wonder trully how many poor
Sons of Bitches with tears in their Eyes have I Seen within
these Six weeks past, Coming from your place ... all declaring
themselves Broken [miserably] but None of them without a
Good Store of [curses which] they bestow (with a very Liberal
hand) on the Good Folks of Newbern, and how can you bear
with all this, can you [2] expect to thrive Under the Heavy
Curses of the Rightious folks of this Country, had Not you
better try to do Something that may entitle you to Our
Blessing Instead of Our Curses, come do (for Godsake) begin
with me, and let us See what you can do.[9]

During the war years Blount stayed active in both public and
business affairs. As an assemblyman, he supported measures that
would further his business interests; at the same time he was making
friends with many influential North Carolinians. In May of 1782, with
an eye to expanding his business contacts beyond the provincial scope
of Carolina, he stood for a seat in Congress, which he won. Other
delegates from his state included Hugh Williamson who, like Blount,
would go to the Constitutional Convention, and Benjamin Hawkins,
with whom Blount would have many future dealings.[10]

In April 1783 Blount resigned his congressional position, from
which he had made many business contacts and defended North
Carolina interests, for a seat in the state assembly. John Gray also
served in the 1783 legislature, and between them the Blounts
managed to win the passage of laws opening North Carolina's western
lands to large-scale speculation. Also around this time the Blount
brothers set up the firm of John Gray & Thomas Blount, Merchants,
in which William Blount, characteristically, was a silent partner. The
Blounts soon began acquiring sizable amounts of property in the
western North Carolina and eastern Tennessee region, which at that
time was Carolina land. By 1786 the brothers were conducting

---

[9]Thomas Hart to William Blount, 25 January 1780, in 1 Alice Barnwell Keith ed.,
The John Gray Blount Papers (Raleigh: State Department of Archives and History,
1952) 8-9. The bracketed words are Keith's editorial corrections.

[10]Masterson, *William Blount* 39-57.

transactions involving hundreds of thousands of acres.[11]

In 1785 Blount returned to Congress, motivated largely by a desire to vote against the ratification of several Indian treaties that could hurt his land ventures. Although arriving after the treaties' ratification, he remained in order to promote other interests, such as tobacco sales. By 1787 he came to have the makings of a Federalist. This was a result of Shays's Rebellion, the abortive revolt of western agrarian against eastern commercial interests in Massachusetts, as well as some radical North Carolina opponents' attacks upon his reputation and business dealings. The increasing scale of interstate and even international operations of the Blount brothers' firm, moreover, probably served to make the concept of a strong national government, and the prospect of a stable economy that it promised, an attractive one. As plans for a convention in Philadelphia solidified, then, John Gray prevailed upon Governor Caswell to name William as a delegate.[12]

Blount played only a small role in the convention. Much of the time he was in New York, where he worked in Congress to protect his property interests in the western Carolina region from the provisions of new Indian treaties. Another of his goals was to secure and maintain an American right to navigate the Mississippi River, along which commerce could flow and settlers and purchasers could make their way to the site of his land holdings. This latter goal, in particular, was to be a key element in the conspiracy that would develop a decade later. He returned to the Philadelphia Convention in early August after a lengthy stay in New York; whatever contributions he then made to the Constitution's drafting remain hidden. On September 17 he signed the finished document, but without enthusiasm. According to Madison's notes he signed it only to attest that it had been properly approved by the state delegations.

---

[11]Ibid., 66-71, 76, 78-79, 89, 99.

[12]Ibid., 110-11, 121-25; 3 Farrand, *Records* 587. For an account of Shays's Rebellion and the struggle between economic interests during the 1780s, see David P. Szatmary, *Shays' Rebellion: The Making of an Agrarian Insurrection* (Amherst: The University of Massachusetts Press, 1980). Around the time of the rebellion, Blount dismissed the New York delegation to Congress as a group of "antifederal Peasants." William Blount to Richard Caswell, 28 January 1787, *in* 8 Edmund Cody Burnett ed., *Letters of Members of the Continental Congress* (Washington: Carnegie Institution of Washington, 1936) 532, 533.

Their duty done, Blount and his fellow delegates then departed.[13]

Back in his native state, Blount continued to work not only for his private interests, but for ratification as well, though his efforts with regard to the latter goal met with defeat until 1789. In respect to land ventures, however, his holdings only increased, although the breakdown of conveyancing machinery under the heavy load of speculation gave rise to some transactions of questionable legality, whether or not Blount realized it. By the end of 1789, however, the Blount interests began looking up in political terms as North Carolina's second ratifying convention, which included a strong Blount-controlled faction, finally approved the Constitution.[14]

Shortly after this convention adjourned, Blount—by now a state senator—backed a plan to cede all North Carolina lands west of the Appalachians to the new federal government. As might be expected, the legislation contained many safeguards for speculators' holdings in the region. In April 1790 the First Congress accepted the cession, and less than two months later it established the new "Territory of the United States South of the River Ohio," which encompassed, among other areas, the present-day state of Tennessee. By this time Blount had his eye on the position of territorial governor. "My Western Lands had become so great an object to me," he wrote, "that it had become absolutely necessary that I should go to the Western Country, to secure them and perhaps my Presence might have enhanced there [sic] Value." He began to do all that was within his power to win the post even before the territory's creation. He had both friends, among whom was the key figure of George Washington, and influence in the national government; he also had a solid record as a Federalist, an interest in the region, a strong acquaintance with prominent Westerners, and a good reputation within the new territory. On June 8, 1790, he got his wish when Washington named him governor. Blount, at home in North Carolina, received the news

---

[13]Masterson, *William Blount*, 126-33; 2 Farrand, *Records* 645-46; McKellar, *Tennessee Senators* 50.

[14]Masterson, *William Blount* 137-38, 140-41, 164-66. For a brief summary of ratification, see Richard B. Morris, *The Founding of the Union 1781-1789* (New York: Harper Torchbooks, 1987) 315-16; for a more thorough study, see Louise Irby Trenholme, *Ratification of the Federal Constitution in North Carolina* (New York: Columbia University Press, 1932).

later that month, and by early September he set out for the territory and the infamy that awaited him.[15]

☙

The Trans-Appalachian West of the late eighteenth century was a remote and isolated place, a wild and unpredictable region. Even years later, after 1800, frontiersmen such as Blount's friend Andrew Jackson would not be able to journey from Philadelphia to the town of Nashville in middle Tennessee in fewer than five weeks. Eastern Tennessee, the other oasis of settlement in the future state, was closer to North Carolina than was the area to the west of the Cumberland Plateau, but being separated from the eastern seaboard by the Smoky Mountains it shared more with the Mississippi and Ohio River Valleys than it did with the Carolinas. The region imported most or all of its goods, and the price of their transportation over the mountains made up a third of their cost.[16]

This isolation, together with nearby vestiges of European presences, helps to explain why the old frontier was a world unto itself, so different from the states to the east. English, French, Spanish, and New World cultures, technologies, and ideologies blended under the dim, sun-dappled canopy of primeval forest that yet spread unbroken from Atlantic settlements to Mississippi River. The prime forces here, outgrowths of European civilization, were mercantile and imperial; the adventurers in their sway were those whom Conrad described much later in *Heart of Darkness* as Marlow and his companions, safe in London, survey a river rather more sedate than the Father of Waters in the dying light of day.

> Hunters for gold or pursuers of fame, they all had gone out on that stream, bearing the sword, and often the torch, messengers of the might within the land, bearers of a spark from the sacred fire. What greatness had not floated on the

---

[15]Masterson, *William Blount* 166-67, 174-78, 182; Act of May 26, 1790, ch. 14, 1 Stat. 123 (1790); Wm Blount to John Steele, 10 July 1790, *in* 1 H.M. Wagstaff ed., *The Papers of John Steele* (Raleigh: Edwards & Broughton Printing Company, 1924) 67-68.

[16]Whitaker, *Mississippi Question* 13; Masterson, *William Blount* 187.

ebb of that river into the mystery of an unknown earth! ...
The dreams of men, the seed of commonwealth, the germs of
empires.

But though far from the eastern seat of the federal government,
and even farther from Europe and its capitals, the frontier could not
escape their influences. The fate of the American West largely hung
upon, and often drove, the decisions of princes and diplomats
hundreds and thousands of miles away, for the reach of Great Powers
of Europe extended along the Mississippi and the Saint Lawrence even
in the years following the War for Independence. "A sinister political
and geographical symmetry," writes Samuel Flagg Bemis, the dean of
American diplomatic historians, "placed the hinterlands of the United
States between two great sovereign millstones that threatened to
grind out the life of the weak confederation."[17] The first of these
millstones was England. To the north of the Ohio River, between the
Mississippi and the Appalachians, lay the Old Northwest and its
scattering of British outposts. According to the definitive treaty of
peace of 1783, this region belonged to the United States, and
England was to evacuate these posts "with all convenient speed" in
the treaty's words, but as of 1790 no such withdrawal had occurred.
The reasons were fairly straightforward: these fortifications provided
essential strategic security for the British fur trade, an extremely
profitable Canadian enterprise. The furs that arrived in Montreal
came from the Old Northwest and its handful of white trappers and
multitude of Indian peoples. Were the British to evacuate these
posts, treaty or no, they would be surrendering control of the most
important points along the fur-trade routes.[18] This was something
that British leaders refused to do in the face of a contrary English
public opinion and the 1784 rise to power of William Pitt the
Younger, who promptly abandoned England's policy of reconciliation

---

[17]Samuel Flagg Bemis, *Pinckney's Treaty: America's Advantage from Europe's
Distress, 1783-1800* (New Haven: Yale University Press, rev. ed. 1960) 41.

[18]Treaty of Paris, 3 September 1783, U.S.-Gr. Brit., art. 7, *in* Fred L. Israel, ed.,
Major Peace Treaties of Modern History 1648-1967 (New York: Chelsea House
Publishers, 1967) 345, 349; Samuel Flagg Bemis, *Jay's Treaty: A Study in
Commerce and Diplomacy* (New Haven: Yale University Press, rev. ed. 1962) 3-10.

with the United States.[19] Here, writes Bemis, lay one of the two major postwar issues between Britain and America, the other being the problem of the Atlantic commerce between the two nations.[20]

Below the Ohio, stretching from the Smoky Mountains to the Mississippi, lay the Old Southwest. To the south were Spanish East and West Floridas; west of the Mississippi, of course, was Louisiana, once French territory, but since 1763 the property of Spain, the second frontier millstone. Here, too, the contest was imperial, but the diplomatic problems surrounding this region were rather more complex than those to the north. Louisiana, that vast expanse of lightly-populated territory sprawling beyond the Mississippi, and straying eastward across it at New Orleans, was a land that Spain hoped to use as a buffer zone to protect her more valuable holdings in and below Mexico from American influence. As the American presence grew, so, too, did Spanish concern. From the banks of the Mississippi, officials of New Spain watched the ominous swelling ranks of the young republic; one Louisiana governor described the ominous, inexorable march of the American frontiersmen with a grim admiration.

> This prestigious and restless population [he wrote], continually forcing the Indian nations backward and upon us, is attempting to get possession of all the vast continent which those nations are occupying between the Ohio and Mississippi Rivers and the Gulf of Mexico and the Appalachian Mountains .... Their method of spreading themselves and their policy are so much to be feared by Spain as are their arms .... Their wandering spirit and the ease with which those people procure their sustenance and shelter quickly form new settlements. A carbine and a little maize in a sack are enough for an American to wander about in the forests alone for a whole month. With his carbine he kills the wild cattle and deer for food and defends himself from the savages. The maize dampened serves him in lieu of bread. With some tree trunks crossed one above other, in the shape of a square, he raises a

---

[19]Jerald A. Combs, *The Jay Treaty: Political Battleground of the Founding Fathers* (Berkeley: University of California Press, 1970) 9-10.

[20]Bemis, *Jay's Treaty* 1; Idem ch. 2.

house, and even a fort that is impregnable to the savages by crossing a story above the ground floor. The cold does not affright him. When a family tires of one location, it moves to another, and there settles with the same ease.... If such men succeed in occupying the shores of the Mississippi ... nothing can prevent them from crossing ... and penetrating into our provinces on the other side.

Against such a threat the Spanish battle was uphill or, more accurately, upstream, for most of Louisiana's forty thousand inhabitants lived in its southern reaches, near New Orleans, and travel against the current was difficult. A line of Spanish garrisons straggled up-river on both banks of the Mississippi and sometimes well to its east: Plaquemines, south of New Orleans; Natchez; Walnut Hills; Chickasaw Bluffs; New Madrid; St. Louis. In Spanish West Florida stood the post at Mobile; further north, below the junction of the Tombigbee and Alabama Rivers, was Fort St. Stephen, and higher up on the Tombigbee lay the remote Fort Confederation. Some of these outposts housed barely more than two dozen troops, who served as tripwires against American incursion—or invasion.[21]

But the easternmost garrisons' location was much more important than was their size. Collectively, the regions that would become Kentucky and Tennessee had a much greater population than Louisiana's, easily amounting to at least 150,000 in 1795 while barely a third that many people lived beyond the river a year earlier.[22] Louisiana's rulers could not hope to withstand the pressure of these numbers should the Americans decide to move westward, as they well might. What Louisiana lacked in population, then, Spain sought to make up for in territorial claims and Indian alliances. West Florida, under Spanish control since 1763, clearly extended as far north as the 31st parallel, or, to put this another way, a line running roughly from just below Natchez eastward to the Chatahoochee River. This was the border that the Anglo-American treaty of 1783 recognized as the line between American and Spanish land. The border of East Florida was

---

[21] Dale Van Every, *Ark of Empire: The American Frontier 1784-1803* (New York: William Morrow and Company, 1963) 26 (quoting Hector, Baron de Carondelet); Whitaker, *Mississippi Question* 27-28, 54, 276.

[22] Whitaker, *Mississippi Question* 8, 10, 276 n.24.

almost as far north, reaching from the Chatahoochee and Appalachicola east to the St. Mary's, which remains today's eastern boundary between Georgia and Florida. Spanish claims for West Florida, however, went considerably farther north, by some estimates as far as the Ohio River. Bemis has shown that the provenance of this claim, at least as far north as the mouth of the Yazoo near present-day Vicksburg, was a fairly sound one, and as of 1790 Spain meant to exploit it, the better to keep the Americans as far away as possible.[23]

In this disputed region Spanish alliances with, and control of, the area's large Indian nations was another leverage point that Spain sought to use. Having only fifteen hundred troops along the Mississippi, the country was anxious for treaties of friendship with the southern tribes, and in 1784 it signed such agreements with the Creek, Choctaw, and Chickasaw. In 1793 came the Treaty of Nogales, which strengthened Spanish-Indian ties as well as extending them to the Cherokee, another of the region's major tribes. These agreements would give the Spanish an entrée into the Indian lands to the east of Louisiana, as well as Indian assistance in those quarters, even though the United States also negotiated similar treaties with these tribes around this same time.[24]

American interest in securing Indian alliances matched Spain's for similar reasons; for the United States, control of the tribes meant control of the territory. The frontiersmen wanted not only to subdue the native population, but to exclude the Spanish. In doing so, they would also move a step nearer the even greater goal of controlling the great Mississippi River itself.

"In the beginning," wrote John Locke, "all the world was America." Accepting the truth of this dictum, one would do well to recall that the world's first civilizations, from the Tigris to the Yalu, were riparian. In a land with few roads or the means with which to build them, freedom of movement on navigable rivers was crucial not only to travel but to commerce, defense, and projection of force.[25]

---

[23]Treaty of Paris, 3 September 1783, U.S.-Gr. Brit., art. 2, *in* Israel, ed., *Major Peace Treaties* 345, 347; Bemis, *Pinckney's Treaty*, 41-43.

[24]Bemis, *Pinckney's Treaty* 48-55; Abraham P. Nasatir, *Spanish War Vessels on the Mississippi 1792-1796* (New Haven: Yale University Press, 1968) 11-12; Whitaker, *Spanish-American Frontier* 181-82 .

[25]John Locke, *Second Treatise of Civil Government* ¶ 49; 1 Clark G. Reynolds,

The Mississippi, to say nothing of its tributaries, was quite literally central to this freedom in the valley that it had carved out over the eons and to which it gave its name, and the frontiersmen knew it. "To the aggressive 'men of the western waters,' as they delighted to call themselves," Bemis observes, "the river was the only practicable route by which they might trade profitably with the outside world. Their whole future prosperity hung on its unrestricted use." Without that use, large-scale trade with outside markets and suppliers, an elemental requirement for an American inland empire, was impossible.[26]

The Spanish knew this as well as the frontiersmen did, and they naturally wished to deny control of the river to the Americans. In 1784, José de Moñino y Redondo, Count of Floridablanca and Secretary of State to Charles III, closed the river to American traffic; though the Treaty of Paris of 1783 recognized United Sates sovereignty from the Mississippi's eastern bank to its center, Spain's conflicting claim to the eastern bank challenged the validity of this title, and at any rate Spanish possession of New Orleans effectively barred American access via the Mississippi to the Gulf of Mexico. Spain reversed this policy in 1788, but it imposed various duties on American commerce on the river for years afterward.[27]

This Spanish concession did little, however, to answer the ultimate question of which of the two powers actually owned the river (leaving aside any claims of the Indian peoples, who could do little to stem the tide of white assimilation of the continent). These ambiguities combined with the wild and remote location to create a precarious world beyond the Smokies, an undiscovered country in both the literal and the Shakespearean sense. The Spanish in the South and hostile English forces in the Northwest often incited Indians to attack American settlers, and the Indians were happy to comply. On the northern frontier thick undergrowth could hide numbers of British-equipped Indians and Canadian militia waiting in ambush for United States troops; farther to the south, Spanish patrols would appear from nowhere and open fire, throwing American forces into

---

Command of the Sea: The History and Strategy of Maritime Empires (Malabar, Florida: Robert E. Krieger Publishing Co., 1974) 19-22.

[26] Bemis, *Pinckney's Treaty* 46.

[27] Whitaker, *Spanish-American Frontier*, 68-70, 101-02; Whitaker, *Mississippi Question* 83-89.

confusion. At night American garrisons would extinguish lights at the first sounds of gunfire in order to escape artillery barrages. In this frontier darkness, this place so far from the refined airs of Philadelphia, of Whitehall, of Versailles and Madrid, almost anything could happen.[28]

Being so far from the civilized world, the Mississippi Valley provided a perfect refuge for any number of social misfits and strange characters from the East and elsewhere. Here one could find men such as "Diving" Dayton, so called because of his feigned suicide by drowning in New England to outwit his creditors, and Philip Nolan, a shadowy trader-adventurer who ultimately met a mysterious end at Spanish hands deep in Louisiana, where one of his captors cut off Nolan's ears and kept them as a memento. Even the terrain itself was hazardous. In 1797 the American surveyor Andrew Ellicott, in Natchez to help fix treaty boundaries, reported that the banks of the Mississippi could cave in without warning, destroying settlements located there, and that navigation of the river itself at night was a dangerous undertaking. On the river appeared one of the few concrete signs that imperial overlords existed in some outside world; the frontiersman who pushed that far into the valley, or floated downstream in a flatboat, might well spy one of the lumbering Spanish galleys of Spain's river fleet, small but lethal.[29] This was the world in which Blount found himself when he crossed the mountains, chose a site for his territorial capital on the eastern rim of the territory, named the new settlement Knoxville, and began to set up his new government.

In establishing and operating a territorial administration Blount had his work cut out for him. Undoubtedly the biggest issue facing him at first was the Indian question. As he traveled throughout the

---

[28]John C. Miller, *The Federalist Era 1789-1801* (New York: Harper Torchbooks, 1960) 184-86; Francis S. Philbrick, *The Rise of the West 1754-1830* (New York; Harper & Row, 1965) 157; Andrew Ellicott, *The Journal of Andrew Ellicott* (Philadelphia: Budd & Bartram, 1803) 111.

[29]Ellicott, *Journal* 29-30, 91; Whitaker, *Mississippi Question* 142, 157, 162; Nasatir, *Spanish War Vessels* ch. 2. Nolan was involved in the mustang trade, which often took him as far into Spanish territory as the Rio Grande. The strange circumstances of his death in 1801, however, and his friendship with James Wilkinson, suggest that he was involved with one of the many frontier conspiracies that simmered from the 1780s to at least 1807. *See* pages 86-88, *infra.*

territory commissioning officers, he made overtures to the Cherokee in hopes of winning more land cessions and avoiding an Indian uprising. While he did eventually conclude some key treaties with the Cherokee, the Creek and Chickamauga tribes continued to be a concern for the territory's thirty-five thousand white inhabitants. Even the Cherokee, although treating with the American government, were largely pro-Spanish. By September 1792, despite further negotiations, peace still eluded the region, and Blount increased the size of the militia while attempting to learn more of Spanish plans. On September 30 came a large Indian attack upon a small settlement to the south of Nashville, and Blount prepared for full-scale war. From Philadelphia, however, Secretary of War Henry Knox sent word that Blount was to limit his operations to defensive maneuvers only.[30]

This policy demanded too much of Blount, and in the spring of 1793 he set out for Philadelphia to ask permission in person to settle the Indian problem, by force, once and for all. Washington and Knox, however, remained dubious, and the latter merely asked Blount to suggest ways of postponing open conflict. Blount was aware that behind the administration's reluctance lay eastern opposition to war—for western campaigns at this point were absorbing the lion's share of federal expenses—as well as a regard for Spanish-American relations. This last consideration in particular grated on the governor, who by now was becoming obsessed with a hatred of Spain.[31]

By this time, however, the political situation was changing. John Jay's unpopular treaty with England, negotiated in 1794 and 1795 and executed by 1796, while sacrificing the United States's neutral shipping rights in the Anglo-French struggle, did provide for a British evacuation of the Northwest. Then in 1795 came a decisive battle in the Northwest Territory in which General "Mad Anthony" Wayne and his federal army routed a force of Indians from several tribes. This Battle of Fallen Timbers led to the American-Indian Treaty of Greenville, which with Jay's Treaty cleared a large part of the Northwest for peaceful settlement.[32]

At the same time, Spanish hostility against the United States was also waning. Manuel de Godoy, Spain's young First Minister and *de*

---

[30]Masterson, *William Blount* 192-98, 203-10, 224-27, 230-32.

[31]Ibid., 247-52; Miller, *Federalist Era* 183.

[32]Miller, *Federalist Era* 164-67, 183.

facto dictator, had kept up pressure against the American Southwest until 1794, hoping that American resistance would collapse and open the way for a Spanish move north and east, but as of 1794 this collapse was nowhere in sight. In 1795, furthermore, fending off revolutionary troops to her north and fearing that its 1793 anti-French alliance with England was too one-sided, Spain ended that alliance and sided with France instead. This diplomatic shift created a danger of an Anglo-Spanish war, however, and with Jay's negotiations came the sudden possibility, as Godoy saw it, of an Anglo-American alliance against Spain.[33]

All these developments made Godoy very anxious to seek some agreement with the United States, and in the fall of 1795 he made several concessions to American negotiator Thomas Pinckney. The resulting Treaty of San Lorenzo, or Pinckney's Treaty, among other things granted to the United States a right of commercial deposit at New Orleans (hitherto a port closed to all but Spanish shipping), and the privilege of navigation upon the Mississippi River, thus making the interior part of the territories more accessible to trade and settlement. Even more important was Spain's retraction of its overextended territorial claims to land east of the Mississippi, and its promise not to incite further Indian attacks. Henceforth the region's southern boundary with West Florida was clearly the 31st parallel. The treaty also required the evacuation of Spanish troops in the Old Southwest.[34]

Pinckney's Treaty came as excellent news to the citizens of the Southwest, and to Blount himself, for by now his financial interests in the area were monumental. By 1794 he was making plans to sell large tracts of his lands, which now spanned an area from the Carolinas to the Mississippi, to European purchasers. The political developments

---

[33]Bemis, *Pinckney's Treaty* 201-04; Miller, *Federalist Era* 186-88. Though Jay's Treaty produced no military alliance, Bradford Perkins has illustrated how the United States and Great Britain did experience a period of improved relations in the decade following the treaty's adoption. *See* Bradford Perkins, *The First Rapprochement: England and the United States 1789-1805* (Berkeley: University of California Press, 1967).

[34]Bemis, *Pinckney's Treaty* 245; Miller, *Federalist Era* 185-89. For a good, brief, recent discussion of the frontier question and its role in foreign relations, see Stanley Elkins & Eric McKitrick, *The Age of Federalism* (New York: Oxford University Press, 1993) 436-49.

of this time were further enhanced by improved relations with several Indian tribes, whose Spanish support was decreasing. Finally, in 1795, Blount decided that the time had come for Tennessee to seek statehood, and by the end of the year a territorial referendum had convinced him to call for a constitutional convention.[35]

In January 1796 the convention met at Knoxville, chose Blount as president, and proceeded to draft a constitution that contained, not surprisingly, large benefits for land speculators. A state legislature met in March and promptly elected Blount and his friend William Cocke as Tennessee's first two United States senators. Simultaneously Blount's territorial administration came to an end, and several days later he departed for Philadelphia to lobby personally for Tennessee's admission into the Union.[36]

By this time Blount was fast becoming a Republican, as the majority of Tennessee citizens already were. He had tried to enforce federal (that is, Federalist) policy in the Southwest despite his divergent outlook on the Indian problem, but his economic stake in the region was growing, and this inevitably began to alienate him from the administration. Blount was still very much the speculator rather than one of the "antifederal Peasants" of whom he had taken such an ill view several years earlier. His commercial interests, however, revolved around the Southwest and its fate, and in the years since the ratification of the federal Constitution, the region had benefited little from the new government, despite the Thomas Pinckney's recent victory at San Lorenzo. As long as Philadelphia sacrificed Western to Eastern interests, few potential buyers for his lands would venture into the Mississippi Valley. This simple fact had to be on his mind, but if it were not enough, in 1795 he came under the scrutiny of the new Secretary of War (soon to be Secretary of State) Timothy Pickering, an ultra-Federalist New Englander who focused much of his attention and criticism upon Blount, his policies, and his expenses now that conditions in the Northwest no longer served as a distraction. "Upon the whole, Sir," Pickering wrote Blount in March, "I cannot refrain from saying that the complexion of some of the Transactions in the Southwest territory appears unfavorable to the

---

[35]Miller, *Federalist Era* 190; Masterson, *William Blount* 249-51, 270, 275, 282-84.

[36]Masterson, *William Blount* 271-75, 288-95.

public interest." As a result of all of this, Blount more or less formally crossed the aisle in 1796. In the course of congressional debates on the question of Tennessee's admission to the Union, Aaron Burr, then a senator from New York, served on a conference committee considering the question. In this election year Blount turned all of his attention and support to Burr to win his favor, and he continued this support after the issue's decision. Endorsing Thomas Jefferson and Burr for the presidency and the vice-presidency, respectively, while at the same time lambasting Pickering, Blount completed his shift to Republicanism by the end of the year. In the meantime, his efforts to win statehood for Tennessee had succeeded, and on May 31, 1796, Congress admitted the territory into the Union, although the Senate denied Blount and Cocke their seats until the following session.[37]

In light of Pinckney's Treaty, the reduction of Indian problems, Tennessee's new status, and Blount's vast land holdings and other financial concerns, not to mention his new place in the federal Senate, his position in the summer of 1796 seemed excellent, at least on the surface. But this same period also saw all of his finances strained to the limit in consequence of his years of vast and complex transactions. His plan to sell lands to European purchasers had failed, and the administration had appointed Benjamin Hawkins as Indian Commissioner in the Southwest. Hawkins, far more sympathetic to the Indians than Blount, was in a position to damage the new senator by settling various Indian property claims. Still another problem lay in Blount's brokerage of lands. He could not take title to several tracts until he had paid cash for them, cash that he did not have; and potential buyers would not pay cash to him until he had conveyed title to them. Although he had some claim to these lands, then, he was powerless to liquidate them. Of additional concern were the financial difficulties of some of his business partners, which in turn

---

[37]Ibid., 271-75, 288-98; Thomas Perkins Abernethy, *From Frontier to Plantation in Tennessee: A Study in Frontier Democracy* (Chapel Hill: The University of North Carolina Press, 1932) 142-43 (quoting Pickering). While flirting with Federalist support, Burr pretty clearly considered himself a Republican, though as Massachusetts Federalist Theodore Sedgwick wrote of other leading Republicans, "'They doubtless respect Burr's talents, but they dread his independence of *them*.'" Herbert S. Parmet & Marie B. Hecht, *Aaron Burr: Portrait of an Ambitious Man* (New York: The Macmillan Company, 1967) 108-11 (quoting Theodore Sedgwick to Jonathan Dayton, 19 Nov. 1796, Hamilton Papers, Library of Congress).

taxed Blount's own credit. Thus, appearances to the contrary, Blount was poised delicately on the edge of financial collapse in October 1796 when Godoy's fears became reality and England and Spain went to war.[38]

≈

The isolation of the Old Southwest in the late eighteenth century, the nearby British and especially Spanish presences, the distant rumblings of revolutionary French interest in regaining mastery of Louisiana, an almost nominal connection to the government in Philadelphia, neglectful federal sovereignty over this region that did not even have the political power of statehood—all of these things conspire to give the modern reader an impression of the area as an imperial plaything, a chunk of raw meat around which circled a pack of ravenous wolves. The picture is partly, but only partly, true. From the 1783 Treaty of Paris at least until the Louisiana Purchase in 1803, and perhaps until the Battle of New Orleans in 1815, the land's ultimate future was in doubt, and the territory often seemed ripe for the taking. Yet the wolves, eyeing each other as well as the meat, could scent the iron jaws of the trap that lay beneath. The Southwest came with not only assets but liabilities, and for years none was willing to take unequivocal steps of shouldering the burden. The Spanish saw the area as a buffer zone, not as a place for settlement or expansion; in the United States, eastern Federalists by the 1790s were more concerned with Atlantic commerce, and frustrated with the high cost of maintaining the frontier. England's principal object lay further north, and for a time in Louisiana itself as the possible prize of an Anglo-Spanish war. France, meanwhile, could not convince Spain to part with the province, and so remained only indirectly involved in the Mississippi Valley.[39] In light of all this, these four powers that ringed the Southwest, none of them possessing the fortitude to dominate the region, begin to resemble not circling wolves, but

---

[38]Masterson, *William Blount*, 298-301.

[39]Whitaker, *Spanish-American Frontier* 185-87; Whitaker, *Mississippi Question*, 102, 182-84; Bemis, *Jay's Treaty* 72-73; Abraham P. Nasatir, *Borderland in Retreat: From Spanish Louisiana to the Far Southwest* (Albuquerque: University of New Mexico Press, 1976) ch. 3.

instead merely sheep in wolves' clothing.

The real wolves lived in the Southwest.

In geopolitical terms, the factors that would decide the fate of the region were clear, and Blount was by no means the only westerner whose interests they threatened. A century ago, amid a Darwinist struggle for empire and on the eve of America's war with Spain, the famed Frederick Jackson Turner curtly stated the equation in the racist language of the day:

> The frontiersmen were about to advance. Their produce was useless if the Mississippi were closed. They were wary of the incessant Indian war on their borders. The federal government discouraged their attacks on the savages and appeared indifferent to the closing of navigation by Spain. To the frontiersmen the essential thing was relief from this intolerable situation. The new government had not yet approved its value to them; the future of a united nation extending from Atlantic to Pacific appealed less to their imagination than did the pressing need of themselves possessing the portals of the great valley which they occupied. There appeared to be two solutions of the difficulty, either to come to an agreement with Spain, which would open the Mississippi, stop the Indian raids and furnish them with liberal land-grants, or to fight their way out.[40]

Such was the equation. The only remaining question was what to do about it.

That an understanding between Spain and the American frontiersmen might be, for the latter, a disloyal and even traitorous act quite possibly ruinous to American interests was, as Turner notes, beside the point, and the region's history shows it. Accounts of the Southwest are rife with tales of plots, conspiracies, and intrigues, beginning even as America won its independence and continuing for a generation. Some of the most famous, and most notorious, names in American history appear in these stories: The revolutionary general George Rogers Clark, the brother of the man who would serve as

---

[40]Frederick J. Turner, "The Origin of Genêt's Projected Attack on Louisiana and the Floridas," 3 *Am. Hist. Rev.* 650, 653 (1898).

Meriwether Lewis's partner in the trek to the Pacific Northwest; Elijah Clarke and Daniel Morgan, two other general officers in the War for Independence; Brigadier General James Wilkinson, commander of the all American military forces in the West; his superior, Major General Alexander Hamilton; Hamilton's nemesis, Vice-President Aaron Burr; William Blount, friend to Burr and, like Hamilton, signer of the Constitution; and Blount's young protégé, Nashville lawyer and planter Andrew Jackson. At one time or another, whether from within the territory or from afar, all of these men plotted revolution in the West.

The list is far from complete. Other names, not quite as impressive but by no means obscure, have a place on it as well: James Robertson, Dr. James White, John Sevier, and Harry Innes, to name a few. One must add European representatives to the list as well, including Baron Friedrich Wilhelm von Steuben, who rendered the Continental Army such great service during the war; Citizen Edmund Charles Genêt, emissary from the new French Republic; Josef de Jáudenes, Spanish agent in Philadelphia; and Hector, Baron de Carondelet, Intendent of Spanish Florida and later Governor at New Orleans. Add to these a host of other figures and the roster is still lacking, for the full extent of some of the intrigues that simmered beyond the mountains may never come to light.

What was the purpose of these conspiracies? The particular details changed from plot to plot, but the common theme was the aggrandizement of the Southwest, either at the expense of one of the contiguous powers,[41] or with the help of one of the contiguous powers, or both. Those who lived on the western waters saw this land as a place of opportunity, if only things would turn out right, and when events threatened to go badly, the frontiersmen had no qualms about doing whatever was necessary to make sure that things did go right.

An exhaustive account of frontier intrigues is impossible here; others have written on the subject in greater depth than we can hope to achieve in this study, though some details of these plots may well have died with their fomenters. A brief sketch of some of the conspiracies, however, will serve to illumine Blount's own plans.

---

[41]This phrase must include the United States, which had only a tenuous hold over the land itself and the loyalties of the frontiersmen.

One of the earliest conspirators was also one of the most constant and most notorious. James Wilkinson, an ambitious young man of twenty-six when he arrived in Kentucky as a mercantile agent in 1784, had served the United States as a brigadier general during the war, and he would do so again in later years. He refused to let his lust for martial fame, however, encumber him on his quest for wealth, but he no doubt had both goals in mind when he sailed down river from Kentucky to New Orleans in 1787. Contacting Governor Esteban Rodriguez Miró, proposing to him the separation of Kentucky, not yet a state, from the Union and its attachment to Spanish territory, Wilkinson also offered himself as Spain's agent. As a sign of his good faith he went so far as to swear an oath of loyalty to the Spanish Crown. "Self-interest regulates the passions of nations as well as individuals," reads the beginning of his self-composed pledge of allegiance, "and he who imputes a different motive to human conduct either deceives himself or endeavors to deceive others."[42]

In this instance Wilkinson's particular motives were plain. He had felt the geopolitical forces at work in the West a mere few months after his arrival in Kentucky, when Spain closed the Mississippi River to American traffic, based on its claim of ownership of both banks of the river. His proposal, at least in 1787, was designed to eliminate this obstacle to Kentucky's prosperity through its partnership with Spain.

Wilkinson's plan was no mere idle fancy. For more than a year he had been putting forth surreptitious proposals of independence among his fellow Kentuckeans, and what he had to say was of interest to Miró. The governor, together with Intendent Martin Navarro, forwarded Wilkinson's proposition on to their masters in Spain, having themselves found it most attractive. The answer was a while in coming, partly because of the matter's importance, and also because Spain's ruling ministers had other irons in the fire. Not until early 1789 did Miró receive orders from that barred him from giving

---

[42]W.L. Shepherd, "Wilkinson and the Spanish Conspiracy," 9 *Am. Hist. Rev.* 490, 492-97 (1903). For biographies of Wilkinson see James Ripley Jacobs, *Tarnished Warrior: Major-General James Wilkinson* (New York: The Macmillan Company, 1938); Thomas Robson Hay & M.R. Werner, *The Admirable Trumpeter: A Biography of General James Wilkinson* (Garden City, New York: Doubleday, Doran & Company, Inc., 1941).

Wilkinson any material support, although they directed him to maintain a correspondence with the frontiersman. The goal was to stir up revolution in the American West, if possible but to avoid direct involvement. By 1789, meanwhile, word of Wilkinson's intrigues had gotten out to too many Kentucky citizens, and a regional convention, under unionist control, had petitioned Congress for statehood. Together with Spanish reticence, this development foiled Wilkinson's plans, at least for the time being.[43]

As Wilkinson was at work in Kentucky, other frontiersmen to the South were attempting similar things. Islands of white settlement on the Holston River, on the southeast of which Knoxville came to stand, and more remote outposts far to the west on the Cumberland River, such as Nashville, had citizens who contemplated dreams of independence, economic and perhaps political. Beleaguered by Alexander McGillivray's Creeks, neglected by the North Carolina government that in the 1780s claimed much of this land, these settlements toyed with following the lead of a trio of Westerners: James Robertson, Dr. James White, and John Sevier. From 1786 to 1789 White carried on a dialogue with Miró and Don Diego de Gardoqui, Spanish Minister Plenipotentiary to the United States; what he sought was an alliance with New Spain that would help the Holston settlements, then part of the separationist state of Franklin, win their independence from North Carolina. This new state might then extend itself farther to the southwest, to Muscle Shoals on the Tennessee River. From that key point, a short portage of a few dozen miles would bring the traveler to the Alabama River, which flowed southward through Spanish Florida to the Gulf. To the Holston settlements, this trade route was closer, more desirable, and with Spanish help more attainable than that of the Mississippi.[44]

---

[43]For a more complete account see Bemis, *Pinckney's Treaty* chs. 6-7 and Whitaker, *Spanish-American Frontier* 97-107.

[44]Abernethy, *From Frontier to Plantation in Tennessee* ch. 6; Van Every, *Ark of Empire* 127-29; Whitaker, *Spanish-American Frontier* 109-12. This was perhaps one of the motives that lay behind Blount's own schemes a decade later, for the Yazoo companies held claims to enormous tracts of land in this area, and Blount was one of the Yazoo speculators. Masterson, *William Blount* 151, 196-97, 304-05; Andrew R.L. Cayton, "'When Shall We Cease to Have Judases?' The Blount Conspiracy and the Limits of the 'Extended Republic,'" *in* Ronald Hoffman & Peter J. Albert, *Launching the Extended Republic: The Federalist Era* (Charlottesville:

While White sought aid from Miró, Sevier, having in mind simular goals, also corresponded with Gardoqui. James Roberston, meanwhile, promoting the interests of the Cumberland settlers, sought an alliance with McGillivray and the Creeks, and through them the Spanish, that would reduce the danger of Indian attacks. Miró, as is clear from Wilkinson's story, had a serious interest in making inroads into the American West, for he could hardly hope to hold Louisiana with the few soldiers he had, and a Western independence movement might well reduce the threat that faced his province across the Mississippi. But his own government's answer to Wilkinson's proposal kept him from taking any active steps to aid these other adventurers, though he said what he could to encourage their efforts. Though Spain had an alliance with the Creeks, moreover, it could not control them. Then in 1789, the same year that Kentucky petitioned for statehood, a convention in Nashville asked North Carolina to cede its western territory to the new federal government, which it did. Congress's organization of the Territory Southwest of the River Ohio, and Washington's appointment of Blount as its governor, effectively ended these sundry intrigues.[45]

The Spanish stood to profit from these plots, though the American frontiersmen were the instigators, but a different sort of machination occurred soon after Edmund Charles Genêt arrived on American shores in 1793. By now the French Revolution had shaken Europe for four years. Louis XVI had just gone to the guillotine, and his nation stood on the brink of the Terror. The effects of this Continental upheaval are so great as to be almost beyond imagining or describing; certainly the clinical accounts of many historians and political scientists fail to convey its true impact. By 1793 the ripples, spreading out from the epicenter, were already crossing the Atlantic, and the Revolution and what followed would be a backdrop for most of the major events in the new American republic until Europe at last

---

Published for the United States Capiol Historical Society by the University Press of Virginia, 1996) 156, 173-77. Thomas P. Abernethy, a leading scholar of the southern frontier, maintains that Blount himself may have been involved in White's plans. *See* Abernethy, *From Frontier to Plantation in Tennessee* 93, 97-98.

[45]Abernethy, *From Frontier to Plantation in Tennessee* ch. 6; Bemis, *Pinckney's Treaty*, 119-21; Whitaker, *Spanish-American Frontier* 99, 109-15.

caged the tiger Napoleon on St. Helena years later.[46]

Many Americans, proud of their own struggle's success, found the French revolutionary ideals attractive. Others, witnessing the horror of the guillotine and a political and social process out of control, believed Great Britain and her fleet one of the last barriers between the thing that France was becoming and the destruction of western civilization. In the East, American commercial interests, tied in strongly to England, dominated both economics and politics, as is evident in Alexander Hamilton's financial policies. Western agrarian interests, however, gave rise to different sentiments, and Blount, Federalist that he was in the early 1790s, was the rare exception among the men of the western waters. The frontiersmen, benefiting little from the federal government and living a life with little security and less restraint, could sympathize more with French ideals. When Genêt made certain overtures to various frontier citizens about the possibility of seizing Spanish Louisiana, then, ears pricked up.[47]

Conflict between England and France, of course, was nothing new. Since 1689 the two countries, along with others, had fought a series of wars that together amounted to nothing less than a struggle for control of globe-spanning empires. What was particularly interesting in 1793, however, was a certain alliance. Spain, Catholic, separated from France only by the Pyrenees and wedded to her by the blood of their sovereigns, was a natural ally of that country and just as natural an enemy of Protestant England since the days of Drake, Hawkins, and the Tudors. The dangerous new ideas breeding in France, however, were at least as odious to European monarchs as Protestantism had been to Catholic nations two centuries earlier, and Spain, like others, saw a grave new danger awakening in the country to her north. The death of Louis XVI on the guillotine in March 1793, followed shortly by a French declaration of war against Spain, shocked the country into action, and later that year Spain and England signed an alliance against republican France.[48]

---

[46]*See* Elkins & McKitrick, *The Age of Federalism* chs. 8-9.

[47]Whitaker, *Spanish-American Frontier*, 187-88.

[48]Robin Ranger, "The Anglo-French Wars 1689-1815," *in* Colin S. Gray & Roger W. Barnett eds., *Seapower and Strategy* (Annapolis: Naval Institute Press, 1989), 159, 159; Bemis, *Pinckney's Treaty*, 168-69; Hilt, *Troubled Trinity* 37-38; Sir A.W. Ward & G.P. Gooch eds., *The Cambridge History of British Foreign Policy 1783-*

This new arrangement made concerted Anglo-Spanish actions in North America, perhaps against the United States, a distinct possibility. At the very least it meant that Spain need not worry about combined Anglo-American pressure against it in the Mississippi Valley. Consequently Godoy, by then Spain's first minister of state, began to spin out negotiations with the United States over the southern boundary question. Simultaneously, however, some Westerners grew eager to entertain Genêt's suggestions for a frontier strike against Louisiana. One of these was George Rogers Clark, a frontier general during America's own recent war against England.[49]

Clark had actually been planning an attack on Louisiana since before Genêt's arrival. A friend of his, Dr. James O'Fallon, had connections to one of the Yazoo companies, the land speculation concerns that had bought vast tracts of lands in present-day Alabama and Mississippi from the Georgia legislature, and the dealings of which would later culminate in the famous case of *Fletcher v. Peck*. Some of the land of interest to O'Fallon lay deep within the disputed area of the Southwest, and by late 1792 Clark had begun planning to help O'Fallon protect his investment by leading an armed expedition against Louisiana. A few months later Genêt arrived in Charleston.[50]

By early 1793 the French Directory was aware of the antagonism against New Spain that smoldered in the American West, and upon dispatching Genêt to America it instructed him to do everything possible to bring the Revolution to Louisiana, either with or without the help of the United States government. As things turned out, that help failed to materialize, so Genêt took matters into his own hands, contacting Clark and commissioning him as "Chief of the Independent and Revolutionary Legion of the Mississippi." Thomas Jefferson for a time seemed to fall under the Frenchman's spell, going so far as to write a letter of introduction for one of Genêt's agents. Though he objected upon learning of Genêt's proposals to Clark and others, Jefferson did not dismiss the possibility of aggression against

---

1919 (New York: The Macmillan Company, 1922) 238.

[49]Bemis, *Pinckney's Treaty*, 196; Whitaker, *Spanish-American Frontier* 187-89.

[50]*Fletcher v. Peck*, 10 U.S. (6 Cranch) 87 (1810); C. Peter Magrath, *Yazoo: Law and Politics in the New Republic: The Case of* Fletcher v. Peck (Providence: Brown University Press, 1966); Whitaker, *Spanish-American Frontier*, 187-89; Philbrick, *Rise of the West*, 187-89.

Louisiana; even his great and sympathetic biographer Dumas Malone quotes him as having told Genêt that as long as the French emissary did not draw the American government into the fray "'I did not care what insurrections should be excited in Louisiana.'"[51]

In the end nothing came of the plot, despite Clark's declarations that he had hundreds of frontiersmen ready to march. Washington, together with Hamilton taking a different view of matters than Jefferson, issued his Proclamation of Neutrality; thereafter the French government, in need of commercial help from the United States, and thus of good relations with it, revoked Genêt's credentials, and his successor Jean Fauchet in turn revoked the commissions that he had issued to the Westerners. With the loss of French backing, Clark's plans collapsed.[52]

In June 1794, as a result of the Genêt/Clark intrigue, Congress passed a new criminal statute. This law contained a provision, now known as the Neutrality Act, which has survived practically unchanged to the present day. In the 1790s it stipulated that any person organizing a military expedition within United States territory aimed at a foreign dominion with which the United States was at peace was guilty of a high misdemeanor, a crime that in this case carried a maximum penalty of three years' imprisonment and a three thousand dollar fine. This act would play a role in the investigation of the Blount Conspiracy a few years later.[53]

Genêt's plans had other ramifications for Blount's schemes as well, for another effect they had was to revive James Wilkinson's interest in winning Western independence, this time either with or without Spanish help, and this plot in turn helped to spawn Blount's. Although Clark had initially told Genêt that he could raise 800 men, which would suffice to capture New Orleans, other frontiersmen put forth somewhat higher figures. Spanish fears of the westerners magnified these numbers far beyond Clark's initial estimate, which itself may well have been inflated. Then, in the wake of Genêt's

---

[51]Whitaker, *Spanish-American Frontier*, 187-89; Philbrick, *Rise of the West* 187-89; Turner, "Genêt's Projected Attack," 652-56; Dumas Malone, *Jefferson and the Ordeal of Liberty,* 104-05 (quoting Jefferson).

[52]Harry Ammon, *The Genêt Mission* (New York: W.W. Norton, 1973) 157-58.

[53]Act of June 5, 1794, ch. 50, § 5, 1 Stat. 381, 384 (1794); Act of March 2, 1797, ch. 5, 1 Stat. 497 (1797); 18 U.S.C. § 960 (1994).

planned attack, against the background of Clark's preparations, Wilkinson wrote again to Carondelet, declaring that his Kentuckeans had resolved to take control of the Mississippi. Whether they did this by seceding from the Union and aligning themselves with New Spain, or instead by conquering Louisiana, was up to the Spanish. Carondelet, apprehensive, sought permission from Godoy to help Wilkinson with his plans to separate Kentucky from the Union; at one point he wrote that a leviathan force of sixty thousand frontiersmen was poised to sweep downriver, overwhelming Spanish posts as it came. The only prevention, Carondelet argued, was to reopen negotiations with the Westerners—particularly the Kentuckeans—to try to win an alliance with those forces instead.[54]

From Godoy's perspective in his European stronghold, however, things appeared very different indeed than they did in the heart of the American wilderness. By the summer of 1794, when he received Carondelet's dispatches, the Anglo-Spanish alliance was faltering, with its replacement by an Anglo-Spanish war a growing likelihood. Such a war might well pit Spain against the United States if it came to an agreement with England, for the latter two countries were by then negotiating the troublesome issues of the Northwestern border and the Anglo-American Atlantic commerce. On the other hand, if the Anglo-Spanish alliance somehow held, and England and the United States came to blows rather than to agreement, England might call for Spain to make war upon the United States as part of its Anglo-Spanish commitments. Either way, the United States stood to do Spanish interests in North America some serious damage. The only solution, Godoy and his council of ministers decided in the summer of 1794, was a *rapprochement* between the United States and Spain.[55]

Godoy's response to Carondelet was thus much the same as Floridablanca's reply to Miró had been in 1789. Carondelet was to work with Wilkinson and his "Secret Committee of Correspondence of the West" only to maintain Spain's good offices among the frontiersmen and to weaken England's. Godoy, meanwhile, shifted his

---

[54]Philbrick, *Rise of the West*, 187-89; Whitaker, *Spanish-American Frontier*, 189-97.

[55]Bemis, *Pinckney's Treaty*, 201-04, 218; Whitaker, *Spanish-American Frontier* 197-200.

attention to the American eastern seaboard, stepping up negotiations with the federal government. The news of Jay's Treaty, arriving in Spain in 1794, sparked Spanish fears that an Anglo-American alliance was in the offing, though in reality the treaty accomplished nothing of the kind. But these fears hastened the conclusion of Pinckney's Treaty the following year, which in turn finished off the Spanish intrigue. Wilkinson's plans stalled again, though he was by no means through with his frontier plots.[56]

This pattern of intrigue, in which everyone on the frontier seemed to know something of someone's schemes, and with both claims and fears of military forces that were often in gross excess of what was feasible, may seem rather amusing to late twentieth century readers. The fact is, however, that these episodes, despite their humorous characteristics, illustrate many important facts of life in the Mississippi Valley, and the Old Southwest in particular, some of which were very grave indeed. In these conspiracies, we see on the part of many of the inhabitants of the western waters an attachment to the Union that was at best equivocal, at worst mercenary. One can also see the lack of exterior constraints on the region and its people. Even after all of these early cabals, the federal government took insufficient steps to reinforce its grip on the region. Finally, one can easily see that the sparse population, the connections among the leading citizens, and the rumor and gossip that formed a major portion of the area's communications not only assured that word of intrigue got around; they also helped give people ideas about what courses of action were possible, desirable, and even acceptable in that howling wilderness. As a social historian or an anthropologist might clinically put it, conspiracy in the Old Southwest was something of a cultural phenomenon. By the end of 1796, as war clouds loomed, a new manifestation of this phenomenon, the most spectacular to date, was about to appear, and this one the federal government would not

---

[56]Bemis, *Pinckney's Treaty* ch. 11; Whitaker, *Spanish-American Frontier* 197-200, 209-13. As to Wilkinson's later activities, see Epilogue, *infra*. In fact, the strange circumstances surrounding Philip Nolan's death in 1800, in combination with his friendship with Wilkinson, suggests that Nolan's final, fatal journey beyond the Mississippi was part of another one of Wilkinson's plots. *See* Noel M. Loomis, "Philip Nolan's Entry into Texas in 1800," *in* John Francis McDermott ed., *The Spanish in the Mississippi Valley 1762-1804* (Urbana: University of Chicago Press, 1974) 120, 132.

ignore.

 ?&

For some time prior to late 1796, many Americans had harbored suspicions that the new Franco-Spanish alliance would result in Spain's retrocession of Louisiana to France, which Spain had taken in 1763. The replacement of decaying Spanish rule with a virile French presence opposed to American interests would be a cause for major concern to the entire country, but especially to the Trans-Appalachian region, the economy and territorial integrity of which was at stake. French control of Louisiana and the Mississippi would jeopardize American trade, travel, and property rights throughout the Southwest. Rumors were widespread and extreme, but behind them lay some truth, for Spain and France had been negotiating the retrocession of Louisiana since 1795. Fears of a French incursion into North America increased in late 1796 as people began to think that Louisiana might be that price that France demanded of Spain for a continued alliance against England. Even though Spain was to hold Louisiana until 1803, the region's immediate future as of 1796 was by no means certain.[57]

As Spain and England came to blows in October that year, Godoy, who up to this point had been faithfully executing Spain's obligations under Pinckney's Treaty, issued orders to delay the evacuation of Spanish posts on the Mississippi. He had come to feel that the United States might join England in its war against his country, and perhaps he did not wish to leave Louisiana undefended in the face of a possible American threat. Although Godoy settled on this new policy in October 1796, Spanish authorities in Louisiana did not receive their new orders until the following February; but even before this new blow to the American frontier, Blount's financial collapse had begun.[58]

Economic conditions throughout the West during the winter of

---

[57]Whitaker, *Mississippi Question* 52-53, 101-02, 186; Miller, *Federalist Era* 190; Elkins & McKitrick, *Age of Federalism* 436-40; Masterson, *William Blount* 302.

[58]Whitaker, *Mississippi Question* 52-58, 101-02; Masterson, *William Blount* 301-02.

1796 were terrible, largely due to speculation as well as rumors of war. Money disappeared; land prices collapsed; credit vanished; speculators went down into ruin. Blount himself, while in North Carolina, was pursued by creditors and escaped two arrest attempts only by pleading his senatorial immunity. The worst of the matter was that no end was in sight to the conditions that had caused this chain of disastrous events. As long as the Trans-Mississippi region, and the river itself, lay in the hands of an unfriendly power, the economic security of the American West was poor.

On top of all this, the Federalist administration's appointment of Benjamin Hawkins as Indian Superintendent threatened white expansionism in the Southwest, with all that that meant for Blount, has lands, and his finances. Hawkins was much too pro-Indian for Blount's tastes. In 1791 Blount had negotiated the Treaty of Holston with various tribes; though this treaty established a line of demarcation between white and Indian lands, as of 1796 that line had yet to be surveyed. The new senator doubtless feared that that with Hawkins in charge, the commissioners might now run the line to white settlers' detriment, adding further damage to an already disastrous season. Such were Blount's circumstances when he returned to Philadelphia in late November 1796 to be confronted with potential salvation, in the form of a proposition set forth by John Chisholm.[59]

Chisholm was the sort of character whom one might expect to meet on the frontier. Arriving in New York during the American Revolution, he proceeded through South Carolina and Georgia into Spanish Florida, where he was prisoner for a time. From thence he found his way into the Cherokee Nation, and finally to Knoxville. Some of his more recent adventures had involved Blount, whom he had served on occasion as a territorial Indian agent.[60] Described by his contemporaries as "a hardy, lusty, brawny, weather-beaten man," and by one historian as "as colorful an example as can be found of the old frontier," Chisholm, though poorly educated, was "enterprising,

---

[59]Masterson, *William Blount* 203-07, 297-302, 304-05.

[60]Declaration of John D. Chisholm, 29 November 1797, *in* Frederick Jackson Turner, "Documents on the Blount Conspiracy, 1795-97," 10 *Am. Hist. Rev.* 574, 595 (1905); Masterson, *William Blount* 262.

resolute, and well-acquainted" with the Southwest.[61] In the autumn of 1796 he journeyed to Philadelphia carrying a petition from a number of British subjects living in the West who sought American citizenship. These petitioners, along with Chisholm, had resolved to commence hostilities against Spanish possessions on their own if the federal government would not begin protecting their interests. When James McHenry, Pickering's successor as Secretary of War, refused to grant their request for citizenship, Chisholm took matters into his own hands.

One of the first people with whom Chisholm discussed his plans was John Rogers, a friend and fellow frontiersman who was in Philadelphia serving as an interpreter for several Indians who had business with President Washington. Rogers grew wary as Chisholm tried to entice him into joining the project. When he refused Chisholm's request to put his ideas before the Indians whom he was attending, the plotter went behind Rogers's back and discussed his plans with them himself. A bit later, visiting Chisholm's lodgings, Rogers saw written versions of Chisholm's proposals lying about in the open. At this point, realizing what had happened and much displeased with Chisholm, Rogers walked out "advising him," he said later, "to take care that he did not get hanged."[62]

Despite this warning, Chisholm apparently thought his neck in no danger, or if he did, he took little heed, for Rogers and the Indians were not the only ones he approached. Even before McHenry's decision, Chisholm had sought out Blount and told him of his group's intentions, as well as indicating that he had Rogers's support, though Rogers was later to deny that this was so. At any rate, Blount was sufficiently interested to entertain thoughts of introducing Chisholm to Robert Liston, British minister to Philadelphia, in order that Chisholm might solicit British support. In the end Blount himself remained in the background, not involving himself with Liston. Chisholm, however, did go to see the minister, possibly at Blount's suggestion, and told him of his plans.[63]

---

[61]8 *Annals of Cong.* 2366 (1797); Philbrick, *Rise of the West* 197; Robert Liston to Lord Grenville, 24 June 1797, *in* Turner, "Documents," 588.

[62]8 *Annals of Cong.* 2393-95 (1798).

[63]Declaration of John D. Chisholm, 29 November 1797, in Turner, "Documents," 596-97, 601-02; 8 *Annals of Cong.* 2350-51, 2378 (1797).

Liston, a veteran Scottish diplomat, had been serving in Philadelphia for only a few months when Chisholm contacted him. He had greeted word of his appointment to his new post with mixed emotions. "I would much rather go anywhere else," he wrote at the time. Still, he was quite aware that America was an important battleground for vying European interests. "The French are making infinite trouble in that quarter," he noted, "so I suppose I must go." He knew that the situation was delicate, for though the Revolution was dragging the nations of Europe into war, the United States, so far, remained a neutral in the contest. Chisholm's revelations made his job in this respect no easier. [64]

A few days after meeting the frontiersman, Liston told Chisholm that the English government could not offer its assistance in the affair. In a later interview, however, Liston did say that he would forward the proposal to England. Late in January 1797 he did in fact write to England's Foreign Secretary, William, Lord Grenville, informing him that Chisholm had over a thousand whites on the frontier prepared to attack Spanish possessions in Florida on England's behalf, if England were to supply a few ships and other equipment.[65]

In view of Genêt's attempts to revolutionize the West, to say nothing of the Spanish intrigues with the Kentuckeans, Chisholm's hope for British intervention is not as far-fetched as it may seem. British interest spanned the continent from Canada, which a French-dominated Louisiana might threaten, to East Florida, which could provide bases for French privateer sorties against Anglo-American merchantmen. To ward off danger of the latter event, the Admiralty was consorting with John McIntosh in Georgia even as the Blount Conspiracy evolved. At his plantation on St. Simons Island, engaging in secret signals with British ships, McIntosh contrived means of enlisting loyalists to help England take East Florida by force. Simultaneously an obscure parish priest in Wexford who knew Enrique White, the Irish-born governor of Pensacola, informed

---

[64]Willson, *Friendly Relations* 19-20, 23-24.

[65]Robert Liston to Lord Grenville, 25 January 1797, *in* Turner, "Documents," 576-77; Declaration of John D. Chisholm, 29 November 1797, *in* Turner, "Documents," 596.

English authorities that White could deliver Pensacola to England.[66] As for Canada, England had begun acting a year before Chisholm and Blount began their intrigues. In October 1795 William Henry Cavendish, 3rd Duke of Portland, instructed Canada's Lieutenant Governor John Graves Simcoe to sound out possible support among American frontier whites for an attack on Spanish possessions, with English backing, in the event of a British rupture with Spain. Liston's knowledge or ignorance of this particular communication notwithstanding, and whatever his personal opinion of Chisholm, he was aware of the strategic outlook in North America and the surrounding waters, and he was determined to prevent French resurgence there.[67] Given this state of affairs, he thought enough of the proposal to tell Grenville about it. In the meantime he left Chisholm hanging, though so far only figuratively.

Chisholm, however, was not one to wait with patience or with silence. In January he traveled to New York in the company of some Indians and British subjects. While there he discussed his plans with several merchants and shopowners. In telling Blount, however, he had unwittingly set off a chain of events that would eclipse his own endeavors.[68]

Exactly when Blount began to envision a more ambitious campaign than Chisholm planned is uncertain. Chisholm was not the only one to go to New York, though, for around the end of January Blount himself journeyed there to see an old friend and business partner, Dr. Nicholas Romayne, about some land matters. Their acquaintance went back to Blount's first term in Congress in the early 1780s. Romayne, a British subject and a physician of note in New York, was the man with whom he had collaborated to sell western lands to European customers, and on this visit Blount spoke of this and other financial concerns. When Blount asked Romayne to make

---

[66] J. Leitch Wright, Jr., *Britain and The American Frontier 1783-1815* (Athens: The University of Georgia Press, 1975) 110-12.

[67]*See* Ibid.; Duke of Portland to Lieutenant-Governor Simcoe, 24 October 1795, *in* Turner, "Documents," 575-76. Shortly after Liston wrote Grenville, in fact, George Rogers Clark asserted that British agents were on the frontier attempting to raise troops for just such an attack. Ibid., 576 n.1. Grenville's reaction to Chisholm's plan, however, suggests that these agents, if they existed at all, were perhaps Chisholm's own cohorts, acting without commissions.

[68]Ibid., 596-97.

renewed efforts to sell property to French buyers the doctor refused, noting that French interests at present were hostile to those of the United States, and that France might even secure Louisiana before long.[69]

During this lengthy conversation Blount apparently grew quite depressed, especially over the renewed rumors of Louisiana's transfer to France. He mentioned his concern with the welfare of Tennessee, and the impact that this event would have on the state. At one point he even burst into tears. A few days later, he followed up this episode by observing that his Tennessee lands had become valueless. Romayne remarked that it was a shame that England did not own Louisiana. In devious fashion Blount concurred heartily, saying that "it was indeed to be regretted that the British did not possess Louisiana, and that such an event might very easily be brought about." To this suggestion Romayne expressed doubt, or so he claimed later. He pointed out that strong anti-British sentiment was to be found in the West. But Blount pressed him further, declaring that Spanish forces were weak and finally revealing Chisholm's plan to the doctor. Apparently this was enough to alleviate Romayne's doubts about becoming involved in Blount's designs, for soon after this discussion the two began a correspondence about the project.[70]

From this point on Blount's program began to run in two somewhat different directions. Chisholm, continuing his negotiations with Liston, had as his primary object Spanish Florida, while Blount and Romayne included Louisiana in their plans. Blount himself remained involved in both parts of the plot, although Chisholm was an independent sort who considered himself the principal figure.[71] In fact the conspiracy, or conspiracies, to secure political and economic stability in the West comprised only a small part of the intrigues to be found in the Mississippi Valley during these months. In Natchez Andrew Ellicott was soon coming across rumors of various sorts, especially after Spain began to delay compliance with Pinckney's Treaty. Simultaneously French General Victor Collot, reconnoitering

---

[69] 8 *Annals of Cong.* 2356-59, 2340 (1797). For a brief sketch of Romayne's life, see 8 Dumas Malone, ed., *Dictionary of American Biography* (1935) 127-28.

[70] 8 *Annals of Cong.* 2356-59, 2340 (1797).

[71] Ibid., 2357-60, 2347, 2368; Outline of Chisholm's Plan, *in* Turner, "Documents," 600-01.

the West, informed Carlos Martinez de Yrujo and Pierre Adet, the Spanish and French ministers in Philadelphia, that the British had plans afoot in the Mississippi Valley. This rampant appearance of rumors may be partly due to Chisholm's vociferations. From 1796 on he told large numbers of people of his plans. Even Blount made inquiries of frontiersmen concerning Spanish fortifications.[72] Plots other than Blount's and Chisholm's may well have been afoot; the history of the region shows, if nothing else, that it was a breeding ground for such cabals. If other would-be conspirators were as obvious as these two, the abundance of such rumors seems unavoidable.

Despite Chisholm's frequent tirades, however, the details of the Blount Conspiracy never came fully to light. As Bemis wrote of one of the Southwest's earlier conspiracies, "The very nature of an intrigue of this kind is to leave as little documentary evidence as possible."[73] The best summary is one that Chisholm rendered months later. According to this account, the plan consisted of three expeditions. The northernmost, composed of forces from New York and Pennsylvania, was to set forth from the Ohio River to attack New Madrid on the west bank of the Mississippi. The second group, to be headed by Blount and composed of Choctaws and frontier whites, would move upon New Orleans from Tennessee. The third force, made up of Creeks, Cherokees, and Florida whites, all under Chisholm's command, was to attack Pensacola. All of these attacks were to take place on the same day. English support would consist of money as well as a number of ships to blockade both Pensacola and New Orleans.[74] Thus would the filibusters clear the way for British rule of Louisiana and Florida.

The general outlines of the conspiracy are fairly clear, but the full details may never emerge from the lengthening shadows. Nevertheless, a few especially tantalizing bits of information lead us to wonder about the relationships between various individuals during the

---

[72]Ellicott, *Journal* 44, 80, 91; Victor Collot to Carlos Martinez de Yrujo, 1 March 1797, *in* Turner, "Documents," 577, 580; General Collot to Carlos Martinez de Yrujo, *in* Turner, "Documents," 585; 2 Victor Collot, *A Journey in North America* (Paris: Arthur Bertrand, 1826) 64-68; 8 *Annals of Cong.* 2368, 2377, 2389 (1797).

[73]Bemis, *Pinckney's Treaty*, 143.

[74]Outline of Chisholm's Plan, *in* Turner, "Documents," 600-01.

months that Blount's plans were developing. An interesting hint or two appear in Romayne's correspondence with Blount; on one occasion the doctor gave the senator news of "Your friend, Mr. Burr," and on another Romayne wrote that "I have spoken to Colonel Burr about a land scheme between you and me."[75] Nothing else appears in the correspondence to implicate this most notorious western conspirator of them all in Blount's plans, but the two did have a friendship, and the details of Burr's own later conspiracy, so similar to Blount's in many ways, are enough to make one wonder.

An even more interesting event occurred around Blount's dinner table one evening. Summoned by the senator's young son, Chisholm strode into the room, expecting to find Blount taking his meal alone, since meetings between the two had always been private. Instead he found Blount in conversation with General James Wilkinson and Vice President Thomas Jefferson. With Wilkinson's schemes we are well acquainted. As for Jefferson, he was the one who would write a few years later, in his characteristically sweeping terms, that "There is on the globe one single spot the possessor of which is our natural and habitual enemy. It is New Orleans, through which the produce of three-eighths of our territory must pass to Market."[76]

What the three men discussed that evening is now lost to us; not even Chisholm knew, or if he did, he dissembled. "It immediately struck me," he mused later, "that Blount had sent for me in order to open my plan to these Gentlemen," though, uncertain, the frontiersman kept his mouth shut for once. Pleading an appointment with Secretary of War McHenry as an excuse to depart, he attempted to extricate himself before the senator ensnared him. Blount urged him to remain, but Chisholm, fearing some sort of trap, departed.[77]

As Blount conspired with Romayne and consulted his western friends, Chisholm continued, not without some miniscule success, to try to win British support. By the end of February 1797 he had convinced Liston to send him to London to present his idea to

---

[75]8 *Annals of Cong.* 2348, 2353 (1797).

[76]Thomas Jefferson to Robert R. Livingston, 18 April 1802, *in* 8 Paul Leicester Ford ed., *The Writings of Thomas Jefferson* (New York: G.P. Putnam's Sons, 1896) 143-47.

[77]Report of Examination of Chisholm by Rufus King, *in* Turner, "Documents," 602.

Grenville personally. On the last day of the month Liston's secretary arranged Chisholm's passage on a brig bound for England. Two weeks later Liston wrote for Chisholm a letter of introduction to Grenville. In this letter Liston stated his belief that he lacked authority to decide whether to agree to Chisholm's proposal. While not actually announcing his support for the plan, Liston nevertheless made suggestions to Grenville as to how the British could aid Chisholm without interfering with American neutrality.[78]

Chisholm, meanwhile, had made his own preparations for the journey. In early March he boarded the ship, and before long he had begun to tell others aboard of his plans. On March 17 he wrote Blount, notifying the senator of his impending departure. That same day he wrote another friend, frontiersman John McKee, once again making his intentions known:

> at nine o'clock to-morrow, I go on board the Ship favorite, & saile for Old England—Rejected by the U S—I now steere for forein Climes— ... to be plaine Jack—I will conquer or be Damnd.[79]

When the day for sailing (actually it was March 19) arrived, however, Chisholm was not aboard. When Liston learned of this, he began to search for the conspirator. That night he found him in a Philadelphia tavern, talking too much as usual, this time to a group of Frenchmen, of all people. Liston then saw to it that Chisholm embarked for England a few days later.[80]

Shortly after Chisholm's departure, however, Grenville penned a response to one of Liston's earlier letters, in which he informed his correspondent that the English government had decided to reject Chisholm's proposal, primarily because such a move would violate American neutrality. Unaware of this decision, Chisholm arrived in England and had to wait several weeks before he saw Grenville, when he finally learned the government's answer.[81]

---

[78]8 *Annals of Cong.* 2366-67 (1797); Robert Liston to Lord Grenville, 16 March 1797, *in* Turner, "Documents," 582-83.

[79]8 *Annals of Cong.* 2366, 2346-47 (1797).

[80]Ibid., 2367-69.

[81]Ibid., 2376; Declaration of John D. Chisholm, 29 November 1797, *in* Turner,

In the meantime, Liston, Blount, and Romayne proceeded in ignorance of the English decision. By mid-March 1797 Blount himself was planning a trip to England, while at the same time intimating even to his wife that he would actually soon be going to Tennessee. Within a few weeks at most, though, he apparently changed his mind, possibly when he learned of Chisholm's voyage, or perhaps because Romayne planned to go, for he never made the trip to England (and in fact neither did the doctor). Instead Blount elected to make good on his promises to go to Tennessee. Before he left Philadelphia at the close of the congressional session, however, Romayne wrote him from New York, enjoining him to keep the plan secret, but to continue circulating rumors of a Spanish cession of Louisiana to France. In this way, said Romayne, Blount could "inflame the minds of the people in a certain way, so as not to let out any of our plan, and yet put things in such a situation as will make our plan, when it takes place, appear as a salvation of the people."[82]

By the spring of 1797 attempts to keep things secret were almost pointless. Even as early as the previous December, while in Philadelphia, Chisholm had told his plans to James Carey, an Indian interpreter and long-time acquaintance of Blount, and Carey had asked the senator what Chisholm had meant. Blount, caught off guard by the inquiry, told Carey to regard the story as the sort of babble that Chisholm was always uttering. Others were learning of the plan as well. By early May Liston, still unaware of the English decision, wrote Grenville that rumors of an English attack upon Louisiana were circulating. Ellicott continued to hear various stories. Yet these were still just rumors, and none of them linked Blount's name to that of Chisholm or Liston. Liston himself probably did not know of Blount's involvement, although the British minister did carry on an oblique correspondence with Romayne.[83]

Ironically, in light of Chisholm's blabbering, Blount himself was the one who would provide the key piece of evidence that would show the rumors to be well-founded. By the end of March 1797 the senator departed Philadelphia for North Carolina, and in April he continued

---

"Documents," 596-97.

[82]8 *Annals of Cong.* 2343, 2353-54, 2359-60, 2345 (1797).

[83]Ibid., 2389-90, 2351-52; Robert Liston to Lord Grenville, 10 May 1797, *in* Turner, "Documents," 588-89; Whitaker, *Mississippi Question* 103.

on toward his adopted state. By April 21 he had reached the Sullivan County iron works of Colonel James King, a business partner, in northeastern Tennessee. Here he learned that the new president, John Adams, had called a special session of Congress to meet on May 15. The summons meant that in order to return to Philadelphia in time for the session Blount would have to depart immediately. This was when he decided to write certain persons on the frontier, Adams's summons having deprived him of his opportunity to meet with them personally. One letter he wrote to Chisholm's friend John Rogers in which he mentioned the conspiracy briefly and in an obscure manner. Another, more detailed letter, he wrote to James Carey.

Colonel King's Iron Works, April 21, 1797.

Dear Carey: I wished to have seen you before I returned to Philadelphia; but I am obliged to return to the session of Congress, which commences on the 15th of May.
Among other things that I wished to have seen you about, was the business Captain Chesholm mentioned to the British Minister last Winter in Philadelphia.
I believe, but am not quite sure, that the plan then talked of will be attempted this fall; and if it is attempted, it will be in a much larger way than then talked of; and if the Indians act their part, I have no doubt but it will succeed. A man of consequence has gone to England about the business, and if he makes arrangements as he expects, I shall myself have a hand in the business, and probably shall be at the head of the business on the part of the British. You are, however, to understand, that it is not yet quite certain that the plan will be attempted; yet, you will do well to keep things in a proper train of action, in case it should be attempted, and to do so, will require all your management—I say require all your management, because you must take care, in whatever you say to Rogers, or any body else, not to let the plan be discovered by Hawkins, Dinsmore, Byers, or any other person in the interest of the United States or Spain.
If I attempt this plan, I shall expect to have you, and all my Indian country and Indian friends, with me; but you are now

99

in good business I hope, and you are not to risk the loss of it by saying anything that will hurt you, until you again hear from me. Where Captain Chesholm is I do not know; I left him in Philadelphia in March, and he frequently visited the Minister and spoke upon the subject; but I believe he will go into the Creek nation by way of South Carolina or Georgia. He gave out he was going to England, but I did not believe him. Among other things that you may safely do, will be to keep up my consequence with Watts, and the Creeks and Cherokees generally, and you must by no means say anything in favor of Hawkins, but, as often as you can, with safety to yourself, you may teach the Creeks to believe he is no better than he should be. Any power or consequence he gets, will be against our plan. Perhaps Rogers, who has no office to lose, is the best man to give out talks against Hawkins. Read the letter to Rogers, and if you think it best to send it to him, put a wafer in it, and forward it to him by a safe hand, or perhaps you had best send for him to come to you, and speak to him yourself respecting the state and prospect of things.

I have advised you, in whatever you do, to take care of yourself. I have now to tell you to take care of me too; for a discovery of the plan would prevent the success and much injure all the parties concerned.

It may be that the Commissioners may not run the line as the Indians expect or wish and, in that case, it is probable the Indians may be taught to blame me for making the treaty. To such complaints against me, if such there are, it may be said by my friends, at proper times and places, that Doublehead confirmed the treaty with the President, at Philadelphia, and receives as much as 5,000 dollars a year, to be paid to the nation, over and above the first price; indeed, it may with truth be said, that, though I made the treaty that I made it by the instructions of the President, and, in fact, it may with truth be said, that I was, by the President, instructed to purchase much more land than the Indians would agree to sell. This sort of talk will be throwing all the blame off me upon the late President, and as he is now out of office, it will be of no consequence how much the Indians blame him.

Among other things that may be said for me is, that I was not at the running of the line, and that if I had been, it would have been run much more to their satisfaction. In short, you understand the subject, and must take care to give out the proper talks, to keep up my consequence with the Creeks and Cherokees. Can't Rogers contrive to get the Creeks to desire the President to take Hawkins out of the nation? for, if he stays in the Creek nation and gets the good will of the nation, he can and will do great injury to our plan. When you have read this letter over three times, then burn it. I shall be at Knoxville in July or August, when I will send for Watts, and give him the whiskey I promised him.

I am, &c.,WILLIAM BLOUNT.[84]

In this one letter Blount linked himself with Chisholm's plans as well as casting aspersions upon Washington, his former sponsor, and Hawkins. The latter things were mere indiscretions, but his talk of Chisholm's plan, and his own involvement with the British, was potentially catastrophic. His prediction that trouble would follow if the plan came to light was correct.

Blount left these letters with King and departed for Philadelphia. A week later, in Washington County, Virginia, he came across James Grant, a government employee from Tellico Blockhouse in Tennessee. Grant was *en route* from Hillsborough, North Carolina back to the frontier, and Blount took him into his confidence, promising to reward Grant for his services. After this meeting Grant headed on to Knoxville and Blount continued his journey to Philadelphia.[85]

In mid-May Grant was preparing to set out for Tellico, about 35 miles to the southwest of Knoxville, and King asked him to take three letters with him, one of which was double-sealed. Grant took the letters and, upon arriving at Tellico, he gave the sealed one to James Carey, who began to read it to himself while in Grant's presence. Grant later maintained that he had occasionally helped Carey with a

[84]7 *Annals of Cong.* 41-43 (1797); 2 *American State Papers, Foreign Rel.* 76-77.

[85]8 *Annals of Cong.* 2395-97 (1797).

difficult word, while Carey claimed that Grant had helped him read it without looking at it himself, leading Carey to believe that Grant already knew its contents. How much Blount told Grant in Virginia is uncertain, so whether Grant read the letter before delivering it to Carey is a question that remains unanswered. According to Carey, Grant told him to be careful, as Blount's letter was confidential, and he advised Carey to burn it, as Blount himself had directed. A few days later Grant wrote Blount, telling him that he had delivered the letter.[86]

At this juncture Carey began to have misgivings. This was obviously the first confirmation that Blount had given him that Chisholm had spoken true in Philadelphia the previous December, and it threw him into turmoil, partly because of the recent oath of loyalty he had taken to the government. "I was much embarrassed," he recounted frankly, "between my regard for Governor Blount and what might possibly be my duty with respect to the letter." Because of his doubts, he asked William L. Lovely, a clerk at Tellico, what he should do, and Lovely simply told him to consider his oath. A few days later Carey unburdened himself to James Byers, a government trader at Tellico and one of the men of whom Blount had warned him; the following day he showed Byers the letter itself. Byers stated that the document should be "disclosed," and Carey gave it to him.[87]

Soon after Carey's dealings with Byers, Grant, along with one or two officers, came to see Carey and asked him what had happened to Blount's letter. Apparently Grant, whose loyalty to Blount seems clear, had learned that it had fallen into other hands. Carey made some answer to the effect that the letter was gone or destroyed, and that no one had gotten it from him unless by robbery.[88] Following this interview Carey met with a Colonel John McClellan from Knoxville, who told Carey that he had heard that Byers had gained possession of the letter while Carey was drunk. Carey finally admitted that Byers had the letter, at which McClellan, apparently a Blount partisan, expressed his disappointment. Several days later Willie Blount and others came to meet with Carey, but the Tellico officers

---

[86]Ibid., 2395-98, 2381, 2390-91, 2354.

[87]Ibid., 2388, 2391.

[88]Ibid., 2391-92, 2385, 2398. All three of these accounts of the meeting differ from each other somewhat.

prevented them from seeing him.[89]

The shock waves that the letter produced spread quickly in Tennessee. When Byers received the letter, he showed it to David Henley, a War Department agent and an old adversary of Blount's. Henley copied the letter and sent the copy to George Washington, while Byers kept the original; Henley also summoned Hawkins to discuss Blount's plans, although Hawkins did not arrive until later.[90] At some point word of Byers's possession of the letter got out, sparking the local uproar. But even as the news began to circulate in the West, Byers departed the frontier to take the letter to McHenry and Pickering.[91]

⁊❧

By the middle of May Blount had returned to Philadelphia and once again he took up his official duties. During this session he roomed with his brother Thomas, who by now was serving in the House as a representative from North Carolina. For the next several weeks Blount occupied himself, both in a public and a private capacity, with routine matters. Occasionally he corresponded with Romayne. One thing with which he did not have to contend was the Turner impeachment investigation, which had stalled in the House earlier in the year without ever reaching the Senate. Throughout May and June, he was oblivious to the events unfolding hundreds of miles away on the Tennessee frontier.[92]

But despite his ignorance of these things, impeachment and conspiracy would soon become overriding concerns; for Byers was riding hard for Philadelphia, and the man and the moment were about to meet.

---

[89]Ibid., 2392.

[90]35 John C. Fitzpatrick, ed., *The Writings of George Washington* (Washington: Government Printing Office, 1970) 483-84; Benjamin Hawkins to David Henley, June 28, 1797, in David Henley Papers, Manuscript Room, Duke University.

[91]Masterson, *William Blount* 316.

[92]8 *Annals of Cong.* 2353-55; Masterson, *William Blount* 314-15.

Chapter 3

The First Session: Clamor
July-November 1797

Tuesday July 4 was a fine cool day in Philadelphia, a perfect day for the many celebrations the city witnessed. Dawn cannonades and bell-ringings marked the arrival of the country's twenty-first birthday, and in the harbor ships flew their flags to honor the United States. In the afternoon the acclaimed French aeronaut Jean-Pierre Blanchard launched a balloon from the debtor's yard, and the contraption (which carried Blanchard, a friend, and assorted animals) landed safely on the Market Street Wharf. Artillery and musket volleys punctuated the day's events, and many public dinners, with their usual elaborate toasts, took place about town.

Abigail Adams had fretted over the approaching festivities for several days. The round of meals that she had given for the members of Congress was nothing, she feared, to the gala that she would have to orchestrate for Independence Day. She had heard that the parties of previous years had cost the Washingtons as much as five hundred dollars, with many guests having to sit outside as the President's mansion would not hold them all. And this year, since Congress was in session, the number of attendants and the expense would both be even greater than before. In the end, though, all went to the first lady's satisfaction. At noon on the 4th Congress adjourned; the senators and representatives then joined with other federal and state officials to call upon and congratulate President Adams, the latter resplendent in full uniform and delighted to receive their respects. After visiting with Adams the men called upon Abigail, who also visited with their wives.[1]

Had members of the public been present while Adams greeted his callers—and some no doubt were—they may have felt some tension in the room. Perhaps they would have taken note of the absence of one of Tennessee's new senators, although they probably would not have given it much thought. Besides these minute imperfections, however, they would have found little wrong with the day as they proceeded to converse with the president. But though the public was yet unaware of the fact, a great deal was wrong, and most of those in attendance at the mansion knew it; for on the previous day Adams, in receipt of Blount's letter to James Carey, had delivered it to both houses of Congress.

Actually administration officials had received the incriminating document in the middle of June.[2] By then rumors of western conspiracies had been running rampant for some time. Months previously the Spanish minister in Philadelphia, Carlos Martinez de Yrujo, having received information from his agents in Louisiana, told Timothy Pickering of his suspicions regarding an Anglo-American plot. The secretary of state denied any knowledge of American involvement in such plans. At the same time, however, Pickering took the precaution of querying Robert Liston. Liston told Pickering that he had no information on such an expedition as Yrujo described; shortly thereafter the British minister warned his own government of the circulating rumors, but he did tell Grenville that Pickering had seemed satisfied with Liston's answers.[3]

When the administration learned of Blount's involvement, however, wheels began to turn. Pickering again approached Liston, this time going so far as to reveal some of the information found in the Carey letter, as well as Blount's name. Liston, by now aware of Grenville's decision denying Chisholm aid, replied truthfully that his

---

[1]*Philadelphia Gazette*, 3 July 1791, p. 3, col. 5; *Claypoole's American Daily Advertiser*, 5 July 1797, p. 3, col. 3; Stewart Mitchell, ed., *New Letters of Abigail Adams, 1788-1801* (Boston: Houghton Mifflin Company, 1947) 98-100.

[2]Byers would probably have reported to James McHenry, his superior, who drafted a cover letter to Adams; but the earliest references to the letter come from Pickering. See note 3, *infra*.

[3]*2 American State Papers, Foreign Rel.* 68-69; 8 *Annals of Cong.* 2372-73 (1797); Robert Liston to Lord Grenville, 10 May 1797, *in* Turner, "Documents," 588-89.

government was not involved in any conspiracy, although he was perhaps somewhat vague as to what the British actually knew. Pickering, an ardent Anglophile, was receptive (according to Liston) to the Englishman's suggestion that the entire affair was a French ruse.[4] For his part the secretary of state was probably willing to accept any explanation from Liston that "would tend to deny or downplay the English connection, for proof of England's involvement would damage Anglo-American relations." Pickering also took steps to warn frontier officers of the danger of a possible plan to bring about a western revolution, although he did not disclose the existence of Blount's letter. For the time being the document remained a secret. Even Liston stayed silent, except for his report to Grenville.[5]

Meanwhile, administration officials began to investigate courses of legal and political action against Blount. On June 20 Adams asked Attorney General Charles Lee his opinion on several questions of law. Lee sought the help of William Rawle, the United States attorney in Philadelphia, and William Lewis, a well-known attorney of the city and friend of the administration. On the 22nd they replied that Blount's letter was evidence of a crime—specifically, a misdemeanor— and that Blount was liable to impeachment for this offense.[6]

Before the end of June Pickering was anxious to deliver Blount's letter to Congress. Liston, however, tried to convince him to avoid aggravating the issue, in order that the government could investigate

---

[4]Robert Liston to Lord Grenville, 24 June 1797, *in* Turner, "Documents," 589-90; 2 *American State Papers, Foreign Rel.* 69. In late July Pickering told members of Congress that Liston had mentioned Chisholm to him as early as April; no other extant document corroborates this statement, however, and Pickering did have motives for portraying the British in a favorable light. 8 *Annals of Cong.* 2373 (1797).

[5]Timothy Pickering to Winthrop Sargent, 30 June 1797, Reel 6, *Pickering Papers* (Film, Massachusetts Historical Society); Declaration of John D. Chisholm, 29 November 1797, *in* Turner, "Documents," 599; Gerard H. Clarfield, *Timothy Pickering and American Diplomacy 1795-1800* (Columbia: University of Missouri Press, 1969) 134.

[6]Letter from Charles Lee, William Lewis, and William Rawle, 22 June 1797, Reel 6, *Pickering Papers* (Film). The matter of when Adams first learned of Blount's letter is open to doubt. Lee's opinion speaks of questions from the president on the 20th, but McHenry drafted a cover letter to Adams, in which he explained the document, that bears the date of June 30. 2 *American State Papers, Foreign Rel.* 72-77.

the plot without scaring the would-be filibusterers into hiding. But either Liston failed to convince Pickering, or Adams took a different view, for on Monday July 3 the president dispatched his secretary to Congress with the letter, other documents describing frontier developments, and a message to both houses.[7]

William Blount was as ignorant of these new developments as everyone else in Congress. On June 30th he carried on as usual, presenting a letter from Tennessee Governor John Sevier to McHenry and going with his fellow senator William Cocke to see the president. Adams, however, was too busy to see the men, or so he said; in fact he may have been avoiding the discomfiture of looking the conspirator in the face. Blount, although exasperated by the denial of an audience, probably attributed it to a busy presidential schedule, or at worst a spirit of partisanship.[8]

On July 3 Blount, still unaware of the blade hanging over his neck, was exiting the Senate when he met Samuel B. Malcolm, Adams's secretary, going into the chamber with a message from the president. Blount asked its contents, but Malcolm only replied that the message was secret and confidential. The two men then went their separate ways. Upon receiving the message, which included a copy of Blount's letter to Carey, the senators had it read aloud, presumably after clearing the chamber, and as they heard the document's contents the room exploded into an uproar.[9]

Some time after the letter's reading, Blount returned to the Senate. On motion, the incriminating document was read once again. Blount turned visibly pale as Thomas Jefferson, the presiding officer, asked him whether he was in fact the letter's author. The senator replied that he had written a letter to Carey on or about the date appearing on the Senate's document, but that he was unable to say whether it was a correct copy. He asked for a copy of the Senate's version as well as for a day's delay so that he might refer to his files.

---

[7]Robert Liston to Lord Grenville, 24 June 1797, in Turner, "Documents," 589-90; Mitchell, *Abigail Adams* 100. Liston later guessed that Adams did not wish to be caught withholding the information, an occurrence that might suggest the administration's complicity in Blount's scheme. Robert Liston to Lord Grenville, 8 July 1797, in Turner, "Documents," 592-94.

[8]William Blount to John Sevier, 30 June 1797, Edward Carey Gardiner Collection, Historical Society of Pennsylvania.

[9]Mitchell, *Abigail Adams* 100; 7 *Annals of Cong.* 33-34 (1797).

These requests the Senate granted.[10]

The House of Representatives also cleared its galleries as the representatives heard Adams's message along with Blount's letter. Unlike the Senate, the lower house did not vote any delay in proceedings; instead it created at once a committee to investigate the affair, and referred to it all of the documents that Adams had sent.[11]

Thus the wheels began to turn in a process that would run for over eighteen months. For a day or two it ran quietly, without the public's knowledge. It also ran for this same period without the active involvement of its principal subject. On July 4, the appointed day for Blount to give an explanation of the letter, the senator did not appear in his place, although Cocke attended and brought with him a letter from his colleague. In this letter Blount asked for still more time to examine his papers. Perhaps he hoped that he could be saved by Congress's adjournment, which was overdue and could only be days away at most.[12] But the Senate was running out of patience. Now it, too, formed a committee on the affair, referring the pertinent materials to this group, empowering it to send for persons and papers, and voting an injunction of secrecy on the entire matter.[13]

This Senate committee, headed by the Pennsylvania Federalist James Ross, soon sent a request that Blount appear on the morning of the 5th to answer its questions. On that day Blount did not appear, instead sending Ross a letter denying his authorship of the Carey missive. Ross's committee then reported to the Senate, after which Jefferson issued a terse letter of command to Blount. "Sir," the vice president wrote, "You are hereby required to attend the Senate in your place without delay." This letter he gave to the doorkeeper to deliver; but the officer was unable to locate Blount, who had bolted.[14]

---

[10]Mitchell, *Abigail Adams* 100; 7 *Annals of Cong.* 33-34 (1797).

[11]*Massachusetts Mercury*, 11 July 1797, p. 2, col. 1; 7 *Annals of Cong.* 440-41 (1797).

[12]Thomas Jefferson to Thomas Mann Randolph, 29 June 1797, 102 (Reel 34) *Jefferson Papers* (Film).

[13]7 *Annals of Cong.* 34-35 (1797). This is perhaps the earliest example of the Senate creating an investigative committee; the House had done so on at least two prior occasions, the first being in 1792. 3 *Annals of Cong.* 490-94 (1792); 5 *Annals of Cong.* 169-70 (1795).

[14]7 *Annals of Cong.* 35-36 (1797); William Blount to James Ross, 5 July 1797, National Archives, Record Group 46 (Film M1704); Thomas Jefferson to William

On the morning of the 5th Blount, rather than appearing before Ross's committee, had made his way to the Philadelphia waterfront and chartered a pilot boat for Ocracoke Inlet, North Carolina, taking some trunks of his papers on board with him. Before the boat sailed, however, several officers came looking for him, having somehow traced him to the waterfront. Not knowing Blount personally, they unwittingly allowed him to escape, although they did find one or two other men aboard who seemed very anxious to conceal Blount's baggage. The Republican newspaper *Aurora* later reported that Pickering had prevailed upon the officers to release these men—one of whom was allegedly English—and from this point no further mention of them appears. The trunks and their contents, however, ultimately found their way to Ross's committee.[15]

By the 5th news of Blount's letter had become public knowledge, and press and citizens began an outcry that would soon spread nationwide. As the word got out in Philadelphia, an interesting phenomenon occurred. The Federalist party was, in general, more sympathetic to British than French interests, while Republicans tended to favor France and its revolutionary principles. Yet on the frontier these alignments often came second to other matters. Blount's interests, for instance, had suffered at the hands of Federalists as well as those of Spain, France's ally. Here then was Blount, by now an avowed Republican, conspiring with the English, who were friends of the Federalists. Clearly Republican and Federalist alike found his actions repugnant, but neither party could throw the blame entirely upon the other because of Blount's peculiar set of associations, although both groups made repeated efforts to do so. The *Aurora* observed that Blount had long been a friend of the administration, Washington having appointed him to his gubernatorial post; it also pointed out that Pickering had given Liston advance warning of the letter's existence. To this the Federalist *Gazette of the United States* retorted that Washington, rising above party spirit, had been known to appoint Antifederalists to office, that

---

Blount, 5 July 1797, National Archives, Record Group 46 (Film M1704).

[15]*Boston Gazette*, 17 July 1797, p. 1, col. 3; *Philadelphia Gazette*, 5 July 1797, supplement; William Blount to James Ross, 7 July 1797, National Archives, Record Group 46 (Film M1704); Mitchell, *Abigail Adams* 100; *Aurora*, 12 July 1797, p. 3, col. 1.

Blount had attacked his former patron in the Carey letter, that at present he was an administration opponent, but that he was not an acquaintance of Liston's. To this salvo the fiercely Federalist "Peter Porcupine," William Cobbett, editor of *Porcupine's Gazette*, soon added the charge that all of Blount's political support in this crisis was coming from Republicans. This partisan squabbling continued for weeks thereafter as the papers screamed their warnings to the nation.[16]

The press was not the only place where Blount's actions met with such a response. Clearly the conspiracy was the talk of the town. Secretary of the Treasury Oliver Wolcott described the senator's actions as treasonous;[17] Ross's fellow senator from Pennsylvania, William Bingham, told Rufus King, United States minister to England, that Blount's plans had convinced the Spanish to delay their compliance with Pinckney's Treaty (an erroneous conclusion).[18] Abigail Adams wrote her sister that the Jacobins, emphasizing the British connection, rejoiced over the affair's disclosure. "When shall we cease to have Judases?" she exclaimed, lamenting that Pennsylvania had no gallows with which to punish the senator for his "diabolical plot." From Mount Vernon Washington joined in this round of denunciations, forwarding his copy of the incriminating letter to McHenry and expressing a desire to see Blount meet with all the punishment to be had under the Constitution and laws of the country.[19]

While this agitation continued Blount himself changed his mind, deciding upon fight rather than flight. On Thursday, the day after his abortive attempt to leave the city, he appeared in his place in the Senate chamber, and he even participated in the routine business of the day. Finally, James Ross read a second report from his investigating committee. This report said that the criminality in this affair transcended Blount's personal actions and related to his

---

[16]*Aurora*, 11 July 1797, p. 3, col. 1; *Gazette of the United States*, 7 July 1797, p. 2, col. 1; *Porcupine's Gazette*, 8 July 1797, p. 3, cols. 3-4.

[17]Oliver Wolcott to James Iredell, 12 July 1797, James Iredell, Sr. and James Iredell, Jr. Papers, Manuscript Room, Duke University.

[18]William Bingham to Rufus King, 10 July 1797, *in* 2 King, *Correspondence* at 199-200; See Chapter 2, *supra*.

[19]Mitchell, *Abigail Adams* 100-01; 35 Fitzpatrick, *Writings of Washington* 490-91.

senatorial capacity, and that the Senate should accordingly expel Blount for committing a high misdemeanor. In response to the report, Blount rose and read a declaration. He said that he understood that the House of Representatives was considering impeachment, and in light of this fact he intended to keep silent during the investigation, while remaining confident that he would ultimately win vindication.[20] The Senate then voted to delay consideration of Ross's report recommending expulsion until the next morning. Blount read his declaration again, stated that he would appear and answer the allegations against him, and asked for a copy of Ross's report as well as permission to be represented by counsel. After an unsuccessful motion to delay consideration of these points, a long debate ensued, and the Senate finally agreed by a good margin to allow Blount to be represented by two attorneys. Blount asked for a third, but to this the Senate unanimously disagreed. The chamber then voted to allow Blount to have copies of various papers, and the affair ended until the following morning.[21]

During this exchange in the Senate, the House of Representatives was also discussing the affair, as Blount himself had noted. As Ross was recommending Blount's expulsion, Representative Samuel Sitgreaves, chairman of the House committee, was introducing into the House a committee resolution calling for Blount's impeachment. This resolution became the subject of a lengthy debate.

As the House of Representatives began to consider this recommendation, the first objection from the floor raised the question of whether the House should involve itself in the matter at all. Sitgreaves, a staunch Federalist from Pennsylvania, answered that Adams had thought the matter serious enough to inform Congress, and he called the chamber's attention to the opinion of Lee, Rawle, and Lewis, which the president had made available. In light of these

---

[20]7 *Annals of Cong.* 37-38 (1797); *Independent Chronicle*, 13 July 1797, p. 3, col. 1; *Massachusetts Mercury*, 14 July 1797, p. 2, col. 1.

[21]*Massachusetts Mercury*, 14 July 1797, p. 2, col. 1; 7 *Annals of Cong.* 37-38 (1797); *Independent Chronicle*, 13 July 1797, p. 3, col. 1. In permitting Blount the assistance of counsel the Senate, either knowingly or unknowingly, followed a House precedent set a year and a half earlier in the investigation of Robert Randall. 5 *Annals of Cong.* 179-85 (1795). Because Senator (then Representative) Theodore Sedgwick was present at the 1795 debate, and later at the proceedings of July 5, 1797, the Senate may well have discussed Randall's case on the latter occasion.

facts, Sitgreaves contended, the House's course was clear. He went on to argue that because the Constitution's impeachment clauses limited only punishments rather than the power as a whole, senators were subject to the process; he added that the purpose of an impeachment was to reach cases not cognizable in a regular court. Because the Senate shared in executive powers and knowledge, he asserted, a senator's interference in the government's diplomatic activities must be an impeachable offense. Sitgreaves also mentioned the Senate's duty of confirming and supervising official appointees. In light of this power, he declared, Blount's encouragement of Carey to break his government oath must be considered a breach of his own duty.[22]

The issues here mentioned, particularly the question of a senator's amenability to the impeachment process, were to give rise to a good bit of controversy in the following months. Sitgreaves failed to resolve the issue of impeachment's scope in this speech, as he learned almost immediately when John Nicholas, a Republican from Virginia, arose.

Nicholas began by attacking Sitgreaves's committee for daring to declare Blount guilty, in effect, without any supporting evidence. If nothing else, he suggested, the House of Representatives should determine whether the script of the Carey letter matched the senator's own handwriting. The House of Representatives, he told his colleagues, should be legally satisfied as to a man's guilt before it impeached him.

Nicholas next took issue with Sitgreaves's arguments as to a senator's impeachability, remarking that the Senate's role in the appointment power was small and its alleged post-appointment supervisory duties nonexistent. Nicholas admitted that these were first thoughts, and he advised the House to delay the entire matter until the following session, when it could deal with procedural matters in a calmer, less hurried, more deliberate fashion. Congress had no need to fear Blount's escape in the meantime, he said, for impeachment, not involving personal punishment, could not be blocked by the impeached party's absence—another controversial remark that would give rise to extensive debates in the months ahead.[23]

---

[22]7 *Annals of Cong.* 448-50 (1797); *Aurora,* 7 July 1797, p. 2, col. 5; *Massachusetts Mercury,* 14 July 1797, p. 2, col. 2.

[23]7 *Annals of Cong.* 450 (1797); *Aurora,* 7 July 1797, p. 3, col. 1; See Chapters 4 and 5, *infra.*

As Nicholas finished, Albert Gallatin stood to speak. A brilliant, dedicated Republican, Gallatin had on the previous day expressed to his wife his desire to pursue the affair if only to discover the extent of Britain's intrigues. Clearly at first he doubted the propriety of impeachment proceedings; he submitted to his colleagues that the Constitution expressly held only civil officers to be subject to impeachment, and he expressed his doubts as to whether legislators fell into this category. But the particular question here, he went on, was whether the House could impeach a senator for an act, such as this one, that lay without the bounds of his official duties. Gallatin argued that since Congress would not impeach and try a private citizen for treason, it should treat a senator who acted in a private capacity no differently. Gallatin then dismissed Sitgreaves's whole argument as to Blount's corruption of an Indian agent.

Gallatin's next point most clearly revealed his interest in the affair. Blount's letter indicated the existence of an English conspiracy, and as such it warranted not only legislative, but executive investigation. An expulsion now would not prevent the House of Representatives from impeaching Blount later, he claimed, so the House should proceed with some deliberation, perhaps waiting until the following session to take action. Finally, the Swiss-born Republican questioned the point of Lee's opinion. The decision to impeach or not to impeach was the decision of the House alone, he said, thus getting into the record a partisan critique of the Federalist administration.[24]

Samuel Dana of Massachusetts spoke next, arguing that just as a judge might be impeached for treason not related to his official duties, so might a senator be impeached for unofficial acts as well. As to whether a legislator was impeachable at all, Dana, echoing Hamilton's arguments in the *Federalist*, maintained that impeachment was a political device designed to protect the government from unworthy men such as Blount. Article II, Section 4 of the Constitution states that all civil officers, in addition to the expressly-named president and vice president, were subject to impeachment; according to this same provision, as well as Article I, Section 3, Clause 7, conviction entailed removal from office, and

---

[24]Albert Gallatin to Hannah Gallatin, 5 July 1797, *Albert Gallatin Papers* (Film, New York Historical Society); 7 *Annals of Cong.* 450-52 (1797); *Aurora*, 7 July 1797, p. 3, cols. 1-2.

possibly disqualification from holding "any Office of honor, Trust or Profit under the United States." Dana apparently believed that legislators did not fit within the definition of officers, at least as the impeachment provisions contemplated it. He held up the absurdity of a former official, impeached, convicted, and barred from holding office in the future, winning election to the Senate or House of Representatives, a consequence logically possible if legislators were not to be considered civil officers. Dana closed by conceding that the House of Representatives should be fully satisfied of the facts before acting, but he also said that the facts here were clear enough to warrant impeachment now and a drafting of articles of impeachment later.[25]

Sitgreaves then responded to Gallatin's arguments. Siding with Dana, he agreed that the facts justified an impeachment, since this process, he claimed, was founded upon the idea of notoriety—the common law concept of a fact so well known to the community as to dispense with the need further proof. The clause respecting judgments in impeachments, he noted, were not found at the same location as the "Civil Officers" Clause, which indicated the wider application of judgment than to just officers. Sitgreaves was here arguing, in effect, that even if a legislator were not constitutionally a civil officer, he might nevertheless be subject to impeachment under a broad construction of the government's powers. That which the Constitution does not expressly prohibit, he practically said, it allows by implication. Sitgreaves's own implication thus hung in the air; because the Constitution did not expressly bar impeachment of a senator, Blount was liable to the process whether he were a civil officer or not. This process, Sitgreaves pointed out, was much more lenient in terms of punishment than that Blount would face in a regular court.[26]

Sitgreaves also agreed with Dana's proposed sequence of impeachment and article drafting, as befitted an accusation based on notoriety, or by clamor, as it was known in the context of English impeachment.[27] John Rutledge, Jr. had attended part of the

---

[25]7 *Annals of Cong.* 453 (1797).

[26]Ibid. at 453-55.

[27]7 *Annals of Cong.* 455-56 (1797); Lambrick, "Abington," 274; Plucknett, "1376," at 157, 159, 161. Cf. Plucknett's analysis of Mortimer's case; Plucknett,

impeachment trial of India's Governor-general Warren Hastings some years earlier. He concurred with Sitgreaves, but he did suggest that the House of Representatives prove the letter's handwriting to be Blount's. Abraham Venable seconded the idea, reminding the representatives that this case would stand as a precedent. At this point Gallatin admitted that Dana's arguments had removed some of his own doubts, but he continued to argue that investigation of the plot was of more importance than the punishment of Blount. The House having reached some agreement, four representatives, including framer and Republican Abraham Baldwin, attested that the handwriting belonged to Blount, and the House adjourned for the day.[28]

This first practical discussion of impeachment on record raises many questions. The first, and for Blount the most important ones, were the issues of whether only civil officers were subject to impeachment, and if so whether a senator was a civil officer. Sitgreaves had best put these questions; because the Constitution's text was vague on this point, expressly extending the process to civil officers but silent about all other persons, the issue was a perfect partisan sparring ground. Federalists, ascendant in the national government at this time, generally took the Hamiltonian view that all was granted except that which was expressly denied. Republicans, the opposition (and an opposition whose loyalty the Federalists doubted), took the other view, holding all to be prohibited which was not expressly granted. This debate, in various forms, would consume a great deal of the Fifth Congress's time in coming months.

The House debate touched upon other points as well. The matter of whether Congress should consider Blount's actions to be private or public—that is, whether they were related to duties in his capacity as senator—was another major issue. Still another was that of the standard of proof involved; the idea that Blount's letter to Carey made his actions notorious, as put forth by Dana and Sitgreaves, apparently met with little if any criticism.

Blount had clearly won the disfavor of everyone who spoke that day. The principal questions seemed to be that of how to deal with him, why an investigation was in order, who should conduct it, and

---

"Origin," 59-61.

[28] 7 *Annals of Cong.* 455-58 (1797); *Aurora*, 7 July 1797, p. 3, col. 2.

when it should take place. At the end of the day those who wished to continue a congressional investigation, both in the Senate and the House, had clearly triumphed, although no one expressed any objection to the idea of a concurrent administration inquiry as well. Attempts to delay the impeachment process failed; by the end of July 6, then, Blount's position was fast deteriorating.

On the 7th the House resumed its debate. One of its first acts was to hear a letter from Thomas Blount, William's brother, in which the representative from North Carolina asked to be excused from voting, a request that the House granted. The representatives then went into a Committee of the Whole, which, after some debate, reported to the House the Sitgreaves committee's impeachment resolution.[29]

This Committee of the Whole—in which the previous day's debates had also taken place—was a parliamentary device that enabled the entire House to sit as a committee, unhampered by the need for a quorum and deciding issues that were not final until voted upon by the House acting in its normal capacity. Since the House of Representatives, acting as such, had thus not yet approved the resolution, it now had to vote upon the question of the impeachment.

As these events transpired in the House, the Senate was also witnessing the drama's unfolding. With news of the conspiracy having become public two days before, spectators packed the galleries as Blount entered the chamber in the company of Jared Ingersoll and Alexander James Dallas, two of the city's finest attorneys.

Though Blount might well have been in fear's grip, what he now displayed was outrage. Earlier in the day he had written an indignant letter to James Ross protesting the seizure of his trunks from the pilot boat as inconsistent with Fourth Amendment principles. "I do not dispute the Power of the Senate to send for papers and witnesses in a cause depending before them," he declared, "yet I do not

---

[29]7 *Annals of Cong.* 458-59 (1797); U.S., Congress, House, Committee on Impeachment of William Blount, *Report of the Committee of the House of Representatives of the United States, Appointed to Prepare and Report Articles of Impeachment against William Blount, a Senator of the United States, Impeached of High Crimes and Misdemeanors* (Philadelphia: John Fenno, 1797) [Evans 34785] 4-5; *The Debates and Interesting Speeches in the Fifth Congress of the United States, at their First Session* (Newbergh, New York: David Denniston, 1797) [Evans 32965] 375.

conceive that a general Power of that Description, in Order to collect Information, can destroy the Right of the People to be secure in their Person, Papers and effects."

The letter apparently had some effect on Ross, although he refused Blount's demand to "Let the trunks therefore be returned to me as my property," and likewise ignored his promise that "I will expose the Contents of them to the Inspection of the Committee." He instead elected to keep the trunks; he did begin the proceedings, however, by telling the Senate that his committee had acquired them, and he requested the Senate's clear authorization before examining any of their contents. This the Senate agreed to after some discussion, expanding the committee's subpoena power to cover those items specifically.[30] This matter out of the way, a table and other accommodations were set up before the chair of the Senate. Senator Uriah Tracy took the liberty of sending a note to the House of Representatives to inform it that the Senate had prepared seats for those representatives who wished to attend. The President *pro tempore*—Jefferson had already departed Congress for the session— asked Blount if he were ready to proceed, and Blount answered in the affirmative, introducing his counsel. The stage was set.[31]

In choosing his attorneys Blount had made his wisest decision of the week. In an age when Philadelphia lawyers were renowned for their abilities, Ingersoll and Dallas were among the best of the best. Jared Ingersoll, the elder of the two at only forty-eight, had served at the Constitutional Convention ten years earlier. The Connecticut

---

[30]*Aurora*, 8 July 1797, p. 3, col. 1; *Massachusetts Mercury*, 14 July 1797, p. 2, col. 1; 7 *Annals of Cong.* 38 (1797); William Blount to James Ross, 7 July 1797, National Archives, Record Group 46 (Film M1704). This grant of a subpoena power to a Senate select investigating committee comes years before the dates usually given for the earliest Senate investigations. See M. Nelson McGeary, "Congressional Investigations: Historical Development," 18 *U. Chi. L. Rev.* 425, 425-26 (1951); Marshall Edward Dimock, "Congressional Investigating Committees," 47 *Johns Hopkins University Studies in Historical and Political Science* 9, 62 (1929).

[31]*Aurora*, 8 July 1797, p. 3, col. 1; *Massachusetts Mercury*, 14 July 1797, p. 2, col. 1; 7 *Annals of Cong.* 38 (1797). Jefferson's early departure gave rise to Federalist whispers that the vice-president had been involved in the Blount affair. *Porcupine's Gazette*, 8 July 1797, p. 3, col. 4; *Independent Chronicle*, 8 January 1798, p. 3, col. 1. The rumors are intriguing, especially in light of the dinner meeting of Blount, Jefferson, and Wilkinson that Chisholm witnessed. Report of Examination of Chisholm by Rufus King, *in* Turner, "Documents," 602-03.

native had received his training at London's Middle Temple in the 1770s, and he had learned his lessons well. His good height, distinct military and self-confident bearing, and rhythmic oratory all served to augment his logical abilities and his power to persuade and manage juries, a power none of his contemporaries could equal. He was given to learning his case so thoroughly that he could seemingly ignore his prepared notes when at bar, and he rarely made tactical mistakes. Alexander James Dallas is perhaps best known to attorneys today for his four volumes of reports, which bear his name, of federal and Pennsylvania judicial opinions. Born in Jamaica in 1759, he was just as skilled as his good friend Ingersoll, with whom he had often collaborated. An excellent courtroom pleader, Dallas was widely recognized as a tenacious, resourceful attorney. This was all to the good, for Blount was in dire need of the two men's combined talents. The fact that each—particularly Dallas—was a leading Republican was lost on no one.[32]

When all was in order, Dallas arose and erected his client's first line of defense. Launching into a "neat and pertinent" argument against expulsion, the lawyer then quickly asked the Senate to grant a delay in the proceedings until Monday to give the attorneys more time to prepare their case. As Blount had sought him out only on the previous afternoon, Dallas pointed out, he had had little time to prepare his arguments. Ingersoll followed his partner, speaking out against expulsion on different grounds, but also ending with a request for more time; in his case he had only gotten the relevant documents that very morning. Once again, then, Blount sought to play the waiting game.[33]

After the attorney's request Theodore Sedgwick, a well-known Federalist senator from New York, arose and moved that Blount's counsel retire while the senators discussed the request. This motion caused quite a tumult, with several senators shouting their

---

[32]Horace Binney, *The Leaders of the Old Bar of Philadelphia* (Philadelphia: Henry B. Ashmead, 1866) 89-91; William Montgomery Meigs, *The Life of Charles Jared Ingersoll* (Philadelphia: J.B. Lippincott Company, 1897) 18-22; Raymond Walters, Jr., *Alexander James Dallas: Lawyer, Politician, Financier 1759-1817* (Philadelphia: University of Pennsylvania Press, 1943) 5, 6, 17, 76-77; *Porcupine's Gazette*, 10 July 1797 p. 2, col. 5.

[33]*Massachusetts Mercury*, 14 July 1797, p. 2, col. 1.

disagreement. Even Cocke ventured to suggest that the proceedings remain open.[34] Open they stayed, as Henry Tazewell, a Virginia Republican, suggested that the Senate delay the expulsion debate until the next morning. At this point Ingersoll said that such a schedule was impossible, as he had to attend a regular court the next day. To this Senator James Hillhouse replied caustically that the United States Senate should not have to wait upon the convenience of an ordinary court. Thus the discussion continued for a time, during which the Senate sent to the House to retrieve the original of the Carey letter. Having procured it, the president *pro tempore* flatly asked Blount if he had written it. Apparently the Senate leadership was tired of delay.[35]

Dallas immediately threw himself into the confrontation, not being one to be bullied. He said that he hoped the Senate would not insist upon asking such a question at that point, for to do so would be to act in derogation of legal principles. (Dallas here apparently referred to his client's constitutional privilege against self-incrimination or his fair trial rights; if so this was not the last time Blount's attorneys, along with others, would invoke provisions of the Bill of Rights against the Senate.)[36] The two lawyers reminded the Senate that an impeachment was pending at that very moment in the House, and forcing Blount to answer the question of the letter's authorship, or to prejudge the issue by expelling him, would be unjust.[37]

During this showdown Samuel Sitgreaves, accompanied by several other representatives, arrived with a message from the House. Proceeding to the bar of the Senate, Sitgreaves announced:

> *Mr. President*: I am commanded, in the name of the House of Representatives, and of all the people of the United States, to impeach William Blount, a Senator of the United States, of

---

[34]Ibid. In allowing Blount's counsel to remain in the chamber the Senate acted contrary to the House's practice in the Randall case. 5 *Annals of Cong.* 194-95 (1796). Perhaps the fact that Blount, unlike Randall, was a member of the deliberative body played a part in the Senate's decision.

[35]*Massachusetts Mercury*, 14 July 1797, p. 2, col. 1.

[36]Ibid.; *Aurora*, 8 July 1797, p. 3, col. 1. See Chapters 4 and 5, *infra*.

[37]*Massachusetts Mercury*, 14 July 1797, p. 2, col. 1; *Aurora*, 8 July 1797, p. 3, col. 1.

high crimes and misdemeanors; and to acquaint the Senate that the House of Representatives will, in due time, exhibit particular articles against him, and make good the same.

I am further commanded to demand that the said William Blount be sequestered from his seat in the Senate; and that the Senate do take order for his appearance to answer the said impeachment.

This message, which carried tidings that the House had just unanimously voted the first federal impeachment in the nation's history, served to break the spell in the Senate, and the legislators promptly agreed to postpone debate on the expulsion question in order to consider the House's requests.[38]

Despite its brevity, the House's statement revealed a great deal about what the representatives thought about the impeachment process. Although the House had agreed to the committee's impeachment resolution quickly, the question of whether to delay the impeachment until after the preparation of articles, or specific charges, was a troublesome one. Gallatin and others had wanted to wait until the articles were ready. But Sitgreaves and others wished to proceed with the impeachment presently in order to secure Blount's person. In adopting this position Sitgreaves relied on precedents spelled out by Blackstone and others, and in the end this view prevailed.[39]

The question of sequestration had also come under debate. Sitgreaves, anxious to deal firmly and efficiently with Blount, had pushed for sequestration, for barring the senator from his seat while the impeachment was pending, as well as suggesting that Blount be held to bail. Some representatives responded that these decisions were matters for the Senate to decide, but Sitgreaves persisted, likening the House of Representatives to a prosecutor who must make the proper motions before the Senate, the court, could take any action at all. The Sitgreaves faction had further maintained that Blount's absence during trial would defeat the impeachment effort.

---

[38]*Massachusetts Mercury*, 14 July 1797, p. 2, col. 1; *Aurora*, 8 July 1797, p. 2, col. 5, p. 3, col. 1; *Claypoole's American Daily Advertiser*, 8 July 1797, p. 2, col. 4; 7 *Annals of Cong.* 38-39, 459 (1797).

[39]7 *Annals of Cong.* 459 (1797).

Because the Senate, moreover, could not act *sua sponte* to compel Blount's appearance, the House must request that the upper chamber take steps to guarantee that appearance. These arguments finally triumphed by a fairly close margin, and the House adjourned to proceed to the Senate chamber.[40]

As Sitgreaves withdrew from the bar of the Senate and that body voted to delay the expulsion proceedings and took up the House's message, the issues that the representatives had recently debated came under new scrutiny. The first to speak was Humphrey Marshall, a Kentucky Federalist. Quoting several constitutional provisions to support his position, he attempted to prove that the House of Representatives had no power to impeach senators, denying that they were civil officers. The President commissions such officers, he pointed out, and legislators held no such commissions. Sedgwick took issue with these claims briefly, but then he voiced his belief that a resolution of such issues should properly take place at Blount's impeachment trial. Sedgwick was followed by Cocke, who sided with Marshall; then Jacob Read and James Ross, both Federalists, spoke out in support of Sedgwick and urged immediate adoption of resolutions to carry the House's demands into effect. Tazewell then rose, and noting that the Senate's decision on these points would become a precedent for "all future time," he asked the Senate to wait until the following day to deliberate upon and decide the issue. This was not good enough for Marshall, who reiterated his objections denying that the Senate could bar a member from his seat in so cavalier a fashion. Challenging the lower house, Marshall asked how it dared to demand anything of the Senate, which was a totally independent body. Invoking the Constitution again, he warned his colleagues that a person could be removed from office only after conviction, and not before, as sequestration would effectively do. To bar Blount from his place on the strength of a mere allegation the Senate need only muster a simple majority vote, which would circumvent the two-thirds majority safeguard that an impeachment conviction required.[41]

That such procedural objections come from a Federalist is

---

[40]Ibid. at 460-62; *Aurora*, 8 July 1797, p. 2, col. 5.

[41]*Claypoole's American Daily Advertiser*, 8 July 1797, p. 2 col 5; *Aurora*, 8 July 1797, p. 3, cols. 1-2.

surprising, since Republicans had raised all other such points. Humphrey Marshall was "an aristocratic lawyer who possessed a sarcastic tongue, a great disdain for the rabble, and kinship to future Chief Justice John Marshall," and a close kinship at that. Like Blount, Marshall was from the West, but this is one of the few characteristics that the two had in common. Another was that Marshall himself had once been the subject of a senatorial investigation. Winning his seat as part of a nativist reaction against Genêt's western activities, Marshall had done his best to expose the Spanish intrigues in Kentucky. His own investigation revealed Benjamin Sebastian, a state judge, to be a Spanish agent. This revelation triggered Sebastian's own allegation that Marshall had once perjured himself in a chancery proceeding. When the affair came before the Senate in early 1796, Marshall asked the chamber to look into the matter in order to clear his name, but the Senate had declined jurisdiction in the affair.[42]

Whether these events colored Marshall's view of the Blount episode, the fact remains that no other Westerner or Federalist in Congress went so out of his way to defend Blount in this fashion.[43] Perhaps Marshall adopted this position because he feared the future possibility of a popularly elected, Republican-controlled House attempting to dominate a Federalist Senate. Such a theory would help explain the Kentuckean's views nicely. That he was the only Federalist to adopt these views, however, is puzzling.[44]

Despite the soundness of many of his arguments, Marshall found himself in opposition to a considerable weight of opinion. Tazewell's motion to delay consideration of the resolutions met with defeat, although William Bingham convinced the Senate to deal separately with the issues of sequestration and bail. The Senate then voted fifteen to ten to delay the issue of sequestration, and next voted

---

[42]Anne M. Butler & Wendy Wolff, *United States Senate Election, Expulsion, and Censure Cases 1793-1990* (Washington: Government Printing Office, 1995) [Serial Set 14216] 8; U.S., Congress, Senate, *Senate Election, Expulsion and Censure Cases from 1793 to 1972*, Richard P. Hupman comp. (Washington: Government Printing Office, 1972) [Serial Set 12935-1] 2; 5 *Annals of Cong.* 54-60 (1796).

[43]See pp. 274-75.

[44]As to allegations that Marshall was himself involved in the Blount Conspiracy, see Epilogue, *infra*.

seventeen to eight to require both bail and sureties of Blount. As the chamber was prepared to hold Blount in custody until he met these requirements, the senator promptly entered into recognizance for twenty thousand dollars—a considerable sum indeed. He also offered his sureties, Thomas Blount and Republican Pierce Butler, who guaranteed the sum of fifteen thousand dollars each, bringing the total to the astronomical amount of fifty thousand dollars, a staggering amount to demand of an insolvent speculator. Having reached this point, the Senate then put aside the entire affair until the following day.[45]

On Saturday the Senate turned once again to the expulsion question. Dispatching the clerk to the House with a message to the effect that Blount had given bail to guarantee his appearance to answer the as-yet-unwritten articles of impeachment, the chamber then took up the Ross committee's report. This report was fairly straightforward; in it the committee members stated their belief that Blount was the author of the Carey letter, which contained evidence that the senator was acting both contrary to the interests of his country and inconsistently with his public duties. Blount's actions, the committee report concluded, constituted a high misdemeanor, rendering him unworthy of continued membership in the Senate, and subject to expulsion.[46]

Before debating the adoption of the report itself—which indicated that two senators had at some point attested to Blount's handwriting—the Senate tried once again to get the Tennesseean to admit outright his authorship of the incriminating document. Read asked Blount directly if the letter was written in his hand, but Marshall, Tazewell, and Samuel Livermore all objected to this question, noting that others had already sworn to this point. Not satisfied with this response, Bingham moved to send for a magistrate. This the Senate did, and a local justice arrived some time later. The justice administered an oath to Cocke and Alexander Martin, both of whom knew Blount quite well, and they, too attested to the writing,

---

[45]*Claypoole's American Daily Advertiser*, 8 July 1797, p. 2, col. 5; *Massachusetts Mercury*, 14 July 1797, p. 2, cols. 1-2; *Aurora*, 8 July 1797, p. 3, col. 2.

[46]U.S., Congress, House, Committee on Impeachment of William Blount, *Report* [Evans 34785] 6; 7 *Annals of Cong.* 40-44 (1797).

while Blount himself departed the chamber for a time. Now that the Senate was fully satisfied, the presiding officer asked Blount upon his return if he were ready to proceed, and Blount stated that his attorneys were prepared to speak.[47]

Dallas rose first, beginning his presentation at about half past eleven and continuing for three hours. He spoke of Blount's character, unblemished up to this point, and he called attention to the way that the senator now conducted himself, as if innocent of the criminality the letter suggested. The document's authorship, Dallas reminded the Senate, had been proved only by a comparison of handwriting, and according to the principles of criminal law that standard of proof was insufficient.

Dallas's next maneuver, as his first had been, was rather technical. Even if Blount's authorship were beyond question, he said, the Senate would bypass the safeguards of the impeachment process—would render impeachment "nugatory" and thus violate the Constitution—if it expelled Blount before the impeachment proceedings ended. The Senate, he said more pointedly, should not judge a cause "by anticipation" when it later had to judge an impeachment growing out of the same incident that had brought about the expulsion.[48] Such an argument, while sound in its appeal to procedural intricacies, and artful in taking advantage of the fact that Blount was the target of two separate and constitutionally distinct proceedings, was probably without merit; even the strict constructionist Marshall on the previous day had emphasized the Senate's independence from the House of Representatives. To maintain that the lower house's voting of an impeachment foreclosed the upper house from exercising a power peculiar to itself was to adopt an untenable and even desperate position. Yet Dallas did have a point in arguing that an expulsion now would prejudice the Senate when it came to Blount's impeachment trial.

At length, in mid-afternoon, Dallas ended his arguments and Ingersoll began. Like Dallas he drew heavily on precedents of former impeachments. In the entire history of the practice, Ingersoll asserted, from 1301 on, no one had ever been expelled from his

---

[47]*Philadelphia Gazette*, 10 July 1797, p. 2, col. 4; 7 *Annals of Cong.* 41 (1797); *Claypoole's American Daily Advertiser*, 10 July 1797, p. 3, col. 2.

[48]*Philadelphia Gazette*, 10 July 1797, p. 2, col. 4.

position while an impeachment was pending. He cited many cases to prove his point. In light of these facts, Ingersoll stated, the question before the Senate was whether it would proceed in a manner that was reasonable, constitutional, and required by conscience, or whether it would punish Blount first and only later try him. Ingersoll's speech took two hours; and at some point either he or Dallas, or both, challenged the power of the House of Representatives to impeach a senator, though the particulars of that line of argument remain unknown.[49]

After Ingersoll had finished, James Ross, one of Blount's more zealous adversaries, rose to reply. In contrast to the logical, technical, procedure-oriented arguments of Blount's counselors, Ross's speech concentrated more upon empirical and emotional matters. Examining and discounting all of Ingersoll's and Dallas's claims, Ross sought to justify an expulsion on the basis of the Senate's evidence of Blount's unworthiness to continue in his seat. He reminded all present of the nature of the crime attributed to Blount, and the potential consequences of such a conspiracy. Ross's oratory "seemed to have great effect" upon the senators; after he concluded some others made a few additional remarks.[50]

By now the hour had grown late, and Cocke and Tazewell suggested yet another postponement. North Carolina Republican Timothy Bloodworth made a motion to this effect, but it met with a sound defeat, the vote going along party lines with only a single Federalist supporting a delay. The Senate had heard the arguments and it was ready to finish the business. At five-thirty the vote on the Ross committee's report began. It was almost unanimous; even those senators who had raised a battery of procedural objections joined in Blount's condemnation. Only Tazewell believed strongly enough in the lawyers' arguments against prejudicing the impeachment trial to vote against expulsion, and even he clearly expressed his belief that Blount was guilty. Not even Cocke stood with his fellow Tennesseean, and as the voting ended Blount found himself expelled by a margin of twenty-five to one.[51]

---

[49]Ibid.; *Claypoole's American Daily Advertiser*, 10 July 1797, p. 3, col. 2.

[50]*Philadelphia Gazette*, 10 July 1797, p. 2, col. 4; *Claypoole's American Daily Advertiser*, 10 July 1797, p. 3, col. 2.

[51]*Philadelphia Gazette*, 10 July 1797, p. 2, col. 5; *Aurora*, 10 July 1797, p. 3,

ح

Throughout the week the speculator's fortunes had grown steadily worse. Impeached one day, expelled the next, still facing the prospect of trial before the Senate, Blount was rapidly achieving a catastrophic series of firsts. As if these congressional proceedings were not bad enough, however, he also faced a criminal action in Federal district court in Pennsylvania. Almost no record of this action has yet come to light; all that we may say for certain is that some time on or before Saturday July 8, and presumably not before Monday the 3rd, someone (probably Lee, Rawle, or some other administration official) instituted an action against Blount for a misdemeanor. The grounds were his alleged disturbance of the peace and tranquillity of the United States. In connection with this charge Lee also mentioned the possibility that Blount had violated the Neutrality Act, which Congress had passed in the wake of Genêt 's abortive efforts to enlist George Rogers Clark's help in revolutionizing Louisiana a few years earlier. A prosecution of Blount under this act would elevate the case to the federal Circuit Court, which had original jurisdiction in all but the most petty criminal cases.[52]

---

col. 3; 7 *Annals of Cong.* 41-44 (1797). Blount, significantly, did not vote on either the motion to delay consideration or the expulsion itself. No clue remains as to whether he voluntarily abstained or whether instead the Senate somehow prevented him from participating.

Blount's was not only the first expulsion from the Senate but, thus far, the only one other than the fourteen Southern senators who shared this fate in the early 1860s. The Senate has begun expulsion proceedings on more than a dozen other occasions without voting an expulsion; the charges have ranged from corruption, embezzlement, and election fraud to Mormonism and disloyalty. See 4 Robert C. Byrd, *The Senate 1789-1989: Historical Statistics 1789-1992* (Washington: Government Printing Office, 1993) [Serial Set 13726] 669-70; Butler & Wolff, *United States Senate Election, Expulsion, and Censure Cases, passim.* One other senator, John Smith of Ohio, faced such proceedings for reasons similar to those in the Blount affair. See Epilogue, *infra*.

[52]*Maryland Gazette*, 3 August 1797, p. 3, col. 1; 1 Op. Att'y Gen 75 (1797); Act of June 5, 1794, ch. 50, § 5, 1 Stat. 381, 384 (1794); Act of March 2, 1797, ch. 5, 1 Stat. 497 (1797); 18 U.S.C. § 960 (1994). In the 1980s, nearly two centuries after its passage, this statute became involved with an issue that later gave rise to possibilities of impeachment; because of the Reagan administration's

As a result of the complaint filed in his court, Judge Richard Peters issued a warrant for Blount's arrest and directed the marshal to take the speculator into custody as soon as the Senate had no more need of his presence. The marshal was on hand as Blount was experiencing the shame of the expulsion vote.[53]

When the voting ended the marshal sought to take custody of the former senator, but the chamber was not yet done with Blount. The Tennesseean, along with others, had complained since the previous day of the excessive amount of his bail. As the expulsion proceedings concluded Saturday evening one senator moved to dispense with the bail and sureties entirely. This motion failed, but the Senate did agree to reduce the amount drastically, requiring a thousand dollars of Blount and half that sum from each of his sureties, who had since surrendered Blount to the Senate. Not until Blount had made good on these new amounts, thus promising to return to the chamber on Monday to answer the articles of impeachment, would Senate officials hand their former colleague over to the marshal.[54]

In light of what he probably expected would happen to him in court, as well as the greatly reduced bail, Blount decided that the time had come for flight. After satisfying the Senate's demands as to bail and sureties, he somehow avoided delivery into the marshal's hands, or else escaped from his custody. Between Saturday evening—probably sometime after midnight—and daybreak Sunday, the conspirator eluded pursuers and struck out for Tennessee, although none knew his destination.[55]

When news of Blount's escape and the Senate's bail reduction

Nicaraguan policy, private citizens filed actions seeking not only private redress, but also prosecutuion of officials under the act. *Sanchez-Espinoza v. Reagan*, 770 F.2d 202 (D.C. Cir. 1985); *Dellums v. Smith*, 577 F. Supp. 1449 (N.D. Cal. 1984), *rev'd on other grounds*, 797 F.2d 818 (9th Cir. 1986); *Dellums v. Smith*, 573 F. Supp. 1489 (N.D. Cal. 1983). See generally Jules Lobel, "The Rise and Decline of the Neutrality Act: Sovereignty and Congressional War Powers in United States Foreign Policy," 24 *Harv. Int'l L.J.* 1 (1983). As to Federal court jurisdiction in 1797, see the Judiciary Act of 1789, ch. 20, §§ 9, 11, 1 Stat. 76-79 (1789).

[53] *Boston Gazette*, 21 August 1797, p. 1, col. 1; *Connecticut Courant*, 21 August 1797, p. 4, col. 2.

[54] *Boston Gazette*, 21 August 1797, p. 1, col. 1; *Connecticut Courant*, 21 August 1797, p. 4, col. 2.

[55] *Maryland Gazette*, 21 August 1797, p. 1, cols. 1-2; Ibid., 3 August 1797, p. 3, col. 1; *Aurora*, 11 July 1797, p. 2, col. 4.

became public, a howl of fury sounded along the eastern seaboard. Editorial writers attacked the Senate for its foolish act regarding the bail money, and some intimated that the mostly Federalist Senate had wished for Blount to escape with his knowledge of the conspiracy still a secret. Others defended the Senate's bail reduction on procedural grounds. Meanwhile Blount was rumored to be heading for Tennessee, or perhaps New York. Nichols, a marshal from Philadelphia, set off in pursuit of the fugitive, but he lost the trail after a few days. When Blount failed to appear on Monday the Senate had no choice but to declare the bail forfeit. Besides sending copies of its records to Adams and Governor Sevier of Tennessee it had no other duty to perform, for the articles of impeachment were still nowhere in sight. Its other business completed, the Senate adjourned until November.[56]

The House of Representatives, too, adjourned on the 10th, but its final days in session saw a flurry of activity centered around the impeachment. Although by the 7th Sitgreaves's committee had fulfilled its duties, on the 8th the Pennsylvania representative moved to appoint a new committee that would have as its task the preparation of articles of impeachment. Sitgreaves asked the House to give this new committee sweeping powers of investigation, including a subpoena power. As the legislators were coming to realize that the drafting of articles would take more than a few days, Sitgreaves also asked that the committee be allowed to continue sitting after the session's end. The House promptly agreed to the committee's creation, but Gallatin and others wished to take further time to consider Sitgreaves's other requests. Sitgreaves was adamant, stating emphatically that the investigation was going to take time. Accounts of the debate from this point on become confused and conflicting; apparently Gallatin and others thought that some representatives were trying to railroad the whole impeachment inquiry through Congress, and at least one legislator questioned the House's power to grant the committee the authority to remain sitting after adjournment. If this is the case, then the possibility of a partisan split is evident; Gallatin, who made this charge, was a Republican, and

---

[56]*Boston Gazette*, 21 August 1797, p. 1, cols. 1-2; *Connecticut Courant*, 21 August 1797, p. 4, cols. 1-2; *Aurora*, 11 July 1797, p. 2, col. 4; Ibid., 17 July 1797, p. 3, col. 2; 7 *Annals of Cong.* 44-45 (1797).

Sitgreaves, who was pressing for a full and prompt investigation, was a Federalist. Certainly debate on at least one of the two provisions was finally put off until Monday, and perhaps both were. In the meantime the House appointed five men to the committee; these were Sitgreaves, Baldwin, Dana, John Dawson, and Robert Goodloe Harper of South Carolina. Dana, in the next day or two, declined to serve, and the House replaced him with Delaware Federalist James A. Bayard, thus fixing the committee membership at three Federalists and two Republicans.[57]

By Monday the impeachment committee had met and examined some of Blount's papers. Some of these had come from Ross's committee in the Senate, which had examined several documents on the afternoon of the 7th pursuant to the Senate's vote of that morning.[58] What the House committee found was sufficient to cause it to make a report to the whole House, in which it again requested authority to sit during Congress's recess and to issue subpoenas. With the galleries cleared the House of Representatives debated the report, replaced Dana with Bayard, and finally gave in to Sitgreaves. Having firmly established the impeachment committee's powers, the House adjourned for the summer.[59]

In the following days and weeks the public outcry continued. By now news of the Blount affair was spreading outward from Philadelphia. Newspapers from New England to North Carolina began to recount the events in the capital. In Boston the *Independent Chronicle* printed headlines linking Blount's "Treason" to "the effect of British Gold," and asserted that Liston knew of the entire plot long before it came to light. Soon thereafter the *Massachusetts Mercury* dismissed the idea of English involvement as outrageous; the editors asked if the word of a traitor were to be believed instead of that of Liston. In Philadelphia publisher Benjamin Franklin Bache had anticipated and answered this question the day before. While admitting that the British minister had declared upon his honor that

---

[57]7 *Annals of Cong.* 462-66 (1797); *Philadelphia Gazette*, 10 July 1797, p. 2, cols. 3-5; *Porcupine's Gazette*, 10 July 1797, p. 2, col. 5.

[58]8 *Annals of Cong.* 2319 (1797); see pp. 116-17, *supra*.

[59]*Aurora*, 13 July 1797, p. 3, col. 1; 8 *Annals of Cong.* 2319 (1797); U.S., Congress, House, Committee on Impeachment of William Blount, *Report* [Evans 34785] 7, 9; 7 *Annals of Cong.* 464 (1797).

he had no knowledge of the affair, Bache stated that the declaration was but "feebly supported" as Liston had no honor upon which to swear. In the North, newspapers published Byers's role in the conspiracy's discovery and identified him as the valiant son of a New York businessman; in the South a Carolina paper charged that Blount had received his orders from the French Directory itself; and in Philadelphia the English pamphleteer, newspaper editor, and devoted Federalist William Cobbett promised an award of ten dollars to anyone who could prove that Dallas did not shame Cobbett by sharing the country of his birth.[60]

Although some of these reactions may seem almost comical to the modern reader, in fact they revealed the presence of a high tension during mid-1797. International pressures were considerable during the late 1790s, and the United States, a weak nation at the time, walked a thin line in its dealings with Britain and France, the greatest powers of Europe, as well as Spain, by no means impotent.[61] Blount's conspiracy, for all anyone knew, could seriously erode America's diplomatic relations with these countries, and the administration's discovery of the plot was no bar to its execution. In Natchez emissaries of Blount continued to appear even after the senator's expulsion, and Andrew Ellicott reported anti-Spanish sentiment in the region to be running dangerously high. In Philadelphia no such reports were needed to fuel politician's fears. Oliver Wolcott

---

[60]*Independent Chronicle*, 13 July 1797, p. 2, col. 3; *Massachusetts Mercury*, 1 August 1797, p. 1, col 2; *Aurora*, 31 July 1797, p. 3, col. 3; *Massachusetts Mercury*, 8 August 1797, p. 2, col. 3; *North Carolina Gazette*, 5 August 1797, p. 3, col. 3; *Porcupine's Gazette*, 10 July 1797, p. 2, col. 5. The importance of the role of newspapers in the Blount impeachment and in other important issues of the day should now be clear to the reader. For further information, though principally from a Republican perspective, see Donald H. Stewart, *The Opposition Press of the Federalist Period* (Albany: State University Press of New York Press, 1969) (containing a treatment of the Blount episode at pages 264-69); Richard N. Rosenfeld, *American Aurora: A Democratic-Republican Returns: The Suppressed History of Our Nation's Beginnings and the Heroic Newspaper that Tried to Report It* (New York: St. Martin's Press, 1997). For a view of the other side, See Daniel Green, *Great Cobbett: The Noblest Agitator* (London: Hodder and Stoughton, 1983) ch. 7; Leonora Nattrass, *William Cobbett: The Politics of Style* (Cambridge: Cambridge University Press, 1995) 43-61.

[61]See generally Elkins & McKitrick, *Age of Federalism* 303-450; Miller, *Federalist Era* 210-27.

mentioned the possibility that Blount's schemes could have resulted in war, and in a letter that fairly shouted urgency Abraham Baldwin wrote Georgia's governor with a request for any helpful information. To the government's way of thinking the danger had merely come to light; it had not dissipated.[62]

Two weeks after Congress's adjournment Philadelphians received new information. On or about July 25, word arrived that a Tennesseean had met Blount about six miles beyond Staunton, Virginia. Proceeding on to town the man mentioned the meeting, and news of the former senator's presence galvanized several of Staunton's citizens into action. Mounting horses, they set off after Blount while news of the contact began its journey to Philadelphia.[63]

Charles Lee, upon hearing of Blount's impending capture, set about making arrangements for getting him back to Philadelphia. On the 28th he transmitted to Pickering Judge Peters's original unexecuted warrant for Blount's arrest, along with other papers that would provide sufficient grounds for a new warrant to issue from a Virginia court. Pickering wasted no time in forwarding these materials to Staunton. Mailing them to Archibald Stewart, an attorney there whom Lee had recommended for the job, Pickering sought to enlist Stewart's aid as a United States Attorney in the Blount case. Pickering warned Stewart that although the present charge was only that of a misdemeanor, it was nevertheless one of "the most dangerous and fatal tendency." He also cautioned Stewart that bail might not secure Blount's presence, as his recent actions in Philadelphia showed.[64]

In the end Lee and Pickering need not have bothered. Despite the Staunton citizens' pursuit, Blount eluded them and made his way to North Carolina, where his wife was recuperating from a carriage accident, and from there he moved on to Knoxville. Pickering had

---

[62]Ellicott, *Journal* 173; Andrew Ellicott to Thomas Jefferson, 25 September 1797, 102 (Reel 34) *Jefferson Papers* (Film); Oliver Wolcott to James Iredell, 12 July 1797, James Iredell, Sr. and James Iredell, Jr. Papers, Manuscript Room, Duke University; Abraham Baldwin to Jared Irwin, 11 July 1797, Jared Irwin Papers, Manuscript Room, Duke University.

[63]*North Carolina Gazette*, 5 August 1797, p. 3, col. 3; *Aurora*, 26 July 1797, p. 3, col. 2.

[64]1 Op. Att'y Gen. 75, 75-76 (1797); Timothy Pickering to Archibald Stewart, 28 July 1797, Reel 6, *Pickering Papers* (Film).

instructed Stewart to forward the warrant and other documents to another lawyer if Blount could be found elsewhere, but the Staunton incident turned out to be the last decent chance to capture the speculator.[65] In Tennessee, beyond the Appalachians, Blount found refuge, and as the excitement died, Pickering settled down to await the outcome of the House impeachment committee's investigation.

ۿ

Throughout the remainder of the rainy, oppressive summer the committee attacked its chore with determination. In the early anxious days following Congress's adjournment, with the threat of conspiracy still hanging in the air, the committee would meet without regard for hours, sometimes sitting for the entire day. Later, as the initial panic wore off, it became more systematic, regularly sitting for four hours around midday. As the inclement weather continued and a bout of yellow fever began to ravage the city, the representatives amassed more and more information, often with Pickering's help. All this information it decided to keep secret until the committee could report to the House in five months' time.[66]

In fact the committee had energetically taken up its duties on the very day of its creation, two days before Congress adjourned. Finding references to Nicholas Romayne in the papers it received from Ross's committee, Sitgreaves and his colleagues promptly determined to deal with the man. Issuing an arrest warrant, the committee asked Pickering to provide a trustworthy messenger, and Pickering

---

[65]Timothy Pickering to Archibald Stewart, 28 July 1797, Reel 6, *Pickering Papers* (Film).

[66]John Dawson to James Madison, 13 August 1797, Reel 6, *James Madison Papers* (Film, Library of Congress); Ibid., 7 September 1797; *Philadelphia Gazette*, 20 July 1797, p. 3, col. 4; *Aurora*, 18 August 1797, p. 3, col. 1; 8 *Annals of Cong.* 2321-22 (1797). In the eighteenth and nineteenth centuries, Philadelphia experienced recurring epidemics of yellow fever, which often wrought havoc upon the city and its inhabitants. Outbreaks were particularly frequent from 1793 to 1805. See J.H. Powell, *Bring Out Your Dead: The Great Plague of Yellow Fever in Philadelphia in 1793* (Philadelphia: University of Pennsylvania Press, reprinted 1993) xiii. During the Federalist era, even the proper medical treatment for the disease was a subject of partisan debate. Ibid., 80-84; Martin S. Pernick, "Politics, Parties, and Pestilence," 29 *Wm. & Mary Q.* (3d Ser.) 565 (October 1972).

responded by placing Captain William Eaton at the committee's service.

Eaton was an army officer who was fast becoming one of Pickering's favorites. A veteran of the War for Independence, the Dartmouth graduate had been with Wayne at Fallen Timbers, where his "mercurial temper and lack of tact" nearly resulted in a duel with the adjutant of his regiment. In 1796 he was serving on the Georgia frontier when his commanding officer, Lieutenant Colonel Henry Gaither, ordered his court-martial. Eaton maintained that this was the result of his refusal to involve himself in certain land speculations, and because he reported directly to Pickering, then Secretary of War, on relations between Georgia and the Creek Nation. This ran counter to Gaither's interests, for the colonel wished much stricter treatment of the Creek than Pickering was prepared to countenance. When Eaton took his case to Pickering, the secretary interceded and arranged his immediate transfer to Philadelphia. To meet the committee's needs in the present crisis, Pickering could think of no better officer.[67]

On Sunday July 9 the committee issued the young captain his orders, which were to seek out Romayne in New York, to seize him and his papers, and to bring him before the representatives. To this end he was to have the assistance of all citizens and officers, both civil and military. The gravity of the situation was clear. Blount might have been removed from office, but his plans to take up arms in the West remained very much alive, for all Congress knew. The impeachment committee, along with Pickering, stood ready to take whatever steps were necessary to ensure that the danger was past.

In addition to his general instructions, Eaton received a letter from Sitgreaves in which the chairman told the captain to go in secret to United States Attorney Richard Harrison in New York to procure assistance before proceeding to Romayne's. These orders confirmed those of Pickering, who also stressed the importance of discretion and who suggested that Eaton seek out Alexander Hamilton, John Jay, or New York's attorney general if Harrison was not to be found. Having

---

[67]5 *Dictionary of American Biography* 613; Louis B. Wright & Julia H. MacLeod, *The First Americans in North Africa: William Eaton's Struggle for a Vigorous Policy Against the Barbary Pirates, 1799-1805* (Princeton: Princeton University Press, 1945) 18-20; 8 *Annals of Cong.* 2325 (1797).

gotten his orders, carrying a letter for Harrison, and well armed, Eaton departed for New York long before dawn on the 10th.[68]

Twenty-one hours later—just after midnight on the 11th—Eaton arrived at Harrison's home. After a brief conference, the two men decided that speed was essential. They feared that Romayne might destroy any papers in his possession if given time. Securing the aid of a marshal and a deputy, they proceeded to Romayne's house.[69]

Shortly after one o'clock the four officers arrived at their destination. The doctor did not seem very surprised at the intrusion, and in fact he said that he supposed Eaton had been instructed to search for papers; he even offered to produce them. He led the men upstairs to his bed-chamber, which was in a state of disarray. Here the officers found a few bundles of papers in which they discovered four letters between Romayne and Blount. The bundles appeared to have been recently examined, and this fact, together with the room's condition, led Eaton to believe that Romayne had destroyed some papers. A bit later Eaton mentioned his suspicions to the doctor, who replied that he was a careless man and thus he may have torn up some letters from Blount several days ago. While Harrison and his men examined the surviving correspondence, Eaton spotted another bundle of letters. Romayne suddenly grew quite agitated and tried to wrest them from the captain, but Eaton secured it. In it he found a letter to Romayne from Robert Liston.

His mission accomplished, Eaton prepared to depart with Romayne and the five letters. Taking with him one of Harrison's assistants, Eaton started back for Philadelphia at three o'clock. His entire stay in New York had lasted something under four hours. The travelers arrived in Philadelphia at three the following morning, and Eaton delivered his charges to the impeachment committee.[70]

Even as Eaton was preparing to set forth on his New York mission, the impeachment committee was also making arrangements to send to Tennessee for evidence and witnesses. Choosing Captain Thomas Lewis as its emissary, the committee gave him a warrant for the arrest of James Grant and precepts to be served on James Carey and Chisholm's friend John Rogers. For some reason (perhaps because of

---

[68]8 *Annals of Cong.* 2324-26 (1797).

[69]Ibid. at 2326-27; *Massachusetts Mercury*, 4 August 1797, p. 2, col. 1.

[70]8 *Annals of Cong.* 2326-28 (1797).

Blount's popularity and influence in that remote region) Sitgreaves and his colleagues decided to take a more lenient course of action with regard to the westerners than they had with Romayne. Since the men were all War Department agents, McHenry as well as Sitgreaves wrote letters to Carey and Rogers, in which they appealed to the men's patriotism and sense of duty, and offered to pay the expenses of a trip to Philadelphia. To Lewis the committee gave instructions to treat Grant as a fellow traveler rather than as a prisoner, but it impressed upon the captain the importance of speed. Lewis also received a letter for David Henley, in which the frontier officer was directed to give Lewis all the assistance that he needed. By the 12th Lewis was ready for the journey, and the following day he set out for Knoxville at a breakneck pace.[71]

Within hours after Lewis's departure, the Chevalier de Yrujo called upon the impeachment committee. The Spanish minister had expressed his outrage and dismay to Pickering several days earlier when he had learned of Blount's plans, and he had demanded the speculator's punishment. This communication was no mere formality, for in the following months Yrujo called upon Sitgreaves's committee on several occasions to deliver individuals and documents that shed light on the plot. On this day Yrujo told the committee of a tall, thin young Tennesseean named Mitchell, whom Yrujo believed to have been in correspondence with John Chisholm. The committee did not question Yrujo; instead it quickly issued a letter and a subpoena for the mysterious conspirator and forwarded them by mail to Lewis, who by now was too far beyond the city to be caught.[72]

---

[71]Ibid. at 2320-21, 2329-34.

[72]Robert Liston to Lord Grenville, 8 July 1797, *in* Turner, "Documents," 592-94; 8 *Annals of Cong.* 2322-23, 2336 (1797). This "Mitchell" may well have been the same man as John Mitchell, a surveyor whom Chisholm met in New York or Philadelphia in early 1797, who may or may not have been involved in other frontier plots as well as having connections to the Whiskey Rebels. As early as 1793 various sources, both American and Spanish, report the involvement of a Thomas, or Medad, Mitchell, in frontier plots including those of Wilkinson and Genêt. See Bemis, *Pinckney's Treaty* 214-17; Whitaker, *Spanish-American Frontier* 196; Thomas P. Abernethy, *The South in the New Nation* (Baton Rouge: Louisiana State University Press, 1961) 175, 181; Abraham P. Nasatir & Ernest R. Liljegren, "Materials Relating to the History of the Mississippi Valley From the Minutes of the Spanish Supreme Councils of State, 1787-1797," 21 *La. Hist. Q.* 5, 34 (1938).

Having seen to Tennessee arrangements, the representatives turned their attention to Romayne, who had recently arrived in town. Such a development, despite the committee's desire for secrecy, could hardly be kept quiet; even in New York in the dead of night some citizens had witnessed Eaton's visit to the doctor's house. In Philadelphia the papers kept up a running commentary on Romayne's appearance, although the committee was apparently successful in keeping the substance of his testimony confidential.[73]

By the 13th the questioning was underway. Romayne was less than cooperative, however, challenging the committee's power to sit after Congress's adjournment and denouncing his seizure and forced appearance before the representatives. Apparently the conspirator, who had been (according to Eaton) so calm while in New York, managed to find his tongue when the committee confronted him with its knowledge. As Romayne told it, his objections to the committee's authority had had an effect on Sitgreaves and the others, who allowed Romayne to speak to them informally while in Pickering's presence. Pickering, though, proved as interested a party as the committee, and at length Romayne gave in and signed a deposition that revealed a great deal about the conspiracy. Perhaps he even capitulated immediately upon his arrival, and only decided to become indignant after the fact. To Romayne's public description of the ordeal, Sitgreaves made no reply other than to say the doctor's version of events was quite false.[74]

Regardless of Romayne's degree of enthusiasm in cooperating with the impeachment committee, in the end he did give it considerable information. Among other things he revealed were the names of some of his New York contacts, notably a Dr. Charles Buxton. Buxton had,

---

[73]8 *Annals of Cong.* 2404 (1797); *Gazette of the United States*, 14 July 1797, p. 3, col. 3; *Philadelphia Gazette*, 14 July 1797, p. 3, col. 4.

[74]*Gazette of the United States*, 14 July 1797, p. 3, col. 3; *Claypoole's American Daily Advertiser*, 15 July 1797, p. 3, col. 5; *Aurora*, 17 July 1797, p. 3, col. 1; *Philadelphia Gazette*, 20 July 1797, p. 3, col. 4; *Massachusetts Mercury*, 4 August 1797, p. 2, cols. 1-2; 8 August 1797, p. 2, col. 3; 8 *Annals of Cong.* 2320 (1797). Romayne's challenge to the committee's authority may have been partly responsible for Congress's passage the following year of a statute authorizing certain members of Congress, including committee chairmen, to administer oaths and affirmations to witnesses, and establishing a penalty for perjury. Act of May 3, 1798, ch. 36, §§ 1-2, 1 Stat. 554 (1798) (current versions at 2 U.S.C. §§ 191-92 [1994]).

in fact, already come to Harrison's attention the day after Romayne's arrest; the attorney heard rumors that Buxton, while drunk, had bragged that Romayne would soon be one of the greatest men in the country. Upon hearing this, Harrison sought out Buxton and asked him of his involvement with Romayne. Buxton related some of the things that his former teacher had said, but he himself denied any involvement. Harrison nevertheless communicated this information to the impeachment committee, which subpoenaed the young physician a few days later. Before long Buxton arrived in Philadelphia to give his own deposition.[75]

This was not the end of the New York investigation; the town was apparently a hotbed of conspiracy, speculation, and rumor that rivaled anything one could find in the West. As the impeachment committee was issuing its call for Buxton, Eaton was traveling through the city on his way to his home in Massachusetts for a visit. While on a ferry, he chanced to overhear a conversation in which the speakers were discussing a meeting in town between Romayne, one Benjamin Winthrop, and a Leonard Bleeker. During this meeting, as Eaton understood it, Romayne had made some comments about an approaching revolution. Intrigued, Eaton made inquiries of the persons whom he had overheard, and then he passed on the information to the impeachment committee.[76]

Unfortunately for Eaton, his involvement in the Blount investigation did not end with the ferry incident. After bringing Romayne before the committee, and before he departed for his home in Brimfield, the captain (like almost everyone else involved in the Blount business from Chisholm to Carey to Buxton) began to talk of what he knew. One man to whom he spoke was John Philips Ripley, an acquaintance he knew slightly from his Dartmouth days and whom he befriended when Ripley came to Philadelphia to seek a consular post. One thing Eaton told Ripley was his belief that Liston's letter to Romayne countenanced the conspiracy. Pickering, later hearing of Eaton's remarks, took his protégé to task for having made this statement, and Eaton, thus rebuked, left for New England.[77]

---

[75]8 *Annals of Cong.* 2379-80, 2404-05 (1797); *Philadelphia Gazette*, 20 July 1797, p. 3, col. 4; *Maryland Gazette*, 3 August 1797, p. 2, col. 3.

[76]8 *Annals of Cong.* 2407-08 (1797).

[77]Ibid. at 2337-39.

By July 24 Yrujo, too, had heard of Eaton's conversations with Ripley and a Thomas Odiorne, and on that day he called upon the committee to introduce these young men to the representatives. Each stated under oath that he had heard Eaton say that he had taken not one, but several letters of Liston from Romayne. Although the committee members apparently had reason to believe that these statements were false, they were in a delicate situation. Pickering, who was Eaton's sponsor, had a well-known affinity for England, and perhaps the representatives thought that he might be trying to shield Liston by arranging for some papers to disappear. On the other hand the committee was not prepared to take Yrujo or his accomplices at their word; probably the tension of July gave rise to a bit of paranoia. At any rate Sitgreaves wrote Eaton a somewhat apologetic letter describing the problem and asking the captain for an explanation.[78]

Eaton promptly wrote a full disclosure of his interviews with Ripley, Odiorne, and Pickering, and swore under oath that he had withheld no evidence from the committee. He volunteered to cooperate with the committee in any way it wished, and he assured the representatives that his relationship with his two accusers had recently soured. These representations apparently satisfied the impeachment committee, which let the matter lie. Eaton had a long memory, though, and just before sailing for a North Africa posting (where he was to have many more adventures) more than a year later he wrote Ripley a vicious letter, charging him with betraying Eaton's trust and confidence, lying, and adhering to the administration's enemies. Having written these things, which tend to support Eaton's side of the story, he took his leave of the country.[79]

While dealing with the Eaton incident, and as it awaited word from Tennessee, the impeachment committee continued its work, examining local tavernkeepers and merchants about John Chisholm's comings and goings, sending to New York for other persons, and reading anonymous letters and bundles of circulars that Pickering and

---

[78]Ibid. at 2322-23, 2337-39, 2399-2401.

[79]Ibid. at 2337-39, 2402-03; 5 *Dictionary of American Biography* 613; William Eaton to John Philips Ripley, 28 November 1798, Dartmouth College Library.

others provided it. One witness the committee interviewed, ironically, was George Turner, by now a former judge. Turner deposed that while he had been in Philadelphia the previous winter to make an appeal to Congress in his own impeachment investigation Blount had approached him, asking his estimates of river navigability, Spanish fortifications, and troop strength in the Northwest region. Blount had taken notes of Turner's answers, and the judge then endorsed the notes.[80]

As Turner and others came forward—sometimes not entirely of their own free will—the committee's evidence steadily accumulated. By early September, committee member John Dawson (who even several weeks earlier had expressed a grim satisfaction in the amount of material) told his good friend James Madison that the committee's work had exceeded his expectations. The final report, Dawson predicted, would come as a "bitter pill" to Liston, Pickering, and the Federalists.[81]

Throughout the investigation the administration's, and most notably Pickering's, cooperation with Congress and the impeachment committee was striking, especially in contrast to more recent inquiries, such as the Watergate and Iran-Contra affairs. Of course Blount was not an executive officer, and so the administration had no need to protect itself. On the contrary, just as the Republican Dawson wished to lay the blame on the Federalists, so Pickering apparently believed that the evidence would ultimately show the Blount Conspiracy to be a Spanish, French, or (better still) a Republican plot. While the parties sought to blame each other, they nevertheless had a common ground, at least for the time being, in their desire to discover all the essentials of the affair.

Pickering did more than his share in attempting to attain this goal. He wrote his men on the frontier, where news of the plot was agitating some groups against the Spanish, to warn of the danger and to solicit information; he received and forwarded to the committee anonymous letters pertaining to the conspiracy; he corresponded with New Yorkers, obtaining additional evidence from that quarter; and he suggested that the committee examine some of Chisholm's local

---

[80]8 *Annals of Cong.* 2355-56, 2321-22, 2365-72, 2376-77 (1797).

[81]Ibid. at 2355-56, 2376-77; John Dawson to James Madison, 13 August 1797, Reel 6, *Madison Papers* (Film); 7 September 1797.

connections, which the committee did. One of his smarter actions was to inform Rufus King of developments. The American minister to the Court of St. James queried Grenville about his knowledge and eventually located Chisholm, extracting a good bit of knowledge from the conspirator. As the committee and the administration grew more enlightened about the plan's elements, the apparent danger of an actual execution of the plot decreased, and tension began to subside.[82]

In late September Captain Lewis, escorting Grant, Carey, and Rogers, arrived in Germantown, Pennsylvania, and he promptly sent word to the committee, which rode to meet him there. Lewis recounted his whole story to the committee, and the representatives then set about the task of examining the new witnesses. The army officer had arrived at Knoxville within two weeks of leaving Philadelphia, and he had soon located Grant. Together with Henley, Lewis had placed Grant's relevant papers under seal while awaiting Carey's arrival from Tellico, from which Henley and Hawkins had summoned him. Rogers, he learned, was somewhere in the Creek Nation, although Henley and Hawkins had sent for him as well. Although searching diligently for the mysterious Mitchell, Lewis could find no evidence of the man's existence. The supposed conspirator thus fades from the records of the Blount Conspiracy as abruptly and mysteriously as he appeared. Rogers never arrived; sending Carey on to Virginia, Lewis waited until August 20, and then set out with Grant, detouring by James King's ironworks. From there the two men went on to rendezvous with Carey, and the group rode for Pennsylvania. Rogers apparently caught up with them at some point.[83]

---

[82]Timothy Pickering to Winthrop Sargent, 30 June 1797, Reel 6, *Pickering Papers* (Film); Timothy Pickering to William Willcocks, 22 July 1797, *id.*; Timothy Pickering to Andrew Ellicott, 28 July 1797, Andrew Ellicott Papers, Manuscript Division, Library of Congress; Ellicott, *Journal* 147-49; Timothy Pickering to Rufus King, 5 August 1797, *in* 2 King, *Correspondence* 209-10; Rufus King to Lord Grenville, 28 August 1797, *in* 2 King, *Correspondence* 216-18; Declaration of John D. Chisholm, 29 November 1797, *in* Turner, "Documents," 595-600; Outline of Chisholm's Plan, *in* Turner, "Documents," 600-01; Report of Examination of Chisholm by Rufus King, *in* Turner, "Documents,"601-05; 8 *Annals of Cong.* 2321-22 (1797).

[83]8 *Annals of Cong.* 2334 (1797). But cf. 8 *Annals of Cong.* 2321, 2393-95

By this time Tennessee was in an uproar. Governor John Sevier, General James Robertson, and other close acquaintances of Blount wrote freely of their dismay, either at the plot or at its discovery. Sevier called Blount's conduct imprudent; Robertson was distressed by the news from Philadelphia but opined that the letter did not evince a high degree of criminality. Hawkins and Henley, conducting an investigation of their own, had taken Carey before a local judge for questioning. In mid-August, Henley had informed Sevier that several letters from Blount to one of Chisholm's correspondents had arrived at Knoxville. At Henley's request, Sevier ordered the postmaster to open and examine the letters and to send to the government any information therein that ran contrary to United States interests. From farther west, surveyor Andrew Ellicott continued to send warnings of conspiracy circulating among frontiersmen. Although one pro-British faction there bestirred itself at the news of Blount's plans, in the end nothing came of it.[84]

In Pennsylvania, the impeachment committee continued its investigations by examining Carey and the others, who made a very full disclosure of the facts as they knew them. The resulting depositions augmented Carey's earlier deposition, which Hawkins had forwarded to Philadelphia some weeks before. Having taken this evidence, the committee had little left to do but to prepare a report to Congress and to draw up the articles of impeachment, although a trickle of material continued to come its way through the end of November. After late September, then, came a lull, similar to that which might accompany the eye of a tropical storm sweeping up the

---

(1797). Lewis's report clearly states that he departed Knoxville without Rogers, but the impeachment committee's records say with equal clarity that Rogers was present in Germantown and underwent an examination on the same day as did Grant and Carey. The only possible conclusions are that Rogers joined Lewis at some point or (less likely) preceded him to Germantown. Why Lewis appeared in Germantown rather than Philadelphia, and why the committee met him there, are mysteries; perhaps the yellow fever epidemic wae responsible. During the 1793 outbreak the village was a refuge for many Philadelphia residents, and Washington and the executive department had removed to it as well. Powell, *Bring Out Your Dead* 105-06, 230-31, 261-64.

[84]"Correspondence of General James Robertson," 4 *American Historical Magazine and Tennessee Historical Society Quarterly* 336, 343-45 (1899); Carl S. Driver, *John Sevier; Pioneer of the Old Southwest* (Chapel Hill; The University of North Carolina Press, 1937) 130-31; Ellicott, *Journal* 147-49.

Mississippi Valley from the Gulf, as the committee digested its information and prepared to report to the House of Representatives.

❧

This first phase of the Blount investigation, which includes administration inquiries, the House impeachment and investigation, the district court criminal action, and the whole of the Senate's expulsion proceedings, tells the modern student much. The first clear conclusion is that Blount held the favor of no one in the government. Administration and Congress, Federalist and Republican alike denounced the speculator's intrigues and sought to punish him, while at the same time they distanced themselves from him. The Senate's expulsion vote was practically unanimous, and the lone dissenter plainly expressed his belief in Blount's guilt. On the House impeachment committee, both Federalists and Republicans displayed at various times a vehement desire to unravel the conspiracy and bring Blount to heel.

And yet some considerable opposition was present in both houses to the conduct of the impeachment and expulsion proceedings. Most of that opposition came from Republicans—the same Republicans who voted to impeach and to expel Blount. Because the Republicans were demonstrably indifferent to the political well-being of Blount himself, and their concern clearly went far beyond that of pleasing their own constituents, their motivations for opposing the House and Senate actions at earlier points must lie elsewhere.

Clearly each party sought to capitalize upon the conspiracy by blaming it upon the other faction. Because of the Republican Blount's connections with England, both Federalists and Republicans could find some elements in the event that suggested that the other party was involved. This meant that each party made continual efforts not only to highlight Blount's association with the other group, but to discover even more evidence of such connections.

This fact, however, does not explain several Republicans' attempts to have Congress delay consideration of both impeachment and expulsion. The desire for such a delay, in fact, seems inconsistent with statements of Baldwin, Dawson, Gallatin, and Tazewell concerning Blount's guilt and the need for an exhaustive investigation. If these and other men wanted an investigation to go forward in order to allow them either to affix blame or to achieve vindication, and if they had no interest in protecting Blount personally, then they must have raised questions of procedure for the sake of procedure itself, as a matter of principle. As at least one author has written, the Republicans by the late 1790s were an opposition party whose only weapon against Federalist policy was the Constitution. They believed that the Constitution, strictly construed, was a device to protect principles of republican government and that policies in derogation of this strict construction endangered those principles. Many Republicans feared an English-style government of an economic aristocracy, to which they feared Hamiltonian policies would lead.[85] Others probably feared the establishment of a strong central government of any sort. For either danger, the principle of strict construction, of *expressio unius est exclusio alterius*, of express and not implied powers, was the constitutional remedy.

Broad construction won the day, however, in at least one significant way. The exposure of the conspiracy resulted in not only the nation's first federal impeachment, but its first senatorial expulsion and one of its earliest congressional investigations. How these processes unfolded in the following days is interesting, and sometimes surprising. The expulsion occurred with breathtaking speed, which speaks much about the fear and anger that Blount's fellow senators felt as the story of his western schemes unfolded. As for the Senate and House investigations, little express basis for such a proceeding appeared in the Constitution's text, but this detail proved no more obstruction to the investigation committee than it had in the proceedings involving St. Clair a few years earlier. Here broad construction won the field completely.

In *The Federalist* Hamilton describes impeachment as a national inquest; in doing so he perhaps had in mind earlier descriptions of Parliament, or at least Commons, as a "Grand Inquest of the Nation," in the Pitt the Elder's phrase, and of impeachment as "a presentment

---

[85]Lance Banning, "Republican Ideology and the Triumph of the Constitution, 1789 to 1793," 31 *Wm. & Mary Q.* (3d. Ser.) 167, 184-88 (April 1974). Banning argues that measures such as the Virginia and Kentucky Resolutions were born of a desire to protect not state rights but instead more general principles of civil rights and republicanism. Ibid. at 184-85.

to the most high and supreme court of criminal jurisdiction by the most solemn grand inquest of the whole kingdom" in the words of Blackstone.[86] The impeachment of Blount, and the ensuing investigation, shows that as of the 1790s many people agreed. For sheer drama, for a sense that national security hung up on the outcome of this inquest, none other, save perhaps Andrew Johnson's, and not counting the near-impeachment of Richard M. Nixon, comes close. The cavalier approach to separation of powers during the early proceedings against Blount, as well as to the separation of civil and military authority, reinforces this picture of impeachment as a means of investigating what for a time seemed a grave national peril.

Congressional investigations had occurred before. The most detailed before Blount's was the examination of Arthur St. Clair's defeat on the banks of the Wabash in 1791, a debacle that one scholar has called "the greatest Indian victory in American history ... dwarfing even Custer's extermination at the Little Big Horn." On that occasion at least two members of the House had observed that such an investigation into the executive branch would be tantamount to an impeachment of Washington, although the House never seriously considered this latter course of action.[87] In July 1797, however, things were different. Except for Albert Gallatin's complaint that a House committee had no authority to sit after the end of a session, little objection arose over either the investigation or the committee's power to compel the appearance of witnesses and papers by subpoena. None suggested that an impeachment was a necessary prerequisite to the House's exercise of such investigatory authority; on the other hand, the Senate's own unilateral investigation reveals many of the same attributes as that of the House. Whatever imprimatur the Supreme Court deigned to give congressional investigations in *Kilbourn v. Thompson*[88] nearly a century later, Congress's near-reflex reactions incident to its exercise of express constitutional powers of impeachment and expulsion do a great deal

---

[86]Telford Taylor, *Grand Inquests: The Story of Congressional Investigations* (New York: Simon and Schuster, 1955) 1 (quoting William Pitt the Elder); 4 William Blackstone, *Commentaries* *256.

[87]Chalou, "St. Clair's Defeat," *in* 1 Schlesinger & Bruns, *Congress Investigates* 3, 4; 3 *Annals of Cong.* 491 (1792).

[88]*Kilbourn v. Thompson*, 103 U.S. 168 (1881).

to illustrate the early understanding of investigations in such instances.

The most interesting twist came with Pickering's, and through him Captain Eaton's and Captain Lewis's, involvement. Because the office of secretary of state is largely a creation of Congress, one might expect the holder of that post to give whatever aid that Congress required, even though heads of executive departments stand on something of an odd relationship to the legislature. With Eaton and Lewis, however, things are different, especially since the former was apparently taking orders not from McHenry but Pickering, the secretary of state. Congress's use of military officers to arrest civilians and search their property comes disturbingly close in concept, if not in scope, to martial law. On the other hand, this incursion of the military into civilian affairs was quite limited, involving only a very few officers who acted directly under civilian authority. One should recall, too, that just as lines between offices and even branches of governments were in many ways fluid at first (Chief Justice Jay serving as minister plenipotentiary to England, and Pickering's own simultaneous service as Secretaries of War and State, for instance), so, too, the division between military and civilian realms was not yet a sharp one. The emergence of the military as a coherent profession occurred late in the United States, principally because the American political tradition has distrusted the armed forces and because the Constitution subjects control of military power to the same decentralization under separation of powers and federalism that it applies to civil authority. Samuel P. Huntington observes that "Washington obeyed the Continental Congress not as a soldier but as a citizen." He further notes that the Federalists in particular were willing to take liberties with military forces not only because of the still-threatening European presence on the frontier as well as on the Atlantic, but because of the spread of the French revolutionary ideas that seemed so dangerous in Federalist eyes.[89] Given this context, the House's use of military officers in the investigation of a conspiracy posing a potential threat to what we would today term national security is more understandable.

What of the processes taking place within the halls of the

---

[89]Samuel P. Huntington, *The Soldier and the State: The Politics of Civil-Military Relations* (Cambridge: The Belknap Press, 1957) 146, 195.

legislature itself? With Blount's impeachment and expulsion Congress ventured into new constitutional territory, unexplored in practice and little discussed even in theory. Tazewell and Venable expressed Republican sentiments at this juncture when they observed that these events would become precedent for future occasions. While Congress adhered to procedures they found proper, the Republicans were more than willing to proceed; in the House of Representatives Baldwin, a Republican, attested to Blount's handwriting in order to satisfy evidentiary (that is, technical) requirements. In the Senate Martin and Cocke did the same, and they were not only Republicans, but Blount's friends.

Even the arguments of Blount's counsel reveal the state of things. Among the members of Congress, among the administration, among members of the public, very little doubt existed in July 1797 that Blount had either planned or committed acts that might be treasonous. Ingersoll and Dallas saw no point in trying to deny the fact. Both lawyers constantly sought avenues of defense that sounded of technicality rather than denial. Even if Blount had done the things of which he stood accused, they maintained (not stopping to dwell on the question of whether he had or not), good legal reasons existed as to why Congress's procedures should not go forward. Not once did they try to deny the fact of their client's actions; their entire defense rested on legal technicality. In adopting this stance they followed an old maxim to the effect that when the law is against an advocate he should appeal to the facts, and when the facts are against him he should argue points of law.

Although this Republican emphasis on procedure was not born of an interest in Blount personally, still it remained a partisan characteristic. The critical student of impeachment may point out that this sort of partisan division among the framers' generation obscures their pure, nonpartisan, original intent as to the power's particulars (assuming, of course, such intent ever existed). In fact this conclusion, although correct in some respects, is quite wrong in others. In Blount's case more than any other, because of the universal, bipartisan acrimony he inspired, we may see a consensus that we could never find in the cases of Samuel Chase, Andrew Johnson, or even Richard M. Nixon. When both parties act so similarly, and so strongly, we find our best indications of what this generation understood the impeachment power to be.

On what points, then, do we find this consensus? The most notable is the actual impeachment. In our age the Judiciary Committee of the House of Representatives may take months to procure and examine evidence before it finally ventures to draw up articles and recommend an impeachment. The fact that in 1797 the House of Representatives impeached Blount within four days on the basis of just a few documents at most is surprising to those who lived through Watergate and its months of hearings. The additional fact that it acted thus without bothering to enunciate formally the grounds for its action is even more so. Yet Federalist and Republican alike agreed to this sequence of events in the end, and in doing so they followed the English tradition of impeachment by clamor, which in itself reveals something of the importance in which they held precedent in such cases. The obvious object of the impeachment itself (as opposed to the trial) was not Blount's protection but that of the nation at large, the established political order, as Dana had pointed out. The House's actions in the Blount impeachment thus stand in sharp contrast to modern practice, suggesting that this practice diverged sharply from that which the framers' generation envisioned.

Another point is found in the impeachment committee's subsequent investigation. As of July 8, Blount was no longer a senator. All an impeachment conviction could accomplish with relation to the speculator was further censure, at most disqualification for office. Admittedly Blount had a following in Tennessee, but the chance of his re-election seems rather small.[90] Had his state returned him to Congress, the Senate had shown that it could deal with him summarily by expulsion, and should he win election to the House, presumably the same was true. Perhaps, however, Congress felt otherwise. Nevertheless, though Blount was gone, the impeachment investigation continued. Its primary target,

---

[90]In November 1797 Blount wrote to his brother John Gray that he could have regained his place in the Senate in the recently-concluded elections, which unseated William Cocke and sent Joseph Anderson and Andrew Jackson to Philadelphia with Blount's "most hearty Concurrence." William Blount to John Gray Blount, 7 November 1797, in 3 William H. Masterson, ed., The John Gray Blount Papers (Raleigh: State Department of Archives and History, 1965) 175. In the end, however, Blount declined to stand for office, and at any rate his enemies claimed that he could not have won the election. Ibid.; Masterson, William Blount 324-27.

however, was apparently not Blount but instead the conspiracy as a whole. Gallatin had adopted this view as early as July 5, and Baldwin, both a framer and a member of the impeachment committee, confirmed it some days later. Even the newspapers soon picked up on the idea that the impeachment was a tool for learning more about the conspiracy.[91] In light of this fact, then, impeachment would seem to have a wider purpose than the removal of a government official; this suggested purpose, in fact, fits in very nicely with the theory that impeachment is a device designed to protect the political order from destructive tendencies.[92] What we see emerging from the House's first full-scale impeachment investigation, then, is a broad impeachment and investigation power, truly the stuff of a grand national inquest, just as in the Senate we see a broad power to expel a member on the basis of notorious fact, without regard for procedural intricacies.

੨ও

As the impeachment committee prepared its report, the future of Blount's case seemed uncertain. The representatives had discovered many of the conspiracy's details, and the danger appeared to be past. Blount himself, now back in Tennessee and apparently not a threat, was no longer the center of attention. The drama's next act would belong to Congress alone, as the nation's lawmakers decided upon a course of action, grafting still more flesh onto impeachment's bones.

---

[91]*Massachusetts Mercury*, 14 July 1797, p. 2, col. 2.

[92]Philip B. Kurland, "Watergate, Impeachment, and the Constitution," 45 *Miss. L.J.* 531, 546-47 (1974).

Chapter 4

The Second Session: Uncertainty December 1797-July1798

Thomas Jefferson arrived late in Philadelphia, well after the beginning of the Fifth Congress's second session. The appointed day for the legislature's first meeting was November 13, 1797, but the Senate had to make do with a president *pro tempore* for a month. Jefferson finally arrived on December 13 to assume his duties. The vice-president blamed the weather for his delay; winter had come early to Virginia, and the November snows and storms had swollen the rivers, making them impassable.[1]

The severe weather followed Jefferson to Philadelphia. Before spring came to the city in 1798 the congressmen had to endure more than one snowstorm, battling their way through drifts that made even walking difficult. The chill, however, did not confine itself to the outdoors but pervaded Congress's deliberations as well, especially the proceedings in Blount's impeachment. By December the passion that had surrounded the conspiracy's investigation had cooled, and except for a few very heated moments the mood was to remain for the next several months.[2]

Certainly the returning congressmen had no clue as to what awaited them. When they left Philadelphia the previous July the

---

[1]7 *Annals of Cong.* 469, 477 (1797); Thomas Jefferson to Henry Tazewell, 28 November 1797, 102 (Reel 34) *Jefferson Papers* (Film).

[2]Henry M. Wagstaff, "Letters of William Barry Grove," 9 *James Sprunt Historical Publications* (No. 2) 45, 70-72 (1910); Thomas Jefferson to James Madison, 22 February 1798, Reel 6, *Madison Papers* (Film); Thomas Jefferson to John Taylor, 23 December 1797, 7 Ford, *The Writings of Thomas Jefferson* 181.

conspiracy had loomed over the town as threatening as one of the summer thunderstorms that had struck the capital that year. On arriving in November, the representatives no doubt expected Sitgreaves's impeachment committee to deliver its report. In Tennessee, Blount anxiously awaited for news from the capital, confident that the state's congressional delegation would keep him informed of impeachment developments. Neither Blount nor the congressmen were to be disappointed in their quest for information, but afterwards the inquiry would change direction.[3]

On November 30 the impeachment committee completed work on its report, organizing its materials and drafting a short account of its investigations. This report Samuel Sitgreaves presented to the House of Representatives four days later. For hours on December 4 and 5 the clerk read aloud the seemingly endless array of materials. Afterwards the House, removing the injunction of secrecy on the committee's activities, ordered printers to prepare six hundred copies of the report. The chamber then tabled the committee's work and the Blount affair died down for a while, at least in Congress.[4]

Despite the legislature's sudden quiescence the public continued to express an interest in the affair, especially when the documents became a matter of public knowledge. Many of these documents found their way into the Philadelphia press, where they attracted considerable attention. One enterprising individual even offered for sale a pamphlet describing "Blount's Curious Business."[5]

In New York people took a more personal interest in Blount's curious business. According to one newspaper account, a broker by the name of Wynhoop had told William Eaton that Nicholas Romayne had criticized the American Revolution. By this account Romayne had declared that the United States ought still to belong to the Empire, and that he himself should be the governor at Natchez. The passage resembles Eaton's earlier story of happening to overhear

---

[3]William Blount to John Gray Blount, 28 November 1797, 3 Masterson, ed., *The John Gray Blount Papers* 188-89; Thomas Blount to John Gray Blount, 25 January 1798, Ibid., 198-99.

[4]8 *Annals of Cong.* 2319-23 (1797); 7 Ibid., 672-79.

[5]*Claypoole's American Daily Advertiser*, 26 December 1797, p. 1, col. 3; Ibid., 2 January 1798, p. 1, col. 5; Ibid., 11 January 1798, p. 1, col. 5, p. 4, col. 5; *Independent Chronicle*, 8 January 1798, p. 1, col. 3; *Porcupine's Gazette*, 30 January 1798, p. 4, col. 4.

a conversation on a ferry linking Romayne with Benjamin Winthrop, and *Porcupine's Gazette* in fact identified this broker as Winthrop. Romayne, learning of these allegations, wrote a public letter calling Winthrop a liar. The following day, December 26, Romayne paid Winthrop a not-so-friendly visit and demanded a written retraction of the statements that the latter had apparently made to Congress. Winthrop refused, and the doctor, in a fit of fury, kicked his accuser down a flight of stairs and then threw him into a gutter.

Romayne, though, had not reckoned with public sentiment. That same afternoon, entering a coffee house in search of Leonard Bleeker, the cohort of Winthrop's that Eaton had described, he found himself confronting a restless crowd, which followed him into the street and which he dared to approach him. The group stood uneasily on the street, the rain pouring down, tempers rising. Then Bleeker arrived upon the scene. Romayne started towards him and the crowd exploded, attacking the physician, who managed to get in some blows of his own before escaping.[6]

As Romayne was adjusting to his new notoriety, others came forward, probably spurred on by the committee's revelations. Near the end of December yet another New Yorker, Abel Holden, Jr., sought out the committee and informed it that he had heard Eaton's nemesis John Phillips Ripley conversing in French, and that the man was an acquaintance of the Chevalier de Yrujo's. The committee duly forwarded this information to the House; but the report caused both Ripley and Yrujo to appear and explain that Ripley's associations with the Spanish minister were minor ones, Ripley once having sought a loan from Yrujo.[7]

---

[6]*Massachusetts Mercury*, 5 January 1798, p. 2, col. 4, p. 3, col. 1; *Porcupine's Gazette*, 29 December 1797, p. 2, col. 4.

[7]7 *Annals of Cong.* 847, 890 (1798); 8 *Annals of Cong.* 2412-15 (1798); U.S. Congress, House, Committee on Impeachment of William Blount, *Further Report from the Committee, Appointed on the Eighth of July Last, to Prepare and Report Articles of Impeachment Against William Blount, a Senator of the United States, Impeached by the House of Representatives of High Crimes and Misdemeanors* (Philadelphia: 1798) [Evans 34793]; U.S. Congress, House, Committee on Impeachment of William Blount, *Further Report from the Committee, Appointed on the Eighth of July Last, to Prepare and Report Articles of Impeachment Against William Blount, a Senator of the United States, Impeached by the House of Representatives of High Crimes and Misdemeanors*

Even at this point the committee's investigations continued. In early February Robert Goodloe Harper announced the committee's intentions to investigate rumors of a British proposition to the American general Elijah Clarke in Georgia, provided that the House agreed to the additional expense. Some representatives observed that the committee, having completed its business, had been discharged, but Harper's continued appeals won the appointment of a new committee, identical in membership to the old one. This new impeachment committee reported in April that Clarke had little or no useful information.[8]

Before the original committee's dissolution, however, it had faced one more task in addition to its preparation of the various reports. This task, seemingly an afterthought, was actually its express original *raison d'être*, the job of drafting articles of impeachment. After it made its report in early December, though, instead of producing the articles, the committee grew strangely silent and inactive. Of course, as Albert Gallatin and others had noted in July, the underlying purpose of the impeachment was to investigate the conspiracy, and the committee accomplished this end by making its report. Yet the ostensible goal of the investigation was the production of charges against Blount. Time was of no concern; in fact several members of Congress mentioned the utter absence of any important business during December that might have kept the committee from its work. Such descriptions of Congress's activity, moreover, also implied that the Blount affair itself lacked importance. The events that had caused such a furor half a year previously were now suddenly useless even as a means to pass the time, much less a subject of serious congressional scrutiny.[9]

Why would such a change in attitude occur? The report's contents may be one factor. The Federalists, largely anti-French, had been generally more zealous, and certainly more heedless, than the Republicans in their efforts to deal with Blount. The report, however,

---

(Philadelphia: 1798) [Evans 34787, OCLC 11275743].

[8]7 *Annals of Cong.* 959-63 (1798); 8 Ibid., 1559, 2413 (1798).

[9]7 Ford, *Writings of Jefferson* 181; William Barry Grove to John Haywood, 18 December 1797, Ernest Haywood Papers, Southern Historical Collection, University of North Carolina; James A. Bayard to Richard Bassett, 30 December 1797, Bayard Papers, Library of Congress.

revealed a link (albeit a tenuous one) between the conspirators and the British government, and no connection at all between Blount and France, or even between Blount and Spain. Because the committee had apparently discovered and exposed the leading conspirators, moreover, the chances that Blount or someone else would try to carry the plot into execution now seemed small. By late 1797, then, the Blount inquiry had lost its air of great urgency, and at the same time it had become an actual embarrassment to the Federalists. Robert Liston wrote Lord Grenville soon after the publication of the December report that Yrujo's efforts to arouse anti-English sentiment in Philadelphia had failed, but the English minister may have been on the defensive. More revealing was his silence as to the report's general impact. John Dawson was more exultant, informing James Madison that the report had produced dismay among the Federalists, and that rumors of French involvement had ceased. December 1797 thus found the Blount impeachment stalled, and the Federalists unwilling to proceed.[10]

But if Blount had become bad press for the Federalists then conversely he had turned out to be an element that the Republicans could exploit. Perhaps even some genuine desire to punish Blount remained among the Republicans; but whatever their motivation, they now found Blount to be a politically safe and advantageous target.

On January 8, 1798, more than a month after the impeachment committee delivered its main report, North Carolina Representative Joseph McDowell, a Republican and a long-time enemy of Blount's, called upon the committee to deliver impeachment articles to the House. The committee had delayed much too long, he maintained, and citizens were becoming agitated. McDowell enjoined the House to act to satisfy the country's honor. Because Sitgreaves, the committee's chairman, was absent, Robert Goodloe Harper rose to answer McDowell.[11]

Harper was well-known to the House, and to Philadelphia in

---

[10]Robert Liston to Lord Grenville, 5 December 1797, *in* Turner, "Documents," 605; John Dawson to James Madison, 10 December 1797, Reel 6, *Madison Papers* (Film).

[11]Masterson, *William Blount* 167-68, 179, 331; 7 *Annals of Cong.* 809-10 (1798); *Aurora*, 11 January 1798, p. 3, cols. 2-3.

general. A native of Virginia, he had represented South Carolina in Congress for three of his thirty-three years; first elected as a Republican, by 1798 he was a devoted Federalist. A rumored monarchist, Harper was considered a man of great talent and even greater vanity. From the first he had been one of Blount's most energetic persecutors, but now he found himself in the position of having to justify a month's delay in the impeachment proceedings. His defense was either good improvisation (something for which he displayed more than a little skill) or else a carefully pre-arranged excuse. He pointed out that Sitgreaves had, some time previously, sought and obtained a ten day leave of absence from the House, and that the committee wished to wait until his return before acting.[12]

At once Harper found himself the target of his fellow committee member John Dawson. Dawson suggested that, because of the absence of not only Sitgreaves but James A. Bayard as well, the House should appoint additional committee members in order to expedite matters. McDowell reiterated his desire to proceed with the matter; when another representative criticized him for not opposing Sitgreaves's request for leave, McDowell responded that he had been unable to do so because of the request's suddenness. He then observed that Sitgreaves at any rate should have returned several days previously. Nevertheless, after these comments, McDowell tabled his motion that the committee proceed.[13]

Three days later McDowell again introduced his resolution, and once again, at Harper's request, he withdrew it. His determination to force the committee to act was clear, however, for Thomas Blount wrote his disgraced brother that day that articles of impeachment would soon be forthcoming. The following Tuesday, January 16, McDowell arose a third time and observed icily that Sitgreaves, even according to his revised schedule, should have appeared in the House the day before. Harper tried to reassure McDowell that in fact Sitgreaves had departed for Philadelphia on the 10th, and thus should

---

[12]Thomas Jefferson, notes, beginning 26 December 1797, 102 (Reel 34) *Jefferson Papers* (Film) (at one point these notes mistakenly label Harper as Hamilton); 22 Harold C. Syrett ed., *The Papers of Alexander Hamilton* (New York: Columbia University Press, 1974) 36-39; 7 *Annals of Cong.* 810 (1798); 8 Malone, *Dictionary of American Biography* 285.

[13]7 *Annals of Cong.* 810 (1798); *Aurora*, 11 January 1798, p. 3, cols. 2-3.

soon make an appearance. This line, however, was apparently growing quite old, for Bayard, who was now present, felt the need to add some observations of his own. As early as December some people—probably Federalists at this juncture—had been heard to deny that the impeachment trial could proceed unless Blount were present, and Robert Liston reported as much to the Foreign Office. "It is probable that the business will rest here," he had written Grenville in late December. "Mr Blount has not made his appearance conformably to the recognizances into which he was obliged to enter at the conclusion of the late Session, and it seems the general opinion that no prosecution can be carried on against him in his absence." Bayard now raised this point, stating his personal belief that Blount's attendance at the proceedings was a necessity. Everyone knew, moreover, that Blount would never appear before the Senate, the representative maintained. In light of these circumstances, said Bayard in a reasonable fashion, the House would achieve little by forcing the pace of things.[14]

Bayard, the sole representative from Delaware and at this point a dedicated Federalist, was a young and respectable gentleman, the son-in-law of framer Richard Bassett. Though somewhat lower-key than Harper, he ranked alongside both Harper and Sitgreaves in his desire to deal with Blount. This desire, along with Bayard's position as impeachment committee member, renders his sudden reversal here—the first such Federalist change of heart on record in the proceedings—quite remarkable. Now the Federalists, rather than the Republicans, were seeking refuge in legal technicality, just as the Republicans had some months earlier.[15]

Many Republicans did indeed express some surprise at Bayard's comments. John Nicholas chided Bayard for taking the view that the impeachment was just a matter of form. Nicholas, for his part, refused to accept the idea that a mere committee could contravene the will of the House of Representatives in this or any other matter, and he

---

[14]7 *Annals of Cong.* 819-21, 837 (1798); Robert Liston to Lord Grenville, 28 December 1797, *in* Turner, "Documents," 606; *Aurora*, 18 January 1798, p. 3, col. 1; *Massachusetts Mercury*, 26 January 1798, p. 2, col. 4.

[15]Theodore Sedgwick to Rufus King, 20 January 1799, Rufus King Correspondence, New York Historical Society; Morton Borden, *The Federalism of James A. Bayard* (New York: Columbia University Press, 1955) 5.

expressly disagreed with Bayard over the need for Blount's presence—the first clear Republican abandonment of procedure for the sake of expediency. Another Republican, Thomas Claiborne of Virginia, reminded the committee that the House would not have given it the power to sit during Congress's recess unless the chamber had considered speed essential. During his speech, Claiborne remarked that he wished to see Blount punished; these sentiments show that Blount had indeed become estranged from his party colleagues. Other Republicans spoke out on the issues of speed and trial in Blount's absence, siding with Nicholas and Claiborne almost without exception. In the end, though, procedure prevailed, as Nicholas successfully proposed that the House give Sitgreaves two more days to arrive.[16]

The next day Sitgreaves finally appeared, and in a somewhat sheepish fashion he acknowledged the chamber's impatience and promised to make a report in a few days. In fact the report did not issue for more than a week. Not until January 25 did the committee deliver to the House five articles of impeachment, all charges therein stemming from statements Blount had made in his fateful letter to James Carey.

Article I charged Blount with conspiring to conduct a military expedition from United States territory against Spain, with whom the country was at peace. The charge was effectively that of conspiracy to violate the Neutrality Act, although that statute required an *actus reus* other than mere conspiracy. Article II averred that Blount had incited Indians to commence hostilities against Spain in derogation of provisions of Pinckney's Treaty as well as American obligations as a neutral power. Article III listed Blount's efforts to destroy the influence of Indian Agent Benjamin Hawkins in derogation of federal laws entrusting Hawkins with his official responsibilities; Article IV similarly charged him with seducing Carey from his duties. Article V related to Blount's attempts to sow discontent with the United States among the Cherokee, specifically in the matters of boundaries and territorial claims.[17]

Debate has raged over the years as to whether high crimes and

---

[16]7 *Annals of Cong.* 838-39 (1798); *Aurora*, 18 January 1798, p. 3, cols. 1-2; *Massachusetts Mercury*, 26 January 1798, p. 2, col. 4.

[17]7 *Annals of Cong.* 948-951 (1798).

misdemeanors encompass only indictable offenses, or whether some broader standard is allowable.[18] Article I relates, or seems to relate, to the Neutrality Act, violation of which was by its express terms a "high misdemeanor." The phrase, by one construction similar to the constitutional language of impeachment (if we understand the word "high" in the latter to modify "misdemeanors" as well as "crimes"), is suggestive of impeachment. Again, however, Article I did not charge Blount with violating the act, that is, with setting on foot an expedition against a friendly power, but instead with conspiring to do so, which the act does not expressly make criminal. Article I, then would seem not to embrace a statutory offense. As to the larger question of indictability, however, one must recall that in 1797 the existence of a federal common law of crimes was still an open question. Not until 1812 would the Supreme Court decide, at least for the purposes of the federal judiciary, that no such law existed.[19] Republicans refused to wait for this ruling; at a later stage of the Blount impeachment, as well as in the face of the Alien and Sedition Acts, they would refuse to recognize any such law. But the Republicans were not in charge of drafting the articles of impeachment. Nor did they hold a majority in the Senate that could automatically block any vote on the issue (although they could, of course, make a two-thirds vote for conviction on Article I, and thus a validation of the offense that the article spelled out, difficult to achieve). In light of the state of the law as well as the political setting, then, this first article says little about whether impeachment as this early generation understood it lay only for indictable crimes.

As for Article II, the international law aspect is interesting. Pinckney's Treaty was clearly positive law on a par, or very nearly so, with congressional statutes by virtue of the Constitution's Supremacy Clause,[20] but this second article discusses more than the treaty. It

---

[18]See, e.g., Theodore Dwight, "Trial by Impeachment," 6 *Am. L. Reg.* (N.S.) 257 (1867) (may also be cited as 15 *Am. L. Reg.* 257 [1867]); William Lawrence, "The Law of Impeachment," 6 *Am. L. Reg.* (N.S.) 641 (1867) (may also be cited as 15 *Am. L. Reg.* 641 (1867)).

[19]Act of June 5, 1794, ch. 50, § 5, 1 Stat. 381, 384 (1794); Act of March 2, 1797, ch. 5, 1 Stat. 497 (1797); 18 U.S.C. § 960 (1994); *United States v. Hudson & Goodwin*, 11 U.S. (7 Cranch) 32 (1812).

[20] U.S. Const. art. VI, cl. 2:
This Constitution, and all the laws of the United States which shall be

also mentions repeatedly the "obligations of neutrality" that Blount's conduct had violated. Article II, furthermore, distinguished these "obligations of neutrality" from "the laws of the United States." Whether the Constitution incorporates customary international law principles into municipal law is still very much under discussion,[21] and in light of this discussion the wording of Article II is intriguing. One can read it as discussing three types of municipal law: the laws of the United States, a treaty, and the obligations of neutrality. The first of these is not generic. That it does not refer generally to "law" as a whole is clear by the article's separate discussion of the treaty, even though a treaty is clearly part of this generic "law" by virtue of the Supremacy Clause. "Laws of the United States," then, must refer to a specific category of municipal law. Perhaps it refers to statutes, although the article's omission of specific statutes renders such a reading suspect. If we adopt this interpretation, however, then, the "obligations of neutrality" may well have indicated in this context that the House impeachment committee considered customary international law to be a third type of municipal law, as it did treaties and statutes, and that impeachment would lie for its violation.

On the other hand, nothing about Article II requires us to read all three of these types of law as municipal law; the committee may have had no thought of arguing here for the incorporation of customary international law into American domestic law. If this is the case, however, then we come to the still more interesting conclusion that the committee considered "high Crimes and Misdemeanors" to include violations of customary international law principles even though those principles form no part of municipal law in the United States. In fact, this seems the likelier reading of Article II.

The other charges offer food for thought as well. Reduction of Hawkins's influence, seduction of Carey from his duty, and fomenting

---

made in Pursuance thereof; and all Treaties made, or which shall be made, under the Authority of the United States, shall be the supreme Law of the Land; and the Judges in every State shall be bound thereby, any Thing in the Constitution or Laws of any State to the Contrary notwithstanding.

[21]*See, e.g., The Paquete Habana*, 175 U.S. 677 (1900); *Filartiga v. Peña-Irala*, 630 F.2d 876 (2d Cir. 1980); Curtis A. Bradley & Jack L. Goldsmith, "Customary International Law as Federal Common Law: A Critique of the Modern Position," 110 *Harv. L. Rev.* 815 (1997); A.M. Weisburd, "State Courts, Federal Courts, and International Cases," 20 *Yale J. Int'l L.* 1, 29-31 (1995).

discontent among Indians would not appear to be indictable offenses, although the articles are worded so as to suggest that Blount violated some statutes in acting in this way; again, however, the articles do not state which statutes these may be.

The articles contain another interesting element. All list as a crucial element of Blount's actions the fact that they were "contrary to the duty of his trust and station as a Senator of the United States."[22] If this is the true impeachable offense, with the specific activities the articles list merely the means by which Blount violated this duty, then the articles at least suggest that private wrongdoing that does not cause the perpetrator to violate such a duty is not impeachable. Of course, this is speculation; these were accusations only, and the Senate had not yet voted on the validity of these charges.

From a political viewpoint the articles contain additional points of interest. The fact that the committee produced them at all reveals that someone—either the House Republicans or the public at large—was sufficiently desirous of seeing the affair concluded to force the committee to act. The articles themselves, however, omit any mention of Blount's involvement with the British. Perhaps the Federalist majority in the committee managed to downplay this element as much as possible. Despite this damage control, though, the articles still made their way to the floor, but the House decided to wait for a few days to consider them.[23]

On Monday the 29th Sitgreaves suggested that the House begin debate. This motion caused some split among the Federalists. Sitgreaves gave signs of wanting to wash his hands of the matter by dropping the whole affair into the Senate's lap. Others, including Harper, wanted to table the articles for a time. Some members of this latter group probably hoped that the Senate would get bogged down in working out the procedural aspects of the impeachment power, perhaps allowing the impeachment to die of neglect in the meantime. While some Federalists, including Sitgreaves, made comments that evinced a desire to proceed, the general impression is one of Federalist indecision as to the best means of sweeping the whole messy affair under the congressional rug. Throughout the debate the

---

[22]7 *Annals of Cong.* 948-51 (1798); *see* Appendix 2, *infra.*
[23]7 *Annals of Cong.* 919 (1798).

Republicans remained silent; their position was clear. Finally the chamber voted—by a bare majority—to consider the articles immediately.[24]

Before long the House, first in the Committee of the Whole and then as the House proper, had agreed to the articles as the impeachment committee had written them, with only one or two very minor and "immaterial verbal alterations" to correct some transcription errors. The House having at last produced the long-awaited articles, the representatives now turned to the proper means for presenting them to the Senate.[25]

Sitgreaves brought up the subject by suggesting that the House appoint eleven impeachment managers, and that the representatives choose these men by ballot, as did the House of Commons. In answer to another representative's suggestion that the House should choose only five managers, Sitgreaves insisted that in light of the impeachment's importance the greater number was desirable. George Thatcher, who had proposed the smaller figure, held that the House should appoint the managers just as it did any other committee. To this Albert Gallatin answered that unlike a committee, the managers were to represent the House in the Senate, and that they should consequently be chosen by ballot. In the end the House agreed to elect eleven managers in the manner that Sitgreaves had set forth.[26]

The following day the voting began, and it continued for about two hours. During the polling, incidentally, came the first famous confrontation between Federalist Roger Griswold of Connecticut and the fanatical democrat Matthew Lyon of Vermont. The hours of balloting must have proved monotonous; during the interlude Jonathan Dayton of New Jersey struck up a conversation with Lyon by the fireplace. During the discussion Lyon commented on the state of politics in Connecticut, proclaiming that he could effect a revolution there in a matter of months were he to open a press. "If you go to Connecticut," called Griswold from nearby, "you had better wear your wooden sword." This was a reference to William Cobbett's charge that during the war General Horatio Gates had

---

[24]Ibid., 947-48.

[25]Ibid., 951; *Universal Gazette*, 1 February 1798, p. 3, col. 3; *Independent Chronicle*, 8 February 1798, p. 2, col. 5.

[26]7 *Annals of Cong.* 951-52 (1798).

forced Lyon to wear such a sword as a mark of cowardice. Lyon did not react, and Griswold walked up to him, took him by the arm, and repeated his gibe. Lyon then responded by turning to Griswold and spitting in his face. This outburst attracted the chamber's attention, and the House almost immediately began a disciplinary proceeding against Lyon.

Disciplinary action was not enough, however, for Griswold. Two weeks later, after the House had voted down a motion to expel Lyon, the enraged Federalist strode into the House and began to beat Lyon with a heavy stick. Lyon reacted by running behind the Speaker's chair, seizing the fire tongs that he found there, and hurling himself at Griswold. The two fell to the floor; the other representatives, whom the assault had stunned into paralysis, finally intervened and pulled the combatants apart just as Lyon was about to beat in Griswold's head. Although arousing the disgust of the Congress, both representatives somehow managed to avoid expulsion.[27]

The rising partisan hostility was also visible, although less spectacularly, in the managers' election. At the end of the balloting on January 20, only nine men, including Sitgreaves, Bayard, Harper, and Abraham Baldwin, had attained a majority. Of the impeachment committee members, only Dawson had not won election. Of the nine legislators who did win, only Baldwin was a Republican. The Georgia representative promptly declined to serve, claiming that because the number of votes he had received was rather low (he was seventh in the standing) he did not have the House's confidence. Despite accusations that he was being unrealistic as well as partisan, Baldwin persisted in his request to be excused from service, and the House finally acquiesced.[28]

The next day voting continued, and finally the House elected the last three managers, none of whom was a Republican.[29] Thus the Federalists, whose enthusiasm had waned over the last two months, used their majority in the House to secure complete control of the group entrusted with the task of prosecuting Blount. This apparent

---

[27]Ibid., 1010-29, 1034, 1048-58; Aleine Austin, *Matthew Lyon: New Man of the Democratic Revolution, 1749-1822* (University Park: The Pennsylvania State University Press, 1981) 93-100.

[28]7 *Annals of Cong.* 953-55 (1798).

[29]Ibid., 957.

change of heart is probably best explained by Federalists' desire to control the process as much as possible. Unable to silence or ignore Republican demands for Blount's punishment, they presumably decided that their best alternative was to play the dominant role in the impeachment and downplay the politically harmful elements as much as possible. Even at this point some Federalists perhaps hoped that if they played along then the entire business would lose momentum. At any rate the Federalists once again found themselves in the front line, at least nominally, in the assault on the disgraced senator.

On February 2 Sitgreaves moved that the managers, when they were ready, proceed to the Senate chamber and in person deliver the impeachment articles. Though the House readily agreed, the managers themselves delayed. Five days later they were prepared. The Senate informed the House that it would receive the delegation at noon. When the appointed hour arrived the representatives adjourned, and Sitgreaves, together with several other managers, went to the Senate. There he read aloud the articles, and Jefferson informed the managers that the Senate would advise the lower house of its actions. Then the managers withdrew, leaving the political ball in the Senate's court.[30]

With the managers' presentation—an act that no doubt gave Sitgreaves great relief—the House concluded the balance of its impeachment activities for the second session. In the upper house, however, things were just beginning to get underway, as the senators started to slog their way through a bewildering morass of procedure.

Between late January and early March, no fewer than four separate select committees met in the Senate to discuss various aspects of Blount's impeachment. Many senators sat on more than one committee, and the bodies rarely confined themselves to a single topic. Only by carefully following the official minutes and supplementing them with unofficial accounts can the reader hope to understand the proper sequence of events.

---

[30]Ibid., 499, 502, 963, 969-70.

From the beginning of the session until January 19, the senators remained almost totally silent with regard to the Blount affair. Perhaps they hoped that the process would die in the House, even as Sitgreaves and others sought to foist the business upon the Senate. Then on the 19th, shortly after Sitgreaves's reappearance and promise to draft articles, Senator Humphrey Marshall announced that he would soon introduce a bill to regulate impeachment procedures. Marshall, the Kentucky Federalist who had sided so strongly with the Republicans the previous summer in demanding that the Senate follow proper procedure, now intended to insure that the chamber did just that in the coming months. On the 22nd he introduced a bill, which proceeded to a second reading that same day.[31]

In an early form this bill, the first of its kind, concerned itself with several subjects. It bestowed various powers upon the House, including the authority to summon witnesses and bind them by recognizance. On the other hand, it also contained restraints upon the arbitrary exercise of authority on the part of each branch of the legislature. It required representatives to send specific allegations to the Senate in any impeachment, along with the names of the managers and witnesses, as well as a description of the evidence. While the Senate received the authority to issue process, the bill's provisions set strict standards for how the process was to be executed. The bill also required each senator, before the trial, to take an oath to do "impartial justice according to law, and my best judgment." The Senate's decision to convict or acquit a defendant was to include a statement of the *ratio decidendi* or grounds for the judgment. Marshall even included provisions that spoke to the defendant's rights. Chief among these was the clause granting the impeached party the right to counsel and also that of compulsory process—the right to subpoena witnesses on his behalf.[32]

---

[31]Ibid., 491.

[32]U.S. Congress, Senate, *A Bill Regulating Certain Procedures in Cases of Impeachment* (Philadelphia: John Fenno, 1798) [Evans 48698]. Marshall's call for a single statement of the grounds for judgment is interesting in light of his cousin John Marshall's adoption of a single opinion of the Court instead of the usual pattern of seriatim opinions when Adams appointed him as Chief Justice a few years later. Perhaps the Kentucky senator told his relative of his experiences with the Blount impeachment and the Senate's foray into judicial territory, and perhaps John Marshall took Humphrey Marshall's experience into consideration when he took over

On the 23rd the Senate delivered this bill to a bipartisan five-man committee, one of whom was Marshall himself. Seven days later the Senate created a second committee, consisting of the three Federalists Samuel Livermore, James Ross, and Uriah Tracy, all of whom also sat on the Marshall bill committee. The Senate commanded this committee of three to report a "form of proceeding in cases of impeachment." In the next few days, things would begin to happen very quickly.[33]

The day after its creation, the three-man committee on the form of proceedings (or "mode" of proceedings, as the Senate's clerk more frequently identified it) made a report. The next day, February 1, Marshall's committee also reported, saying that it had amended the Marshall bill. The Senate's main interest at this point devolved upon the report of the committee on the mode of proceedings, debating it on the 1st and adopting it in part on the 2nd. No record of this report remains, but on the next day the Senate recommitted the unadopted part to a third committee, this one consisting of Federalists James Hillhouse, Jacob Read, and Elijah Paine. Meanwhile the Marshall committee report languished.[34]

On February 5 the third committee made not one, but two reports. The first of these dealt with relatively minor matters; it designated the Senate doorkeeper to be sergeant-at-arms and charged him with executing Senate process and other commands. The report also permitted managers to attend Senate impeachment proceedings, and prescribed the opening sentences by which the chamber would transform itself into a court of impeachment. This report the Senate adopted quickly.[35]

The second report was another matter. It was a resolution prescribing the oath that senators would take pursuant to the constitutional requirement that senators hearing an impeachment "be on oath or affirmation." This oath would require each member to do "impartial justice, according to law." More stringent than Marshall's proposed oath, this version made no allowance for the latitude of

---

the Supreme Court.

[33]7 *Annals of Cong.* 491, 494 (1798).
[34]Ibid., 495-96.
[35]Ibid., 496-97.

individual judgment. The Senate took up this report on February 8.[36]

The central issue regarding this report was simple: did the Senate have the constitutional authority to prescribe such an oath by resolution, or must that oath be the product of a statute, in which the House necessarily concurred? The Constitution required the senators, when hearing an impeachment trial, to be under oath, but it said nothing else about the matter.[37] Though the question of oaths alone would seem to be a small one, the larger issue was great indeed. Was the Senate to be the judge of the extent of its impeachment powers, or could the House exercise checks on those powers? To put this another way, the question was whether "the sole Power to try all Impeachments" allowed the Senate to make its own rules about the process once the House had begun the process by voting the impeachment, or whether instead the process was subject to regulation through legislation, in which the House of course had a voice, but which the Senate could presumably block.

From the first a partisan pattern characterized the Senate's debate. Federalists argued that the Senate could establish the oath by unilateral resolution, while Republicans demanded that the oath pass through the normal, bicameral legislative processes. Unlike the House, then, where substantial changes in partisan sentiment had occurred in recent months, the Senate continued to follow the pattern into which it had fallen in July 1797. Federalists wished to adopt the course that was both faster and more protective of Senate power; Republicans emphasized procedural propriety.

Humphrey Marshall, interestingly enough, sided with the Republicans once again, as he had in the first session. In July Marshall's emphasis on procedure could be explained by his desire to keep senators safe from House attacks. In February 1798, however, Marshall's insistence on a statutory oath suggested that he did not object to lower house incursions on senatorial power, at least as long as the Senate retained a veto over the process. Although this time Marshall was not the only Federalist to appeal to procedural stringency, he still had very little company, and he was by far the most outspoken and persistent. In fact his enthusiasm even surpassed that of most Republicans. In light of his unflagging efforts to

---

[36]Ibid., 503; U.S. Const. art. I, § 3, cl.6.
[37]U.S. Const. art. I, § 3, cl. 6.

implement tougher legal standards, then, Marshall is probably best described as a Federalist to whom the most important issue in the impeachment was neither Blount's punishment (or escape), nor even senatorial immunity from the process, but instead procedural regularity. In an age without clearly defined and established party organizations, politicians—even those of the sort that later ages would consider party regulars—could still turn renegade on certain issues.[38]

In the oath debate, the Federalists, among them Jacob Read, Samuel Livermore, Theodore Sedgwick, and Richard Stockton, argued that the Constitution delegated the "sole Power to try all impeachments" to the Senate, and that this grant included the power to prescribe oaths. Read stated that if a statute was necessary then the House, by refusing to cooperate, could frustrate an impeachment effort. Livermore stressed the constitutional wording, asserting that the Senate clearly had exclusive jurisdiction in the matter. In answer Republican Timothy Bloodworth conceded that each house could and did make its own internal rules, but he argued that impeachment was different in that it affected the lives and liberties of American citizens. Then Marshall made a long speech, sweeping aside the state precedents that Livermore had cited and appealing instead to Parliamentary history. To Read's comments Marshall gave the obvious reply; the House of Representatives, as the prosecuting agency that had first brought the impeachment, surely would not wish to frustrate the process now. (In fact many representatives would doubtless have been happy to do so, and Marshall probably knew it.) Marshall also

---

[38]At least one study of early party development suggests that parties as such did not exist in the day of the Fifth Congress. John F. Hoadley, *Origins of American Political Parties, 1789-1803* (Lexington: The University Press of Kentucky, 1986) 156. Another suggests that in the absence of well-developed parties, legislators' allegiances could shift considerably in this period depending on the issue. Rudolph M. Bell, *Party and Faction in American Politics: The House of Representatives, 1789-1801* (Westport, Conn.: Greenwood Press, 1973) 168-80. Bell's thesis certainly seems applicable to Marshall; nevertheless the fact remains that in the Blount impeachment a consistent split in debating and voting patterns is undeniably present, Marshall's being by far the greatest aberration. This split corresponds to partisan composition in each house as listed in Kenneth C. Martis, ed., *The Historical Atlas of Political Parties in the United States Congress 1789-1989* (New York: MacMillan Publishing Company, 1989) 74, 261-63, and Congressional Quarterly, *Guide to U.S. Elections*, 2d ed. (Washington: Congressional Quarterly, Inc., 1985) 579-606.

challenged the assertion that the Constitution contemplated oaths when it spoke of the Senate's sole power to try impeachments. When, asked Marshall rhetorically, had any agency or individual ever been allowed to prescribe an oath for itself or himself? Marshall's final point was probably more revealing of his sentiments than any of his others. This was his observation that he believed the oath issue to be so important that an impeached party "would under the constitution have the right to deny the jurisdiction of the Senate, sitting under an oath of their own making."[39]

Sedgwick took issue with Marshall over the latter's assertion that no officer prescribed his own oaths, naming magistrates and customs-house officials as two examples. Stockton spoke up next. Having come to the decision that the constitutional oath requirement obviated the need for a statute, he considered that such a statute would be redundant. In answer to Sedgwick, and in support of Marshall, Bloodworth demanded that the former produce a single specific case of a magistrate prescribing an oath not for other magistrates but for himself. Sedgwick made no response. Finally Henry Tazewell, the Virginian who had so strongly defended the importance of procedure in July, spoke up. Tazewell voiced his agreement to the oath's form, but he wished to see it enacted rather than adopted by resolution. He then moved a postponement, and the discussion ended for the day.[40]

As debate resumed on the 9th, Marshall made another speech in which he refuted assertions, both actual and anticipated, that officers in England and America had made their own oaths. Blount's successor, Joseph Anderson of Tennessee, produced even more evidence to help Marshall. Then Tazewell took the floor once more to begin an intense, logical analysis of the Constitution's relevant provisions.

Tazewell, an attorney and former Chief Justice of the old Virginia General Court, was descended from a long line of lawyers. Both dignified and genial, he was the one of the most popular Virginians of his time.[41] He was also gifted; certainly in the winter of 1798 he

---

[39]*Aurora*, 10 February 1798, p. 2, cols. 2-3 (the paper mistakenly lists this debate as taking place on February 1); U.S. Const. art. I, § 3, cl. 6.

[40]*Aurora*, 10 February 1798, p. 2, cols. 2-3.

[41]18 Malone, *Dictionary of American Biography* 354-55.

showed a rare talent for logical discourse. Tazewell first mentioned his opponent's claim that the Constitution prescribed the oath. In response, he asked simply where in the document it appeared. Answering his own question, playing his own devil's advocate, he cited the clause giving the Senate the sole power to try impeachments, which, he claimed, gave the chamber an implicit power to make oaths. An implied oath power, argued Tazewell, could not possibly destroy Congress's express powers of legislation; even if the Senate did possess an implied oath power, he thus concluded, Congress could still enact an oath by law.

In light of the Senate's uncertainty, Tazewell urged, it should act by statute and remove all doubts of impropriety. He then delivered a veiled threat, suggesting that some senators might otherwise refuse to take the oath if they felt that the Senate had unconstitutionally prescribed it. Such an oath, if improper, might even allow the defendant to challenge the Senate's jurisdiction, as Marshall had pointed out.[42]

If Tazewell used this argument to protect procedure he spoke well; if he used it to protect Blount, he spoke brilliantly, warning Congress that its best chance of convicting the former senator lay in extending him ever greater procedural safeguards. He had not yet finished, however, going on to observe that if the House refused to agree to the statute then the Senate could always institute the oath by resolution. Here the Virginian committed an error, though, for in admitting that the Senate could prescribe an oath for itself without House approval in at least one instance, he gave his opponents ammunition. Ross immediately exclaimed that he would never share an admitted Senate power with the House. In a calmer fashion he cited several state impeachments in which the upper house had acted unilaterally.[43]

Tazewell quickly announced that he had not conceded the Senate to have the implied power; he stated that he had merely granted the premise *arguendo*.[44] By now, however, the Federalists had reached

---

[42]*Aurora*, 11 February 1798, p. 2, cols. 2-3.

[43]Ibid. cols. 3-4.

[44]The account of Tazewell's speech contained in the *Aurora*, a Republican newspaper, does not support Tazewell's denial; he clearly admitted the existence of an implied Senate oath power, or else he gave that impression to more than one person present.

the central issue. They refused to part with any power they saw as rightfully belonging to the Senate. Read reiterated his belief that the Sole Power Clause was final on this point, and that a Senate agreement to this effect would override the defendant's subsequent plea to jurisdiction. He also objected to Tazewell's insinuations that some senators might refuse to take an oath that the majority had approved. Such an attitude, he sneered, would be quite anti-republican. Read even threw the Constitution right back at Tazewell; the true unconstitutionality, he charged, would lie in the Senate's parting with a constitutionally granted power. If the House refused to pass the oath and the Senate then prescribed it by resolution, moreover, the senators might expose themselves to charges that they were trying to circumvent the Constitution. As Read finished Bloodworth rose to deny the existence of such a delegated power, Marshall denounced Ross's earlier use of state precedents, and half a dozen other senators joined in on both sides of the debate.[45]

Finally the Senate voted on a resolution to postpone further consideration of the oath question. To vote a postponement would be to delay impeachment proceedings by another day, and this action might also ward off the measure's passage altogether, perhaps necessitating a statutory institution of an oath. (The Federalists possessed roughly a two-to one majority in the Senate.) The vote was quite partisan, with only four cross-overs, one of whom, predictably, was Marshall. Postponement having failed, the chamber next voted on, and approved, the resolution itself. Although some Republicans— including Tazewell, surprisingly—finally sided with the Federalists, all of the six dissenting votes except Marshall's were those of Republicans. Then someone moved that the Senate bring a bill conforming to the resolution, which Tazewell had suggested earlier; but this time Tazewell himself objected, noting that the Marshall bill already contained such a provision. This new motion thus failed miserably, and the Federalists had won another round.[46]

꽃

---

[45]*Aurora*, 11 February 1798, p. 2, col. 4.
[46]Ibid. cols. 2-5; 7 *Annals of Cong.* 503 (1798).

Monday February 12 was the beginning of an eventful week in Congress. On that day the senators agreed to discuss Marshall's bill, which had lain dormant for weeks, two days hence. On Thursday came Griswold's attack upon Lyon. In the Senate a different sort of battle occurred. Just before the Marshall bill came up on the 14th, Jacob Read introduced a startling document:

> *Resolved*, That the duty or trust imposed by the Constitution of the United States, on a Senator of the United States, is not of such a nature as to render a Senator impeachable, or subject to any examination or trial for crimes or offenses alleged to have been committed against the laws and peace of the United States, other than any citizen of the United States not a member of either House of Congress, and not having any office under the said States.[47]

This resolution, its wording tying in to the various phrases found in the articles of impeachment, would clearly work to bar any continuation of the proceedings against Blount. Whether Blount's escape was Read's object is somewhat questionable. The vehemence with which Read debated the provision on oaths bespeaks an interest in the process that he might not have possessed had he been trying simply to end the proceedings against Blount. A fear that the House might frustrate the impeachment process by refusing to help prescribe an oath by statute may also have been driving him. If this is the case, then the best explanation for his introduction of the resolution is that in protecting Blount, he protected himself and all other senators as well from the reach of impeachment and a popularly elected House. On the other hand, if he wished merely to end the Blount impeachment as quickly as possible, then this resolution was a good way to do it. One may reconcile his position in the oath debate with this stance by realizing that waiting for the passage of a statute prescribing oaths might well take longer than a unilateral adoption of an oath by Senate resolution.

The other senators, surprisingly, showed little enthusiasm for the

---

[47]7 *Annals of Cong.* 1034, 505-06 (1798); U.S., Congress, Senate, *Resolved, that the Duty or Trust Imposed by the Constitution* . . . (Philadelphia: John Fenno, 1798) [Evans 48715].

measure at first, taking no immediate action. Instead they voted to discharge the three-man committee on the mode of proceedings that they had commissioned on January 30. This left Marshall's committee and the second committee on the mode of proceedings still theoretically in existence, although after delivering the oath resolution the latter was never again to report. The Senate then turned its attention to Marshall's bill.[48]

First the senators discussed a proposed amendment to the bill that would require the House to use managers. Federalists argued, to their credit and consistently with their oath arguments, that the lower house was free to decide for itself what procedures to follow. Marshall, on the other hand, told the senators to give the House the chance to speak for itself on this provision. His was a voice in the wilderness as the Senate struck the amendment.[49]

Next came a proposal to grant a subpoena power to the lower house. Predictably, the debate followed the same lines that had appeared in the oath controversy. Federalists argued that the Constitution already gave this power to the House and that enabling legislation would be redundant. One senator, Bingham of Pennsylvania, even explicitly stated that the Senate had decided in the oath debate that each house should act independently. Marshall and others, including some Federalists, argued that the law was necessary to demonstrate clearly that federal marshals executing House process were acting legally. Again the pro-procedure faction lost. Things appeared to be settling into a regular routine.[50]

Then came Henry Tazewell's bombshell.

For several weeks some members of Congress had been mentioning, informally, the possibility that the Sixth Amendment requirement of a jury trial in criminal prosecutions extended to impeachment trials. Jefferson had mentioned the issue in a private letter to Madison as early as mid-January. Many senators were probably acquainted with the subject; Jefferson had even ventured to give Madison an estimate of Senate support for the use of juries. What the senators probably did not know, however, was that Jefferson had

---

[48]7 *Annals of Cong.* 506 (1798).

[49]*Aurora*, 16 February 1798, p. 2, col. 2 (the paper mistakenly lists this debate as taking place on February 1).

[50]Ibid. cols. 2-3.

devoted an evening to researching the question, and had then secretly transmitted the results (complete with a long list of citations) to Tazewell. The great English commentators Blackstone and Richard Wooddeson, Jefferson told his fellow Virginian, held impeachment to be a criminal prosecution. This fact, together with the Constitution's phrase "high Crimes and Misdemeanors," was more than enough to convince the vice-president that the Constitution required a jury in the Blount impeachment.[51]

Now Tazewell formally introduced the issue, during a discussion of a Marshall bill provision that dealt not with the Senate but instead with the House's presentation of its case. The result his motion produced was a combination of amazement and contempt. Jacob Read, who seemed to be leading the Federalist assault on procedure, demanded sarcastically that Tazewell elaborate upon his "extraordinary proposition." He insisted that he wished to hear all that Tazewell could say to prove that "such a monster" as a jury of twelve and a court of thirty-two (the latter referring to the senators) belonged within the Senate's walls. Bloodworth sprang to Tazewell's defense, retorting that perhaps not everyone was as anxious as Read to dismiss the issue without mature deliberation. Then Elijah Paine reiterated Read's comments, daring Tazewell to prove the need for a jury. After this posturing, the Senate decided to delay debate on the motion for two days.[52] On the 15th Tazewell again brought up his proposal, and the Senate addressed for the first time an issue that has undergone debate in scholarly circles ever since—the issue of whether

---

[51]Thomas Jefferson to James Madison, 24 January 1798, Reel 6, *Madison Papers* (Film); 7 Ford, *Writings of Jefferson* 191-95; Thomas Jefferson to Henry Tazewell, 27 January 1798, 102 (Reel 34) *Jefferson Papers* (Film); U.S. Const. art. II, § 4. Jefferson clearly wished to appear nonpartisan in the affair, as befitted a man in his position; his correspondence regarding impeachment also includes a letter to Livermore, a member of the Marshall bill committee, in which he recommended that the committee use Jefferson's impeachment notes, as found in his Parliamentary Pocket-book, as a guide. Thomas Jefferson to Judge Livermore, 28 January 1798, 102 (Reel 34) *Jefferson Papers* (Film) (actual date is probably January 29, and the listed recipient is incorrect); Wilbur Samuel Howell, ed., *Jefferson's Parliamentary Writings: "Parliamentary Pocket-Book" and A Manual of Parliamentary Practice* (Princeton: Princeton University Press, 1988) 12, 153-56, 419, 422-26.

[52]*Aurora*, 16 February 1798, p. 2, col. 3.

impeachment is a criminal process.[53]

Tazewell was the first of several men to speak that day, and he was well-equipped for battle. At the outset he discounted the validity of both English and state precedent, and then he decried the passions that drove men, by whom he obviously meant the Federalists, to increase rather than restrain their power. Having made those preliminary observations, Tazewell proceeded to deliver a long argument that marks him as perhaps the most innovative and logical rhetorician to be involved in Blount's case.

The original Constitution, Tazewell observed, contained two phrases that were on point. These were the Senate's Sole Power Clause and the passage in Article III, Section 2 that required a jury in the trials of all crimes except in impeachment cases. Under the unamended Constitution, Tazewell conceded, the impeachment process did not require the use of juries. And yet, he continued, the Sixth Amendment stipulated that all criminal trials involve juries; that new clause made no express exception for impeachment, as had Article III. Therefore the entire issue rested on two questions: 1) was impeachment a criminal prosecution and 2) if so, did the Sixth Amendment abrogate the Article III provision?[54]

Tazewell turned first to the question of impeachment's criminal nature. Appealing to three standards—constitutional usage, English history, and analogy—Tazewell recited argument after argument to

---

[53]Although the jury issue never re-emerged in the Senate after 1798, the closely-related broader questions of impeachment's criminal nature and the applicability of Bill of Rights criminal procedure guaranties remained as major issues through the impeachments and related litigation in the 1980s and early 1990s. See, e.g., Wrisley Brown, "The Impeachment of the Federal Judiciary." 26 *Harv. L. Rev.* 684 (1913); Dwight, "Trial by Impeachment;" George H. Ethridge, "The Law of Impeachment," 8 *Miss. L.J.* 283 (1936); Philip B. Kurland, "Watergate, Impeachment, and the Constitution," 45 *Miss. L.J.* 531 (1974); Lawrence, "Law of Impeachment;" *Hastings v. United States Senate*, No. 89-1602 (D.D.C. June 1, 1989) (Complaint for Declaratory and Injunctive Relief) 28-29, 38-39.

[54]*Universal Gazette*, 1 March 1798, p. 4, col. 1. Throughout the Blount impeachment all parties referred to the present-day Sixth Amendment as the Eighth Amendment. This is so because in September 1789 Congress submitted twelve articles to the states, two of which failed to win enough support for ratification. The current Sixth Amendment was originally eighth in the list. Alfred H. Kelly et al., *The American Constitution: Its Origins and Development*, 6th ed. (New York: W.W. Norton & Company, Inc., 1983) 122; 1 *Annals of Cong.* 948 (J. Gales ed. 1789).

prove that impeachment was a criminal prosecution. Discussing constitutional terminology, the senator stressed phrases such as "high Crimes and Misdemeanors" and the express exception of impeachments from the Article III provision respecting criminal trials. This exception, he stated forcefully, revealed that the framers considered it to be criminal, for otherwise an exception would have been unnecessary. Turning to English law, which in light of his earlier statements he now introduced as persuasive and not controlling authority, he reeled off a string of citations from Blackstone and Wooddeson that must have made Jefferson smile with satisfaction. Then Tazewell turned to analogy, attempting to show that impeachment bore a number of similarities to indictment. Each process, Tazewell maintained, had as its object the punishment of a defendant; often both processes would reach the same sorts of offenses. An impeachment tried before a regular court would possess every essential element of an indictment. Because impeachments and indictments were procedurally indistinguishable, the senator concluded, the former must be criminal in nature, for the place of trial had no effect upon that nature. Finally Tazewell discounted the possibility that impeachment was *sui generis*, a one-of-a-kind procedure. Only two types of process existed, he claimed; these were the civil and the criminal. Impeachment was clearly not civil; and if it were *sui generis*, he continued, then it was a dangerous device, not subject to any legal control. (This sentiment lay at the heart of Republican objections to the Federalist program.) He expressed a strong hope that the Senate "would not this day create such a monster, but confine impeachments to that class of prosecutions which alone could restain [*sic*] its ferocity."[55]

Tazewell then moved on to the second major question and endeavored to show that the Sixth Amendment clause modified the original Constitution and extended the jury trial requirement to all criminal prosecutions including impeachment. Tazewell's primary attack consisted of an analysis of both the Constitution's language and the framers' intent. In the first place, he observed, the Sixth Amendment contained no impeachment exception. This alone would seem to overrule the original Article III provision, but Tazewell went

---

[55]*Universal Gazette*, 1 March 1798, p. 4, col. 1. The context of this last sentence clearly indicates the proper reading to be "restrain."

further. He argued that besides the impeachment exception, no difference existed between the two clauses. A fundamental maxim of legal interpretation, Tazewell reminded his audience, was that no clause of a document should be considered meaningless, and if the Sixth Amendment had not modified the original clause so as to extend juries to impeachments, it served no purpose at all.

Turning to the drafters' intent, Tazewell noted that the Sixth Amendment provision, as James Madison first proposed it, did contain the impeachment exception, but that a Senate committee had subsequently removed that exception. Tazewell urged that this deletion of an express exception constituted a denial of an exception, and that impeachments therefore required juries. Tazewell then reminded the Senate of the case of Jay's Treaty, in which the House of Representatives, attempting to involve itself in treaty concerns, sought papers on Jay's negotiations from Washington's administration. Some senators now opposing Tazewell's motion had opposed the House on that occasion, Tazewell observed. But in that instance Washington had noted that the framers in 1787 had first approved, and then deleted, a constitutional clause that would have given the House a role in the treaty process. Washington interpreted this deletion to mean that the House did not have the power, and he thus refused to comply with the representatives' request. Tazewell's message was obvious. The Federalist senators who approved Washington's actions in 1796 should now, in the name of consistency, adhere to the rule of construction that Washington had then invoked.[56]

The Virginia senator then moved on to argue from more general principles, such as the need to guarantee impartiality. A jury, he proclaimed, was "the best shield against judicial oppression," and an impeachment defendant, with his reputation and office at stake, should have the benefit of such protection.[57]

Tazewell then answered some arguments that apparently had been circulating lately. He distinguished state practice from federal

---

[56]*Universal Gazette*, 1 March 1798, p. 4, col. 2; see Miller, *Federalist Era* 171-74; Elkins & McKitrick, *Age of Federalism* 440-46; David P. Currie, *The Constitution in Congress: The Federalist Period 1789-1801* (Chicago: The University of Chicago Press, 1997) 211-17.

[57]*Universal Gazette*, 1 March 1798, p. 4, col. 3.

impeachment, and then he dismissed as insufficient the suggestion that the use of a jury would prove inconvenient. Ruling authorities, he said, would always find inconvenient the sharing of their power with other groups. Inconvenience was not a bar to the exercise of a right.[58]

As Tazewell concluded his harangue, a number of Republicans immediately requested a postponement in order to consider the senator's arguments. This motion itself blossomed into a major issue; all Republicans who spoke, together with Marshall, either sought a postponement, or demanded a Federalist answer to Tazewell's speech, or both. The Federalists were torn. Though all of them who spoke claimed to have made up their minds, some wished to have an opportunity to respond. Read was not one of the latter. He belligerently remarked that when Tazewell first brought up the jury issue, he, Read, had "really tho't it was for merriment." When he had realized that Tazewell was sincere, he had listened but had heard nothing to make him change his mind.

Despite Read's outburst, those senators who desired to allow time for a rebuttal prevailed. For these men the need for a reply seemed a matter of honor. At least two of them denied Republican charges that the Federalists had already secretly agreed to defeat Tazewell's motion. After the debate on postponement had run for some time, James Ross, followed by Richard Stockton, rose to reply to Tazewell. The fact that either of them could prepare an answer so quickly is suspicious. Each speech, moreover, seems well thought out. The Federalists, their denials notwithstanding, probably did decide beforehand at least to prepare answers to Tazewell's argument.[59]

In his own presentation Ross did almost exactly what Tazewell had counseled the Senate to avoid. He distinguished impeachment from regular civil and criminal processes, declaring it to be a unique instrument. Ross delineated various types of Anglo-American legal proceeding. He mentioned trials at common law, trials in chancery, and trials in admiralty. To these he added trials by impeachment. All of these, he stated, were substantively and procedurally different from each other. Impeachment, then, was by no means the only example of a process other than a civil or criminal common law proceeding.

---

[58]Ibid.

[59]Ibid; *Aurora*, 20 February 1798, p. 3, col. 1; U.S. Const. art. I, § 3, cl. 6.

Impeachment was not a criminal prosecution, but instead a trial of a government officer for breach of duty.

Ross then asked the Senate to consider the result if an impeachment jury voted to acquit a defendant but two-thirds of the Senate then voted for a conviction. Not pausing to dwell on this point he noted that impeachment defendants were liable to criminal prosecution in the regular courts in addition to undergoing the impeachment process. This fact alone indicated impeachment to be something other than a criminal action. Tazewell's motion, Ross concluded, would also violate the Senate Sole Power Clause, presumably by allowing a jury to supplant the Senate's role under this clause of determining the trial's outcome.[60]

Stockton's argument rested on different grounds. The Sixth Amendment respected judicial matters, he maintained. Impeachment was a legislative matter. In no way did the jury trial provision affect the Senate's sole power to try impeachments. To hold otherwise would be to permit an implied interpretation of the Sixth Amendment to override an express constitutional grant of power to the Senate. Stockton even cited the amendment's history in the First Congress to show that it related to regular judicial processes and not to impeachment.[61]

Now that Tazewell had heard these answers to his arguments, he wished to make a reply. Once again he asked for a postponement in order to compose a rebuttal. Read, still bellicose, announced that he was prepared to stay in the chamber until midnight if it meant that the Senate could finish the business that day. The South Carolinian's attitude notwithstanding, the Republicans managed to win a postponement until Monday the 19th.

On Monday the first man to speak in the next long round of discussion was Elijah Paine, a Federalist from Vermont. He, like his colleagues before him, emphasized the Senate's sole jurisdiction in impeachment trials; he categorized impeachments as a political rather than a criminal process; then he examined the impeachment provisions of half a dozen state constitutions to show how the citizens of these states viewed impeachments. Only in Tazewell's Virginia did the process possess an undeniable judicial character, and there the

---

[60]*Aurora*, 28 February 1798, p. 3, cols. 2-3; U.S. Const. art. I, § 3, cl. 6.

[61]*Aurora*, 28 February 1798, p. 2, col. 3.

state constitution expressly vested impeachment jurisdiction in the regular court system. Nowhere in state practice, declared Paine, had juries ever found their way into impeachment trials.[62]

Then Read rose yet again, but he confined his comments to restatements of the anti-jury position and further observations about the disgraceful nature of the entire issue. Tazewell followed Read in order to present his rebuttal. First he attacked Ross's conclusion that impeachment must not be criminal because of regular courts' concurrent jurisdiction. Tazewell drew exactly the opposite conclusion from the clause in question; because a civil action could never bar a subsequent criminal proceeding, the framers would have had no need to approve concurrent jurisdiction expressly in Article I, Section 3 unless they held impeachment to be criminal. Having thus tried once again to demonstrate impeachment's criminal nature, Tazewell returned to the second question of whether the Sixth Amendment modified the original jury trial provision.[63]

The Virginian made a reference to the broad construction approach that Ross and others had taken regarding the Senate's implied power to make oaths by resolution. In that case, he said accusingly, the Federalists had not objected to overriding the Senate's express power of legislation with an implied reading of the Sole Power Clause.[64] And yet, Tazewell continued, these same senators now denied that the Sixth Amendment could likewise implicitly overrule the express Article III provision. The rule, Tazewell commented, appeared to be that implied readings were acceptable only when they served to increase the Senate's power.

At any rate, the Virginian continued, implied constructions were unnecessary. The Sixth Amendment explicitly required the use of juries in all criminal prosecutions, and surely impeachment was such a process. Tazewell, answering Stockton's assertions, even reconciled the Sixth Amendment with the Sole Power Clause. The latter was a grant of jurisdiction, he explained, and though a chancery court may have exclusive jurisdiction in equity cases, and admiralty courts in admiralty cases, the Senate has exclusive jurisdiction in impeachment.

---

[62]*Universal Gazette*, 29 March 1798, p. 4, col. 1; Va. Const. of 1776, *in* 10 Swindler, *Sources* 55.

[63]*Universal Gazette*, 29 March 1798, p. 4, col. 2.

[64]*See* pp. 164-69, *supra*.

But, warned Tazewell, chancery and admiralty courts both used juries. Under this reading the two clauses did not conflict at all, and the true nature of the Sole Power Clause stood revealed.[65]

Tazewell then proceeded to answer more objections that Ross, Paine, and Stockton had raised. He challenged Stockton's interpretation of the First Congress debates, and he argued that he would not object to the extension of other Bill of Rights guaranties to impeachment as well. He attacked Paine's citation of some state precedents. Finally he tried with only partial success to deal with the danger of a conflict between juries and senators, of which Ross had warned. A jury vote of conviction, Tazewell argued, was alone never sufficient to convict a defendant unless the court agreed; hence the use of a jury would not abrogate the clause requiring a vote of two-thirds of the Senate in order to punish the party on trial. This argument, however, failed to address the hypothetical problem that Ross had posed of a jury that voted for acquittal and a Senate that voted for conviction.[66]

At long last Tazewell concluded by saying that he had simply attempted to show why he thought the use of a jury to be necessary, and that the Senate was the body to decide whether he had done so effectively. In fact his analysis was for the most part excellent. His arguments, moreover, had elicited Federalist responses that were often equally impressive. Now the time for decision had come. The matter upon which the Senate was about to rule was not just the jury issue but the broad question of whether constitutional criminal procedure applied perforce to the impeachment process. The precedent that it set, while not irreversible, would carry great weight.

The vote was not even close.

The defeat of the Virginian's motion was no mere partisan

---

[65]*Universal Gazette*, 29 March 1798, p. 4, cols. 3-4 One must take Tazewell's statement about juries in chancery and admiralty courts with a grain of salt. Generally, of course, neither type of court used a jury, and the question had been a subject of discussion during the ratification debates. *See* 1 Holdsworth, *A History of English Law* 550; Peter Charles Hoffer, *The Law's Conscience: Equitable Constitutionalism in America* (Chapel Hill: University of North Carolina Press, 1990) 96, 250 & nn.45-47; John Phillip Reid, *Constitutional History of the American Revolution: The Authority of Rights* (Madison: The University of Wisconsin Press, 1986) 52-55.

[66]*Universal Gazette*, 29 March 1798, p. 4, cols. 4-5.

decision, for Tazewell's all along had been almost the only voice to speak in support of the jury concept. Even when Republicans had defended him, they were defending not so much his position as his right to speak. Of the twenty-nine senators present, only Tazewell, the other Virginia senator Stevens T. Mason, and Blount's protégé Andrew Jackson voted in favor of the measure.[67] One can perhaps argue that the votes of Tazewell and Mason, together with their fellow Virginia citizen Thomas Jefferson's original suggestion of the need for a jury, sprang at least partly from the fairly clear judicial nature of impeachment in that commonwealth. Tazewell, moreover, had served in Virginia's constitutional convention, and this may well have strengthened the provision's influence on his thought. On the other hand, Jefferson's position may have reflected the unpleasant experience he had had as Virginia's governor in 1781 when his actions became the subject of a legislative investigation. Certainly his attempt to pin down the procedural requirements of impeachment, thus restricting partisan influences, in his *Manual of Parliamentary Practice* during the days of the Blount proceedings suggests as much; what he wrote there also reflected, perhaps, his reactions to what he saw of the Blount impeachment. Jackson's vote, moreover, was clearly partisan. He had long been a supporter of Blount, and during his short time in the Senate he consistently voted in Blount's favor. Other than these exceptions, the Senate showed as much unanimity in this decision as it had at any other time during the Blount proceedings. If politics played a role, it was an exceedingly small one.[68]

The vote's outcome could have rested on a failure in either of Tazewell's two arguments. Either the senators felt that impeachment was not a criminal process, or they felt that it was a criminal process but that the Sixth Amendment provision did not nullify the Article III clause. If the outcome rested on the latter grounds, then it said nothing about other criminal provisions in the Bill of Rights; if it rested on the former reason, then it was far broader in its rami-

---

[67]7 *Annals of Cong.* 508 (1798).

[68]Hoffer & Hull, *Impeachment* 71-73, 85-86; Dumas Malone, *Jefferson the Virginian* (Boston: Little, Brown and Company, 1948) 361-66; Malone, *Ordeal of Liberty* 317-18; Howell, *Jefferson's Parliamentary Writings* 153-57, 419-26; Appendix 3, *infra*; *supra* note 62.

fications, potentially applying to the other criminal clauses as well. The Senate expressed no formal reason, of course, for its decision. But most of the arguments that Tazewell's opponents had made went to the broader issue. The question of impeachment's criminal nature, additionally, was a much more basic and complex issue in both theoretical and practical terms than the second concern. The question of the Sixth Amendment's meaning was a relatively simple and common matter, an exercise in principles of construction. Surely the outpouring of strong feelings came about because of a deeper dispute than a conflict in generally-accepted theories of interpretation, for Tazewell introduced no radical new maxims of construction. Both the senators' comments, then, and their clear attitudes, indicate that their defeat of Tazewell's motion constituted a decision that impeachment was not a criminal process.

⁊❦

The day after Tazewell submitted his jury proposal, Jefferson gloomily observed that the two-to-one Federalist majority would make short work of the measure. In fact the vice-president overestimated his party's support for the motion, as the final vote revealed. The heavy preponderance of opinion against the use of a jury no doubt bothered Jefferson, who saw impeachments thus unchecked as instruments "more of passion than justice." Shortly after the final vote Jefferson wrote to Madison to tell him of the outcome and that Federalist support for a completely unchecked impeachment power was growing, Read's motion notwithstanding. Jefferson probably felt surprise as well as disappointment when Madison, the original author of the Sixth Amendment, answered that Tazewell's jury arguments had failed to convince him. "My impression," he told the vice-president, "has always been that impeachments were somewhat sui generis, and excluded the use of Juries."[69]

While Jefferson unburdened himself to Madison, Andrew Jackson was venting his anger to Willie Blount. The majority, Jackson wrote

---

[69]7 Ford, *Writings of Jefferson* 202-03, 207; James Madison to Thomas Jefferson, 4 March 1798, Reel 6, *Madison Papers* (Film).

furiously, had decided that the Senate was not to be bound by laws, but that it instead would make its own impeachment rules. But though the "Solomons" had spoken, Jackson continued, he himself doubted that the Senate could make its own laws in this fashion, in violation of due process. Despite the brash young senator's feelings on the issue, however, the chamber had made its decision, and it was now moving on to other impeachment issues.[70]

The Senate resumed its attack on procedure on February 20, to the Republicans' consternation, resuming its discussion of the Marshall bill. Republicans made further futile efforts to amend the document, most of the changes being relatively minor. Interestingly enough, Marshall and several leading Republicans attempted to attach one clause to the bill that would have expressly permitted a trial in Blount's absence, but only if government officers had first given him actual or constructive notice of the trial beforehand. In the end Marshall and his faction not only failed to win these concessions; they failed to win passage of the bill as well, the Senate refusing to give it a third reading. Thus the Marshall bill, the source of so much debate on procedure, died on the 20th.[71] In refusing to pass the provision that would have given Blount the statutory right to counsel, not to mention the right to subpoena witnesses, the Senate had dealt another severe blow to the theory that impeachment was a criminal process to which Bill of Rights guaranties attached. One could argue that the Senate saw no need to extend these guaranties to Blount by statute since the Bill of Rights also provided them, but in light of the fate of Tazewell's jury gambit, the opposite inference is the better.

The Republicans, though, still had a slim chance to influence the development of impeachment procedure. Even as the jury debate raged, Samuel Livermore had moved that the Senate appoint a new committee to consider what actions the chamber should take specifically concerning the articles of impeachment. On the 20th the

---

[70]Andrew Jackson to Willie Blount, 21 February 1798, William Blount Papers, Library of Congress.

[71]7 *Annals of Cong.* 508-09 (1798); U.S. Congress, Senate, *A Bill Regulating Certain Procedures in Cases of Impeachment* (Philadelphia: John Fenno, 1798) [Evans 48698] 1-2; U.S. Congress, Senate, Committee to Whom was Referred the Bill Regulating Certain Proceedings in Cases of Impeachment, *Report of Amendments* (Philadelphia: John Fenno, 1798[?]) [Evans 48660].

senators agreed, appointing Livermore, Ross, and Stockton to the committee. The following day the Senate referred Read's motion on senatorial amenability to impeachment to this committee. The Republicans would have an opportunity to debate any measures that this new committee reported when those measures reached the floor; but the committee itself, composed of all Federalists, would seem to be an agency to iron out policy differences within the majority party.

By late February these differences were growing more pronounced. While penning a letter to Madison, Jefferson remarked that the Federalist view was that the Senate must remain independent of popular passions. To this end the Read resolution would certainly contribute. On the other hand, the day before the new committee's appointment, Jefferson had heard someone declare that not only civil officers, but all citizens of the country, were subject to impeachment. Jefferson noted the existence of considerable Federalist support of this concept, which only fueled his fears of the power's abuse. Theories of an unchecked impeachment power also circulated among the public, a fact that could only have agitated the Republicans further.[72]

To the Federalists, who clearly controlled Congress at this point, the dilemma was obvious. In adopting Read's view that senators were not subject to impeachment, they could protect the Senate from House attacks in the future. This was an attractive prospect, for the partisan division in the popularly-elected lower house was much closer than in the Senate. On the other hand, Federalists still controlled both branches of Congress, and in the Senate they probably possessed a two-thirds majority, which would suffice for impeachment convictions. Just possibly the Federalists, by adopting a very broad construction of the doctrine, could do what Jefferson feared most and turn impeachment into an unchecked partisan tool from which not even private citizens would be safe. Were this construction to prevail, and if impeachments lay for political as well as indictable offenses, then the process could well become a means for conducting state trials of politically unpopular citizens. The problem, of course, was that a universal impeachment power, as Jefferson called it, might well be incompatible with Read's proposed senatorial

---

[72]7 Ford, *Writings of Jefferson* 207-08; *North Carolina Gazette*, 24 February 1798, p. 2, cols. 1-2.

exemption. The Federalists, then, had to decide which course to adopt, and Livermore's new committee seemed to be an instrumental part of the decision process.

On February 22 the committee recommended that the Senate set aside a day to discuss on the floor the issue of a senator's amenability to impeachment. The committee's report contained an elaborate adversarial process for the debate, which would include the House managers and Blount or his counsel if any of these wished to participate. Besides dealing with Read's resolution the report also detailed a procedure for issuing a writ of summons for Blount. The committee recommended that the summons travel via special messenger to Blount's residence in Knoxville.[73]

The next day the Senate debated and recommitted the measure. On the 27th Livermore made a partial, modified report. No record of this document exists, but from the form of a subsequently-adopted measure we may assume that all traces of the Read resolution and the plan for an adversarial debate had disappeared. On March 1 the Senate, after amending the partial report, adopted it. In doing so the senators agreed to a form for the summons, and to the date that it, and Blount, should return to the Senate for trial: Monday, December 17, 1798. James Mathers, the chamber's doorkeeper and sergeant-at-arms, was to deliver the writ to Blount.[74]

Read's proposal to bar impeachments of senators failed to resurface in the final version of Livermore's report. Records of floor debates on the report's adoption have not come to light; the views of individuals and factions on the issue remain unknown. No group, though, won a victory in killing the resolution, for the whole question would arise again before the Blount affair concluded. For now, however, the Senate had spent its energy. With the adoption of the Livermore committee report on March 1, the long parade of impeachment procedure debates ended for the session.

ɕ

---

[73] *7 Annals of Cong.* 511 (1798); U.S., Congress, Senate, *Report of the Committee Appointed to Report the Proper Measures . . . William Blount . . .* (Philadelphia: W. Ross, 1798) [Evans 48714] 3, 6.

[74] *7 Annals of Cong.* 511-14 (1798); 8 Ibid., 2245.

Before Congress finished, at least for the moment, with the Blount affair, it had to deal with a few loose ends. One, seemingly mundane, was a question respecting the examination of witnesses. In late February 1798, Representative John Wilkes Kittera had remarked on the inconvenience that the House and some of its committees had experienced the previous session while examining witnesses before them; specifically, the problem was that of who had authority to administer oaths to these persons. Quite possibly he had the impeachment investigation committee in mind, though he had not been one of its members. At any rate, and perhaps concerned with not only the past session but the next one, which would see Blount's trial in the Senate, he proposed that the House look into the issue, which it did. Within a few months, Congress had approved a statute empowering the President of the Senate (though not the President *pro tempore*), the Speaker of the House, and the chairmen of the Committee of the Whole and all select committees to administer oaths and affirmations to witnesses under examination. The statute also subjected such witnesses to criminal sanctions in the event of perjury. These statutory provisions, perhaps the first relating to the congressional investigatory power, remain in force today in modified versions, the perjury provision especially becoming one of the building blocks for the growth of that power.[75] Debate on this statute twice occurred just before some aspect of the Blount impeachment came up for discussion, suggesting a relationship between the two.[76]

Something similar happened with Congress's consideration of a bill organizing what remained of federal territory below the Ohio after the admission of Tennessee into the Union. Shortly after discussing this bill, which would later that year organize this region into the Mississippi Territory, the Senate turned its attention to the Blount affair. The conspiracy had given Congress, and the nation, a glimpse of what was happening, and what might yet happen, in the land beyond the mountains. Now that Spain had withdrawn its claims to the region, a strengthening of the ties between Philadelphia and the Southwest by establishing a new territorial government perhaps

---

[75]7 Ibid., 537, 539, 544, 546, 1069 (1798); 8 Ibid., 1371, 1376, 1380, 1560 (1998); Act of May 3, 1798, ch. 36, §§ 1-2, 1 Stat. 554 (1798) (current versions at 2 U.S.C. §§ 191-92 [1994]).

[76]7 *Annals of Cong.* 537 (1798); 8 Ibid., 1376 (1798).

seemed a useful countermeasure for preventing, or at least discouraging, other intrigues.[77]

On March 2 the House received a Senate message informing it of the writ's December return day. Samuel Sitgreaves now came to fear that the trial would outlast the Fifth Congress, which would adjourn in March 1799, and he moved that the House instruct the managers to request that the Senate name an earlier day to begin. Sitgreaves probably harbored a belief that an impeachment voted in one Congress would be invalid in the next, or perhaps he feared that a change in the Senate's composition might make a conviction more difficult. Several representatives agreed with Sitgreaves's suggestion, and now for a time the House began to discuss the possibility of itself introducing an impeachment law designed to prevent the Senate from frustrating a House impeachment. The representatives complied with Sitgreaves's request, but thereafter no further mention of an impeachment bill appears, and indeed the subject of an earlier return day itself lay dormant for over a month.[78]

Why the House Federalists, after first apparently wishing that the Blount business would go away, changed their minds and pushed for a faster resolution of the affair is unclear. Perhaps by this point they were resigned to the fact that the impeachment was going to go forward, and they wished to move this political embarrassment along as quickly as possible, the better to remove it from the public eye. On the other hand, perhaps the potential of an unlimited impeachment power, which would tempt them in the coming months, had already begun to dawn upon them. If this is so, then the sooner that Blount came to trial, the sooner the Federalists could test and then wield this new weapon. Possibly they were feeling a mixture of the two sentiments in the spring of 1798.

Whatever the Federalist agenda, as the House waited to hear from the Senate regarding its request for an earlier return day for the writ, Senate strict-constructionists made a last effort to establish some checks on the impeachment process as well as upon the budding investigatory power. On March 12, the chamber discussed an

---

[77]7 Ibid., 511, 515, 532-33 (1798); 8 Ibid., 1249, 1277-84, 1296, 1298, 1313, 1318; Act of April 7, 1798, ch. 28, §§ 3-4, 6-8, 1 Stat. 549, 549-50 (1798).

[78]7 *Annals of Cong.* at 1143-45 (1798); *Massachusetts Mercury*, 13 March 1798, p. 2, col. 1.

appropriations bill that included a provision to set aside over twenty-six hundred dollars to cover the expenses of the House committee that had investigated the conspiracy the previous summer and fall. Joseph Anderson of Tennessee moved to strike the provision, an obvious attempt to discourage the formation of such committees in the future. No committee, exclaimed Anderson, could sit during a recess unless Congress authorized the action by law. Federalist Uriah Tracy sided with Anderson, in a move reminiscent of the opinions of Marshall and Read. Tracy warned that at this rate the House might soon be sending committees to Europe to make treaties—a clear reference to the House's earlier attempt to interfere in the Jay Treaty negotiations. Ultimately, said Tracy, the House might convene as the Committee of the Whole and sit while Congress was nominally in recess. Anderson's motion failed by a large margin, in a mixed vote. Tracy and Hillhouse, in addition to Marshall, sided with Anderson; Tazewell voted with the majority in voting to approve the appropriation, and three other Republicans joined him.[79]

On April 6 the question of the summons arose again in the House. Sitgreaves proposed that a Senate/House conference committee meet to decide on a new return day for the writ. The House agreed to a conference, as did the Senate, but Sitgreaves was to be disappointed. During the week of April 9 the managers met with Livermore and Ross, who refused to change the return date. The current session, they pointed out to the representatives, would probably not last long enough to allow Mathers and Blount to return in time for a spring trial. Congress's only option was thus to begin the process early in the third session. The managers had no choice but to agree.[80]

❧

By April 1798, international tensions, particularly between the United States and France, were rising. Congress consequently turned away from domestic and frontier concerns and looked eastward to the Atlantic and Europe. The long winter debate over the Blount affair,

---

[79] 7 *Annals of Cong.* 520-21 (1798); Thomas Jefferson, notes, beginning 26 December 1797, 102 (Reel 34) *Jefferson Papers* (Film); Act of March 19, 1798, ch. 18, § 1, 1 Stat. 542, 544 (1798).

[80] 7 *Annals of Cong.* 537, 541 (1798); 8 Ibid., 1376-77, 1412-13, 1426.

so diverting in the absence of more important business, had provided excellent opportunities for partisan intrigue. But as America's envoys to France reported their reception by the notorious agents X, Y, and Z, Congress and the nation suddenly found themselves facing matters of far graver concern.[81] In April, then, for the first time since it had come to light, the Blount affair became an issue of secondary importance. By this time, though, Congress had taken several decisive steps with regard to both Blount and impeachment. A few of these developments are particularly prominent.

The first important turn was in the House of Representatives, where Federalist desires to make an example of Blount cooled markedly after the impeachment committee's revelations. Although impeachment may seem to have many things in common with a judicial proceeding, this partisan reversal in December 1797 and January 1798 reveals the practical difficulty of separating impeachment from politics.

An issue of much greater importance arose in the Senate. In general terms this was the question of how far Senate power extended over impeachment procedure. By repeatedly voting down efforts to circumscribe the Senate's free hand in conducting the impeachment, the Federalist majority revealed a determination to retain all discretionary authority in the upper house. These senators found the concept of limitations imposed by the lower house to be unacceptable. Few Federalist senators cared to admit even the existence of constitutional limitations. While not adhering to demonstrably unconstitutional views, most Federalists did adopt very broad interpretations of Senate impeachment power, justifying all by frequent recourse to the Sole Power Clause.

A modern critic might respond to this pattern of Senate voting by observing that even if the partisan votes serve as precedent, the Senate is free to reverse itself at any time. Such an argument is not without merit. But the single most crucial vote, which followed the most protracted debate, was the vote on Tazewell's motion to use juries. This vote did not go along party lines. Instead almost every senator voted against it. Some of these senators had been present in the 1787 Convention, and others had sat in the Congress that framed

---

[81]7 Ibid., 535-36, 1373-80; *Claypoole's American Daily Advertiser*, 10 April 1798, 1-4.

the Bill of Rights. This group of men was in an excellent position to know the meaning behind the constitutional phrases at issue. Almost all of them decided that the Sixth Amendment Jury Trial Clause did not apply to impeachments. At the very least the outcome of the jury debate creates a considerable presumption that impeachment is not a process to which constitutional standards of regular criminal procedure apply. This presumption is all the greater in light of the Senate's subsequent defeat of Marshall's bill, which would have expressly extended key Sixth Amendment rights to the impeachment process.

The third issue of major importance to arise in early 1798 was the dispute over what individuals were subject to impeachment. During the second session this issue was mainly of concern to the Federalists. Possessing as they did a majority in both houses, but wary of the possibility that they might suffer losses in the lower chamber, the Federalists—or at least their numbers in the Senate—had to decide whether to forge a broad impeachment power that might someday prove to be double-edged, or whether instead to blunt the sword, denying themselves a partisan weapon while depriving their opponents of it as well. Whatever their decision, a future Congress could probably reverse it; but even the Federalists revealed, in their statements in Congress, a respect for precedent that made them hesitant to decide matters arbitrarily. In early 1798 the Federalist Party was not particularly popular, and the majority senators perhaps wished to avoid taking a stance that might arouse the indignation of voters, especially in an election year that might see the rise of a Republican majority in the House of Representatives. In the end, the Federalists skirted the issue, at least until the following session.

In mid-July 1798, more than a year after Blount's conspiracy first became public knowledge, the Fifth Congress adjourned its second session. The Senate had issued a command for Blount to appear in December. Until then the country could do nothing but await both the Tennesseean's return to Philadelphia and the steady, ominous approach of war with one of the world's most powerful nations.

Chapter 5

The Third Session: Resolution
August 1798-January 1799

❧

Jean Conrad Hottinguer, Pierre Bellamy, and Lucien Hauteval are names almost unknown to twentieth century Americans. Not a citizen in a million, one suspects, would be able to identify any of them if asked to do so. Even in earlier ages this ratio would probably have been about right, for these names never really came to the public's attention. Hottinguer, Bellamy, and Hauteval, when they strode briefly onto the stage of American politics in 1798, did so under the pseudonyms X, Y, and Z.[1]

Despite popular unfamiliarity with these men's identities, one hopes that some higher percentage of Americans have at least heard of the XYZ affair. The incident, after all, did help to bring about the famous, undeclared naval war between the United States and France. Other factors were involved as well, but the last straw was the episode involving these three relatively insignificant Europeans.[2]

In fact relations between the United States and France had been poor ever since 1794, when the Washington administration negotiated Jay's Treaty. While America and England grew closer, or at least averted an open breach, France stepped up her war with the island nation, seeking to strangle her maritime trade. The French did not limit their attacks to British shipping alone; in their eyes, the United States was acting in violation of its 1778 Treaty of Amity and Commerce with France, and they acted accordingly. On Christmas

---

[1]William Stinchcombe, *The XYZ Affair* (Westport, Connecticut: Greenwood Press, 1980) 4-5; Elkins & McKitrick, *Age of Federalism* 571-73.

[2]Elkins & McKitrick, *Age of Federalism* 549-79; Miller, *Federalist Era* 212-13; Stinchcombe, *XYZ Affair* 115-16.

Day 1796, a French privateer fired a broadside into the American merchant ship *Commerce*; early the following year an armed brig captured the *Cincinnatus*, the French crew torturing the American captain into the bargain. By 1797 the Directory did not care who suffered from its campaign, and the United States and its citizens, though technically neutral, were no exception. By 1798 French picaroons, sailing from West Indies ports, harassed American merchant shipping in United States coastal waters, where they captured large numbers of merchantmen. The economic cost to the United States was considerable.[3]

Violations of neutral shipping rights have often led the United States into war. The French crisis was to be the first such occasion. But John Adams's initial instinct, which the arch-Federalist Alexander Hamilton shared, was to negotiate a settlement. To this end the president chose Elbridge Gerry, John Marshall, and Charles Cotesworth Pinckney as envoys extraordinary to France, and sent them on their way with instructions to find a peaceful solution to the conflict. The notorious French Foreign Minister Talleyrand, however, was not disposed to make such a settlement, at least right away. Day after day, amid the turmoil of Republican Paris, the envoys sought in vain a meeting with the minister. Instead of receiving them, however, Talleyrand approached them unofficially through Hottinguer, Bellamy, and Hauteval, who suggested that the Americans arrange a considerable loan to the French government in order to procure an audience with him. This course the American delegation rejected, even as the gravity of the situation became clear and the emissaries threatened them with allusions to the "power and violence of France." Finally, in an exchange that the Americans reported in great detail to Philadelphia, Hottinguer grew most forthright.

> Said he, gentlemen, you do not speak to the point; it is money: it is expected that you will offer money. We said that we had spoken to that point very explicitly: we had given an answer. No, said he, you have not: what is your answer? We

---

[3]Miller, *Federalist Era* 205-07, 213-15; Stinchcombe, *XYZ Affair* 13, 14, 19, 32-46; Alexander DeConde, *The Quasi-War: The Politics and Diplomacy of the Undeclared War with France 1797-1801* (New York: Charles Scribner's Sons, 1966) 8-10.

replied, it is no; no; not a sixpence.

Further efforts to secure money from the delegation also proved futile, despite eventual face-to-face meetings with Talleyrand. After receiving word of what had happened, President Adams disclosed the information to the Senate and then to the public in April 1798.[4]

The country soon grew outraged at such cavalier treatment. Not even news of the Blount Conspiracy had had such an effect. Over the next few months the nation began to gear up for war. Congress provided for a drastic enlargement of the army to over sixty thousand men, and Adams persuaded George Washington to leave retirement and take command of these forces. At the same time the Navy fitted out and commissioned the three recently-launched frigates *United States*, *Constellation*, and *Constitution*, which carried an American naval presence into the Atlantic for the first time in well over a decade. But the Federalists, traditionally anti-French, wisely avoided an American declaration of war. Many Republican votes would no doubt go against such a move, and a prior French declaration would at any rate have a more unifying effect. Because of this turn of events the Federalist party, which had been losing its grip on the national government, suddenly found itself at the height of its popularity.[5]

France itself, the more extreme Federalists believed, was not the only source of danger. A considerable number of French and pro-French foreigners and sympathizers lived within America's borders, and almost all of these supported the Republicans. This "Jacobin" influence the Federalists perceived as diabolical and dangerous, spreading notions of democracy and atheism, and (according to rumor) plotting even to destroy Philadelphia by fire and massacre. The Federalists believed, quite naturally, that they must deal with such a threat. Congress's response was to pass in June and July 1798 a group of four statutes now known collectively as the Alien and

---

[4] Elkins & McKitrick, *Age of Federalism* 581-88; DeConde, *The Quasi-War* 46-73; Stinchcombe, *XYZ Affair* 106-17; 2 *American State Papers, For. Rel.* 161.

[5] Elkins & McKitrick, *Age of Federalism* 588-90; Miller, *Federalist Era* 210-18; DeConde, *The Quasi-War* 89-98; Stinchcombe, *XYZ Affair* 118-21; Marshall Smelser, *The Congress Founds the Navy 1787-1798* (Westport, Connecticut: Greenwood Press, 1959) chs. 7-14. For a history of hostilities, see Michael A. Palmer, *Stoddert's War: Naval Operations During the Quasi-War with France, 1798-1801* (Columbia: University of South Carolina Press, 1987).

Sedition Acts.[6]

Despite their infamous reputation, these statutes were not as severe as many writers have portrayed them. The Naturalization Act merely extended the residency requirements for aliens wishing to become naturalized citizens. Two of the other laws authorized the president to deport or otherwise restrain dangerous or enemy aliens. One of these Adams never employed; the other one, operative only in wartime, never came into effect. Even the fourth law, the Sedition Act, was not as extreme as some commentators suggest. In seeking to punish false writings intended to defame the federal government, it in fact ameliorated some of the more extreme aspects of the common law of seditious libel. Under the new act, for example, defendants could plead truth of an utterance as an effective affirmative defense, and juries rather than judges were to determine whether a statement was defamatory. Nevertheless the Republicans, who found themselves the primary target of the measure, screamed their opposition to the statutes, which they labeled unconstitutional. These objections were fruitless, for the Adams administration managed not only to bring fifteen indictments under the Sedition Act, but also to win ten of the cases. Chief among the defendants were leaders of the Republican press on the East Coast. The most famous victim of the act, however, was Matthew Lyon, whom the Federalists finally succeeded in jailing in the summer of 1798.[7] Thus by the end of the Fifth Congress's second session the Federalists, at the very height of their power, capitalizing on their new popularity, actively sought to consolidate their political position by bringing the fullest possible weight of federal authority to bear on their Republican opponents. For a time the possibilities must have seemed endless.

---

[6]Elkins & McKitrick, *Age of Federalism* 590-93; Miller, *Federalist Era* 228-29; Act of June 18, 1798, ch. 54, 1 Stat. 566 (1798); Act of June 25, 1798, ch. 58, 1 Stat. 570 (1798); Act of July 6, 1798, ch. 66, 1 Stat. 577 (1798); Act of July 14, 1798, ch. 74, 1 Stat. 596 (1798).

[7]Miller, *Federalist Era* 228-37. The best history of these acts is James Morton Smith, *Freedom's Fetters: The Alien and Sedition Laws and American Civil Liberties* (Ithaca: Cornell University Press, 1956); for the Lyon episode, see Austin, *Matthew Lyon* chs. 10-11.

The uproar on the East Coast had not yet fully pervaded the Trans-Appalachian region when James Mathers arrived at Knoxville in late August 1798. Proceeding to Blount's home, the Senate sergeant-at-arms found the former senator absent, and he left a copy of the summons with Blount's wife. The next day he located Blount himself nearby and served the writ upon him.[8]

Some historians maintain that Mathers accompanied Blount back to the latter's home, where he became the Tennesseean's guest while he attempted to convince Blount to go with him to Philadelphia. According to these sources Blount showed Mathers great hospitality but refused to let himself be taken prisoner. Mathers turned in frustration to Blount's local opponents David Henley and Benjamin Hawkins, and the federal marshal also, but all were either unable or unwilling to assist him. Mathers's further efforts to raise a *posse* to take Blount by force proved futile. Finally Mathers departed Knoxville, escorted by some of the town's citizens who assured him that he could not take Blount back to the East.[9]

The accuracy of this story is questionable, but particulars notwithstanding the fact remains that Mathers returned to Philadelphia empty-handed, and Blount stayed in Tennessee. The former senator even resumed some political activity later in 1798 when he won election to the state legislature.[10] Whatever the circumstances by late 1798, one thing seemed certain: Blount would not be present for any of Congress's subsequent impeachment proceedings.

A few months later, in early December 1798, the Fifth Congress began its third and final session. Unlike the climate of the previous winter, the atmosphere in the new session was tension-charged. The naval war with France was escalating. Sedition Act prosecutions were underway. As Republicans uniformly denounced the high-handed Federalist enactments, party lines finally acquired a clear definition centered on the Alien and Sedition laws. During this session word

---

[8]8 *Annals of Cong.* 2245 (1798).

[9]J.G.M. Ramsey, *The Annals of Tennessee* (Philadelphia: J.B. Lippincott & Co., 1860) 699-700; Isabel Thompson, "The Blount Conspiracy," 2 *East Tennessee Historical Society Publications* 3, 12 (1930); Masterson, *William Blount* 339.

[10]Masterson, *William Blount* 338-39.

arrived of Nelson's defeat of the French fleet off the coast of Egypt, and with that news, the nation came to realize that danger of a French invasion of the United States had ended for the time being. With this threat from the Atlantic reduced, Hamilton and other extreme Federalists, ironically, began to envision an Anglo-American invasion of Louisiana, the Floridas, and even South America, all of which the decaying Spanish empire still held. In the end nothing came of these plans, for Adams wished to avoid such foreign entanglements, but this was neither the last time nor the first that Americans dreamed of western conquests.[11]

In light of all these developments one might expect the Blount impeachment to be as dead an issue in 1798 as it had been in December 1797. But by this time the more extreme Federalists, still seeking to improve their political position, had grand plans in store for the impeachment power. Soon, then, proceedings began to move at a brisk pace.

On December 6 the Senate learned of Mathers's adventures in the West, and Jared Ingersoll and Alexander James Dallas, Blount's attorneys, informed the president *pro tempore* that they were ready for trial. The Senate promptly told the House that Mathers had returned the writ, and the day for the trial's beginning approached.[12]

Each chamber had to make a few more arrangements, however, before the appointed day arrived. In the House the representatives elected a new manager—John Wilkes Kittera—to replace Samuel Sitgreaves, who had resigned the previous summer to accept an appointment as a commissioner to Great Britain. Though a Federalist like all the other managers, Kittera was a minor figure, and Bayard and Harper became the leading prosecutors.[13]

On Monday the 17th, the day set for the writ's return, the Senate created a committee consisting of James Ross, Samuel Livermore, and Jacob Read to report a proper trial procedure. This new committee swiftly produced a recommendation that the chamber should set aside all legislative and executive business by taking the oath upon which it had earlier agreed. It should then call Blount to appear and record his appearance or default. The Senate should inform the

---

[11]Miller, *Federalist Era* 216-20, 234-35, 237.
[12]8 *Annals of Cong.* 2189-90, 2194 (1798).
[13]9 Ibid., 2440-41.

managers as to whether Blount was present and schedule them to appear the following noon. This report the Senate adopted in short order, and then the chamber, seventeen months after Blount's exposure, at last formed itself into a court of impeachment.[14]

Pursuant to the committee report, the Senate's first action was to take the oath that it had prescribed for itself in February. On the 17th twenty senators were present to swear to do "impartial justice, according to law." As senators continued to arrive in the next few weeks they, too, took the oath. Some of those legislators failed to appear until after all arguments before the court had ended, yet they participated in the debate and the final votes.[15] This curious fact suggests that at least some of the first generation of senators did not believe their presence for all of the proceedings to be necessary in order to participate.[16]

The next order of business was for the sergeant-at-arms to command the defendant to appear. After nearly a year and a half, the moment had at last arrived. The doors of the chamber swung open.

"Hear ye! Hear ye! Hear ye!" called Mathers. "William Blount, late a Senator from the State of Tennessee, come forward and answer the Articles of Impeachment exhibited against you by the House of Representatives."

To no one's surprise, Blount failed to materialize. Twice Mathers repeated the cry, but still it failed to produce the Tennesseean. Blount was hundreds of miles away in Knoxville, safely ensconced behind the Appalachians' high wall. Everyone present was almost certainly aware of this fact; the oral summons was strictly *pro*

---

[14]8 *Annals of Cong.* 2196, 2245 (1798).

[15]3 U.S. Congress, Senate, *Journal of the Senate of the United States of America; Being the First Session of the Sixth Congress; Begun and Held at the City of Philadelphia, December 2, 1799, and in the Twenty-Fourth Year of the Independence of the Said States* (Washington: Gales and Seaton, 1821) [SuDocs Z3.4:3] (hereinafter cited as *Senate Journal*) 483, 486, 491.

[16]This fact may help to justify the Senate's recent, controversial use of evidentiary committees, a practice in which all but a dozen senators receive only a report of testimony and other evidence. *See generally* Napoleon B. Williams, Jr., "The Historical and Constitutional Bases for the Senate's Power to Use Masters or Committees to Receive Evidence in Impeachment Trials," 50 *N.Y.U. L. Rev.* 512 (1975); *see also* Epilogue, *infra* (discussing recent developments regarding impeachment trial committees).

forma.[17]

Continuing to follow the prescribed procedure, the court now adjourned until the following noon. On the 18th, before reconvening in this capacity, the Senate created the last of its long line of impeachment committees, this one consisting of Livermore, Ross, and Stockton. This committee, like most of its predecessors, the Senate charged with reporting rules of procedure. No doubt the upper house wished to make some provision for trying the impeachment in Blount's absence. Before this committee reported, however (which it did on the 20th), Congress faced two related problems of great importance.

After hearing a letter from Nicholas Romayne in which the doctor stated his readiness to appear at the trial to give evidence, the senators, now convened as a court, turned their attention to the managers and the defendant's counsel. The Senate had summoned the managers, and about noon most of them arrived. Ingersoll and Dallas had preceded them, requesting the court to admit them as Blount's attorneys, and to this request the senators agreed. Jefferson was not in attendance; John Laurance, the president *pro tempore*, addressed the managers. He notified them that the Senate was ready to proceed with the trial, that Ingersoll and Dallas were to serve as Blount's counsel, and that Blount, despite the service of summons, was absent. He also read aloud the articles of impeachment.[18]

Bayard being elsewhere, Harper arose, asking the Senate for a delay. Because the court had only recently notified the House that it would convene today, he explained, the managers were unprepared. Harper then mentioned the specific problem troubling the representatives. The managers, he said, believed that they must consult the House of Representatives on "a very important preliminary question." This, he said, was the matter of whether the court could try Blount in his absence. The managers believed themselves not competent to decide such a weighty issue, he continued. They must instead confer with the other representatives.

---

[17]8 *Annals of Cong.* 2245, 2196 (1798).

[18]National Archives, Record Group 46, "Journal of Impeachment Proceedings Before the U.S. Senate, 1798-1805" (Film M1253) 14, 17; 9 *Annals of Cong.* 2457-58 (1798); 8 Ibid., 2245; *Independent Chronicle*, 27 December 1798, p. 2, col. 3; *Claypoole's American Daily Advertiser*, 19 December 1798, p. 3, col. 4.

Read asked Harper what day the managers wished to reappear before the Senate, and Harper suggested the following Monday, Christmas Eve. Laurance was about to call for a vote when Dallas spoke up and raised a second issue. Both he and his partner, he reminded the senators, were appearing on the defendant's behalf, and he voiced a hope that the Senate had thus not recorded Blount as being in default. Laurance admonished the lawyers that Blount had not appeared on the previous day, as the summons had required. Ingersoll pressed the point. He had notified the Senate's clerk weeks ago, he said, that he and Dallas would appear for Blount, and he had also sent a letter on the matter to the Senate proper. The attorney emphasized that he and his partner had always been ready to appear, and he trusted that the Senate would thus not make Blount to suffer for his absence.

Laurance, attempting to reassure the lawyers, notified them that the Senate only now had begun to take action on the impeachment. This was enough for the defense, at least for the time being. Laurance then prepared once again to call for a vote on Harper's request, and once again came an interruption, as Read suggested that the presiding officer poll each member of the Senate. Irritated, Laurance answered that the Senate had made no provision for polling, and that the vote would thus be in the normal fashion. He then put the question, the court agreed unanimously to reconvene on the 24th, and the managers withdrew.[19]

As the representatives departed, Read raised objections to how Laurance had conducted the vote. It was undignified, he charged. In every court of justice, judges usually gave separate opinions. He moved that in the future the court of impeachment do likewise, but William Bingham countered that the court should decide such motions while sitting as the Senate. Others spoke up, and then Elijah Paine noted that as none had seconded Read's original motion that the whole discussion was out of order. Chastened, Read grew silent, and Laurance adjourned the court.[20]

The debate over Blount's absence and its effect on the proceedings by no means ended on the 18th. Blount himself would certainly

[19]*Claypoole's American Daily Advertiser*, 19 December 1798, p. 3, cols. 4-5; *Gazette of the United States*, 19 December 1798, p. 3, cols. 3-4.

[20]*Claypoole's American Daily Advertiser*, 19 December 1798, p. 3, col. 5.

remain in Tennessee, having recently entered the state senate (where he was currently presiding, ironically, over the impeachment of a state judge).[21] The House, then, had to decide on a course of action.

On December 20 Harper gave the House an account of the Senate proceedings of the 18th, asking that the chamber instruct the managers to request the Senate to issue further process against Blount. That day the managers prepared a report to this effect, which they submitted to the House on the 21st. A serious difference of opinion arose on the subject, and the representatives engaged in a protracted debate over the report.

First to speak was John Nicholas. If the House asked the Senate to issue an arrest warrant and Blount escaped capture, he argued, then the House might be estopped from going forward in Blount's absence. At any rate, he continued, in this case the Senate could effect judgment even though Blount was not present, so the issue was unimportant.[22]

Samuel Sewall, answering Nicholas, asserted that the Senate was bound by common law principles of criminal procedure in the absence of any specific rule on the subject. These principles required the court to extend Blount an opportunity to plead his case. To try an absent defendant would be to set a dangerous precedent, he warned. He also suggested, however, that Congress should enact a statute establishing a punishment for contempt in impeachment trials, in order to protect the integrity of the process.[23]

These two speeches reveal a reversal of the traditional Federalist-Republican division on procedure, but partisan positions on this measure were soon to grow even more muddled. Next to speak was Harrison Gray Otis, a Federalist from Massachusetts. Otis raised a new point. The House of Representatives, he said, acted only as a prosecutor, whereas the Senate, as the court, exercised final authority. As prosecutors, the managers should not seek obstacles to their presentation of the case. "[I]t is our duty," remarked Otis, "to

---

[21]Masterson, *William Blount* 339-41; *Philadelphia Gazette*, 15 January 1799, p. 3, col. 2.

[22]9 *Annals of Cong.* 2471-73 (1798); *Philadelphia Gazette*, 22 December 1798, p. 2, col. 3.

[23]9 *Annals of Cong.* 2472-73 (1798); *Philadelphia Gazette*, 22 December 1798, p. 2, cols. 3-4.

present ourselves before the Senate, and there to insist upon our prosecution. If our cause should be overruled, we must submit; but it is not for us to start difficulties."

Otis gave another reason why he found a trial in absentia to be acceptable. Impeachment, he observed, was similar to an *actio in rem*, an action aimed not at Blount but at the former senator's office—in effect, a property action, a case of forfeiture. Because the process had no effect on Blount's person, he postulated, Blount need not be present.[24]

Samuel Dana then joined his fellow New Englander on this last point. The purpose of a personal appearance, he theorized, was to allow the court to visit judgment upon the defendant. Here the judgment, presumably one of disqualification, would be just as effective regardless of whether Blount was present. The prospect of the Senate arresting and convicting Blount, only to then release him, Dana remarked, was rather silly.[25]

Then Harper began to speak. From the first the South Carolinian had been anxious to punish Blount, although his vigor had abated for a time after the publication of the impeachment committee's report the previous December. Now, as a leading manager, and holding a position of some responsibility, Harper sought the support of his fellow representatives. Perhaps he reasoned that if he acted under House instructions, he could escape blame if the decision proved erroneous. Whatever his motivation, he now began to make an eloquent case for passing his resolution.

The true reason why courts required defendants' presence, Harper said, attached to impeachment as well as common law proceedings. This reason, he said, was the importance of the defendant's right to confront his judge and his accusers. Courts held this principle in such regard that they even refused defendants the right to waive it. Harper

---

[24] 9 *Annals of Cong.* 2473-74 (1798); *Philadelphia Gazette*, p. 2, cols. 3-4. Had Blount still been a senator, this argument would carry more force, for one might then regard impeachment as a means of divesting Blount's present possessory interest in the office. As the goal of the impeachment was now not removal but disqualification, however, the process would effect Blount's right to acquire property in the future. This would seem to defeat Otis's argument, although none of his opponents raised this specific objection.

[25] 9 *Annals of Cong.* 2474-75 (1798); *Philadelphia Gazette*, 24 December 1798, p. 2, col. 3.

acknowledged that neither Blount's person nor his property was in danger here, but something of even greater importance—his reputation, his public character—was.

Harper beseeched his colleagues to follow the wisdom of precedent. Were the House to "depart from the maxims of experience," he warned,

> we [would] subject ourselves to the dominion of our passions—to revenge on one side, or to favoritism on the other, and our reasonings will lead us this way or that, according to our enmity or affection towards the party accused. It is true, on one day the decision may be in our favor, but it may be against us on the next; and though our favorite be screened today, he may tomorrow, when the popular opinion, which is ever varying, shall have changed, be overwhelmed by this departure from established principle.

To act at variance with precedent, Harper warned, would be to set foot upon a slippery slope that would lead to disastrous consequences, not the least of which would be the destruction of impeachment's solemnity and effectiveness.[26]

Otis, opposing Harper, reiterated that the Senate was the proper judge of the question. The House's decision on this point would be moot. As for Harper's emphasis on the defendant's reputation, Otis dismissed it. "[T]he law," he noted, "does not compare the reputation of a man to life or limb" no matter how much importance Harper might attach to honor.[27]

These assertions did not suffice to convince William Gordon. This Federalist openly disagreed with Otis's characterization of impeachment as an *actio in rem*, for in his own view the process did affect Blount's person in depriving him of a property interest, the office being the property. This also meant, Gordon continued, that impeachment was a criminal process, for divestiture of a property interest certainly constituted a punishment. Impeachment resembled

---

[26]9 *Annals of Cong.* 2475-78 (1798); *Philadelphia Gazette*, 24 December 1798, p. 2, cols. 3-4.

[27]9 *Annals of Cong.* 2478-79 (1798); *Philadelphia Gazette*, 24 December 1798, p. 2, col. 5.

a criminal prosecution in other ways, Gordon also said, and all would admit the need for Blount's attendance, he argued, if impeachment were indeed a criminal process.

Gordon next drew for his listeners a grim picture that illustrated the need for Blount's presence. What if, he asked, attorneys claiming to be a defendant's agents entered a plea of guilty to an impeachment charge of treason? This plea would certainly bar the defendant from proclaiming his innocence when the matter arose in a regular court. In this way a lawyer's actions before the court of impeachment could condemn the defendant to death. This point had its weaknesses, yet Gordon pressed on. If the current law was insufficient to compel Blount's attendance, he argued, then Congress could pass a new law, perhaps a law to the effect that a defendant having constructive notice of the trial would, by his absence, assent to the truth of the managers' factual allegations. But by no means, he cautioned, should the House attempt to railroad the impeachment through the Senate for fear that Blount might escape. "Let us not be so much for the severity of justice," he advised, "as to do away the principle of law."[28]

Gordon's characterization of impeachment as a criminal process provoked a reaction from William Edmond. The Federalist representative pointed out the numerous procedural difficulties the House would encounter if it acknowledged impeachment to be a criminal trial. Reading the Constitution's impeachment provisions, he went over much of the same ground that senators opposing Tazewell's February jury motion had covered.[29] The crucial difference between impeachment and criminal trials, Edmond noted, was in the nature of the offenses for which impeachment would lie. This nature, he said, was political. To decide that criminal safeguards attached to the impeachment process, he argued, was to venture into very dangerous territory. Here Edmond set forth the hypothetical example of a treasonous president who fled to another country while remaining in office. If Congress decided that the defendant's presence was essential, he warned, this president would be beyond its reach. Edmond assured the House that he wished to extend Blount every

---

[28]9 *Annals of Cong.* 2479-82 (1798); *Gazette of the United States*, 27 December 1798, p. 2, cols. 3-4; *Philadelphia Gazette*, 26 December 1798, p. 1, cols. 3-4.

[29]*See* Chapter 4, *supra.*

legal privilege possible, but that Blount should not have the power to defeat the impeachment by remaining absent.[30]

In answer to Edmond, Samuel Sewall posed a hypothetical problem of his own. Blount's attorneys were skillful counselors, he observed. Conceivably they could appear on his behalf and argue their case, and then, if they lost, they might seek to arrest judgment on the grounds that the common law bound the Senate and that Blount's presence was thus necessary after all.[31]

Otis declared still again that the motion was irrelevant, the Senate having the final word, but Nicholas demanded that the House resolve the issue and provide the managers with some guidance. After further comments on both sides, the House voted sixty-nine to eleven to deny Harper's request for instructions.[32]

This vote, however, was not the end of the issue. Sewall now introduced a resolution that was the opposite of Harper's, instructing the managers to proceed to trial regardless of Blount's absence. Some representatives raised relatively small objections to the new resolution, to which others, most notably Harper, replied in exasperation that the House should give the managers *some* sort—any sort—of indication as to how to proceed. Harper announced that he viewed himself as a counselor, with the House his client; this drew him a lecture from Dana to the effect that the managers were just another committee. At last Albert Gallatin spoke up and announced that, as long as Blount had the right to attend the trial, and as long as his duly authorized counsel were present, he would agree to the instruction. The issue thus being joined, the representatives voted on Sewall's resolution. As had Harper's, it met with defeat, although by a considerably narrower margin.[33] The House thus ended the day by refusing to give the managers any instructions on how to proceed.

The entire debate is quite confusing; no doubt Harper and his fellow managers thought so. The vote on Harper's motion to have the

---

[30] 9 *Annals of Cong.* 2482-83 (1798); *Philadelphia Gazette*, 26 December 1798, p. 1, cols. 3-4.

[31] 9 *Annals of Cong.* 2483-84 (1798); *Philadelphia Gazette*, 26 December 1798, p. 1, col. 5.

[32] 9 *Annals of Cong.* 2485 (1798); *Philadelphia Gazette*, 26 December 1798, p. 1, cols. 4-5, p. 2, col. 1.

[33] 9 *Annals of Cong.* 2485-87 (1798); *Philadelphia Gazette*, 26 December 1798, p. 2, cols. 1-2.

managers seek an arrest warrant was by itself fairly clear; all of the motion's few supporters were Federalists, and most were managers. On the other hand a large number of Federalists joined the Republicans in opposing the instruction. Although the vote on Sewall's measure (to instruct the managers to proceed in Blount's absence) was much closer, it too ended with the motion's defeat, but no roll is extant.

Various possible motives for voting exist. In supporting Harper's resolution, the managers may have been seeking to share the responsibility for their actions with the rest of the House, or they may have wished to stretch out and eventually kill the impeachment, or they may have honestly wished to extend Blount procedural safeguards. Despite Harper's appeals to law, though, this last possibility is a slim one. Not once up to this point had House Federalists allowed procedure to stand in their way. If this were their true goal, moreover, they could have asked the Senate for an arrest warrant immediately, without consulting the other representatives. Both of the first two explanations involve political expediency. The first, however, seems more likely, for near the end of the debate Harper and others were clearly anxious to receive some kind of guidance, even if it was an instruction to proceed to trial.

While the voting analysis is further complicated by the lack of sufficient evidence, it still suggests that the managers' primary motivation was to share responsibility for their actions, and, additionally, that the House wished to avoid this responsibility. The very fact that the representatives defeated a measure diametrically opposed to Harper's indicates that they wished the managers to decide. In this way, any blame for future errors of pleading would rest not on the House, but on Bayard, Harper, and their fellows. Another indication that this outlook controlled the day's voting is that all representatives remained silent on a certain point. During the 1797 impeachment investigation, the House itself, acting through the impeachment committee, had issued warrants; by its direction William Eaton had arrested Nicholas Romayne and brought him to Philadelphia, and Thomas Lewis had likewise apprehended James Grant.[34] This fact suggests that the House itself may have had the power to issue a warrant for Blount's arrest. One could argue, of

---

[34] 8 *Annals of Cong.* 2320, 2324, 2329 (1797).

course, that the matter was now before the Senate, to which the Constitution gave sole power in the affair, and that it barred the House from acting here in this fashion. Some members of the House, on the other hand, may have challenged such a view. The central point, however, is not that the argument would have found such opposition, but that no one raised the question at all, as if no one wanted to take a decisive step.

The House's decisions on the 21st, then, probably were based in political expediency rather than theoretical concerns. But this was no comfort to the managers, who were free, by virtue of the House's inaction, to decide their own course. Many of them no doubt feared that whatever path they chose would lead into quicksand.

ʒ❧

On December 20 the second Senate impeachment committee of the session reported a form of trial procedure. It was fairly straightforward, providing for a sequence of pleadings including answer, reply, and rejoinder, an oath for witnesses, and a system of direct and cross-examination. The report also provided that senators themselves could serve as witnesses, and that the Senate would decide all questions of procedure behind closed doors. The document thus epitomizes impeachment's nature, incorporating legalistic elements but accommodating political factors as well. On the 21st the Senate adopted the report.[35]

Finally the preliminaries came to an end. On the 24th the Court of Impeachment convened again and the managers and Blount's counsel appeared before it. Pursuant to the latest report, the presiding officers asked the managers if they had any statements to make before counsel for the defendant answered the impeachment articles. In response Harper moved that Ingersoll and Dallas exhibit the instrument by which Blount had authorized them to appear.

Dallas displayed a collection of papers, informing the senators that

---

[35] 8 *Annals of Cong.* 2197-98 (1798); U.S. Congress, Senate, Committee on Impeachment of William Blount, *Report, in Part, of the Committee, Appointed on the 18th Instant, to Consider What Rules are Necessary to be Adopted by the Senate in the Trial of William Blount* (Philadelphia: Way and Groff, 1798) [Evans 34789] 3-4.

Blount had appointed the lawyers as his attorneys in two separate letters. These letters, said Dallas, also contained the Tennesseean's confidential instructions, which the lawyers naturally wished to keep secret. He expressed a willingness, however, to show them to the court's presiding officer in order to satisfy the Senate that the authorization was proper.

Harper, raising a point that at least one representative had uttered on the 21st, stated that he simply wished the court to be satisfied as to Dallas's and Ingersoll's standing so that Blount might not later plead that he had had no representation at trial. Laurance, on the Senate's instruction, cleared the chamber, and the senators began a confidential debate.[36]

Taken in conjunction with the counselors' statements of December 18, the meaning of this exchange is clear. Ingersoll and Dallas wished to prevent the possibility that the Senate might render a default judgment against their client, while the managers sought to ensure that Blount could not later plead his absence in bar of an unfavorable judgment. In desiring an authoritative decision of the necessity of the defendant's presence, then, the adversaries were of a single mind.

About an hour later the Senate readmitted the parties, and Laurance declared Ingersoll and Dallas to be Blount's duly appointed counsel, with no further warrant of attorney being necessary. The vote had been nearly unanimous, with only the Federalists Livermore and Tracy dissenting. The Senate having settled this point, and presumably the question of the need for Blount's presence as well, Laurance asked the managers if they had any more requests. They answered in the negative, and he then instructed Blount's counsel to enter their plea. Jared Ingersoll brought a document forward, and the clerk of the Senate read it aloud.[37]

Many students of common law pleading are familiar with the apocryphal Case of the Kettle. This legendary controversy is a study in alternative pleading, the practice of making, in the same plea,

---

[36]8 *Annals of Cong.* 2246 (1798); *Claypoole's American Daily Advertiser*, 25 December 1798, p. 3, col. 5; *Gazette of the United States*, 24 December 1798, p. 3, col. 4: National Archives, "Journal," 15-16.

[37]*Claypoole's American Daily Advertiser*, 25 December 1798, p. 3, col. 5; National Archives, "Journal," 16-17; 3 *Senate Journal* 487; 8 *Annals of Cong.* 2246-48 (1798).

several inconsistent and contradictory defenses to an opponent's allegations. In the Case of the Kettle, the plaintiff averred that he had lent his kettle to the defendant, who had cracked it before returning it to its owner. In answer the defendant made three statements: first, that he had never borrowed the kettle; second, that he had not cracked the kettle; and third, that it already had been cracked at the time he borrowed it. Although modern procedure is lenient in such matters, alternative pleading at common law was usually fatal to an attorney's case.[38]

Ingersoll, surprisingly, ignored this danger in his answer. This fact alone shows that the Senate did not observe strictness of form in pleading. Generally Blount's answer was a challenge to the Senate's jurisdiction. It first argued that the Sixth Amendment requirement of a jury trial for crimes barred the Senate's jurisdiction. It argued that impeachment proceedings lay only against civil officers, and then only for high crimes and misdemeanors. Blount, however, was no longer a senator, and he had never been a civil officer, for senators were not such under the Constitution. Impeachment, therefore, was not the proper procedure in this instance. Then Ingersoll went on to make an argument that at common law would have voided his entire answer. In asserting that the regular courts, under the Sixth Amendment, had jurisdiction in this case, Ingersoll denied that Blount had committed any of the acts alleged, and then he claimed that none of the acts that Blount had allegedly committed were pursuant to the execution of his official duties. Thus in a single document did Ingersoll deny that Blount had committed any of the acts charged, but also that those acts, which he now admitted *arguendo* that Blount *had* committed, were not impeachable offenses because they were acts done in a private rather than a public capacity. More signal was his assertion that senators were not civil officers.[39]

With this barrage of detailed and sometimes contradictory defenses confronting him, Harper asked that the court give the managers time

---

[38]See, e.g., *United States v. Henry*, 749 F.2d 203, 215 n.2 (5th Cir. 1984); Rudd v. Dewey, 121 Iowa 454 458-59, 96 N.W. 973, 975 (1903); Joseph H. Koffler & Alison Reppy, *Handbook of Common Law Pleading* (St. Paul: West Publishing Co., 1969) 146-47; Roy W. McDonald, "Alternative Pleading: 1," 48 *Mich. L. Rev.* 311, 314-17 (1950).

[39]8 *Annals of Cong.* 2246-48 (1798).

to prepare a reply. The court, after discussing the motion privately, agreed unanimously to hear the reply on January 3, and then it adjourned for the day.[40]

Two days later the Senate conveyed a copy of the answer to the House, and on Bayard's motion the representatives referred it to the managers. Bayard also asked the House to instruct the managers to take such action on the measure as they thought fit. Otherwise, he warned, the managers would feel compelled to ask the House for specific instructions. The threat worked. Facing the prospect of another debate of the sort that had occurred on the 21st, the representatives complied with Bayard's request by a large margin. To go with their responsibility, then the managers now had express clearance to act at their discretion.[41]

On December 31 Bayard reported the text of a reply, or "replication," to the House. Perhaps this was a managerial attempt to drag the whole chamber into the affair. At any rate the representatives agreed to the document in a short time. Then on January 3, 1799, as the first impeachment lurched into its third calendar year, all eleven managers proceeded to the Senate chamber. The Senate, before forming itself into the court, had resolved to decide requests for adjournment and delays without the normal secret debate. This vote would simplify matters over the next few days. The court was now prepared to hear the managers' reply.[42]

In contrast to Blount's answer, the manager's reply was short. It was, in effect, a demurrer, charging that because of the House's sole power to prefer impeachments, and the Senate's sole power to try them, Blount's allegations were legally insufficient to suspend the process. In response to a question from Laurance, Ingersoll commented that, because the reply appeared to be a demurrer, he and Dallas believed a rejoinder to be necessary. Not long before the attorney had eschewed common law principles of procedure by pleading in the alternative; now, however, he seemed to think those principles relevant. Whether or not it noticed the inconsistency, the

---

[40]Ibid., 2248; National Archives, "Journal," 20.

[41]9 *Annals of Cong.* 2490-92 (1798); *Philadelphia Gazette*, 27 December 1798, p. 3, col. 1; *Massachusetts Mercury*, 4 January 1799, p. 2, col. 3.

[42]9 *Annals of Cong.* 2564 (1798); 8 Ibid., 2199-2200 (1799); 3 *Senate Journal* 488.

Senate agreed with Ingersoll's request.[43]

The rejoinder that Blount's attorneys offered disputed the managers' contentions and reemphasized the sufficiency of the earlier plea. The issue was joined; managers and counsel faced the prospect of debating whether Blount's assertions were sufficient to bar the Senate's jurisdiction. The battle lines were drawn.

Bayard conferred briefly with Ingersoll, under whom he had once studied law. Together they decided agreed that the managers should open the debate, and afterwards reply to the defense's arguments. Bayard informed the court of this agreed-upon order, and with the Senate's leave, he began.[44]

᠀

The previous spring, many Senate Federalists had come to view impeachment in a broad fashion, subject only to limitations that the senators themselves decided upon. Soon afterward, as partisan tension increased during the French crisis, the Federalists used their superior numbers in Congress to pass laws effectively increasing national power and adversely affecting the Republican opposition. For both of these reasons, the Republicans bitterly opposed the Alien and Sedition Acts—which Bayard, and especially Harper, had supported—but the Federalists had other plans for extending the national government's power as well. First Bayard, and then Harper, would now adopt a position in the impeachment arguments that would certainly impress some of these extreme Senate Federalists.[45]

Bayard first dealt with a topic that the Senate had decided months earlier, but which Blount's lawyers had raised again. This was the contention that the Sixth Amendment required that Blount have the opportunity of a jury trial. The sole issue under discussion at this time, Bayard said, was the question of the Senate's jurisdiction. The jury issue had nothing to do with jurisdiction. If Blount were correct in contending that the lack of a jury robbed the Senate of its

---

[43]8 *Annals of Cong.* 2248 (1799); *Claypoole's American Daily Advertiser,* 5 January 1799, p. 2, col. 4.

[44]8 *Annals of Cong.* 2248-49 (1799); Borden, *Bayard* 20.

[45]Smith, *Freedom's Fetters* 54-56, 151; Miller, *Federalist Era* 229; Borden, *Bayard* 39-43.

jurisdiction, then his interpretation extinguished all of the upper house's judicial functions. The Constitution clearly did not contemplate such a circumstance. Bayard then attacked, rather belatedly, the constitutional analysis that Tazewell had set forth months ago. The original Constitution, in Article III, contained an express exception of impeachment to jury trial requirements, he noted. As maxims of construction dictated that the Sixth Amendment be considered an original part of the Constitution, the Senate should not read it as contradicting the Article III provision. Next Bayard described impeachment's function. Impeachment was a political proceeding, he argued, designed to protect the state rather than punish the defendant. In such a process a jury would be out of place.[46]

So far Bayard's task had been easy, especially as the Senate had already effectively decided this point. Now he moved on to address the heart of Blount's argument, the contention that a senator was not a civil officer and thus not subject to impeachment.

In answer to these claims Bayard made two assertions of his own, either of which would suffice to defeat Blount's plea. The first, and the more extravagant, was that no part of the Constitution limited impeachment to civil officers. This argument, though extreme, has more merit than is first evident. Article II, Section 4 prescribes that the "President, Vice President and all civil Officers of the United States, shall be removed from Office on Impeachment for, and Conviction of, Treason, Bribery, or other high Crimes and Misdemeanors." This phrase, argued Bayard, did not confine the process to these persons but instead merely required a certain punishment—removal—when one of these named individuals was the defendant.

The Constitution was silent on many subjects, he said, and in such matters the framers intended that the interpreter look to the common law for guidance. As examples he threw out a series of terms: *felony, habeas corpus, bill of attainder, corruption of blood*. The Constitution defined none of these, said the representative. In all these instances, common law interpretations controlled. As for impeachment, the Constitution prescribed who would impeach, who

---

[46]8 *Annals of Cong.* 2250-51 (1799); *Claypoole's American Daily Advertiser*, 5 January 1799, p. 2, cols. 4-5.

would try, and what the limits of punishment would be, but it was silent as to whom Congress could impeach. Because the House of Representatives corresponded to the House of Commons, and the latter could impeach whomever it pleased, the House of Representatives was free to do the same.[47]

Bayard further supported his point by showing why impeachment of non-civil officers was a desirable power. Suppose, he suggested, that a very influential private individual, possessing ambition and wealth, should conspire with the "disaffected" among the citizenry, or even foreign agents, with the goal of subverting the political process. This person might even stir the country to insurrection in the hopes of elevating himself to the presidency. (Obviously Bayard employed this scenario to play upon the same Federalist fears that had produced the Alien and Sedition Acts; whether or not he actually thought it likely in the wake of the disturbing Blount Conspiracy and the current partisan turmoil is an interesting question to ponder.) In such a circumstance, said Bayard forcefully, the best weapon against the evildoer would be a vote of perpetual disqualification from public office, imposed via impeachment.[48]

Bayard's argument served to reveal the allure of a broadly-construed impeachment power to any Federalist senator who might not yet have heard the theory. In the hands of a Federalist Congress, such a power could terminate the political career of any subversive individual. And to more than a few Federalists, all Republicans seemed subversive.[49] With this power a determined Congress could virtually guarantee permanent Federalist ascendancy.[50]

Bayard then turned to his second answer to Blount's contention. This argument was both weaker and more intricate than the relatively straightforward universal impeachment theory. In short, Bayard averred that (contrary to Blount's argument) senators *were* civil officers of the United States. Senators acted at various times, he said,

---

[47]8 *Annals of Cong.* 2251-54 (1799); *Claypoole's American Daily Advertiser*, 5 January 1799, p. 2, col. 5.

[48]8 *Annals of Cong.* 2254 (1799); *Claypoole's American Daily Advertiser*, 5 January 1799, p. 2, col. 5.

[49]Miller, *Federalist Era* 233.

[50]Cf. Hoffer & Hull, *Impeachment* 151-62 (discussing the universal impeachment theory as it evolved in the Blount proceedings).

as legislators, as executive advisors, and, as was now the case, as judges. In other words, they exercised every sort of government authority. As an office was nothing more than the exercise of authority, senators were obviously civil officers. If this argument was insufficient to remove doubt, he continued, let the doubters examine the Northwest Ordinance of 1787, of which Blount himself had voted in support. That statute, dating from the same year as the Constitutional Convention, spoke of territorial legislators as being government officers; this revealed the framers' understanding of the term. That Blount now differed from his earlier interpretation, Bayard noted with irony, only attested to his treachery.[51]

Bayard's second main argument, so far, was a good one, but it brought him into conflict with a number of constitutional clauses, and now he had to resolve these conflicts. First he noted the Article II, Section 3 provision stipulating that the president was to commission all officers. The president obviously did not commission senators. And yet, Bayard pointed out, this clause merely delegated executive authority, located as it was in the executive article. Its true meaning was that the president was to commission all officers whom *he* appointed. Other officers, not serving by virtue of presidential appointment, might also exist. Both the president and the vice-president, argued the representative, were officers, but neither of these held commissions from the chief executive. By an act of 1792, he continued, Congress had designated the Speaker of the House as a presidential successor, pursuant to the constitutional clause empowering Congress to choose an officer for this purpose. Thus Congress had admitted in 1792 that the Speaker was an officer; but the Speaker held no presidential commission.[52]

Another clause, in Article I, Section 6, gave Bayard more trouble. This was the provision that no member of Congress could assume "any civil Office under the Authority of the United States" created while he was in Congress. The clause challenged Bayard's

---

[51]8 *Annals of Cong.* 2254-55 (1799); *Claypoole's American Daily Advertiser,* 5 January 1799, p. 2, col 5, p. 3, col. 1; *see* Act of Aug. 7, 1789, ch. 8, 1 Stat. 50, 51-52 (1789).

[52]8 *Annals of Cong.* 2258 (1799); *Claypoole's American Daily Advertiser,* 5 January 1799, p. 3, col. 1; *see* U.S. Const. art. II, § 1, cl. 6; Act of March 1, 1792, ch. 8, § 9, 1 Stat. 239, 240 (1792).

characterization of senators as civil officers. To escape this danger, Bayard stressed the word "under." A difference existed, he explained, between officers *of* the United States and officers *under* the United States, or under the government. A senator is not under the government but is instead part of the government, which consisted of legislature, executive, and judiciary. A member of Congress, then, was an officer of the government, although he was not an officer under the government. Article I, Section 6 spoke only to the latter sort of office.[53]

Having reached this point, Bayard now faced another difficulty. Article I, Section 3, Clause 7 prohibited the Senate from imposing judgments more extreme than removal and future barring of persons from office *under* the United States. According to Bayard's distinction between the two sorts of officers, this wording meant that Congress could not disqualify persons from serving as president, vice-president, members of Congress or the judiciary, or as any other officer *of* the United States. Bayard now adopted a common sense outlook to circumvent this problem. The framers never could have intended such a result, he said; otherwise persons barred from the office of Senate doorkeeper could still become a senator. (One can imagine Mathers's thoughts at this point.) Bayard thus employed at this juncture the "golden rule" of language-based construction, refusing to extend the letter of the Constitution to the degree that an absurdity would result. Surely, he said, the Senate should not read the document in such a way as to allow the wrongdoer access to the higher sort of office.[54]

Bayard now targeted Blount's next defense, consequently reaching safer ground for himself. Blount claimed that he was a senator but not an officer at the time he allegedly committed his offenses; but if the Senate adopted either of Bayard's two previous impeachment theories, this defense must fall. Blount's claim that he was no longer a senator, and thus no longer subject to impeachment, was similarly defective, and Bayard warned of the dire consequences of establishing the precedent that a defendant could escape the process, and

---

[53] 8 *Annals of Cong.* 2257-58 (1799); *Claypoole's American Daily Advertiser*, 5 January 1799, p. 3, col. 1.

[54] 8 *Annals of Cong.* 2258-59 (1799); *Claypoole's American Daily Advertiser*, 5 January 1799, p. 3, col. 1; see Prologue, *supra*.

potential disqualification, through resignation. Then Bayard turned to Blount's last defense—the claim that he had not performed the alleged acts within the context of his duties as a senator. Bayard replied that the Constitution did not limit impeachable offenses to acts done in a public capacity, for such a limitation would work "against the plain dictates of common sense." If the Senate adopted Blount's position, then a judge, acting privately with criminals to break the law, would be beyond Congress's reach.

The final point Bayard discussed was Blount's assertion that the regular court system was the proper place to hear these allegations. Bayard stated that the charges were of a political nature, and that the remedy of disqualification was also political. Impeachment was thus the proper process. At any rate, the manager noted, the Constitution expressly provided for a regular court trial in addition to impeachment, so the defendant could not plead one process in bar of another. Bayard then concluded by asking the Senate to overrule Blount's plea and compel the Tennessean to answer the articles of impeachment. Ingersoll moved for a delay before the defense responded to Bayard; the Senate cleared the galleries, debated the motion, and unanimously decided to reconvene the following morning.[55]

Shortly after court met on the 4th, Dallas began a three-and-a-half hour speech. If Bayard's broad-construction argument had represented the Federalist view of impeachment and national power, then Dallas's entire argument comprised a Republican *credo* concerning the central government. A logically sounder speech than Bayard's, Dallas's presentation shows why he enjoyed his high reputation.

The attorney first paid tribute to Bayard's eloquence even as he expressed amazement at some of the principles that the representative had put forward. Dallas himself set forth only three general arguments in direct opposition to Bayard's views, although all of them were the basis for elaboration and digression. His first contention was that only civil officers were amenable to impeachment. The central government, he charged, as a creature of the states, was a government of express powers only, designed to act

---

[55] 8 *Annals of Cong.* 2261-62 (1799); *Claypoole's American Daily Advertiser*, 5 January 1799, p. 3, cols. 1, 2; 3 *Senate Journal* 489.

when independent state action was not desirable. To this end the government possessed only those powers that the framers had explicitly given it, in conformity to the principle *expressio unius est exclusio alterius*. These statements epitomized Republican beliefs. If Bayard's assertions were correct—if impeachment could reach civil and criminal offenses, national and state matters, martial and non-martial subjects—one would expect to find an express constitutional statement to this effect. But Bayard, unable to produce such a statement, turned instead to an implied construction, resting that construction upon the common law. By this shaky means, said Dallas, the managers sought to extend impeachment even to state officers and offenses, which even the federal judiciary could not reach, to say nothing of private citizens. This was indeed an extreme reading of the impeachment power.[56]

To justify this theory, Dallas reiterated, Bayard and his colleagues resorted not to the letter of the Constitution but to the common law. To this he replied: What common law? No federal common law of crimes existed, he asserted, and each state had adopted different parts of the British common law. Should the Senate turn to the law of a particular state, he asked, in which case it would destroy the uniformity that was the whole point of a federal Constitution? "Or," he suggested,

> is it to be the common law of England, and at what period? Are we to take it from the dark and barbarous pages of the common law, with all the feudal rigor and appendages; or is it to be taken as it has been ameliorated by the refinements of modern legislation?[57]

If he had to choose one of these options, Dallas would probably have chosen the latter. He was a notorious opponent of the common law tradition, embracing instead Enlightenment and continental code law concepts. But here his endeavor was to avert the need to resort to the British system to any degree. The Constitution, he told his audience,

---

[56]8 *Annals of Cong.* 2262-64 (1799); *Claypoole's American Daily Advertiser*, 8 January 1799, p. 2, col. 2.

[57]8 *Annals of Cong.* 2264-65 (1799); *Claypoole's American Daily Advertiser*, 8 January 1799, p. 2, col. 2.

contained in itself all of the principles and information necessary for Congress to fix the limits of its impeachment power.[58]

The provisions were clear, Dallas said. The Constitution listed in Article II, Section 4 those persons who were subject to impeachment, and it did not mention members of Congress. The lawyer noted that the document contained an analogous grant of cognizance to the judiciary branch in Article III. Would Bayard contend, he asked, that the judiciary could likewise exercise jurisdiction even when it had no express authority? Even if the Senate did find the common law to control here, Dallas commented, the English authorities revealed impeachment to lie only for abuses of government power. As private citizens were not in a position to commit such offenses, Dallas continued, so Congress had no authority to try Blount.[59]

Dallas was not yet finished with his first point. He proceeded to ask why the Constitution limited judgment in impeachments to removal and disqualification. Obviously this limitation meant that the process applied only to officeholders, and specifically to presidential appointees. Regular courts could not affect an officeholder's tenure, yet they did have concurrent jurisdiction over impeachable offenses. Clearly then, Dallas concluded, impeachment was a congressional device designed to check executive abuses of power. An extension of this weapon to include persons other than presidential appointees, he said, would be absurd.[60]

Dallas now moved on to his second argument, namely, that impeachable offenses were limited to acts an officer committed within his official capacity. The attorney had already demonstrated that impeachment reached only civil officers, and lay only for abuses of power. Obviously the offenses that impeachment contemplated were those that officers were in a unique position to commit. These could be none other than public acts. Even the House of Representatives had acknowledged this to be the case, said Dallas, in its choice of language in the articles of impeachment. These articles charged, as an

---

[58]Walters, *Dallas* 105-06; 8 *Annals of Cong.* 2265 (1799); *Claypoole's American Daily Advertiser*, 8 January 1799, p. 2, col. 2.

[59]8 *Annals of Cong.* 2365-67 (1799); *Claypoole's American Daily Advertiser*, 8 January 1799, p. 2, col. 2.

[60]8 *Annals of Cong.* 2267-68 (1799); *Claypoole's American Daily Advertiser*, 8 January 1799, p. 2, col. 2.

important part of the evil acts, that Blount had acted contrary to his duties as a senator.[61]

Dallas began his third major argument by stating clearly that senators were not civil officers. Here Bayard's argument had been weakest, and now Dallas delivered a devastating rebuttal. In some places, he observed, the Constitution spoke of officers of the United States, while in other places it mentioned officers under the United States. If the document actually contemplated two separate classes of officers, then numerous inconsistencies would result. Only officers of the United States would be subject to impeachment, but their disqualification would be from offices under the United States. The president would have the power to appoint officers of, but not officers under, the United States. These and other illustrations Dallas employed to show that Bayard had relied on a mere play of words to establish a false dichotomy. Clearly the Constitution contemplated only one type of officer despite its use of two different words. The 1792 presidential succession law he explained away by describing the Speaker as an officer not of the United States but instead of the House of Representatives.[62]

Dallas did not stop here, continuing instead to hammer away at Bayard's theory. If Article II, Section 4 expressly named the president and vice-president as impeachable he asked, why did it not name senators if the power did in fact apply to them? Legislators, he said, were not officers of the government, were no mere functionaries; they were collectively the representatives of the country's very sovereignty. The framers intended that impeachment reach not the sovereign, but its agents, that is, the officers holding executive commissions. Senators, holding no such commissions, were not officers. Bayard, said Dallas parenthetically, had argued that neither president nor vice-president held presidential commissions, though both were impeachable. The fact that they did not have executive commissions, Dallas countered, was the precise reason for their express inclusion in Article II, Section 4, for if the Constitution had not explicitly named

---

[61]8 *Annals of Cong.* 2269 (1799); for a discussion of this issue, see pages 156-59, *supra.*

[62]8 *Annals of Cong.* 2269-70 (1799); *Claypoole's American Daily Advertiser*, 8 January 1799, p. 2, cols. 3-4.

them they would not have been subject to the process.[63]

Although these arguments seemed sufficient to call Bayard's assertions into question, Dallas had still more to say, relying on the Constitution's text to draw several other distinctions between senators and civil officers. He returned to his point about the legislature as the representative of the sovereign, proclaiming in true Republican fashion that congressmen were responsible only to the electorate. The people, through election or expulsion, could remove legislators of whom they disapproved. An expelled senator or representative could then return to Congress if the people wished to re-elect him. Theirs was the last word. The people could not, however, directly reach members of the other government branches; this was the reason, Dallas maintained, that the framers had incorporated impeachment into the Constitution. To extend the power of disqualification to cover members of Congress, however, would be to limit the sovereignty of the people, their power to choose the representatives that they wished. The Senate had already expressed, through the process of expulsion, its opinion of Blount, the attorney stated. If the people disagreed with that opinion, they should be free to return him to Congress.[64]

Here, then, was Dallas's ideological response to Bayard's broad construction arguments. Bayard had averred that the government could act to protect itself, even to the point of impeaching private citizens; Dallas responded that the government could act against all but the sovereignty of the people whom it served. Clearly the jurisdiction dispute was becoming a contest between Federalist and Republican philosophies.

In closing Dallas offered another blanket statement of the strict construction principle. Through implication, interpreters could make the Constitution say almost anything, he argued, but such arbitrary descriptions of legislators as government officers did not change the basic nature of the legislative function. Dallas then sat down, and the

---

[63]8 *Annals of Cong.* 2270-71 (1799); *Claypoole's American Daily Advertiser*, 8 January 1799, p. 2, cols. 3-4.

[64]8 *Annals of Cong.* 2272-76 (1799); *Claypoole's American Daily Advertiser*, 8 January 1799, p. 2, col. 4; cf. *Powell v. McCormack*, 395 U.S. 486 (1969) (addressing a very similar problem).

Senate adjourned until the next morning.[65]

ॐ

Because the managers would have an opportunity to present a rebuttal, Jared Ingersoll was the next man to address the Court of Impeachment. As had his partner, Ingersoll made three principal arguments. Not once did he expressly refer to any inside knowledge that he might have possessed of the Constitutional Convention's deliberations; but his stature as a framer, no doubt, gave great weight to his pronouncements.

Ingersoll first examined the nature of the impeachment power, dismissing Bayard's broad construction and universal impeachment claims as extravagant. Such theories, Ingersoll told the court, had stirred him, and now he saw himself as more than just Blount's attorney. To his way of thinking, danger loomed over the country. "This is the first and last opportunity to pause and consider before the irretrievable step is taken," he declared. "The interest of my client is lost in the consideration, how the event of this hearing may affect the public."[66]

A trial by jury, Ingersoll stated, was one of the essential freedoms that the Anglo-American legal tradition granted. Magna Carta, he asserted, implicitly guaranteed the right of a jury trial; England's denial of this right to colonists was one of the grievances to be found in the Declaration of Independence. Impeachment, on the other hand, was a vague and dangerous power, more open to abuse than trials incorporating juries. If the Senate doubted that the Constitution required a jury for this proceeding, he entreated, it should give the defendant the benefit of the doubt and summon one.[67]

"I read in Magna Charta," the attorney continued, "that no man shall be condemned but by the lawful judgment of his peers, or the *law of the land*. What was this law of the land?" he asked his senatorial audience. "What other mode of proceeding in criminal

---

[65]8 *Annals of Cong.* 2276-78 (1799); *Claypoole's American Daily Advertiser*, 8 January 1799, p. 2, cols. 4-5.

[66]8 *Annals of Cong.* 2278-79 (1799).

[67]Ibid., 2278-79.

causes was then in practice, except trial by jury?" Examining the options, including trial by ordeal and battle, he denounced them all as products of "the ages of dark superstition." Magna Carta predated the earliest impeachments, which according to Ingersoll was not that of Roger Mortimer but rather those of two of his victims, the Despensers. The attorney thus concluded disingenuously that the provisions of Magna Carta, which called for a jury trial, required the use of one in impeachments.[68]

Having addressed the nature of the impeachment power, Ingersoll next concerned himself with its extent. The attorney, like Dallas before him, now adopted the strict construction theory in full force. Before the Constitution's ratification, he argued, Congress had had no impeachment power, and now the legislature could only exercise that power which the Constitution had conferred upon it. The Constitution had granted only limited power, he continued, citing several illustrative passages. In light of this fact, the possibility that impeachment was of such a scope as Bayard suggested was remote.

To enlighten the court still further, Ingersoll brought up Bayard's interpretation of Article II, Section 4. Bayard, he said, maintained that the clause merely required the Senate to impose removal in cases involving the president, vice-president, and civil officers. But in that case, Ingersoll countered, the clause was redundant. Article I, Section 3, Clause 7 stipulated that removal (and its extension of disqualification) was the only punishment in impeachments, so that penalty would of necessity apply to the individuals named in the Article II provision. The only way to give the Article II clause any meaning, then, said Ingersoll, was to read it as a definition of who was subject to impeachment.[69]

As to impeachment's extent regarding offenses, Ingersoll in effect stated that the crime should fit the punishment. Impeachment's sanctions related to an individual's public capacity; it deprived him of his office. Surely this punishment should attach for official wrongdoing, then, and leave redress for private acts to the regular courts. In support of this point Ingersoll turned to English commentators to show that impeachment's traditional purpose had been to deal with the improper acts that government officers had

---

[68]Ibid., 2279-80.
[69]Ibid., 2283-86.

committed. Because Parliament's power was limited, he said, Congress should view its impeachment power accordingly.[70]

Now Ingersoll reached his third and final point—impeachment's object. As he had earlier set forth his view that impeachment was limited to civil officers, he now began to discuss who he believed fell within this category. The attorney's definition of a civil officer had three parts: 1) civil officers were presidential appointees; 2) they held presidential commissions; and 3) they were not military officers. Senators, he pointed out unnecessarily, met none of these criteria. Senators were legislators. Congress possessed powers of expulsion to deal with its own members. Impeachment, he argued, was designed to deal with the executive branch. This last statement, coming from a framer, was quite an authoritative one, although when Ingersoll made it he was speaking not only eleven and a half years after the fact but as an advocate.[71]

If senators held no presidential commission, Ingersoll went on, their executive and judicial functions were insufficient to make them officers. Senators did not appoint officers. Instead they merely consented to the appointment. As for the Senate's judicial powers, Ingersoll said, the powers of the House of Lords in that respect were far greater, yet no one had ever considered the Lords to be officers. The Senate was a legislative body, he said in short, and its other functions were only incidental.

Ingersoll had now worked himself up to a last appeal. If the Senate decided that its own members were subject to impeachment, he told the court, then in destroying constitutional distinctions between the government's branches the senators delivered their own independence into the hands of the House of Representatives. Such a grant of power to the lower chamber, he suggested clearly, some senators might find objectionable. By these statements he obviously hoped to exploit the split in Federalist opinion that had existed since the previous spring. Appealing to the senators to help to preserve the principles of the Constitution, Ingersoll yielded the floor to the opposition with a final appeal: "I say of the Constitution of the United States, in its true sense and genuine exposition, *Esto perpetua!*"[72]

---

[70]Ibid., 2286-87.
[71]Ibid., 2288-91.
[72]Ibid., 2291-94.

Without missing a beat, Harper began his argument. "And I, too," he proclaimed, "say of this Constitution of the United States, *Esto perpetua!*" He chided Ingersoll, however, for intimating that the Federalists' contentions threatened the document, for this debate, he said, involved only a difference of opinion between the Constitution's friends.

Harper then seized upon one of Dallas's utterances in order to make his first point. In attempting to limit impeachment to cover civil officers only, he said, Dallas had denounced Bayard's appeal to common law principles. His contempt of " 'the dark and barbarous pages of the common law,' " Harper said, was quite unjust. How, asked the manager, were the senators to understand any term of art in the Constitution without resorting to " 'the dark and barbarous pages of the common law?' " The rights of greatest importance to American citizens lived within those pages, he exclaimed. He began to reel off a string of examples, locating right after right, principle after principle, in " 'the dark and barbarous pages of the common law,' " uttering the refrain again and again.[73]

Dallas, Harper finally said, would turn to the Constitution itself to discover meanings. But the Constitution alone was insufficient for this purpose. The document did provide that the House could impeach and the Senate would try impeachments, and that the punishment would not go beyond removal and disqualification. On other matters, though, it was silent. The common law, said Harper, was thus the proper guide to the power's extent; and under the common law, impeachment was an unlimited power. In supporting this statement Harper cited the 1709 case of Dr. Henry Sacheverell, which Dallas had overlooked. In this case Parliament tried a clergyman, not a government officer, for preaching a seditious sermon.[74]

Not only officers, Harper said to emphasize this last point, could act in such a way as to injure the government. And judgment of removal and disqualification was more than a political action; it was a punishment, a punishment "pronounced by the highest and most awful judicature known to the Constitution." Because the political

---

[73]Ibid., 2294-98.

[74]Ibid., 2298-99; see Sir George Clark, *The Later Stuarts, 1660-1714*, 2d ed. (Oxford: Clarendon Press, 1956) 226-27.

elements of impeachment therefore respected the defendant and not the office, the defendant need not be an officer. As for the office from which the defendant could be removed, Harper argued, the Constitution used that term in the broadest sense, to encompass any sort of duty. This could include the duties not only of executive officers, but legislative and even military officers as well. Mindful, perhaps, of Blount's new position in the Tennessee legislature, and the Virginia and Kentucky Resolutions' assertion of state authority, Harper did not exclude state officers from the reach of federal impeachments. Such impeachments "must be founded on offences against the United States," he conceded, but "if such offences were committed by state officers, I cannot see why they ought not to be punished, as well as in any other case. Surely they would not be less dangerous." Removal and disqualification, moreover, were not the only penalties, as Ingersoll claimed, but only the maximum allowable penalties. Thus could the power reach those who held no office, or some office other than executive posts. If the Senate agreed on either point, Blount was amenable to Senate jurisdiction.[75]

Even if the senators insisted upon giving Article II, Section 4 a restricted reading and holding only civil officers to be impeachable, Harper said, senators were still subject to the process. Here he cited several examples of legislators being characterized as officers. Because an office included any sort of exercise of duty, including legislative duty, and senators carried out civil rather than military duties, senators were thus civil officers. Then Harper engaged in the same sort of constitutional analysis that Bayard had performed to show that the Constitution contemplated different classes of officers. Harper's logic on this point was as tortured as Bayard's had been, as he tried to show that legislators, while officers in some contexts, belonged in a different category from other officers.[76]

At length Harper moved on to other subjects. Ingersoll and Dallas had suggested that impeachment's purpose was to allow the people to reach executive officers, since they could exercise sufficiently direct control over legislators by other means. But the people, argued the South Carolinian, elected the president more directly than they did senators, so impeachment, by this rationale, should *a fortiori* reach

---

[75]8 *Annals of Cong.* 2299-2305 (1799).
[76]Ibid., 2311-14.

senators as well. As to the character of Blount's acts, Harper largely reiterated Bayard's arguments. Finally Harper, like Ingersoll before him, made a more pointed argument. The Senate, he said, occupied a high station. Surely in light of this circumstance it could best inspire public confidence in itself by admitting its own members' amenability to the process, rather than by attempting to shield them with a doubtful constitutional interpretation. "I confess," he said,

> that feeling, as I do, for the dignity of this honorable body; deeply impressed, as I am, with the awful nature of its trust, and the essential importance of its inspiring the nation with the most unlimited confidence, I tremble to think of its declaring, by a solemn decision, that the conduct of its members shall be exempt from inquiry by impeachment.

With this Harper announced his own confidence that the Senate would reach the right decision, and then he ended his presentation. As had Ingersoll's, his arguments had lasted for two hours.[77]

The president now turned to Bayard and asked if the managers had anything more to say. Bayard conferred in private with his colleagues and then answered in the negative. After three days of exhaustive oral argument the confrontation was over. The court adjourned until Monday January 7.[78]

During the proceedings against Blount, the Federalists had never concealed their desire to establish impeachment as a weapon that could reach any person, public or private, and deprive him of office; on the contrary, they were quite vocal about it. As they went about laying the groundwork for this doctrine, however, they may well have been also contemplating the possibility of a similar, more subtle, constitutional development.

A few years after the Blount impeachment, the Federalist John Marshall, in perhaps the most famous opinion the Supreme Court has

---

[77]Ibid., 2314-18.
[78]Ibid., 2318.

ever written, penned the sentiment that epitomizes that opinion: "It is emphatically the province and duty of the judicial department to say what the law is." That statement did more than any other single action to put the federal courts, and the Supreme Court in particular, at the heart of the American constitutional system. Many other cases, among them Marshall Court decisions such as *Fletcher v. Peck* and *Martin v. Hunter's Lessee*, of course played important roles, but the germ of all of these is what Marshall decided in 1803. The validity of the results of *Marbury v. Madison* has ever since been a subject of hot debate, but most of that debate has centered in the classroom. For the most part the American legal community, especially in the twentieth century, has accepted the truth of a fairly broad reading of the power of judicial review of legislative, executive, and administrative acts.[79]

In the nineteenth century, however, things were not so clear. The question of who had the last word involved not merely a struggle between branches of the federal government, but between federal and state government as well. Federalism and separation of powers are in many ways distinct subjects, but their common goal is to grant governing power while restraining it at the same time. The judicial review debate, then, is one facet of the question of where, in the United States, ultimate sovereignty lies. The question is largely theoretical, for in every age since 1789 one finds not one but many institutions engaging in sovereign actions. If one reads Marshall's opinion as a claim that the federal courts are the ultimate locus of that sovereignty, then one must also recall that whatever its theoretical merits, in practice the claim has limits. Examples range from Andrew Jackson's fabled reply to Marshall's decision in *Worcester v. Georgia*, and his refusal to enforce the Court's ruling in favor of the Cherokee in the 1830s, to the triumph of Roosevelt and New Dealers over the Four Horsemen a century later.[80] A theorist

---

[79]*Marbury v. Madison*, 5 U.S. (1 Cranch) 137, 176-78 (1803); *Fletcher v. Peck*, 10 U.S. (6 Cranch) 87 (1810); *Martin v. Hunter's Lessee*, 14 U.S. (1 Wheat.) 304 (1816). For alternate readings of *Marbury*, see William Van Alstyne, "A Critical Guide to *Marbury v. Madison*," 1969 *Duke L.J.* 1.

[80]*Worcester v. Georgia*, 31 U.S. (6 Pet.) 515 (1832); William E. Leuchtenburg, *Franklin D. Roosevelt and the New Deal 1932-1940* (New York: Harper Torchbooks, 1963) 231-39.

might well respond that these events amounted to violations of judicial review principles in the name of politics, and that they fail to alter the judiciary's theoretical supremacy. This may be perfectly true, but if actual events curtail this theory's perfect application, as has often happened, then it is also irrelevant. Even the Court recognizes this, imposing self-restraint through variety of prudential doctrines such as the political question rule.

The struggle in *Marbury* between the Court and the presidency, into which Marshall dragged Congress and the Judiciary Act of 1789, is the point of introduction for most students of constitutional law and history today. In 1799, however, few people had heard of William Marbury, and at any rate the Federalists controlled all three branches. They had nothing to fear from the federal courts. The states, however, presented another problem. The Alien and Sedition Acts, against which Republicans objected so strongly, occasioned one of the earliest debates on this question of sovereignty. The Virginia and Kentucky Resolutions, largely the product of Madison and Jefferson respectively, claimed a right, albeit a vague one, of state governments to judge the constitutionality of federal acts. For nearly a decade the Federalists had had their way with the national government, enacting a rather Burkean agenda; now, with these resolutions, came the realization that they might face some constitutional limitations on their powers.[81] The theoretical question of the locus of sovereignty suddenly presented a practical, if potential, obstacle. The solution was to find some device that would ensure national supremacy, the rule of law, and the rule of Federalist principles. A likely partial solution, in a day in which the Federalists controlled Congress, was the *lex Parliamenti*.[82]

This Law of Parliament—another name for it is *Lex et consuetudo Parliamenti*—was something quite distinct, according to many jurists and scholars, from the common law. As such, it was a system over

---

[81]Elkins & McKitrick, *Age of Federalism* 719-26; John C. Miller, *Crisis in Freedom: The Alien and Sedition Acts* (Boston: Little, Brown and Company, 1951) 169-81.

[82]*See generally* Carl Wittke, *The History of English Parliamentary Privilege* (New York: Da Capo Press, reprint 1970); Charles Howard McIlwain, *The High Court of Parliament and Its Supremacy: An Historical Essay on the Boundaries Between Legislation and Adjudication in England* (New Haven: Yale University Press, 1910).

which common law courts had no jurisdiction. This in itself was nothing remarkable; one can say the same thing of other legal systems in England, including admiralty, equity, ecclesiastical law, the *lex mercatoria* or Law Merchant, the *lex forestae* or Law of the Forests, and others.[83] These separate "laws" emerged at different times, under different circumstances, and for different reasons than those giving rise to the common law and the royal courts. While these last two did a great deal to help the monarchy establish a central control over England's governmental and legal systems, the other systems remained more or less distinct. What sets the *lex Parliamenti* apart from these others, however, is its claim to supremacy.

Many leading figures recognized the separate station of the *lex Parliamenti*; Coke, for instance, wrote that "judges ought not to give any opinion of a matter of Parliment, because it is not to be decided by the common laws." In 1675, in an extreme statement of the doctrine, Commons maintained that not even Magna Carta superseded the *lex Parliamenti*. Shortly after the Glorious Revolution, George Petyt declared, drawing upon Coke as authority, that "Matters of *Parliament* are not to be ruled by the Common-Law . . . . It doth not belong to the *Judges* to judge of any Law, Custom, or Privilege of *Parliament*," and that "The Prerogative of *Parliament* is so great, That all Acts and Processes coming out of any inferior Courts, must cease, and give place to the highest." These statements were products of the century of the Stuarts, of course, and one must keep that in mind, but Blackstone, who had such a powerful hold on the American legal system, took a similar view. "It will be sufficient to observe," he wrote, "that the whole of the law and custom of Parliment has it's [*sic*] original from this one maxim, 'that whatever matter arises concerning either house of Parliment, ought to be examined, discussed, and adjudged in that house to which it relates, and not elsewhere.' "[84] In an American context, this *lex Parliamenti* would likely prove invulnerable from attack by any other jurisdiction,

---

[83] 1 Holdsworth, *A History of English Law* 94-108; Ibid. ch 7.

[84] Coke, 4th inst., Fo. 50; 3 Com. J. 354; George Petyt, *Lex Parliamentaria: Or, a Treatise of the Law and Custom of the Parliaments of England* (London: Printed for Tim. Goodwin, 1690) 9, 17; 1 William Blackstone, Commentaries *158-59. On the relationship between the *lex Parliamenti* and the law of the land, or *lex terrae*, see Wittke, *Parliamentary Privilege* chs. 5-6.

federal or state.

But what was the substance of this law? What matters did it reach? As the name might suggest, its principal objects lay in matters that particularly concerned Parliment, especially those rights and duties of its members that fell under the heading of Parlimentary privilege. This included such rights as a member of Parliment's freedom of speech and freedom from arrest, and both his and his servants' freedom from molestation. Eventually Parlimentary privilege came to include jurisdiction over various questions of disputed elections, even going so far as to flirt with the possibility of deciding voter qualifications, which, were we to consider Parliament to be a representative institution in the modern sense, would be a wonderful instance of the tail wagging the dog. With the exception of this last development, most of this list seems fairly innocuous. Over time, however, the *lex Parliamenti* grew in scope. At times Parliament extended the power to shield nonmembers from ordinary common law processes; the sixteenth and seventeenth centuries witnessed a veritable "traffic in 'protections' " that allowed friends, relatives, and patrons of Parliament's members to violate other subjects' personal and property rights with impunity. Those on the receiving end found themselves at the bar of Parliment answering charges of having hunted upon a member's lands or having broken his fence. The trump card lay in Blackstone's observation, which some Federalists may have had in mind when they formulated the idea of a universal impeachment power, that no definitive list of Parlimentary privilege existed; the power had to remain fluid enough to respond to new executive abuses.[85]

The idea of creating an American *lex Parliamenti*, and using it to shield men of means and political power from Jacobin attacks, might seem far-fetched today, but no more so than the theory of universal impeachment that was such a blatant and important part of the managers' campaign against Blount. For a Federalist, particularly a Federalist who served in Congress or who had friend who did, this sort of protection might have seemed very desirable, especially if he feared that his interests might soon become the victim of republicanized state legislatures. Blackstone's discussion of the *lex*

---

[85]Wittke, *Parliamentary Privilege* 40-43; 1 William Blackstone, *Commentaries* *159.

Parliamenti was readily available, and no doubt well known, to many of them, so they lacked no exposure to the idea. One objection that opponents might raise is that the Constitution expressly established many of the features of Parlimentary privilege, as well as a few other areas in which Congress was clearly supreme. Among the passages to do so were the Speech or Debate Clause in Article I, Section 6; the provisions in section 5 of that article making each house the sole judge of its members' elections, returns, and qualifications; the expulsion power, also in Section 5; and, of course, each house's respective powers relating to impeachment. An argument that these provisions comprised the full extent of the *lex Parliamenti*'s application in the United States would have been no problem for the Federalists who sought to convict Blount, just as they saw no limitation of the impeachment power itself to the expressly-named civil officers. The possibility of instituting an American version of this law might well have been on some Federalists' minds during the Fifth Congress's third session, especially with the Blount impeachment underway, for the *lex Parliamenti* did possess one weakness from an American perspective: it was essentially judicial in character, arising out of Parliament's judicial functions.[86]

Unlike Parliament, Congress did not evolve into a legislative body from some earlier *Curia Regis* that exercised undifferentiated legislative, executive, and judicial powers. Its genesis, rather, while not quite *ex nihil*, was considerably more definite and express. To develop the *lex Parliamenti*, Congress needed some judicial machinery; no clearer such machinery existed than impeachment; and an impeachment just happened to be underway at the very moment when Federalists needed one.

To develop this legal concept, the House would need the Senate's

---

[86]*See* Wittke, *Parliamentary Privilege* 13-20. On a discussion of the relation of the judicial to the legislative functions of Parliament, and a comparison to the tension between legislation and judicature in the United States written during the height of substantive due process, see McIlwain, *High Court of Parliament* ch. 4. For a recent study of the application of law to Congress, see Harold H. Bruff, "That the Laws Shall Bind Equally on All: Congressional and Executive Roles in Applying Laws to Congress," 48 *Ark. L. Rev.* 105 (1994); for a modern view of congressional self-discipline, see Laura Krugman Ray, "Discipline Through Delegation: Solving the Problem of Congressional Housecleaning," 55 *U. Pitt. L. Rev.* 389 (1994).

complicity, and while this was a possibility it was by no means a certainty. Conflict between houses on such points was nothing new. Over a century earlier, when the Commons had impeached the Catholic agitator Edward Fitzsimmons for high treason, the Lords refused to hear the impeachment, maintaining that the trial ought to take place in a court of common law. A constitutional crisis seemed at hand until Charles II ended the confrontation by dissolving Parliament.[87]

This episode aside, the possibility that the managers and other Federalists were contemplating the development of an American *lex Parliamenti* is conjectural, for one finds little if any express mention of it in the Blount proceedings. Nevertheless, the managers' arguments on occasion hinted that this sort of development was in their thoughts. The whole idea of universal impeachment seems perfectly suited to it. Harper's discussion of the impeachability of state officers, and his related emphasis upon impeachment's judicial nature, likewise suggest that state legislators in general, and not merely Blount, were a cause for Federalist concern. Even Ingersoll was aware of the danger of a wedding between *lex Parliamenti* and impeachment, appealing as he did to Magna Carta, though some would argue that his argument was ineffective, for the *lex Parliamenti* was by most accounts distinct from the *lex terrae* of which Magna Carta spoke.[88] The House select committee's investigation of Blount in the summer and fall of 1797, its effective arrest of Nicholas Romayne, its swearing and examination of witnesses, the extensive debate in March 1798 on Henry Tazewell's motion to summon a jury, Congress's passage of statutory oath-administering and perjury provisions a few months later, the repeated references to the "Court" in December 1798 and January 1799, even Ingersoll's and Dallas's use of a judicial-style caption, "United States v. William Blount," on some of their pleadings—all of these developments show that many people were thinking very carefully about the extent of Congress's judicial functions throughout the impeachment. After all of this, the only question was whether the Senate was prepared to follow this course to its unknown conclusions, to realize the full, unplumbed potential of the impeachment power.

---

[87]Howell, *Jefferson's Parliamentary Writings* 318 n. 5.
[88]*See* Wittke, *Parliamentary Privilege* chs. 5-6.

ᘖ

On Monday January 7, three days after Ingersoll and Harper had concluded their presentations, the court began secret deliberations on Blount's plea to the Senate's jurisdiction. Almost no record remains of this debate, but the Senate did discuss the plea's sufficiency intermittently throughout the entire week. By this time interest in the affair, at least among some Republicans, was flagging. Other matters, such as attacks on the Alien and Sedition acts, preoccupied them instead. The public, however, continued to pay some attention to the proceedings, and one or two analytical editorials on the subject of Blount's plea appeared in Philadelphia.[89]

On Thursday January 10, a motion by Richard Stockton, seconded by James Ross, came up for a vote. This motion was a resolution to the effect that Blount was a civil officer, that his acts had been of a public nature, and that the defendant's plea was thus insufficient to defeat the Senate's jurisdiction. Almost certainly this resolution, or at least the principles found therein, had been the subject of the three previous days of debate. Because the measure was a procedural issue rather than a decision on the merits of the case, a simple majority would suffice to pass it.

This motion, however, received only eleven of the twenty-five votes cast. All of its supporters were Federalists, and their number included the men who had all along most strongly advocated a broad Senate impeachment power, men such as Paine, Ross, Sedgwick, Stockton, and Tracy. Voting against them, in addition to every Republican present, were seven Federalists including Humphrey Marshall and Jacob Read, the latter having introduced the February 1798 motion to bar impeachment of senators. Thus the split in the Federalist ranks, and Federalist philosophy, that had surfaced almost a year ago once more became apparent. That the broad-construction Federalists were now fighting an uphill battle was obvious even from the text of

---

[89]John Dawson to James Madison, 7 January 1799, Reel 6, *Madison Papers* (Film); Richard Dobbs Spaight to John Haywood, 6 January 1799, Ernest Haywood Papers, Southern Historical Collection, University of North Carolina; *Gazette of the United States*, 12 January 1799, p. 3, cols. 1-2; Ibid., 14 January 1799, p. 3, cols. 1-2.

their failed resolution. Rather than stating that Blount was impeachable regardless of his status as a civil officer, it expressly defined him as a member of this category, suggesting that even the extreme Federalists did not accept the idea of universal impeachment. Even if they did, however, they nevertheless adopted this middle ground, perhaps in the hope of attracting other Federalist votes. With the defeat of Stockton's resolution, debate went on.

On Monday January 14 the managers, in response to a Senate message of the previous Friday, filed into the Senate chamber as the Court of Impeachment convened. On Friday an unknown senator had introduced a resolution declaring Blount's plea sufficient to show that the Senate lacked jurisdiction over the case, though the resolution did not say whether this was because Blount was no longer a senator, because senators were not civil officers, or because of some other reason. Despite its imprecision the senators had approved the resolution by a vote of fourteen to eleven. The vote's composition, without a single exception, was a mirror image of the previous day's decision. Ingersoll, Dallas, and the managers now stood silently as Jefferson intoned the formula that heralded the end of the eighteen-month-old drama. "Gentlemen, Managers of the House of Representatives, and Gentlemen, Counsel for William Blount," he pronounced,

> The Court, after having given the most mature and serious consideration to the question, and to the full and able arguments urged on both sides, has come to the decision which I am now about to deliver.
>
> The Court is of the opinion that the matter alleged in the plea of the defendant is sufficient in law to show that this Court ought not to hold jurisdiction of the said impeachment, and that the impeachment is dismissed.

Bayard and the others departed to inform the House of the decision, and the court adjourned *sine die*. The Blount impeachment was over.[90]

---

[90]8 *Annals of Cong.* 2318-19 (1799); 9 Ibid., 2626, 2648-49.

Epilogue

The Legacy of the Blount Impeachment

On March 30, 1798, as the Blount affair reached its midway point in Congress, Andrew Ellicott awoke half a continent away in Natchez. The hour was not yet four o'clock; dawn was nowhere in sight; but the surveyor had his reasons to be up. The previous evening he had learned that the Spanish garrison in that vipers' nest of intrigue was at last about to take its leave, two and a half years of the signing of Pinckney's Treaty, which obligated it to do so.

Ellicott walked to the Spanish fort, arriving in time to see off the rear guard. The departing troops did not even bother to shut the gate behind them. "I went in," he wrote, "and enjoyed from the parapet, the pleasing prospect of the gallies and boats leaving the shore, and getting underway: they were out of sight of the town before daylight."[1]

As Ellicott went about his business the sun began to rise. For him the early spring day had scarcely begun, but for the Spanish the long shadows seemed not of morning but of *Götterdämmerung*. Though the Blount impeachment proceedings would drag on for another nine months, the frontier that had produced it was witnessing in Natchez the autumn twilight of Spain's stay on the western waters.

A year later the country's memory of the impeachment had already begun to fade as well, following the Spanish frontier posts into

---

[1] Ellicott, *Journal* 176.

oblivion. The evaporation of interest was not quite total; several weeks after the Senate dismissed Blount's impeachment, Theodore Sedgwick wrote an acquaintance of his great disappointment in the chamber's final decision. Sedgwick, a Federalist, had voted with the minority on each of the last two resolutions in a futile attempt to exercise jurisdiction over his former colleague. But though Sedgwick had no choice other than to admit the defeat of the universal impeachment theory, he continued to maintain that the Senate's decision was "as erroneous as possibly could be."[2]

Opinions quite to the contrary flourished elsewhere. Almost simultaneously with Sedgwick's comments, Willie Blount expressed his own amazement that so many senators had taken the broad view of the power. The only explanation, he believed, was that the eleven dissenters were simply ignorant of the Constitution. He did take some comfort, however, in the fact that none of these men were from the South or West.[3]

Despite these observations, controversy over the affair died down very quickly after the Senate's January 14 dismissal. Occasionally one finds a reference to the dispute in later years; editors of the *Aurora* and the *Philadelphia Gazette*, for instance, engaged in a sparring match over the subject in early 1801. For days these party organs carried charges and counter-charges, each of the papers attempting to associate Blount with the other's political faction. Two years later a member of the Senate, Republican James Jackson of Georgia, cited in passing the Blount affair as an example of Federalist intrigues. In 1812 John Adams placed Blount's name prominently in a list of unsavory Americans, lamenting the speculator's escape from justice. Except for these rare mutterings, however, little evidence suggests that the public dwelt upon the incident for more than a few days after the dismissal, in sharp contrast to the uproar that greeted Blount's 1797 exposure.[4]

---

[2]Theodore Sedgwick to Peter Van Schaack, 12 March 1799, Sedgwick Papers, Massachusetts Historical Society.

[3]Willie Blount to Moses Fisk, 14 March 1799, *John Overton Papers* (Film), Southern Historical Collection, University of North Carolina.

[4]*Philadelphia Gazette*, 19 January 1801, p. 3, col. 3; Ibid., 20 January 1801, p. 3, col. 2; Ibid., 21 January 1801, p. 3, col. 2; Ibid., 22 January 1801, p. 3, col. 2; *Aurora*, 20 January 1801, p. 2, cols. 1-2; Ibid., 21 January 1801, p. 2, cols. 1-2; Ibid., 22 January 1801, p. 2, cols. 1-2; 12 *Annals of Cong.* 245-46 (1803); 2 Lester

One of the more interesting references came in the midst of Aaron Burr's trial in 1807.[5] Kentucky judge Thomas Todd, in Richmond as a witness, declared to fellow jurist Harry Innes that Humphrey Marshall had been involved in Blount's affair. "I have been informed," he wrote Innes, who remained in Kentucky, "that H. Marshall was connected with Blount in his Conspiracy, that letters from Doctr Romaine will clearly prove it, as well as letters from H.M. to B." Todd went on to allege that Blount's executor had copies of the damning letters; in a later missive, he renewed his charge that "that abandoned & profligate villain" Marshall "had been engaged in Blount's Conspiracy" and that a public investigation was appropriate. The possibility is intriguing, especially in light of a statement of John Chisholm to Rufus King in 1797 that he suspected that, in addition to Blount, "some of the Members [of Congress] who owned Lands on the Western Waters, would favor my plan." While Marshall's complicity might help to explain why the Kentucky Federalist sided with the Republicans so often during the Blount impeachment, nothing came of Todd's allegations.[6]

Blount himself was party to none of these communications. Of most of them he never even had an opportunity to be aware. As 1799 wore on he experienced a sharp decline in his political power and his health. His financial state remained as abysmal as it had been throughout the preceding years. He remained a celebrity in Tennessee, but popularity could furnish no remedy for the illness he contracted barely a year after the Senate dismissed the charges against him. On the evening of March 21, 1800, Blount suffered the last of a week-long series of seizures. Tears sprang from his eyes, and he turned

---

J. Cappon, ed., *The Adams-Jefferson Letters* (Chapel Hill: University of North Carolina Press, 1959) 300-01.

[5]For a discussion of the Burr episode, see pages 241-47 *infra*.

[6]Thomas Todd to Harry Innes, 23 September 1807; Thomas Todd to Harry Innes, 27 September 1807, The Papers of Harry Innes, Manuscript Division, Library of Congress; Report of Examination of Chisholm by Rufus King, *in* Turner, "Documents" 602. Turner has raised the possibility, based on a letter of the French general Victor Collot, that Samuel Livermore and John Rutherford may somehow have been involved in the conspiracy. *See* General Collot to Chevalier de Yrujo, in Turner, "Documents," 585 & n.3. One should here note that Livermore in particular took an active role in debate and committee work during the Blount impeachment and expulsion proceedings. See chapters 3-5, *supra*.

his face to the wall and died.[7]

❧

While these events transpired, things continued to change on the frontier. As Ellicott had witnessed, many of the circumstances that had brought about the Blount Conspiracy and shaped the course of the impeachment were themselves disappearing, to be replaced by startlingly new ones. By 1800 Spain was desperate to be rid of Louisiana. As the nineteenth century dawned, the would-be buffer against United States power was far less populous and defensible than the eastern side of the Mississippi. Even as early as August 1797, with revelations of the Blount affair coming to light, Manuel de Godoy had glumly observed that "You can't lock up an open field"—a good description of the Mississippi Valley. Blount's was not the last of the frontier intrigues, and even Blount himself stayed in contact with some of his agents in the year before his death. Louisiana was simply too open to foreign incursions, whether official or private in origin. Even more important was Louisiana's financial condition. Its expenses consistently outran its revenues by a margin of five to one.[8]

In light of these and other concerns, Godoy determined to cede Louisiana back to France, by now under Napoleon's control, in exchange for French territorial concessions in Europe. After a series of negotiations and maneuvers, France took possession of Louisiana in November 1803, just in time to transfer it to the United States. Various considerations—dangers of British sea power, France's overexertion in Santo Domingo against the rebellious forces of Toussaint L'Ouverture, and others—played a role in Napoleon's decision to part with the region. Whatever the cause, however, the effect was clear. The United States instantly doubled its territory, encompassing most of the region the allure of which had drawn Blount into financial and political ruin.[9]

By 1803, too, the naval war between France and America had long

---

[7]Masterson, *William Blount* 342-46; 3 Masterson, *John Gray Blount Papers* 352-54.

[8]Whitaker, *Mississippi Question* 176-80 (quoting Godoy); Masterson, *William Blount* 344-45.

[9]Whitaker, *Mississippi Question* 180-86, 234-36, 250-53.

since abated. Even by early 1799, increasing American naval strength had cleared United States coastal waters of French privateers and moved into the West Indies to harass French shipping there. The economic cost to France soon greatly outweighed the profits the country had expected to reap from the wrecking of American commerce, and by 1799 the French government sought peace. By 1801, in adopting the Convention of Môrtefontaine, the two countries reached a settlement which, while somewhat unsatisfactory, at least brought an end to the conflict.[10]

Though the naval war had cost the French a considerable sum, it also drained a large amount from the American Treasury. By 1800 the war was unpopular. It had brought new taxes, an increased national debt, and the Federalist high-handedness evident in the Alien and Sedition Acts and the Blount impeachment. The Federalists, so recently at the apex of popularity, now found themselves in great trouble at the polls because of these and other matters. In the presidential election of 1800 came Adams's defeat and the triumph of Jefferson, and the Federalist party began the long decline from which it would never recover. The Alien Friends Act expired in 1800, two years after its passage, and the Sedition Act followed in early 1801. The Republicans, now ascendant in Congress, repealed the Naturalization Act soon thereafter. Only the Alien Enemies Act, the wartime measure that had never taken effect, survived.[11]

The Alien and Sedition Acts, and the extreme Federalist doctrine of universal impeachment, were all born largely of a Federalist desire to maintain control over the organs of the national government. All failed to help them achieve this goal, and indeed the statutes were actually counterproductive, as was probably true of the universal impeachment theory as well. The Federalists did act to secure long-term control of the national judiciary by creating and filling a large number of new judgeships in early 1801, but after Thomas Jefferson's March inauguration they found themselves the opposition party in the two political branches.[12] Now the Republicans controlled not only

---

[10]DeConde, *The Quasi-War* chs. 5-10; Elkins & McKitrick, *The Age of Federalism* ch. 14; Miller, *Federalist Era* 217, 242-46.

[11]Elkins & McKitrick, *The Age of Federalism* ch. 15; Miller, *Federalist Era* 217, 242, 257.

[12]Elkins & McKitrick, *The Age of Federalism* 750-52; Miller, *Federalist Era* 275.

the legislative power but the impeachment power as well, and the next few years would see a new turn of events as the Republicans exercised the latter in an attempt to wrest the judicial branch from the Federalists' grip.

ઝ

The first impeachment to follow Blount's was that of Judge John Pickering of the District Court for New Hampshire. Pickering, a Federalist, had had a long and distinguished career in his home state, but by 1794 he had begun to show signs of insanity. By 1803 his behavior on the bench was often quite bizarre, and finally Jefferson himself brought the matter to the House's attention. In October 1803, with a minority of eight Federalists facing a bipartisan majority of forty-five, the House voted its second impeachment, although as had been the case in Blount's affair the chamber only much later approved specific charges.[13]

Pickering's impeachment bore many similarities to Blount's. The voting was at least partly according to party lines, with the pro-impeachment faction emphasizing the facts of the matter and the opposition party invoking points of law in an attempt to frustrate the process. The articles of impeachment, although not charging Pickering with madness, did allege that he acted "contrary to his trust and duty" while on the bench, a veritable repetition of the phrase that appeared in the Blount articles.[14]

Another similarity between the Blount and Pickering episodes was that of the defendant's absence. Neither Pickering nor anyone representing him appeared before the Senate at any point of the trial. The upper house did debate whether impeachment was a criminal proceeding that required the defendant's participation, but in the end it followed the same course that it had taken in the Blount episode, this time, in fact, going still further, since it proceeded without even waiting for Pickering to appear by proxy.[15] In so doing, the senators dealt another blow to the theory that impeachment was a process

---

[13]Hoffer & Hull, *Impeachment* 206-08. For a recent history of the Pickering impeachment, see Bushnell, *Impeachment Trials* ch. 3.

[14]Hoffer & Hull, *Impeachment* 208-10, 214-15.

[15]Ibid., 214-16.

subject to Bill of Rights criminal guaranties.

The most interesting similarity between the two impeachments, however, was the participation of James A. Bayard and Robert Goodloe Harper in leading roles. Bayard served on the House's initial committee of inquiry, where he attempted to slow the process as he had in Blount's impeachment proceedings in early 1798. Harper, by early 1804 a private attorney, appeared before the Senate to intercede on Pickering's behalf, although he did not officially represent the judge. During the Blount episode Harper occasionally had shown a concern for procedural safeguards, and his actions in Pickering's impeachment were consistent with those of earlier moments. His principal argument was that the Senate could not try an insane defendant who lacked the necessary capacity.[16]

Of course Pickering's impeachment also differed in some respects from Blount's, but these differences generally gave greater weight to Congress's decisions in the earlier incident, rather than negating those decisions' importance. Pickering's case, for instance, did reach trial on the merits, and the Senate did convict and remove him. Blount had at least had attorneys present during pre-trial arguments, but the lack of counsel for Pickering during a trial on the facts greatly reinforces the view that procedural laxity, at least regarding the defendant's presence, was the norm in impeachment. The parties were reversed, with Republicans generally seeking Pickering's removal and Federalists making up the bulk of the opposition.[17] This fact reveals one common denominator of these two impeachments, at least; in each instance the pro-impeachment group relied on the particular facts and the opposition tended to appeal to points of law.

In the Pickering and Blount impeachments, then, one sees an interesting trend. Both of the proceedings had a definite factional element, but this factionalism did not exactly correspond to the established political parties. Willis A. Estrich has observed that

---

[16]Ibid., 213-15.

[17]Ibid., 217, 219-20. The authors argue that the Pickering impeachment was not partisan in origin, but rather that Pickering was an incompetent judge who needed removing regardless of partisan issues. This assertion may be true, but the fact remains that the episode demonstrated the doctrine's utility. This was the first instance of impeachment of a federal judge as well as the first conviction, and these facts could be lost on no one.

impeachment presents a very good occasion for a bipolar division, and the Blount and Pickering impeachments seem to support this argument.[18] The division in those cases, however, essentially arose out of legislators' views on procedural requirements rather than party alignment.

Political parties did play a prominent role, however, in the third and final federal impeachment of the early national era. The very day of Pickering's conviction, two representatives arrived at the bar of the Senate to announce the House's impeachment of Samuel Chase, an associate justice of the United States Supreme Court. Of the first three defendants, Chase was clearly the most partisan. His "virulent Federalism" often spurred him to behave in a scandalous fashion on the bench, especially when he rode circuit. Chase frequently resorted to bullying Republican defendants and their attorneys, a fact to which Alexander James Dallas, having once been the justice's target, could personally attest. Often Chase's rulings at trial were so restrictive as to amount to a prejudging of the controversy. He invariably subjected Republicans to his ploys. In 1803, when charging a grand jury in Baltimore, Chase even went so far as to deliver a diatribe against the Jefferson administration. This sort of behavior the Republicans in Congress would not tolerate, and by convicting Pickering they had forged a weapon with which they could attack Chase.[19]

Pickering's removal and Chase's impeachment came in March 1804, but the Senate did not begin the latter's trial until the following February. Unlike his predecessors, Chase was present for at least a part of the trial, and like Blount he had the assistance of counsel, among whom, ironically, was Robert Goodloe Harper. Once again the defense sought to fight off fact-based frontal assaults by employing procedural intricacies. Because the charges stemmed directly from Chase's political statements and conduct in the courtroom, this impeachment was clearly much more overtly partisan than either of the two earlier episodes.

---

[18]Willis A. Estrich, "The Law of Impeachment," 20 *Cas. & Com.* 454, 454-55 (1913).

[19]Hoffer & Hull, *Impeachment* 217, 228-231. For a recent history of the Chase impeachment, see Bushnell, *Impeachment Trials* ch. 4; William H. Rehnquist, *Grand Inquests: The Historic Impeachments of Justice Samuel Chase and President Andrew Johnson* (New York: William Morrow and Company, Inc., 1992).

Throughout the month of February 1805 the Senate heard an impressive battery of arguments. Chase's attorneys were more talented than their adversaries, and their use of the law was often exceptional. Finally came the vote, a very partisan one, on the impeachment articles. Although the Republicans obtained majorities on a number of the charges, in no case did two-thirds of the Senate vote to convict the associate justice, thanks in part to a few Republicans who consistently sided with the Federalists. Chase thus escaped the full force of Congress's wrath, but the episode had a sobering effect on him, and he was never the same man afterwards.[20] If the House used impeachment in 1797 to investigate an international conspiracy, then the Republicans used it in 1805 to silence one of their most vociferous critics on issues of domestic and foreign policy. In doing so they achieved the goal that had eluded the arch-Federalists in their quest for universal impeachment.

Despite the Republicans' success in their campaign against Chase, however, they failed as completely as the Federalists had to make the impeachment process into a workable mechanism for the maintenance of party hegemony and control. By the conclusion of the proceedings against the associate justice, impeachment's eight-year history revealed its limitations, and the desirability of some alternative, or at least supplementary, forum for dealing with great offenders was necessary. To see this, one only need look to the trial of former Vice President Aaron Burr, which took place in an Article III court. Jefferson and his administration had no desire to disqualify Burr from holding political office in the future, as the Federalists had professed to want during the Blount impeachment. Jefferson's goal was more straightforward; he wanted to see Burr on the gallows.

Aaron Burr, one of the most notorious Americans of his day, no doubt knew something of Blount's plans, certainly from the publicity his friend Blount had received in the summer days of 1797, and perhaps directly from Blount himself. His acquaintance with the Tennesseean dated back at least to his failed bid for the vice-

---

[20]Hoffer & Hull, *Impeachment* 236-55.

presidency in 1796, when Blount, in support of Jefferson and Burr, had crossed the aisle, and Burr's name had after all cropped up now and then in the correspondence between Blount and Nicholas Romayne. All of this, admittedly, is scant evidence with which to implicate him in the Blount Conspiracy whether or not he had a hand in that business, though his own scheme resembled the details of Blount's plan closely enough to make contemporary observes comment on the fact.[21]

Despite his dislike of Jefferson, and his anger with Hamilton, Burr did share at least one thing with these two; this was a sense of the possibilities, both good and evil, that the West held for the United States. Jefferson wrote in 1802 of the key importance of New Orleans to the Union; Hamilton looked even farther, writing in the late 1790s that "'we ought to squint at South America.'"[22] Burr may have antagonized the one and murdered the other, but he heartily concurred in their sentiments, at least on this point.

The same is true of Blount, James Wilkinson, and others, of course, and on this spectrum Burr lay much closer to the latter two than to Hamilton and Jefferson. Indeed, he lay even beyond them, for he went farther down the road to action than any of them.

Failing to secure the vice-presidency in 1796, Burr won it in 1801, but only by losing the presidency, largely through Hamilton's opposition, to Jefferson. During his tenure came the open rupture with Hamilton, who called him, according to one witness, "a dangerous man, and one who ought not to be trusted with the reins of government." This statement led directly to the heights of Weehawken on the New Jersey side of the Hudson, where Burr felled Hamilton in the duel of July 11, 1804.[23] The vice-president was as cool as a surgeon about the episode; a relative had visited with him following the duel, only learning about it afterwards. "Impossible!" he exclaimed, remembering Burr's matter-of-fact comportment. "I have

---

[21]Thomas Perkins Abernethy, *The Burr Conspiracy* (New York: Oxford University Press, 1954) 33.

[22]Thomas Jefferson to Robert R. Livingston, 18 April 1802, *in* 8 Ford, *Writings of Thomas Jefferson* 143-47; Whitaker, *Mississippi Question* 117; Miller, *Hamilton* ch. 32 (quoting Hamilton).

[23]Miller, *Hamilton* 526-29, 570-74 (quoting Charles D. Cooper); 1 Milton Lomask, *Aaron Burr: The Years from Princeton to Vice President 1756-1805* (New York: Farrar Straus Giroux, 1979) ch. 15.

just had breakfast with the Colonel and he said nothing about it." Upon receiving word of the indictment for murder that New Jersey issued against him, however, and the charge of misdemeanor in his own state of New York, he looked to the western bank of another river, the Father of Waters far to the west, as his new promised land.[24]

Burr went first to St. Simons Island, just off the Georgia coast and, not coincidentally, near the borders of Spanish East Florida. In the fall of 1804 he embarked on an intelligence mission into the region, and then he set out for Washington, where the Senate was about to come into session. One of his last activities there as vice-president was to preside over Chase's impeachment trial; the day after the proceeding ended he said his farewells to the chamber and began his travels westward. Louisiana, and New Orleans, might now belong to the United States, but other Spanish lands lay beyond them, and American westerners found them, too, alluring. In New Orleans a strange mix of frontiersmen, French émigrés, expansionism, and revolutionary zeal combined to produce great support for a move into Spanish lands. Edward Livingston, among others, was a leader of the Mexican Association of New Orleans, a group of several hundred people dedicated to the invasion, or liberation, or acquisition (whichever word fits) of Mexico. Others ranging from newspaper editors to Ursuline nuns also supported the plan, so deep did sentiments run.[25]

Burr lost no time in tapping this vein of public sentiment and proposing an expedition into Spanish territory. His own plans, however, also apparently included the separation of New Orleans from the Union and the creation of an independent, or at least a British-backed, state in the interior, though he often espoused differing objectives depending upon his audience and when he spoke or wrote. Voyaging down the Ohio and the Mississippi on an ornate flatboat, he contacted leading frontier citizens along the rivers' length. On his trips back to the East, he got in touch with leading political figures and on both sides of the mountains he sought the aid of officers in the army and navy alike.[26]

---

[24]2 Lomask, *Aaron Burr* ch. 1; Francis F. Bierne, *Shout Treason: The Trial of Aaron Burr* (New York: Hastings House, 1959) 14-16.

[25]1 Lomask, *Aaron Burr* 358-69; Abernethy, *Burr Conspiracy* 24-35.

[26]Abernethy, *Burr Conspiracy* 24-40.

One of these contacts was William Eaton, who had only recently returned from his adventures in North Africa and the Mediterranean. Having played his role in the Blount investigation, he had moved on to serve as consul in Tripoli, where he had occupied himself with attempting to topple the Barbary regimes that were preying upon American commerce. Hoping to set up a friendly government in the area, making his way to Egypt in 1804, he located Hamet Karamanli, whom he described as the "rightful Pasha of Tripoli," and convinced him to accompany the American to Derna and overthrow the usurper there, who happened to be Hamet's brother. Setting out from Alexandria for Derna at the head of a motley army of about 400, many of whom he had hired in the back streets of the city, Eaton had only a midshipman and eight marines to keep this cutthroat group in line. A biographer writing in 1945 observed that Eaton's course across North Africa was the same route as Montgomery's, but the better comparison is to the exploits of Lawrence of Arabia. Short on food and water, yet somehow keeping the mutinous mercenaries in line, Eaton marched his group hundreds of miles and at the end of it took Derna with the help of American naval forces, including *Hornet* and *Constellation*. He was poised to take the rest of Tripoli when orders came from across the Atlantic summoning him home.[27]

Disgruntled at the federal government's reluctance to put an end to the North African piracy by force, and failing to convince Congress to honor his claims for reimbursement of funds he had expended, Eaton was a ripe target for Burr, and for a time he seemed willing to go along with this new conspiracy. Burr initially declared that he was acting with government approval; but Eaton soon grew wary, and when Burr confessed that he had no such support, the hero of North Africa pulled back, perhaps remembering from personal observation what had befallen Blount and Romayne.[28]

Others who had had some involvement in the Blount Conspiracy, or the impeachment, also played roles in Burr's plot. These included Andrew Jackson in Nashville, who at first had a hand in equipping Burr's men for their trip downriver; Indian agent John McKee, friend

---

[27]Wright & MacLeod, *North Africa* chs. 7-8; *cf.* Jeremy Wilson, *Lawrence of Arabia: The Authorised Biography of T.E. Lawrence* (London: Heinemann, 1989) chs. 14-26.

[28]Abernethy, *The Burr Conspiracy* 41-43.

and confidant of John Chisholm, to whom Burr made overtures; and Jonathan Dayton, a friend of Burr's from their Princeton days, who had signed the articles of impeachment against Blount when he was Speaker of the House, and who had just left the Senate when Burr enlisted his aid in 1806. Burr also sought the help of sitting senator John Smith of Ohio, as well as approaching Anthony Merry, Robert Liston's successor as British Minister to the United States, about the possibility of securing the aid of the Royal Navy, among other things. Finally, Burr had as one of his key partners Major General James Wilkinson.[29]

Wilkinson, still in the pay of Spain, had been on hand to take possession of New Orleans, and with it Louisiana, in the name of the United States in 1803. This triumph, however, had whetted rather than slaked his thirst for acquisition and self-aggrandizement. As Burr set his scheme in motion, and Wilkinson at long last came to the brink of carrying out the plans of which he had long dreamed, in the end he turned against Burr. This, too, was no doubt at least partly due to self-interest and not just patriotism, for Wilkinson was constantly calculating the odds of success and failure. Even as Burr was raising his troops, Wilkinson wrote to Jefferson that New Orleans was in danger.[30]

The administration had heard many things about Burr, and not all of them from the frontier. Indeed, the Chevalier de Yrujo, another holdover from the Blount days, had gotten word of such plans in 1805 and pressed Jefferson to investigate. Jackson, upon learning that Burr's objective was western separation from the Union, immediately sounded the alarm in Nashville and sent word to Washington. Wilkinson's communication, however, was what finally got Jefferson's attention, and the president sent orders to the general and to other American officers on the Mississippi to take all necessary steps to stop Burr. By this time Burr had raised hundreds of troops, and he was already descending the river toward New Orleans with sixty of them. Just above Natchez, however, the conspirator learned that the federal government was moving against him. Deserting his men, fleeing southeast across the Mississippi Territory, he came to within a

---

[29]Ibid., 22, 26-28, 36-37, 56, 116-17; 2 Lomask, *Aaron Burr* 49-52, 65-67.
[30]Abernethy, *The Burr Conspiracy* 150-60; Parmet & Hecht, *Aaron Burr* 108.

few miles of Spanish West Florida before Americans captured him.[31]

Burr's trial for treason took place in Richmond in 1807, with John Marshall on the bench. Facing the defendant on the witness stand, among others, were William Eaton, sporting (shades of T.E. Lawrence at Versailles) a Turkish sash over his uniform, and James Wilkinson, the government's star witness. Washington Irving, reporting on the trial, likened Wilkinson's appearance to that of a swelling turkey-cock. Luckily for Burr, the trial became a battle of wills between Marshall and his hated cousin Jefferson. During this contest Marshall constructed a restrictive definition of treason that ensured Burr's discharge.[32]

By now Congress had gotten into the act. Senator John Smith had escaped from his own indictment when Burr won acquittal, but in November 1807 the Senate began to investigate his involvement with the conspiracy. For a few months in early 1808 the chamber debated a resolution that John Quincy Adams had put forward, which called for Smith's expulsion. Smith procured attorneys, one of whom was Robert Goodloe Harper, who by virtue of this appearance and his experiences in the three federal impeachments to have occurred so far, would seem well on his way to becoming an early leading authority on the American *lex Parliamenti*. On April 9 an expulsion vote, but no expulsion, occurred, with the majority who favored Smith's removal falling one vote short of the necessary two-thirds. Later in the month, however, Smith resigned his seat.[33]

Near the end of 1807 Wilkinson, too, came under congressional scrutiny. On December 31, John Randolph introduced a House resolution calling for an investigation into the general's alleged Spanish connections. A chapter from Wilkinson's earlier days had come to light when Randolph acquired some 1796 correspondence between Wilkinson and Spanish authorities in Louisiana that

---

[31]2 Lomask, *Aaron Burr* 52-54; Abernethy, *The Burr Conspiracy* 197-226. A good overview of what befell Burr as he made for New Orleans and afterward appears in Robert V. Remini, *Andrew Jackson and the Course of American Empire, 1767-1821* (New York: Harper & Row, 1977) ch. 10.

[32]Abernethy, *The Burr Conspiracy* ch. 14; 2 Lomask, *Aaron Burr* chs. 11-12; *United States v. Burr*, 25 F. Cas. 55 (C.C.D. Va. 1807) (No. 14693); Wilson, *Lawrence of Arabia* 605.

[33]Abernethy, *The Burr Conspiracy* 262-63; 17 *Annals of Cong.* 55-98 (1807-08); Ibid., 164-331 (1808).

implicated him in treachery. Randolph's action touched off three years of on-again, off-again congressional investigations of Wilkinson that in the end, as had his western cabals, came to nothing. "Rarely in our history was a full public investigation more appropriate," writes one chronicler of these proceedings, "and rarely did Congress fail more completely, than in the Wilkinson case." As had occurred in the Blount, Chase, and Burr proceedings, however, the investigation's abortive end was yet sufficient to wreak havoc upon the subject's public life. After the Congressional investigations ended in 1811, Wilkinson underwent two courts-martial on charges ranging from poor tactical judgment to lying and drunkenness, and though he won acquittal each time, the end of the War of 1812 brought about a reduction in the army's size and Wilkinson's consequent discharge. To the end of his days he worked on business enterprises and land deals in the United States and Mexico.[34]

By 1813, with Blount dead, Louisiana safe in American hands, the Burr Conspiracy in ruins, Wilkinson's career finished and impeachment having shown its limitations as a grand inquest, at least as Congress had allowed it to develop, and insofar as one equates conviction with success, we would seem to be approaching the end of the story of the first impeachment and the circumstances that produced it. But one last scene of expansionist intrigue remains before we close the door and examine the legacy that the episode has left for modern impeachments. This final scene belongs to Blount's friend and protégé Andrew Jackson.

Jackson, the nation's great "Old Hero," a man who, unlike Washington or Jefferson, earned the sometimes almost fanatical esteem of his countrymen, a man who held his fellow citizens in such thrall that some continued to vote for him for president fifteen years after his death—Jackson was an ill-read, tempestous, bullying frontiersman whose passions often got the better of him. During his brief senatorial career in the midst of the Blount impeachment, Jefferson daily watched him on the floor. "When I was President of the Senate," the Sage of Monticello remarked much later, "he could never speak on account of the rashness of his feelings. I have seen him

---

[34] Jacobs, *Tarnished Warrior* chs. 11-12; George C. Chalou, "James Wilkinson— The Spanish Connection," *in* 1 Schlesinger & Bruns, *Congress Investigates* 105, 105.

attempt it repeatedly, and as often choke with rage. . . . [H]e is a dangerous man." Lacking the polish of Burr, the political acumen of Blount, and the wiles of Wilkinson, Jackson had two things that they did not: an unswerving patriotism that allowed him to unite the sentiments of nationalism and expansionism, and the sense to act on it at the right time.[35]

In the years following the Louisiana Purchase, Americans in both East and West argued that the cession had included the westernmost part of Florida. By 1813 United States claims to the region had expanded in the face of crumbling Spanish power, and that year Jackson, on his own initiative but with administration backing after the fact, invaded what was left of Spanish West Florida. He had learned, no doubt from the Blount and Burr Conspiracies, that without the political and logistical support of the government, such schemes were both fruitless and dangerous. He had never ceased to be an expansionist, however, and he chose his moment well, for in 1813 Florida showed signs of becoming a British staging area for a campaign against Louisiana. Of all who had come before him in the saga of American invasion of Spanish holdings, he alone succeeded, and his success was largely due to his timing.[36]

Five years later, during the First Seminole War, Jackson repeated his performance, this time in East Florida. Again, he secured administration support, although in an ironic twist he failed to win the approval of Secretary of War John C. Calhoun, who believed Jackson to be exceeding his orders. Unlike Wilkinson, Blount, and Burr, Jackson refused to sacrifice Union to expansion, as his conduct during the Burr Conspiracy shows. The irony is that his reconciliation of these two things drew him an attack from the future architect of the most comprehensive theory of constitutional secession that an American ever produced, a theory that Jackson's predecessors might

---

[35]Remini, *Empire* 1-2, 104-05, 164, 311. Daniel Webster, Memorandum of Mr. Jefferson's Conversations, December 1824, 17 Fletcher Webster, ed., *The Writings and Speeches of Daniel Webster* (Boston: Little, Brown & Company, 1903) 364, 371. One should note that this is a second-hand account that Webster wrote in an election year.

[36]Remini, *Empire* ch. 15; Cayton, "Judases," at 188. On the Florida question prior to Jackson's invasion, see Wanjohi Waciuma, *Intervention in Spanish Floridas 1801-1813: A Study in Jeffersonian Foreign Policy* (Boston: Branden Press, 1976).

have been quite happy to employ, had they any desire to concern themselves with constitutional niceties at all.[37]

Jackson's victories were the *coup de grâce* to the Spanish presence in North America. In 1819, largely as a result of events in the Floridas, and Spain's all-too-obviously flagging powers in the New World, Secretary of State John Quincy Adams and the Spanish minister Luis de Onís concluded the treaty that bears their names. Its other name is the Transcontinental Treaty, which aptly describes its result, for in it Spain recognized American territorial claims not only to the Floridas, but to all the land from the Mississippi northwest to the Pacific coast. Texas and points westward remained, but by the time those regions came up as issues, the United States would be discussing them, sometimes at gunpoint, with an independent Mexico. As of 1819 the frontiersmen were at long last free to build their new civilization in the wilderness that would help to ensure America's emergence as a Great Power and ultimately a superpower, or to lay waste to that wilderness, its people, and its ecology (depending upon one's point of view). The epilogue of this story would ultimately play itself out in tropical places with names such as Cavite, Manila, El Caney, Santiago de Cuba, and of course San Juan and Kettle Hills, almost precisely a century after Andrew Ellicott watched the Spanish galleys depart Natchez in the predawn gloom.[38]

∂∾

---

[37]Remini, *Empire* chs. 22-23; William W. Freehling, *The Road to Disunion: Secessionists at Bay 1776-1854* (New York: Oxford University Press, 1990) ch. 14. Southern theories of states' rights, nullification, and secession resembled what the Westerners tried to accomplish only superficially. As Andrew R.L. Cayton has suggested, the southern motivation for secession in the mid-nineteenth century was fear of a federal government that would undertake to do too much, that is, the abolition of slavery; the conspirators of the old Southwest, on the other hand, were willing to take matters into their own hands because of their belief that the national government was doing too little for the frontier. Cayton, "Judases" at 163.

[38]*See generally* Philip Coolidge Brooks, *Diplomacy and the Borderlands: The Adams-Onís Treaty of 1819* (Berkeley: University of California Press, 1939); French Ensor Chadwick, *The Relations of the United States and Spain* (New York: Charles Scribner's Sons, 1909); James W. Cortada, *Two Nations Over Time: Spain and the United States, 1776-1977* (Westport, Connecticut: Greenwood Press, 1978) chs. 2-7.

Meanwhile, with the conclusion of the Chase trial, national impeachments disappeared for many years. Hoffer and Hull cite practical reasons for the Republicans' sudden abandonment of the process, at least on the national level. Among these are the fact that impeachments were by 1805 obviously capable of reaching the highest offices, and that consequently no officeholder would be safe if his opposition gained a majority in Congress. Another possible explanation is the lengthiness and inefficiency of the process. Blount's case had taken place, sporadically, over a year-and-a-half; Chase's had immobilized the Senate for an entire month. These and other factors, argue Hoffer and Hull, brought an end to the Republicans' experimentation with impeachment.[39]

Regardless of the adequacy of these explanations, the fact that Chase's was the last federal impeachment for 25 years is inescapable.[40] Not until Andrew Johnson found himself the target of the process in 1868, moreover, did impeachment regain the importance that it had held in 1805.[41] Then came seven decades when Congress preferred only a handful of impeachments, all of them except one aimed at inferior court judges. Based on this record, Raoul Berger's observation about the power's decline appeared to have some validity. "Once employed to topple giants," he wrote on the eve of events that would disprove him, "impeachment has sunk in this country to the ouster of dreary little judges for squalid misconduct."[42]

After the Senate's conviction of District Court Judge Halsted L. Ritter in 1936, impeachment again disappeared, this time for nearly forty years. The most activity in this period came in the early 1970s when Congress discussed the possibility of impeaching Supreme Court Justice William O. Douglas for a variety of alleged

---

[39]Hoffer & Hull, *Impeachment* 256-62.

[40]Arthur J. Stansbury, *Report of the Trial of James H. Peck* (Boston: Hilliard, Gray and Co., 1833) 45-49.

[41]*See generally* David Miller Dewitt, *The Impeachment and Trial of Andrew Johnson* (New York: The MacMillan Company, 1903); Michael Les Benedict, *The Impeachment and Trial of Andrew Johnson* (New York: W.W. Norton & Company, Inc., 1973).

[42]Berger, *Impeachment* 3.

improprieties. Nothing came of the debate.[43]

Then in 1972 began the great constitutional crisis that will forever be known as Watergate. For many years politicians and scholars had spoken ill of impeachment, and some writers had recently recommended that the rusty machinery be stricken from the Constitution entirely.[44] But with the contest between Congress and Richard M. Nixon's administration the process once again acquired a useful purpose and the threat of an impending impeachment played a key role in bringing about Nixon's resignation.[45]

Whether or not the Watergate crisis was a stimulus for Congress to reassert its initiative, in 1980 the legislature adopted a course of action that would help to revive impeachment still further. By this time the federal judiciary had grown quite large, and Congress set up a statutory process whereby judges would investigate their own ranks and alert the House to the presence of circumstances in which impeachment might be proper.[46] Among so large a number of judges some were bound to commit offenses in Congress's eyes. The first who merited its full attention in the post-Watergate era was District Judge Harry E. Claiborne of Nevada, who refused to resign even after his indictment, conviction, and imprisonment for bribery. For this problem—a sitting federal judge imprisoned and still drawing salary—Congress had only one remedy readily available, and in July 1986 Claiborne became the first person in half a century to suffer impeachment. By October of that same year the Senate had convicted and removed him from office.[47]

By 1986 Congress's workload was much greater than it had been in 1805, and to conduct the impeachment as efficiently as possible the Senate invoked for the first time Rule XI, which it had passed in

---

[43]Albert Broderick, "A Citizen's Guide to Impeachment of a President: Problem Areas," 23 *Cath. U. L. Rev.* 205, 223-29 (1973); Berger, *Impeachment* 53, 86, 94.

[44]*See, e.g.*, Francis X. Wright, "The Trial of Presidential Impeachments: Should the Ghost be Laid to Rest?" 44 *Notre Dame Law.* 1089 (1969).

[45]Gerhardt, *Federal Impeachment Process* 23.

[46]28 U.S.C. § 372(c) (1994); *see generally* Steven Flanders, "Judicial Discipline, Criminal Prosecution and Impeachment," 11 *Just. Sys. J.* 394 (1986).

[47]Flanders, "Judicial Discipline," 395, 397-400; 132 *Cong. Rec.* S29870-73 (1986). For a discussion of the Claiborne proceedings, see Bushnell, *Impeachment Trials* ch. 13; Mary L. Volcansek, *Judicial Impeachment: None Called for Justice* (Urbana: University of Illinois Press, 1993) chs. 2-3.

1936. This rule provided for the use of a committee to collect evidence, hear testimony, and examine witnesses. The committee was to serve as a trial body, in effect, which would report its findings to the whole Senate, and the Senate would then vote upon the defendant's guilt or innocence based on the evidence contained in the committee report.[48]

Even as the impeachment was pending, Claiborne turned to the regular courts, albeit unsuccessfully, to challenge this new procedure. His main claim in federal district court was that the Constitution, in conferring the sole power to try impeachments upon the Senate, barred the Senate from delegating this authority, which, he charged, it did by using an evidentiary committee. Ironically, the courts turned this very argument against Claiborne, dismissing his complaint for lack of jurisdiction in matters of impeachment. Because the Senate had the sole power to try impeachments, one district judge wrote, the regular courts were powerless to intervene in the process. This pronouncement echoed that of the United States Court of Claims, to which Ritter appealed in 1936 in an attempt to continue collecting his judge's salary.[49]

In recent years, however, both before and after the 1980s impeachments, several writers have asserted that the federal courts, and particularly the Supreme Court, have the right to intervene in impeachments. The arguments are diverse. Some scholars rest their contentions on the Court's opinion in *Powell v. McCormack*. In that

---

[48]*See generally* Napoleon B. Williams, Jr. "The Historical and Constitutional Bases for the Senate's Power to Use Masters or Committees to Receive Evidence in Impeachment Trials," 50 *N.Y.U. L. Rev.* 512 (1975). For a recent critique of Senate Rule XI, which provides for the use of impeachment trial committees, see Daniel Luchsinger, Note, "Committee Impeachment Trials: The Best Solution?," 80 *Geo. L.J.* 163-90 (1991). For a convenient reprinting of the senate rules, see *Hastings v. United States*, 802 F. Supp. 490, 501-05 (D.D.C. 1992), *vacated and remanded*, 988 F.2d 1280, 1993 WL 81273 (D.C. Cir.), *dismissed*, 837 F. Supp. 3 (D.D.C. 1993).

[49]*Claiborne v. United States Senate*, No. 86-2780 (D.D.C. Oct. 8, 1986); *Claiborne v. United States Senate*, No. 86-5622 (D.C. Cir. Oct. 9, 1986); *Claiborne v. United States Senate*, No. A-275 (U.S., Oct. 9, 1986); *Ritter v. United States*, 84 Ct. Cl. 293 (1936), *cert. denied*, 300 U.S. 668 (1937). For a brief discussion of *Ritter*, see Prologue, *supra; see also* Buckner F. Melton, Jr., "Federal Impeachment and Criminal Procedure: The Framers' Intent," 52 *Md. L. Rev.* 437, 437-38 (1993).

1969 case the court involved itself in the House's exclusion of the duly elected Adam Clayton Powell, despite the constitutional provision that each house shall be the judge of its members' qualifications.[50] Others have distinguished *Powell* from the impeachment issue or have otherwise discounted it, often with devastating force.[51] Other arguments range from general statements that judicial review would serve to guard the rights of defendants to the distinction that some authors draw between the concept of trial and that of appellate review. The Constitution, the latter argument goes, only gives the Senate sole power to *try* impeachments on the merits. It says nothing about appellate review.[52]

The practical answer to these questions came in 1993 as a result of two more impeachments. After the Claiborne case the House brought charges against Alcee L. Hastings and Walter L. Nixon, Jr., both federal district judges. Like Claiborne, these men underwent criminal trials before they faced impeachment; as a result of these trials Nixon suffered conviction, while Hastings won acquittal. The House impeached Hastings in August 1988 and Nixon in May 1989.[53]

Hastings, like Claiborne before him, brought a civil action to stay the Senate impeachment proceedings. In this suit he charged, *inter alia*, that impeachment following his acquittal in a regular court violated the Fifth Amendment's double jeopardy provision, and that the Senate's delegation of power to an evidentiary committee was unconstitutional. Nixon joined in Hastings's arguments in this case, and before it ended the parties had engaged in an extensive series of arguments concerning the nature of the impeachment power.[54]

---

[50]*Powell v. McCormack*, 395 U.S. 486 (1969); U.S. Const. art. I, § 5, cl. 1; Berger, *Impeachment* 104-05.

[51]Charles L. Black, Jr., *Impeachment: A Handbook* (New Haven: Yale University Press, 1974) 53-63; *See generally* Ira M. Goldberg, "An Essay on Raoul Berger's Thesis for Judicial Intervention in the Process of the Removal of the President of the United States," 1975 *Wis. L. Rev.* 414 (1975); *see generally* J. P. Sweeney, "Presidential Impeachment and Judicial Review," 23 *Am. U.L. Rev.* 959 (1974).

[52]Berger, *Impeachment* 53, 111-12, 116-17.

[53]Flanders, "Judicial Discipline," 394-97; 134 *Cong. Rec.* H20206-24 (1988); 135 *Cong. Rec.* 8814-24 (1989). For a study of the Hastings proceedings, see Volcansek, *Judicial Impeachment* chs. 4-5; for Walter Nixon's story, see Ibid. chs. 6-7.

[54]*Hastings v. United States Senate*, No. 89-1602 (D.D.C. June 1, 1989) (Complaint for Declaratory and Injunctive Relief) 28-29, 32-34; *Hastings v. United*

Although the District Court finally dismissed the judges' case, it did so on the grounds that the suit presented the court with a nonjusticiable political question. This more discretionary, or prudential, "political question" test presents a lower bar to judicial involvement than the outright dismissal for lack of jurisdiction that occurred in the *Ritter* and *Claiborne* cases. By finding that the court had jurisdiction but that the questions were best left to Congress to resolve, Judge Gerhard A. Gesell in effect hinted that the court had some discretion as to its involvement the impeachment process, and that the judiciary itself determined the extent of the restraints upon it.

Before reaching this decision, furthermore, Gesell analyzed and approved of the Senate's use of evidentiary committees, and he also labeled the impeachment process as *sui generis* (and thus not subject to the full weight of criminal procedural guaranties). Despite his findings on the point of justiciability, then, Gesell discussed in dictum the constitutionality of the Senate's impeachment procedures.[55] Dictum aside, however, Hastings and Nixon still lost, and although they won appellate review, the United States Court of Appeals for the District of Columbia Circuit declined to reverse Gesell's decision. This court, in fact, voiced a somewhat stronger regard for the Senate's independence than had Gesell.[56] Following these judicial setbacks the judges went on to hear the Senate pronounce their conviction and removal from office, Hastings in October 1989 and Nixon the following month.[57]

After the courts rejected the two judges' effort to enjoin the

---

States Senate, No. 89-1602 (D.D.C. June 14, 1989) (Order Granting Motion of Walter L. Nixon, Jr., to Intervene as Party Plaintiff); U.S., Congress, Senate, *Proceedings of the United States Senate in the Impeachment Trial of Alcee L. Hastings* ... (Washington: Government Printing Office, 1989) [SuDocs Y1.1/3:101-18] at 862-63, 866-68, 903.

[55]*Hastings v. United States Senate, Impeachment Trial Committee*, 716 F. Supp. 38, 39-41 (D.D.C.), *aff'd*, 887 F.2d 332, 1989 WL 122685 (D.C. Cir. 1989); U.S., Congress, Senate, *Proceedings of the Senate* 909-17.

[56]*Hastings v. United States Senate, Impeachment Trial Committee*, 887 F.2d 332, 1989 WL 122685 (D.C. Cir. 1989); *Nixon v. United States Senate*, 887 F.2d 332 (D.C. Cir. 1989); U.S., Congress, Senate, *Proceedings of the Senate* [SuDocs Y1.1/3:101-18] at 1247-49, 1281-83.

[57]135 *Cong. Rec.* S25329-35 (1989); 135 *Cong. Rec.* 27101-06 (1989).

impeachment proceedings, and after those proceeding had ended, both men again sought judicial redress, challenging the constitutionality of their removals. Hastings even succeeded, at least in district court, in clearing the political question hurdle and having the court invalidate the Senate's use of its Impeachment Trial Committee. The court emphasized that the Senate's constitutional power to "try all impeachments" required the Senate to employ "at least the rudimentary hallmarks of judicial fact-finding." Use of an evidentiary committee, the court stated, denied the 88 senators who did not sit on that committee any first-hand knowledge of the evidence against Hastings or of witness credibility. Thus the process did not meet the either the standards that the word "try" required, or the standards of due process to which Hastings was entitled.[58]

Hastings's victory was short-lived, however, because of the outcome in the litigation that Nixon was simultaneously conducting. Unlike Hastings, Nixon failed to convince the district court that the Impeachment Trial Committee process was so clearly a departure from constitutional standards as to make his claim justiciable. Also unlike Hastings, however, as well as Claiborne and Ritter before him, Nixon managed to take his case before the Supreme Court. There, however, the frantic efforts of several years to subject the impeachment process to judicial review came to an end. In 1993 the Court announced without dissent that, while the judicial branch had jurisdiction, impeachment presented a nonjusticiable political question. The Senate's final decision in Nixon's impeachment thus stood. By year's end Hastings consequently saw the dismissal of his own suit.[59]

From a practical viewpoint the courts' reticence, while praiseworthy, should have been much stronger and more unequivocal. Were the courts to approve and attempt to enforce a judicial intrusion into the impeachment process, it would set a precedent that could have grave political consequences, especially in the case of a presidential impeachment. Court intervention in each succeeding impeachment might well become discretionary, based upon policy or

---

[58]*Nixon v. United States*, 506 U.S. 224 (1993); *Hastings v. United States*, 802 F. Supp. 490, 501-05 (D.D.C. 1992), *vacated and remanded*, 988 F.2d 1280, 1993 WL 81273 (D.C. Cir.), *dismissed*, 837 F. Supp. 3 (D.D.C. 1993).

[59]*Nixon* 506 U.S. at 224; *Hastings*, 837 F. Supp at 3.

even the whim of the judge involved. Such discretion, in eroding finality and certainty, would be dangerous in the extreme. Charles L. Black, Jr., has given the best illustration of the hazards of such judicial involvement. If Congress impeached, convicted, and removed a president, he argues, and the former chief executive brought suit to reclaim his office, and the court sided with the plaintiff, the country might find itself with two claimants to the presidency, one in power, supported by Congress, and one possessing the backing of the courts.[60] Such an event would be a constitutional crisis beside which most previous ones would pale. At best, moreover, the judiciary would be powerless to enforce its decree, accomplishing nothing, but creating a critical uncertainty in the popular mind. One hesitates to imagine the worst.

The same sort of dispute, on a smaller scale, would arise if the judiciary intervened in impeachments of lesser officials. The best way to avoid such difficulties is for the courts to remain clear of the process completely. One may argue that nonreviewability opens the door to Congress's abuse of the power. But Congress has for the most part shown considerable restraint in exercising its impeachment powers, especially compared to the days of Blount, Pickering, and Chase, when those who wrote and originally debated the meaning of the impeachment provisions were sometimes far more procedurally lax than recent politicians. With Congress itself, then, and not with the courts, lies the best promise for a responsible use of impeachment.

Impeachments, however, have increased markedly in number in recent years. Between 1986 and 1989 the House of Representatives voted three of them, and the Senate convicted all three of the defendants. So far in the waning 1990s, Congress has also investigated two federal District Court judges, Robert Aguilar of the Northern District of California and Robert Collins of the Eastern District of Louisiana, with an eye to impeachment.[61] Never, before or since, have impeachment or conviction rates been so high. The existence of the new process for judicial investigations, the Senate's use of evidentiary committees, and the growing number of federal officials, furthermore, all go to suggest that this trend may continue, if

---

[60]Black, *Handbook* 53-55.
[61]Gerhardt, *Federal Impeachment Process* 30.

Congress has not recently found the process too cumbersome. Perhaps, then, if Congress targets judges and officials of particular races or political persuasions, the process might someday pose a threat to Americans' civil liberties.

Before using this argument to justify judicial oversight of impeachment, however, or to deny the validity of an originalist study of the subject, one should at least become an originalist for a time, examining federal impeachment's early history to see what that history might have to say to us. This approach, in fact, is all the more important in the wake of *Nixon v. United States*, for that decision has made the arguments in favor of judicial review of impeachment academic. Henceforth, barring an overruling of, or exception to, *Nixon*, Congress has a free hand in how it conducts impeachments. The only restraints upon the process will be those that Congress not only willingly accepts, but willingly imposes. Those who would argue in favor of fair trial guaranties and due process would do well to argue for the importance of congressional precedent in impeachments, citing decisions in past impeachments in order to shape outcomes in future ones, much as one cites cases in regular courts. When the framers wrote and adopted the impeachment provisions, they no doubt thought and spoke in terms of hypotheticals; Blount's conspiracy was the first real opportunity their generation had to flesh out the process. A summary of how they approached that affair may yet be one of our most useful guides. We may find, in fact, the procedural safeguards that they imposed as surprising as the lack of restraint they showed in other instances.

The first main characteristic of the Blount episode is the instinctive, emotional response in Congress and among the public that gave rise not only to Blount's impeachment, but to his expulsion and the criminal proceedings against him as well. That these events essentially resulted from the information contained in a single letter, and transpired within scant days of Blount's exposure, reveals something of the early generation's view of the accusation process. A related and even more striking characteristic is the House's formulation of specific charges months after it actually preferred the impeachment. That the lower house repeated this pattern in the Pickering and Chase impeachments adds to the impression that the framers and their generation viewed the accusation process as a spontaneous, instinctive reaction to the defendant's perceived wrongdoing. The House has always been the final judge of what grounds are sufficient for impeachment, and if it wished to investigate the matter beforehand, as it did in Judge George Turner's case, it was free to do so. No one, however, gave any indication that the House's actions or speed in July of 1797 were improper except insofar as they might cause the impeachment and expulsion processes to run afoul of each other. In light of this sort of action, recent House proceedings (notably those of the Judiciary Committee during the Watergate crisis) seem to deviate from the early pattern. In 1973 and 1974 the Judiciary Committee debated the issue for months before reporting articles of impeachment, and the House took no steps to impeach Richard M. Nixon before the committee made its report—an exact reversal of the process the chamber followed in the first three impeachments.[62] The House's concern for procedural propriety, and its probable concern for the gravity of a presidential impeachment, are laudable. The Blount impeachment, however, strongly indicates that were we to follow the framers' lead, the House could properly invoke the impeachment power with much more abandon, especially when would-be defendants occupy less sensitive posts than that of chief executive.

A related element is the fact that in the Blount impeachment, and the Pickering and Chase episodes too, each house often departed from criminal procedural guaranties of the common law and the Bill of Rights. Chief among these departures were the Senate's near-unanimous condemnation of Henry Tazewell's jury trial theory, its rejection of Humphrey Marshall's bill that would have given defendants various statutory procedural rights (and also the Sixth Amendment right to compulsory process), and each house's willingness to conduct a trial in Blount's absence. From these and other aspects of the impeachment, one may conclude that impeachment is not as closely bound by procedural details as other criminal proceedings, and even that impeachment is not a criminal process at all. Still another departure from judicial principles is apparent in the factional and often partisan voting that often took place throughout the impeachment.

Oddly enough, in the absence of mandatory procedural guaranties,

---

[62]*See* Ibid., 29.

the factional aspect of impeachment is the element that afforded Blount, and his two successors, their greatest protection. Congress's decision to grant or withhold what we may term due process rights to Blount was completely discretionary, if we assume that no higher authority could overrule this decision. (Once again, we should recall that at no point in the Blount episode do we find the slightest suggestion that Article III courts could review Congress's impeachment activities.) In light of this congressional discretion Blount's best defense was to gain support among legislators who would seek to extend to him whatever safeguards they could. Although few members of Congress possessed any regard for Blount after July 1797, many did believe some procedural limitations to be of great importance, and in the end this belief helped save Blount from the further humiliation of conviction and disqualification to hold office.

Though the framers may not have foreseen the evolution of a two-party system, they did contemplate the possibility of factional conflict.[63] Various elements of the impeachment process, furthermore, indicate that they intended the factions to check each other during such a trial. Chief among the indications of this fact are the requirement of a two-thirds vote for conviction, and an implicit recognition (as the use of common law terms to describe the process illustrates) that impeachment was an adversarial function. In short, the Blount impeachment reflected the framers' intention that a strong congressional impetus for impeachment would meet with congressional opposition, and that this opposition, strengthened by the need for an extraordinary vote for conviction, would act as a check upon the pro-impeachment group's abuse of the power.

Ultimately this adversarial process came to involve Congress's bicameral structure. After a period of uncertainty, the House adopted a very broad view of impeachment, and, in the fashion of good prosecuting attorneys, the managers zealously pressed this point upon the Senate. Had their views prevailed, almost every person in America would have become subject to impeachment, and a highly politicized use of the process might well have followed. The Senate, however, took a different view, although the wording of its final decision in the Blount impeachment has always obscured the reason why it declined

---

[63]See, e.g., The Federalist No. 10 (J. Madison).

jurisdiction. If one views this decision as an exercise in legal logic rather than as a result of politics (assuming the two things to be separable) then only a few explanations are possible. The Senate must have concluded that it lacked authority either because Blount was no longer a senator, or because senators (or perhaps members of Congress) are not civil officers. Perhaps some senators who voted to decline jurisdiction believed only one or another of these things, while others believed them all. Any of these reasons, however, necessarily entails the notion that the senators who voted against jurisdiction considered some persons to be beyond the reach of the process, thus quashing the theory of universal impeachment.[64] But whatever their reasons, they came between Blount and the managers' will, ensuring a victory for the strict constructionists that stands to this day. More than a little of the senators' incentive probably grew from their realization that in protecting Blount, they protected themselves from future impeachments that would originate in the more politically volatile lower house. In the end, then, factional conflict kept the process from reaching an extreme.

The central point of factional controversy in the Blount impeachment, which also arose in Pickering's, Chase's, and other impeachments, was the conflict between facts and law. Because the number of national impeachments is small, and each case unique, impeachment proponents generally focus on the facts of the case, especially since the Constitution contains little definite law on the subject. Impeachment opponents, on the other hand, generally turn to this law—however vague it may be—in an attempt to invalidate the impeachment. This was clearly the pattern of Blount's impeachment, as well the two that immediately followed, and others.

Whether the framers anticipated this specific pattern is unclear, but in the Blount impeachment at least this factional division served to give effect to their intentions; for the evidence of the constitutional and ratifying conventions suggests that the framers intended senators to be impeachable, but only by virtue of their

---

[64]Some writers, including producers of official documents, have failed to grasp that the Senate gave no clear reason for its decision. In 1882, for instance, Attorney General Benjamin H. Brewster declared that the chamber had decided that senators were not civil officers. *See* Member of Congress, 17 Op. Att'y Gen. 419, 420 (1882).

quasi-executive functions. Absent these functions, the framers probably would not have entertained the thought that senators were to be subject to the process. By 1797 the Senate had failed to develop its executive duties to the degree that the framers evidently anticipated. Whatever the reasons for its dismissal of the Blount impeachment, the effect of that decision—to shield a senator from impeachment—is perhaps reconcilable with what the framers had in mind, even as it illustrates how an originalist theory by itself would have been inadequate only a decade after the Constitution's drafting, in light of the Senate's changed circumstances.

This observation leads to the most basic point of all. Faced with the proposition that impeachment was a power without limits, a bipartisan Senate majority, including two framers, decided that limitations did in fact exist. While the process was then, and still is, flexible in procedural terms, this early impeachment nevertheless stands for the principle that very broad constructions of the power are not in keeping with the framers' intent.

॰ঌ

The Blount episode, then, gives us the following picture of the process as the framers understood it, not only in theory, but in practice. Impeachment is born spontaneously, and may proceed legitimately at first in accordance with the principles of clamor and notoriety. The House, as the agency that prefers and prosecutes the impeachment, may act with little procedural restraint and with a zeal that befits an advocate. The Senate is the locus of factional debate, where impeachment opponents exercise checks on the process through appeals to, and application of, discretionary procedural safeguards. In this adversarial opposition lies the defendant's best security. While strict rules of criminal procedure do not apply, the impeachment power does have substantive limitations.

If the process is unreviewable, of course, no remedy for Congress's abuse or perversion of the impeachment power exists, at least outside the halls of Congress itself. The point, however, is that checks do exist within Congress, for one can hardly expect such a large number of legislators to agree upon all of the issues surrounding the process. Even in the most violently emotional moments of impeachment, the moments of the least restraint—notably early in the Blount case and the time of the vote on Andrew Johnson's guilt or innocence—factional conflict acted to check the excesses of the process. Alexander Hamilton's observation that impeachments are political is at least partly true.[65] In this fact lies impeachment's greatest threat to the evildoer, and its greatest safeguards for the defendant. As a partisan process, impeachment is an accurate reflection of our political as well as our human natures, for ultimately the final restraint lies within ourselves. No constitution can endure if those under it, or those party to it, have no regard for it. If Congress chooses to exercise its impeachment powers in the proper fashion, judicial review is unnecessary; if Congress is determined to violate the restrictions upon it, judicial review is useless.[66]

The framers and the other participants in the Blount impeachment are long since dead. But in that early episode they gave a definition to the impeachment power that rested in experience, a knowledge of law and government, and practical insights into human nature. Insofar as the present generation continues to deal with the issues surrounding impeachment, it will find the Blount episode an invaluable guide to this process that remains a viable, if not a vital, part of American constitutional government. William Blount lies in a Tennessee grave, and the frontier has moved far beyond the western waters. But others will no doubt appear among the ranks of federal officials to make Congress confront again the same questions that it once faced in the first impeachment.

---

[65]*The Federalist* No. 65 (A. Hamilton).

[66]"The laws reach but a very little way. Constitute government how you please, infinitely the greater part of it must depend upon the exercise of powers, which are left at large to the prudence and uprightness of ministers of state." Edmund Burke, *Thoughts on the Cause of the Present Discontents*, 1770, in 2 Paul Langford ed., *The Writings and Speeches of Edmund Burke* (Oxford: Clarendon Press, 1981) 241, 277.

જી

They looking back, all th' Eastern side beheld
Of Paradise, so late thir happie seat,
Wav'd over by that flaming Brand, the Gate
With dreadful Faces throng'd and fierie Armes:
Som natural tears they drop'd, but wip'd them soon;
The World was all before them, where to choose
Thir place of rest, and Providence thir guide:
They hand in hand with wandring steps and slow,
Through *Eden* took thir solitarie way.

Appendix 1

Constitutional Clauses Relating to the Blount Impeachment

ARTICLE I

Section 2, clause 5.
The House of Representatives shall chuse their Speaker and other Officers; and shall have the sole Power of Impeachment.

Section 3, clauses 6-7.
The Senate shall have the sole Power to try all Impeachments. When sitting for that Purpose, they shall be on Oath or Affirmation. When the President of the United States is tried, the Chief Justice shall preside: And no Person shall be convicted without the Concurrence of two thirds of the Members present.

Judgment in Cases of Impeachment shall not extend further than to removal from Office, and disqualification to hold and enjoy any Office of honor, Trust or Profit under the United States: but the Party convicted shall nevertheless be liable and subject to Indictment, Trial, Judgment and Punishment, according to Law.

Section 5, clause 2.
Each House may determine the Rules of its Proceedings, punish its Members for disorderly Behaviour, and with the Concurrence of two thirds, expel a Member.

ARTICLE II

Section 2, clause 1.

The President shall be Commander in Chief of the Army and Navy of the United States, and of the Militia of the several States, when called into the actual Service of the United States; he may require the Opinion, in writing, of the principal Officer in each of the executive Departments, upon any Subject relating to the Duties of their respective Offices, and he shall have Power to grant Reprieves and Pardons for Offences against the United States, except in Cases of Impeachment.

Section 4.

The President, Vice President and all civil Officers of the United States, shall be removed from Office on Impeachment for, and Conviction of, Treason, Bribery, or other high Crimes and Misdemeanors.

ARTICLE III

Section 2, clause 3.

The Trial of all Crimes, except in Cases of Impeachment, shall be by Jury; and such Trial shall be held in the State where the said Crimes shall have been committed; but when not committed within any State, the trial shall be at such Place or Places as the Congress may by Law have directed.

AMENDMENT 6

In all criminal prosecutions, the accused shall enjoy the right to a speedy and public trial, by an impartial jury of the State and district wherein the crime shall have been committed, which district shall have been previously ascertained by law, and to be informed of the nature and cause of the accusation; to be confronted with the witnesses against him; to have compulsory process for obtaining witnesses in his favor, and to have the Assistance of Counsel for his defence.

Appendix 2

Articles of Impeachment Against William Blount

ৡ

Articles exhibited by the House of Representatives of the United States, in the name of themselves and of all the people of the United States, against William Blount, in maintenance of their impeachment against him for high crimes and misdemeanors.

ARTICLE 1. That, whereas the United States, in the months of February, March, April, May, and June, in the year of our Lord one thousand seven hundred and ninety-seven, and for many years then past, were at peace with His Catholic Majesty, the King of Spain; and whereas, during the months aforesaid, His said Catholic Majesty and the King of Great Britain were at war with each other; yet the said William Blount, on or about the months aforesaid, then being a Senator of the United States, and well knowing the premises, but disregarding the duties and obligations of his high station, and designing and intending to disturb the peace and tranquillity [sic] of the United States, and to violate and infringe the neutrality thereof, did conspire, and contrive to create, promote, and set on foot, within the jurisdiction and territory of the United States, and to conduct and carry on from thence, a military hostile expedition against the territories and dominions of His said Catholic Majesty in the Floridas and Louisiana, or a part thereof, for the purpose of wresting the same from His Catholic Majesty, and of conquering the same for the King of Great Britain, with whom His said Catholic Majesty was then at war as aforesaid, contrary to the duty of his trust and station as a Senator of the United States, in violation of the obligations of neutrality, and against the laws of the United States, and the peace and interests thereof.

ARTICLE 2. That, whereas, on the twenty-seventh day of October, in the year of our Lord one thousand seven hundred and ninety-five, a Treaty of Friendship, Limits, and Navigation, had been made and concluded between the United States and His Catholic Majesty, by the fifth article whereof it is stipulated and agreed, "that the two high contracting parties shall, by all the means in their power, maintain peace and harmony among the several Indian nations who inhabit the country adjacent to the lines and rivers, which, by the preceding articles, form the boundaries of the two Floridas: And the better to obtain this effect, both parties oblige themselves expressly to restrain by force all hostilities on the part of the Indian nations living within their boundary; so that Spain will not suffer her Indians to attack the citizens of the United States, nor the Indians inhabiting their territory; nor will the United States permit these last mentioned Indians to commence hostilities against the subjects of His Catholic Majesty or his Indians, in any manner whatever:" Yet, the said William Blount, on or about the months of February, March, April, May, and June, in the year of our Lord one thousand seven hundred and ninety-seven, then being a Senator of the United States, and well knowing the premises, and that the United States were then at peace with His said Catholic Majesty, and that His Catholic Majesty was at war with the King of Great Britain, but disregarding the duties of his high station, and the stipulations of the said treaty, and the obligations of neutrality, did conspire and contrive to excite the Creek and Cherokee nations of Indians, then inhabiting within the territorial boundary of the United States, to commence hostilities against the subjects and possessions of His Catholic Majesty, in the Floridas and Louisiana, for the purpose of reducing the same to the dominion of the King of Great Britain, with whom His Catholic majesty was then at war as aforesaid: contrary to the duty of his trust and station as a Senator of the United States, in violation of the said Treaty of Friendship, Limits, and Navigation, and of the obligations of neutrality, and against the laws of the United States, and the peace and interests thereof.

ARTICLE 3. That, whereas, by the ordinances and acts of Congress for regulating trade and intercourse with the Indian tribes, and for preserving peace on the frontiers, it has been made lawful for the President of the United States, in order to secure the continuance of the friendship of the said Indian tribes, to appoint such persons, from time to time, as temporary agents, to reside among the Indians, as he shall think fit; and whereas, in pursuance of the said authority, the President of the United States, on or about the eighth day of September, in the year of our Lord one thousand seven hundred and ninety-six, did appoint Benjamin Hawkins, to be principal temporary agent for Indian affairs, within the Indian nations south of the river Ohio, and north of the territorial line of the United States; and whereas the said Benjamin Hawkins accepted the said appointment, and on the 21st day of April, in the year of our Lord one thousand seven hundred and ninety-seven, and for a long time before and afterwards, did exercise the functions, powers and duties attached to the same; yet, the same Wm. Blount, on or about the said twenty-first day of April, in the year of our Lord one thousand seven hundred and ninety-seven, then being a Senator of the United States, and well knowing the premises, did, in the prosecution of his criminal designs and of his conspiracies aforesaid, and the more effectually to accomplish his intention of exciting the Creek and Cherokee nations of Indians to commence hostilities against the subjects of His Catholic Majesty, further conspire and contrive to alienate and divert the confidence of the said Indian tribes or nations from the said Benjamin Hawkins, the principal temporary agent aforesaid, and to diminish, impair, and destroy the influence of the said Benjamin Hawkins with the said Indian tribes, and their friendly intercourse and understanding with him, contrary to the duty of his trust and station as a Senator of the United States, and against the ordinances and laws of the United States, and the peace and interests thereof.

ARTICLE 4. That, whereas, by the ordinances and acts of Congress aforesaid, it is made lawful for the President of the United States to establish trading houses at such places and posts on the western and southwestern frontiers, or in the Indian country, as he shall judge most convenient, for the purpose of carrying on a liberal trade with the several Indian nations within the limits of the United States, and to appoint an agent at each trading house established as aforesaid, with such clerks and assistants as may be necessary for the execution of the said acts: And, whereas, by a treaty, made and concluded on the second day of July, in the year of our Lord one thousand seven hundred and ninety-one, between the United States and the Cherokee nation of Indians, inhabiting within the limits of the United States, it is stipulated and agreed, that "the United States will send such, and so many persons to reside in said nation, as they may judge proper, not exceeding four, who shall qualify themselves to act as interpreters." And whereas the President of the United States, as well in pursuance of the authorities in this article mentioned, as of the acts of Congress referred to in the third article, did appoint James Carey to be interpreter for the United States to the said Cherokee nation of Indians, and assistant at the public trading house established at the Tellico blockhouse, in the State of Tennessee: And whereas the said James Carey did accept the said appointments, and on the twenty-first day of April, in the year of our Lord one thousand seven hundred and ninety-seven, and for a long time before and afterwards, did exercise the functions, and duties attached to the same; yet the said William Blount, on or about the twenty-first day of April, in the year last aforesaid, then being a Senator of the United States, and well knowing the premises, did, in prosecution of his criminal designs, and in furtherance of his conspiracies aforesaid, conspire and contrive to seduce the said James Carey from the duty and trust of his said appointments, and to engage the said James Carey to assist in the promotion and execution of his said criminal intentions and conspiracies aforesaid, contrary to the duty of his trust and station as a Senator of the United States, and against the laws and treaties of the United States, and the peace and interests thereof.

ARTICLE 5. That whereas certain tribes or nations of Indians inhabit within the territorial limits of the United States, between whom, or many of them, and the settlements of the United States, certain boundary lines have, by successive treaties, been stipulated and agreed upon, to separate the lands and possessions of the said Indians from the lands and possessions of the United States, and the citizens thereof: And whereas, particularly, by the treaty in the last article mentioned to have been made with the Cherokee nation, on the second day of July, in the year of our Lord one thousand seven hundred and ninety-one, the boundary line between the United States and the said Cherokee nation was agreed and defined; and it was further stipulated, that the same should be ascertained and marked plainly by three persons appointed on the part of the United States, and three Cherokees on the part of their nation: And whereas, by another treaty made with the said Cherokee nation, on the twenty-sixth day of June, in the year of our Lord one thousand seven hundred and ninety-four, the said hereinbefore recited treaty, of the second day of July, in the year of our Lord one thousand seven hundred and ninety-one, was confirmed and established; and it was mutually agreed that the said boundary line should be actually ascertained and marked in the manner prescribed by the said last mentioned treaty: And whereas, in pursuance of the said treaties, commissioners were duly nominated and appointed, on the part of the United States, to ascertain and mark the said boundary line; yet, the said William Blount, on or about the twenty-first day of April, in the year of our Lord one thousand seven hundred and ninety-seven, then being a Senator of the United States, and well knowing the premises, in further prosecution of his said criminal designs, and of his conspiracies aforesaid, and the more effectually to accomplish his intention of exciting the said Indians to commence hostilities against the subjects of His Catholic Majesty, did further conspire and contrive to diminish and impair the confidence of the said Cherokee nation in the Government of the United States, and to create and foment discontents and disaffection among the said Indians towards the Government of the United States, in relation to the ascertainment and marking of the said boundary line, contrary to the duty of his trust and station as a Senator of the United States, and against the peace and interests thereof.

And the House of Representatives, by protestation, saving to themselves the liberty of exhibiting at any time hereafter, any further articles, or other accusation, or impeachment, against the said William Blount, and also of replying to his answers, which he shall make unto the said articles, or any of them, and of offering proof to all and every the aforesaid articles, and to all and every other articles of impeachment, or accusation, which shall be exhibited by them, as the case shall require, do demand that the said William Blount may be put to answer the said crimes and misdemeanors, and that such proceedings, examinations, trials, and judgments, may be thereupon had and given, as are agreeable to law and justice.

Signed by order and in behalf of the House.

JONATHAN DAYTON, *Speaker.*

Attest, JONATHAN W. CONDY, *Clerk.*

Appendix 3

Senate Voting Record, Blount Expulsion, and Impeachment[1]

჻

The *Annals of Congress* contain various Senate votes by roll on various aspects of the Blount expulsion and impeachment. Not all votes are so listed; the votes counted here, then, constitute an incomplete record. House votes by roll are so scarce as to make quantitative analysis of them meaningless.

In this table, each senator voting in an ascertainable manner is represented by a list showing the total number of ascertainable votes that he cast, the number of times he voted for and against Blount, and the breakdown of these numbers by percentage. Totals by party and by overall membership also appear. Votes "for Blount" are those in support of either additional procedural safeguards or further delays in the expulsion or impeachment processes.

---

[1]. References: 7 *Annals of Cong.* 41, 44 (1797); 7 *Annals of Cong.* 503, 508-09, 521 (1798); 8 *Annals of Cong.* 2318-19 (1799).

Name	Federalist	Republican	Votes cast	Votes for Blount	Votes against Blount	Percentage for Blount	Percentage against Blount
Anderson, Joseph		R	7	6	1	86%	14%
Bingham, William	F		8	2	6	25%	75%
Bloodworth, Timothy		R	9	7	2	78%	22%
Bradford, William	F		2	0	2	0%	100%
Brown, John		R	9	6	3	67%	33%
Chipman, Nathaniel	F		6	0	6	0%	100%
Clayton, Joshua	F		2	0	2	0%	100%
Cocke, William		R	2	1	1	50%	50%
Davenport, Franklin	F		2	0	2	0%	100%
Foster, Theodore	F		9	4	5	44%	56%
Goodhue, Benjamin	F		8	0	8	0%	100%
Greene, Ray	F		6	2	4	33%	67%
Gunn, James	F		6	3	3	50%	50%
Henry, John	F		2	0	2	0%	100%
Hillhouse, James	F		8	3	5	38%	63%
Hobart, John Sloss	F		4	0	4	0%	100%
Howard, John E.	F		7	2	5	29%	71%
Hunter, John		R	5	0	5	0%	100%
Jackson, Andrew		R	4	4	0	100%	0%
Langdon, John		R	8	5	3	63%	38%
Latimer, Henry	F		4	0	4	0%	100%
Laurance, John	F		3	0	3	0%	100%
Livermore, Samuel	F		8	0	8	0%	100%
Lloyd, James	F		5	0	5	0%	100%
Marshall, Humphrey	F		9	6	3	67%	33%
Martin, Alexander		R	8	5	3	63%	38%
Mason, Stevens T.		R	6	6	0	100%	0%
Paine, Elijah	F		5	0	5	0%	100%
Read, Jacob	F		8	2	6	25%	75%
Ross, James	F		8	0	8	0%	100%
Rutherford, John	F		2	0	2	0%	100%
Sedgwick, Theodore	F		8	0	8	0%	100%
Stockton, Richard	F		6	0	6	0%	100%
Tattnall, Josiah		R	4	1	3	25%	75%
Tazewell, Henry		R	5	4	1	80%	20%
Tichenor, Isaac	F		2	0	2	0%	100%
Tracy, Uriah	F		8	1	7	13%	88%
Vining, John	F		2	0	2	0%	100%
Total (Federalist)	27		148	25	123	17%	83%
Total (Republican)		11	67	45	22	67%	33%
GRAND TOTALS:	71%	29%	215	70	145	33%	67%

Sources

I. Bibliographical Essay

The two most likely citation manuals for this project would seem to be *The Chicago Manual of Style* (Chicago: The University of Chicago Press, 14th ed. 1993) and *The Bluebook: A Uniform System of Citation* (Cambridge, Massachusetts: The Harvard Law Review Association, 16th ed. 1996). Unfortunately, each has deficiencies for a work that partakes of both law and history. Section 15.312 of the *Chicago Manual* recognizes that predominately legal works would be better off following the *Bluebook*, but the latter, while usually adequate for law review editors and legal scholars, has serious deficiencies for the historian. The citation style in this book thus reflects an attempt to combine the best that each has to offer, with the overarching rule being that of consistency. One major point requires particular mention; in light of the confusion that the *Bluebook*'s 16th edition has caused in some quarters regarding its revised Rule 1.2, which concerns introductory signals, the use of such signals in this book's footnotes conforms to rule 2.1 as it appears in the 15th edition.

A knowledge of both diplomatic and frontier history is necessary to understand the forces that produced the Blount Conspiracy, and consequently the Blount impeachment. Likewise, a background in the politics of 1790s America is essential for the researcher to be able to view this impeachment in its proper context. To that end, the narrative gives some account of these subjects. This book, however, does not pretend to be a general political history of the Federalist period, much less a work of diplomatic or frontier history. The sources below that relate to these subjects, therefore, are highly selective, although the goal has been to include among them any work that gives significant attention to the Blount Conspiracy.

The secondary literature on impeachment, while voluminous, is not unmanageable. Because of impeachment's particularly close relationship to other issues surrounding judicial tenure and removal, however, the author has here necessarily excluded material principally dealing with the latter subject, which is quite extensive in its own right. Those works on judicial tenure and removal containing some significant discussion of impeachment, however, do appear here. Literature and legal materials on state impeachments are likewise omitted, although several entries located in the section on special finding aids will introduce the interested researcher to the subject, particularly state case law.

The primary sources listed comprise only a fraction of the manuscript and microfilm collections that potentially relate to William Blount, the conspiracy, or the impeachment. In theory, all collections of all persons present in Philadelphia from July 1797 to January 1799 are potential sources for impeachment material. Those included here are the most obvious and presumably the most important, the author having selected them from the *National Union Catalog of Manuscript Collections* and a large number of other manuscript guides. The selection criterion was a list of names of individuals heavily involved in the impeachment or sufficiently placed to have considerable knowledge of the proceedings.

Secondary government documents, while reasonably complete regarding impeachment generally, are subject to the same judicial tenure exclusions that apply to nongovernmental secondary literature. Listings of material relating to the Watergate impeachment investigation and the Claiborne, Hastings, and Walter L. Nixon impeachments are not exhaustive, but merely serve to introduce the reader to the subject. The listing of primary source government documents, or those that contain first-hand material relating directly to the Blount episode, is comprehensive.

Newspapers collectively comprise the most important primary source after government documents. Various papers' coverage of congressional debates often include large amounts of material not appearing in the *Annals of Congress* or any other public source. This fact is especially true of the Senate debates, for the clerk of the upper house during this time kept a much more abbreviated record than did the House of Representatives' clerk.

As a guideline for selection the author generally adhered to the newspaper list in Volume 1, Section 8.9 of *The Harvard Guide to American History*, Revised edition (Cambridge, Massachusetts: The Belknap Press of Harvard University Press, 1974). Some exceptions and additional inclusions, however, do appear, and availability of newspapers was also a factor.

Government documents, especially old ones, are often difficult to locate. The various, often differing versions of those documents relating specifically to the Blount impeachment, furthermore, are often highly elusive. So that the researcher may utilize this bibliography more easily, the author has often elected to include parenthetical information that should remove all doubt as to a source's particular identity and location. The parenthetical information furnished usually refers to Superintendent of Documents (SuDocs) or Serial Set numbers, OCLC record numbers, or numbers appearing in the microfilm edition of American Antiquarian Society, editor, *Early American Imprints, 1639-1800*. This latter collection is based on a list of titles originally recorded by Charles Evans, and citations thereto consequently bear his name.

II. Special Finding Aids

A. Bibliography

Dick, Barrett. "A Researcher's Guide to the 'Watergate Affair' Part 1." 71 *Law Library Journal* 77-82 (1978). A brief survey of constitutional questions raised by Watergate, followed by an extensive bibliography of articles relating to impeachment, separation of powers, and executive privilege. Enormously useful to students not only of Watergate but of these constitutional issues in general.

_____. "A Researcher's Guide to the 'Watergate Affair' Part 2." 71 *Law Library Journal* 266-69 (1978). An exhaustive bibliography of books relating to the above subjects.

_____. "A Researcher's Guide to the 'Watergate Affair' Part 3." 71 *Law Library Journal* 420-24 (1978). A similarly comprehensive bibliography of government publications.

Hall, Kermit L. *A Comprehensive Bibliography of American Constitutional and Legal History, 1896-1979.* 5 vols. Millwood, New York: Kraus International Publications, 1984. Together with its supplements the most extensive bibliography on various subjects of constitutional and legal history currently available; Volume 1 contains a section on impeachment. Includes citations to dissertations.

Shaw, James Kevin. *The Impact of Politics on United States Senate Voting on Impeachment.* Diss. University of Nevada at Reno, 1980. Although the bibliography of this work contains inaccuracies of various types, it does include a section on popular periodicals not cited elsewhere. The user is advised, however, to be wary of faulty citations. See also entry under United States impeachments, *infra*.

U.S. Library of Congress. *Select List of References on Impeachment.* Washington: Government Printing Office, 1905. (SuDocs LC2.2:Im7). Contains citations to information on impeachment found in larger, more general works, as well as information on English impeachments and United States government materials relating to various impeachment proceedings.

_____. *Select List of References on Impeachment.* 2d ed. (SuDocs

LC2.2:Im7/2). Washington: Government Printing Office, 1912. A more complete bibliography than the first edition, especially regarding the records of particular impeachments.

B. Other

Guarino, Glenn A. "Constitutional Issues Relating to Federal Criminal Prosecution of Federal Judges." 65 *American Law Reports (Federal)* 819-22 (1983). A summary of case law on the point of amenability of sitting federal judges to indictment; deals with what promises to be a major issue in future impeachments. Also consult pocket part for latest information.

"Judges." 46 *American Jurisprudence 2d* 106-08 (§§ 18-19) (1969). These sections of the entry on judges in this legal encyclopedia comprise a digest, with commentary, of state case law and authority respecting the impeachment of state judges. Also consult pocket part for latest information.

"Officers and Public Employees." 67 *Corpus Juris Secundum* 532-34, 619-21 (§§ 145, 179-81) (1978). Deals with state case law and authority on impeachment generally. Also consult pocket part for latest information.

"Public Officers and Employees." 63A *American Jurisprudence 2d* 821-24 (§§ 211-18) (1984). Deals with state case law and authority on impeachment generally. Also consult pocket part for latest information.

Shipton, Clifford K., & Mooney, Jemes E. *National Index of American Imprints Through 1800: The Short Title Evans.* 2 Vols. Worcester, Massachusetts: American Antiquarian Society and Barre Publishers, 1969. Author index to the microfiche edition of Evans, Early American Imprints.

III. SECONDARY SOURCES

A. Constitutional and Statutory Interpretation

Banning, Lance. "Republican Ideology and the Triumph of the Constitution, 1789 to 1793." 31 *William and Mary Quarterly* (3d. Ser.) 167-88 (April 1974). Provides one possible explanation for the Republicans' adoption of strict construction principles during the early national period.

Symposium, "Fidelity in Constitutional Theory," 65 *Fordham Law Review* 1247 (March 1997). A series of pieces examining the concept of fidelity, paying considerable to questions of interpretation, including the use of history as an interpretive theory.

Fuller, Lon. "The Case of the Speluncean Explorers." 62 *Harvard Law Review* 616-45 (February 1949). This famous article, dealing with a hypothetical case involving appellate court judges' diverse interpretations of a murder statute, reveals the practical difficulties and ongoing controversy of statutory construction.

Llewellyn, Karl N. "Remarks on the Theory of Appellate Decision and the Rules or Canons about How Statutes are to be Construed." 3 *Vanderbilt Law Review* 395-406 (April 1950). A listing of myriad canons of statutory interpretation set in juxtaposition to one another. Reveals courts' practical use of original intent as well as many other standards to discover (or otherwise determine) the meaning of positive law.

Plucknett, Theodore Frank Thomas. *A Concise History of the Common Law*. 5th ed. Boston: Little, Brown, and Company, 1956. Contains a good discussion of judicial interpretation of legislation in England in both medieval and early modern times.

_____. *Statutes and Their Interpretation in the First Half of the Fourteenth Century*. Cambridge: Cambridge University Press, 1922. A good examination of the relationship between statute and common law during the period in question; chapter two in particular contains an interesting exploration of the genesis of the original intent doctrine.

Rakove, Jack N., ed. *Interpreting the Constitution: The Debate Over Original Intent*. Boston: Northeastern University Press, 1990. A compendium of works by writers with different perspectives on the subject; very useful in light of the ever-growing literature in this field.

Willis, John. "Statutory Interpretation in a Nutshell." 16 *Canadian Bar Review* 1-27 (January 1938). A lucid, well-organized summary of the broad rules and maxims of statutory construction, designed for the practitioner and advocate but extremely useful for the scholar as well. Compares, in disinterested fashion, the merits and disadvantages of the various rules of interpretation.

B. Biographies

1. William Blount

Chandler, David Leon. *The Natural Superiority of Southern Politicians: A Revisionist History.* Garden City, New York: Doubleday and Company, 1977. Chandler, in his section on Blount, concludes (conformably to his general thesis that southern politicians have been underrated) that Blount was a scapegoat for sectional and party conflict, with the Republicans and southerners winning the impeachment contest by employing a strict construction of Congress's powers.

Craige, Burton. *The Federal Convention of 1787: North Carolina in the Great Crisis.* Richmond: Archibald Craige, 1987. This study, which dates from the 1930s, contains sketches of North Carolina's delegates to the Constitutional Convention. The sketch of Blount is dated and uncritically sympathetic.

Goodpasture, A.V. "William Blount and the Old Southwest Territory." 8 *American Historical Magazine* 1-13 (January 1903). A dated, undocumented account of Blount's career in the Southwest Territory and a short summary of the conspiracy.

Keith, Alice Barnwell. *Three North Carolina Blount Brothers in Business and Politics, 1783-1812.* Diss. University of North Carolina at Chapel Hill, 1940. Conatins little or no information on the Blount Conspiracy, but does provide useful background information on Blount himself, as well as his family.

"Letter from Dr. J.G.M. Ramsay." 7 *American Historical Magazine* 38 (January 1902). A defense of Blount penned in the late nineteenth century. No note material.

McKellar, Kenneth. *Tennessee Senators as Seen by One of Their Successors.* Kingsport, Tennessee: Southern Publishers, 1942. Takes the view that Blount had nothing to do with the alleged conspiracy, of which the Adams administration unjustly accused him. A view reminiscent of the above nineteenth century pro-Blount apologies.

Masterson, William H. *William Blount*. Baton Rouge: Louisiana State University Press, 1954. The only adequate biography of Blount. Masterson views Blount as being first and foremost an entrepreneur, a businessman, with almost all of his actions, including the conspiracy, flowing from these characteristics. Masterson's account of the conspiracy is fair to marginal; his account of the impeachment is borderline at best, focusing on Blount rather than the proceedings against him. Contains some factual errors.

Ramsey, J.G.M. *The Annals of Tennessee*. Philadelphia: J.B. Lippincott & Co., 1860. An early history of the state that includes a poorly documented account of the Blount episode.

Wright, Marcus Joseph. *Some Account of the Life and Services of William Blount*. Washington: E.J. Gray, 1884. An uncritical attempt to vindicate Blount; consists mainly of excerpts from the evidence gathered by the House and other material from the record of Blount's impeachment and expulsion. Useless for serious research.

2. Other

Borden, Morton. *The Federalism of James A. Bayard*. New York: Columbia University Press, 1955. An account of Bayard's political life, containing a good deal of information on events and personalities of the day; labels Bayard as a political moderate. The scholarship is stained by frequent large inferential leaps.

Cox, Joseph W. *Champion of Southern Federalism: Robert Goodloe Harper of South Carolina*. Port Washington, New York: Kennikat Press, 1972. Views Harper as a moderate Federalist who was undergoing a shift to a more extreme outlook in the late 1790s. Cox's overlooking of the Blount impeachment and Harper's role therein contains significant omissions that render the book useless for study in this context.

Dallas, George Mifflin. *Life and Writings of Alexander James Dallas*. Philadelphia: J.B. Lippincott & Co., 1871. Contains among other things accounts of Dallas's role in the Blount and Pennsylvania impeachments, the former being drawn mainly from information in *Annals of Congress*.

Meigs, William Montgomery. *The Life of Charles Jared Ingersoll.* Philadelphia: J.B. Lippincott Company, 1897. A biography of Jared Ingersoll's son, which contains some information on the elder Ingersoll in the early part of the book.

Phillips, Ulrich B. "The South Carolina Federalists." 14 *American Historical Review* 731-43 (July 1909). Includes a few paragraphs on Harper.

U.S. Congress. *Biographical Directory of the American Congress 1774-1971.* Washington: Government Printing Office, 1971. Contains capsule biographies of almost all members of the Fifth Congress.

Walters, Raymond, Jr. *Alexander James Dallas: Lawyer, Politician, Financier 1759-1817.* Philadelphia: University of Pennsylvania Press, 1943. The only good scholarly biography of Dallas. Characterizes him as primarily a lawyer, as the title suggests, who broke with the more radical elements of the Republican Party after 1800. A very positive portrayal, with a decent bibliography but no notes at all.

C. The Old Southwest and the Blount Conspiracy

Abernethy, Thomas P. *The South in the New Nation 1789-1819.* Louisiana State University Press, 1961. Chapter 7 comprises a history of the Blount Conspiracy, emphasizing the competition rather than the cooperation between Blount and John Chisholm. Worth reading.

Bemis, Samuel Flagg. *Pinckney's Treaty: America's Advantage from Europe's Distress, 1783-1800.* New Haven: Yale University Press, revised edition 1960. Includes extended discussions of the several pre-1796 conspiracies, and sets the Old Southwest's history in the larger context of international relations. Essential reading for anyone having an interest in the subject.

Cayton Andrew R.L. " 'When Shall We Cease to Have Judases?' The Blount Conspiracy and the Limits of the 'Extended Republic,' " *in* Ronald Hoffman & Peter J. Albert, *Launching the "Extended Republic": The Federalist Era.* Charlottesville: The University Press of Virginia, 1996. Views Blount not so much as an evildoer as a product of the forces at work in the Old Southwest.

Cobbett, William. *Porcupine's Works*. 12 Vols. London: Printed for Cobbett and Morgan, at the Crown and Mitre, Pall Mall, May 1801. Contains accounts of various events in the U.S during the 1790s; Volume 9 includes a summary of the Blount conspiracy and excerpts from the November 1797 report of the House impeachment committee.

Elkins, Stanley, & McKitrick, Eric. *The Age of Federalism*. New York: Oxford University Press, 1993. The most comprehensive political history of 1790s United States, and indispensable for serious study of the era; like other works on this subject, however, it fails to give any attention to the Blount affair.

Gibbs, George, ed. *Memoirs of the Administrations of Washington and John Adams Edited from the Papers of Oliver Wolcott, Secretary of the Treasury*. 2 Vols. New York: William Van Norden, 1846. Volume 1 contains a two-page summary of the conspiracy and impeachment viewed in the context of Spanish-American relations.

Hamer, Philip M. *Tennessee: A History 1673-1932*. 4 Vols. New York: The American Historical Society, Inc., 1933. Volume 1 contains a fairly accurate account of the conspiracy from a frontier perspective, as well as information on Spanish and Indian intrigues in the Tennessee area in the last quarter of the eighteenth century.

Henderson, Archibald. "The Spanish Conspiracy in Tennessee." 3 *Tennessee Historical Magazine* 229-43 (December 1917). While containing no information on Blount or his conspiracy, this article does recount some earlier intrigues involving the Spanish pursued by John Sevier, James Robertson and others from 1788 to 1790.

Knox, J. Wendell. *Conspiracy in American Politics, 1787-1815*. New York: Arno Press, 1972. This reprint of a 1964 University of North Carolina history dissertation contains a section exploring partisan reactions to the Blount Conspiracy.

Lobel, Jules. "The Rise and Decline of the Neutrality Act: Sovereignty and Congressional War Powers in United States Foreign Policy." 24 *Harvard International Law Journal* 1-71 (Summer 1983). A history of the statute that impeachment Article 1, and the District Court complainant, effectively charged Blount with violating.

McMaster, John Bach. *A History of the People of the United States*. 8 Vols. New York: D. Appleton and Company, 1886-1926. Volume 2 holds a colorful but somewhat inaccurate account of the conspiracy and the impeachment, focusing on the partisan aspects.

Miller, John C. *The Federalist Era 1789-1801*. New York: Harper Torchbooks, 1960. In addition to a short section devoted to the Blount conspiracy, Miller's book is an excellent background source for the political setting of the 1790s, until recently comprising the standard introductory work on the subject.

Philbrick, Francis S. *The Rise of the West 1754-1830*. New York: Harper Torchbooks, 1965. Examines the history of the Old Southwest in a larger frontier context, resulting in more limited treatment of the region than some other sources. Nevertheless, a useful introduction.

Posey, Walter Brownlow. "The Blount Conspiracy." 21 *Birmingham-Southern College Bulletin* 11-21 (December 1928). A good summary of the conspiracy, based mainly on evidence gathered by the House which appears in *Annals of Congress*.

Thompson, Isabel. "The Blount Conspiracy." 2 *East Tennessee Historical Society Publications* 3-21 (1930). A marginal treatment of the circumstances surrounding Blount's impeachment, and a less well-done account of the impeachment itself. Poor documentation.

Turner, Frederick Jackson. "The Policy of France Toward the Mississippi Valley in the Period of Washington and Adams." 10 *American Historical Review* 249-79 (January 1905). Describes French intrigues and efforts to discover elements of the Blount and other conspiracies.

Whitaker, A.P. *The Mississippi Question, 1795-1803: A Study in Trade, Politics, and Diplomacy*. New York: D. Appleton-Century Company, Inc., 1934. A well-documented portrait of activity in the Mississippi Valley during the period in question, including perhaps the best account of the Blount Conspiracy, as well as other plots. Required reading for those wishing to gain a background in the history of the Old Southwest.

_____.*The Spanish-American Frontier: 1783-1795: The Westward Movement and the Spanish Retreat in the Mississippi Valley*. Boston: Houghton Mifflin Company, 1927. An equally-well-done account of the subject, this one examining the events in the years leading up to Pinckney's Treaty. Like the above work, and Bemis's study *supra*, indispensable reading.

Wright, J. Leitch, Jr. *Britain and the American Frontier 1783-1815.* Athens: University of Georgia Press, 1975. Contains an account of the Blount Conspiracy, and provides an overview of frontier concerns from the British perspective.

D. Impeachment—General

1. England

Blackstone, William. *Commentaries on the Laws of England.* 4 vols. Oxford: The Clarendon Press, 1765-69. Arguably the best-known series of commentaries on English law ever penned (and certainly the leading eighteenth century work), Blackstone's books (including their information on impeachment and related topics) exercised a powerful influence upon the legal education and ideas of the early generations of American lawyers.

Clarke, Maude Violet. "The Origin of Impeachment." *Oxford Essays in Medieval History Presented to Herbert Edward Salter.* Oxford: The Clarendon Press, 1934. Traces the origin of impeachment back to the 1200s, concluding that it was a revolutionary device for Parliamentary control of executive prerogative that was accepted and incorporated into English law because of its similarity to established devices.

Cobbett's Parliamentary History of England. 36 Vols. London: T. Curson Hansard, 1806-1820. Volume 1 describes, among other things, the life and death of Roger Mortimer.

Hatsell, John. *Precedents of Proceedings in the House of Commons.* 5 Vols. London: Luke Hansard and Sons, 1818. Volume 4 contains a digest of English impeachments, bills of attainder, and bills of pains and penalties down to 1780.

McKisack, May, *The Fourteenth Century 1307-1399.* Oxford: The Clarendon Press, 1959. Contains background information on the Mortimer, Lyon and Latimer episodes.

Plucknett, Theodore Frank Thomas. "Impeachment and Attainder." 3 *Transactions of the Royal Historical Society* (5th Ser.) 145-58 (1953). The author, probably the best recent authority on English impeachment, here argues that Parliament began to rely on treason as a justification for impeachment in the late 1300s, seizing the initiative from the Crown, which at the time was too weak to enforce the requirement that impeachments proceed only with executive approval.

_____. "The Impeachments of 1376." 1 *Transactions of the Royal Historical Society* (5th Ser.) 153-64 (1951). Traces the beginning of impeachment to the proceedings of 1376, wherein Parliament originated an adversarial process to redress notorious offenses that resembled, but was not bound by the legal requirements of, regular criminal proceedings.

_____. "The Origin of Impeachment." 24 *Transactions of the Royal Historical Society* (4th Ser.) 47-71 (1942). Examines regular judicial processes of the mid–1300s and concludes that impeachment grew not out of the process of indictment but instead out of notoriety.

_____. "The Rise of the English State Trial." 2 *Politica* 542-59 (December 1937). Identifies English impeachment as a political or state trial, completely distinct procedurally from common and criminal law processes. Some arguable assertions.

_____. *Studies in English Legal History*. London: The Hambledon Press, 1983. Consists of reprints of Plucknett's articles, including many of the above.

Riddell, William Renwick. "Impeachment in England and English Colonies." 7 *New York University Law Quarterly Review* 702-08 (March 1930). Identifies impeachment as one of three means of instituting a criminal process in England, the other two being indictment and private appeal; this is an interpretation somewhat at odds with that of Plucknett.

_____. "Powers of a Colonial Legislature in Impeachment and Contempt." 21 *Proceedings and Transactions of the Royal Society of Canada* (3d Ser.) (Section 2) 83-90 (May 1927). Traces the origins of impeachment back to 1329-30. See also this entry under United States impeachments, *infra*.

Roberts, Clayton. "The Law of Impeachment in Stuart England—A Reply to Raoul Berger." 84 *Yale Law Journal* 1419-39 (June 1975). Reveals some major errors in Berger's arguments, especially as to the English definition of the phrase "high Crimes and Misdemeanors," but possesses some inconsistencies and unreasonable inferences of its own.

Sutherland, Lucy Stuart, & McKisack, May. *Fourteenth Century Studies*. Oxford: The Clarendon Press, 1937. Clarke's essay also appears in this volume. See Clarke, Maude Violet, this section, *supra*.

Tite, Colin Gerald Calder. *Impeachment and Parliamentary Judicature in Early Stuart England*. London: Athlone Press, 1974. Contends that impeachment in the Stuart period took a different turn from what it had been in medieval times, although the seventeenth century lawyers availed themselves of medieval precedents when they suited Parliament's purpose. The most comprehensive work available on impeachment in early modern England.

2. United States

Alexander, De Alva Stanwood. *History and Practice of the House of Representatives*. Boston: Houghton Mifflin Company, 1916. A survey of the impeachment powers of the House, containing nothing out of the ordinary, although a few factual errors within.

Amrine, Thomas D., Recent Development. "Judicial Review Of Impeachment Proceedings: Nixon v. United States, 113 S. Ct. 732." 16 *Harvard Journal of Law and Public Policy* 809-20 (Autumn 1993). Examining *Nixon*, Armine warns of the dangers to due process that might result from the Supreme Court's decision not to review impeachments.

April, Nathan. "Basis for a Federal Impeachment." A1 *Corporate Reorganizations and Bankruptcy Review* 170-76 (January 1938). Discusses from a broad construction viewpoint the definition of impeachable offences and the question of judicial review. Contains no notes and evinces a poor understanding of English precedent.

Auslander, Rose, Note. "Impeaching the Senate's Use of Trial Committees." 67 *New York University Law Review* 68-107 (April 1992). Argues that the Senate's use of impeachment trial committees overemphasizes efficiency at the expense of judicial independence, and that the issue should be justiciable in Article III courts.

Bates, William III. "Vagueness in the Constitution: The Impeachment Power." 25 *Stanford Law Review* 908-26 (June 1973). A comparative critique of Berger's and Brant's arguments, *infra*, on impeachable offences and judicial review.

Battisti, Frank J. "An Independent Judiciary or an Evanescent Dream." 25 *Case Western Reserve Law Review* 711-46 (Summer 1975). An examination, by a United States district judge, of impeachment and recent proposals for alternate means of removal of federal judges. Concludes that the framers' original intent was to prevent any other means of removal but impeachment.

Berger, Raoul. "Impeachment: A Countercritique." 49 *Washington Law Review* 845-70 (May 1974). A point-by-point rebuttal of Arthur Bestor's critique of Berger's volume on impeachment (*infra*); re-asserts Berger's position that the category of impeachable offenses is not without limits.

_____. "Impeachment for High Crimes and Misdemeanors." 44 *Southern California Law Review* 395-460 (1971). An initial discussion of the point pursued in the above work, this article is substantially the same as chapter 2 of Berger's main book on the subject.

_____. *Impeachment: the Constitutional Problems*. Cambridge: Harvard University Press, 1973. Regarded since its publication as the leading work on American federal impeachment, Berger's volume had its genesis in the congressional investigation of Supreme Court Justice William O. Douglas. Essentially a legal brief, this book attempts to establish limits on the impeachment power, including an argument that impeachment proceedings are subject to review by the federal courts. Some conclusions and research in this volume are questionable.

Bestor, Arthur. "Book Review, Berger, *Impeachment: The Constitutional Problems*." 49 *Washington Law Review* 255-85 (November 1973). Strong critique of Berger, especially his arguments that impeachable offenses are of limited scope and that impeachment proceedings are judicially reviewable. Arguments, based mainly on Berger's text rather than primary sources, occasionally become confusing.

Black, Charles L. *Impeachment: A Handbook*. New Haven: Yale University Press, 1974. A book designed during the Watergate crisis for the layman; contains no notes or bibliography, and is often very subjective, though quite readable. Argues that practicality is the proper guide in determining the scope of the impeachment power (and contains an especially good argument on this ground attacking judicial review.)

Borkin, Joseph. *The Corrupt Judge.* New York: C.N. Potter, 1962. A book by a practicing attorney; contains in one chapter a superficial discussion of the process and policy of the impeachment and removal of federal judges. Concludes that impeachment is an outmoded procedure.

Brant, Irving. *Impeachment: Trials and Errors.* New York: Alfred A. Knopf, 1972. A biased, sketchily researched and documented survey of impeachment. Brant, probably writing in defense of Supreme Court Justice William O. Douglas, adopts a very strict interpretation of the impeachment power, especially regarding impeachable offences, which Brant asserts should be limited to indictable acts.

Broderick, Albert. "Citizen's Guide to Impeachment of a President: Problems." 23 *Catholic University Law Review* 205-54 (Winter 1973). A survey of impeachment that takes a moderate view of the "impeachable offenses" question; argues that public opinion should play a major role in the outcome of the process. Research is uncritical and at times logically inconsistent.

Brown, Wrisley. "The Impeachment of the Federal Judiciary." 26 *Harvard Law Review* 684-706 (June 1913). Based almost exclusively on secondary sources; evidently a justification of the 1912 impeachment and conviction of Archbald. Argues that impeachment is designed to protect the public welfare, and to that end that impeachment provisions should be construed broadly.

Broyde, Michael J. "Expediting Impeachment: Removing Article III Federal Judges After Criminal Conviction." 17 *Harvard Journal of Law and Public Policy* 157-222 (Winter 1994). Proposes the adoption of a streamlined system of impeachment when the subject of that impeachment is a federal judge whom the regular courts have already convicted of a crime.

Burbank, Stephen B. "Alternative Career Resolution: An Essay on the Removal of Federal Judges." 76 *Kentucky Law Journal* 643-700 (Spring 1987-88). A survey of the various means in existence for such removal. Argues that impeachment should be the only means and that Congress should follow precedent in exercising its impeachment powers, which the courts may not oversee.

Bushnell, Eleanore. *Crimes, Follies, and Misfortunes: The Federal Impeachment Trials.* Urbana: University of Illinois Press, 1992. Contains discrete chapters on each impeachment on each impeachment that the House has actually voted through that of Claiborne. See entry under the heading of the Blount impeachment, *infra.*

Cohodas, Nadine. "House Judiciary feels the Burden of Impeachment." 46 *Congressional Quarterly Weekly Report* 1277-79 (14 May 1988). A summary of opinions regarding the impeachment power with a discussion of the 1980 judicial investigation legislation and its first 8 years.

Note. "Constitutional Law—Power of Courts to Review Impeachment Proceedings." 85 *University of Pennsylvania Law Review* 423-24 (February 1937). A two-page note commenting on *Ritter v. United States.*

Costello, Mary. "Presidential Impeachment." 2 *Editorial Research Reports* 923-46 (5 December 1973). A survey of impeachment, in light of Watergate, that concludes that impeachment is primarily a political process. Contains few notes and has a misquotation or two.

Currie, David P. *The Constitution in Congress: The Federalist Period 1789-1801.* Chicago: The University of Chicago Press, 1997. Chapter 6 contains a brief account of the Blount impeachment proceedings that draws principally upon the materials in the *Annals of Congress.*

Danielson, George E. "Presidential Immunity from Criminal Prosecution." 63 *Georgetown Law Journal* 1065-81 (1975). A poorly reasoned article that contends that indictments will lie against the president prior to impeachment.

Dennis, David W. "Impeachment Revisited." 9 *Indiana Law Review* 579-93 (March 1976). Written by a member of the House Judiciary Committee of the Watergate era, this article contains the general argument that impeachment is a criminal process subject to due process and other procedural guaranties. Makes particular reference to the impeachment articles against Richard M. Nixon.

Diamond, Robert A., ed. *Impeachment and the U.S. Congress.* Washington: Congressional Quarterly, Inc., 1974. A pamphlet prepared for public consumption designed to inform the reader about impeachment in general and Watergate in particular.

_____. *Powers of Congress.* Washington: Congressional Quarterly, Inc., 1976. Chapters 11 and 12 contain constitutional and historical analyses of impeachment based on secondary sources and government documents. A fair-to-good introduction to the subject.

Dougherty, J. Hampden. "Inherent Limitations Upon Impeachment." 23 *Yale Law Journal* 60-87 (November 1913). Poorly documented argument to the effect that acts done prior to the assumption of office should not serve as grounds for impeachment.

Duram, James C. *Impeachment: Historical Perspectives and Recent Prospects.* Wichita, Kansas: Wichita State University, 1976. A short pamphlet describing impeachment originally to have been a partisan weapon which Watergate transformed into a bipartisan device to control presidential power.

Dwight, Theodore. "Trial by Impeachment." 6 *American Law Register* (N.S.) 257-83 (March 1867). (May also be cited as 15 *American Law Register* 257 (March 1867)). One of the earliest and most influential scholarly articles on American impeachment, having its origin in the Reconstruction battles between President and Congress. Dwight's work is an argument for a strict "indictable crimes only" impeachment standard.

Ehrlich, Walter. *Presidential Impeachment: An American Dilemma.* St Charles, Missouri: Forum Press, 1974. A general overview, with liberal excerpts from primary sources, of impeachment; views the process as a crucial element of the constitutional system.

Estrich, Willis A. "The Law of Impeachment." 20 *Case and Comment* 454-60 (December 1913). A superficial but well-done survey of the basic problems of impeachment which includes an explanation of why the process so often becomes a tool (or a source) of partisan struggle.

Ethridge, George H. "The Law of Impeachment." 8 *Mississippi Law Journal* 283-303 (February 1936). While focusing on Mississippi impeachment provisions, Ethridge appeals to the law of the national government and other states, finding that the process in general is a criminal one, and as such that it should be attended by the elements of due process.

Feerick, John. "Impeaching Federal Judges: A Study of the

Constitutional Provisions." 39 *Fordham Law Review* 1-58 (October 1970). A moderate article, apparently written in defense of Douglas, that sets breach of public trust—as opposed to private acts—as the standard of impeachable offenses. Surveys impeachment from early English cases through recent federal episodes.

Fenton, Paul S. "The Scope of the Impeachment Power." 65 *Northwestern University Law Review* 719-58 (November-December 1970). Written by the House Minority Counsel, this much-cited analysis of what constitutes an impeachable offense (by reference to English law, the Constitutional Convention, and federal impeachment articles) asserts, in a well-reasoned fashion, a flexible "public misconduct" standard.

Firmage, Edwin Brown. "The Law of Presidential Impeachment." 1973 *Utah Law Review* 681-704 (Winter 1973). Another examination of impeachable offenses. Firmage argues for a vague standard that would protect public interests, the balance of power between branches, and the executive who follows the precedents of his predecessors. Relies on Berger uncritically.

Firmage, Edwin Brown & Mangrum, R. Collin. "Removal of the President; Resignation and the Procedural Law of Impeachment." 1974 *Duke Law Journal* 1023-1116 (January 1974). A detailed description of the processes of impeachment in the House, along with discussions of pardon, judicial review, indictment prior to impeachment, executive privilege, and the application of due process to impeachment. Views the process as a workable constitutional check upon the executive.

Flanders, Steven. "Judicial Discipline, Criminal Prosecution, and Impeachment." 11 *Justice System Journal* 394-400 (Winter 1986). A discussion of the new judicial investigation legislation, the Claiborne, Hastings, and Walter Nixon cases, and the relationship between judicial investigation, impeachment, and indictment.

Foster, Roger. *Commentaries on the Constitution of the United States, Historical and Juridical.* 2 Vols. Boston: The Boston Book Company, 1895. Volume 1 contains a long survey of impeachment which, while dated, contains summaries of federal impeachments as well as discussions of the history, procedure, and general nature of impeachment. Raises several interesting questions regarding impeachable offenses.

Fox, Brendan C. "The Justiciability Of Challenges To The Senate Rules Of Procedure For Impeachment Trials." 60 *George Washington Law Review* 1275-1310 (June 1992). Examines *Nixon v. United States*, concluding that impeachment cases are, or at any rate should be, justiciable.

Franklin, Mitchell. "Further Considerations Relating to Romanist Infamy and the American Constitutional Conception of Impeachment." 24 *Buffalo Law Review* 29-76 (Fall 1974). See entry below.

_____. "Romanist Infamy and the American Constitutional Conception of Impeachment." 23 *Buffalo Law Review* 313-41 (Winter 1974). An attempt to link English and American impeachment with the Roman law concept of infamy, or public disgrace, with an argument that impeachment emerged in England as a popular tool to control the bourgeoisie (the executive); contains a number of unsupported assertions and relies upon an artificially great distinction between English and Roman law.

Freedman, Eric M. "The Law As King And The King As Law: Is a President Immune From Criminal Prosecution Before Impeachment?." 20 *Hastings Constitutional Law Quarterly* 7-68 (1992). Using both historical and analytical approaches, Freedman concludes that criminal prosecution before impeachment is constitutionally permissible.

Futterman, Stanley N. "The Rules of Impeachment." 24 *University of Kansas Law Review* 105-42 (1975). Contains a plea for fairer and more consistent rules of impeachment procedure. Generally relies on precedent but suggests some innovations.

Gerhardt, Michael J. "The Constitutional Limits to Impeachment and Its Alternatives," 68 *Texas Law Review* 1-104 (November 1989). Discusses impeachment as the subject of interpretive theories such as originalism, concluding that history is a good starting point for understabnding the process.

___. *The Federal Impeachment Process: A Constitutional and Historical Analysis*. Princeton: Princeton University Press, 1996. A good recent survey of the subject, but little coverage of the pre-Watergate impeachments.

_____. "Rediscovering Nonjusticiability: Judicial Review Of

Impeachments After *Nixon.*" 44 *Duke Law Journal* 231-76 (1994). Views *Nixon v. United States* as a reminder that the Political Question doctrine is still alive; argues that in deciding the case as it did, the Supreme Court simply maintained the separation-of-powers status quo regarding impeachments.

Goldberg, Arthur J. "The Question of Impeachment." 1 *Hastings Constitutional Law Quarterly* 5 (1974). Selects evidence that supports the contention that the president is not subject to indictment prior to impeachment; argues that Congress should ensure that impeachment is conducted in a scrupulously fair manner, and that impeachment proceedings could be judicially reviewable if Congress does not observe due process guaranties.

Goldberg, Ira M. "An Essay on Raoul Berger's Thesis for Judicial Intervention in the Process of the Removal of the President of the United States." 1975 *Wisconsin Law Review* 414-83 (1975). An intensive critique and rebuttal to Berger's argument for judicial review of impeachment. Marred by excess verbiage and poor writing style.

Greene, Richard S. "The Balance of Power, the Impeachment Powers and the Supreme Power of Congress." 34 *Federal Bar Journal* 42-53 (Winter 1975). Argues that Congress rightfully exercises the great preponderance of power under the Constitution, and should not hesitate to exercise its great powers of impeachment in defense of the public. Contains confusing attempts to distinguish quality from quantity of power exercised by each branch of government.

Grimes, Warren S. "Hundred-Ton-Gun Control: Preserving Impeachment As The Exclusive Removal Mechanism For Federal Judges." 38 *UCLA Law Review* 1209-55 (June 1991). Concludes that while a workable impeachment process would be a valuable device for the preservation of judicial independence, certain reforms such as increased efficiency in House investigation and Senate fact-finding are necessary to make impeachment as useful as other recent judicial disciplinary procedures.

Havens, Murray Clark & McNeil, Dixie Mercer. "Presidents, Impeachment, and Political Accountability." 8 *Presidential Studies Quarterly* 5-18 (Winter 1978). An examination of impeachment and other devices for legislative control of the executive; concludes that impeachment is a political device that Congress and the public must not be afraid to use when other means fail.

Hawkins, Wallace. "'During Good Behavior'—the National Judiciary." 21 *Mississippi Law Journal* 446-54 (October 1950). Essentially a McCarthy-era diatribe in support of extensive congressional power.

Haynes, George H. *The Senate of the United States: Its History and Practice.* 2 Vols. Boston: Houghton Mifflin Company, 1938. An adequate introductory survey to the Senate side of impeachment procedure.

Heflin, Howell T. "The Impeachment Process: Modernizing an Archaic System." 71 *Judicature* 123-25 (August/September 1987). Heflin's personal thoughts and observations concerning alternate forms of removal of judges in light of his experience in the Claiborne impeachment.

High Crimes and Misdemeanors: Selected Materials on Impeachment. New York: Funk and Wagnalls, 1974. A brief survey of impeachment followed by the articles of impeachment in all federal cases, together with an extended treatment of the Johnson impeachment; argues that the president is liable for noncriminal wrongdoing.

Hoffer, Peter C. & Hull, N. E. H. "The First American Impeachments." 35 *William and Mary Quarterly* (3d Ser.) 653-67 (October 1978). An examination of seventeenth century American impeachments. This article is substantially the same as the discussion that appears in the authors' volume below.

_____. *Impeachment in America, 1635-1805.* New Haven: Yale University Press, 1984. One of the best works yet written on American impeachment, and without question the leading account of this time period. Presents impeachment as being at first a device mainly to control corruption in office and later a partisan tool, emerging finally after the Chase impeachment as a constitutional apparatus less subject to political abuse. The arguments are occasionally plagued by attempts, made in the name of consistency of argument, to place particular impeachments into categories in which they clearly do not belong.

_____. "Power and Precedent in the Creation of an American Impeachment Tradition; The Eighteenth Century Colonial Record." 36 *William and Mary Quarterly* (3d Ser.) 51-77 (January 1979). Essentially contained in the above work.

Note. "Impeachment of the President." 7 *Law Reporter* 161-77 (August 1844). A summary of the federal impeachment process, and past impeachments, in light of an abortive attempt to impeach President John Tyler, that prescribes a common law limitation on the Senate's impeachment power. Allows a rare historical view of the early impeachments unencumbered by the Johnson and later episodes, but contains some factual errors.

Note. "Impeachment of U.S. Judges." 7 *Western Jurist* 323-24 (June 1873). An article apparently designed to threaten federal bankruptcy judges with impeachment for their failure to follow the will of the people as expressed through the legislature; the influence of the Johnson impeachment upon the author is obvious.

Isenbergh, Joseph. "The Scope of the Power to Impeach." 84 *Yale Law Journal* 1316-37 (May 1975). Adopts a broad-construction view of the impeachment power reminiscent of Robert Goodloe Harper's positions. Plagued by quotations out of context and strained interpretations of some passages. Contains as broad-construction a view of impeachment as is to be found anywhere in recent literature.

Kainec, Lisa A., Comment. "Judicial Review Of Senate Impeachment Proceedings: Hands Off Approach Appropriate?." 43 *Case Western Reserve Law Review* 1499-1527 (1993). Concludes that in light of practical considerations, as well as the well-reasoned lower court statements in *Hastings v. United States*, the Supreme Court should have found impeachments to be justiciable.

Kastenmeier, Robert W. & Remington, Michael J. "Judicial Discipline: A Legislative Perspective." 76 *Kentucky Law Journal* 763-97 (Spring 1987-88). Although not directly discussing impeachment, this article does present an adequate discussion of the 1980 act.

Kurland, Philip B. "The Constitution and the Tenure of Federal Judges: Some Notes From History." 36 *University of Chicago Law Review* 665-98 (Summer 1969). While not dealing directly with impeachment, Kurland's article is worthy of perusal for its discussion of various historical proposals for alternate means of removal of judges; concludes that no other means should be adopted.

_____. "Watergate, Impeachment, and the Constitution." 45

Mississippi Law Journal 531-600 (April 1974). A discussion of the major modern issues of impeachment. Sound conclusions, well-reasoned, but tinged with some anti-executive bias (Kurland, as a participant in the Watergate impeachment investigation, writes almost as an advocate).

Labovitz, John R. *Presidential Impeachment.* New Haven: Yale University Press, 1978. Although written by a member of the House Judiciary Committee staff, and originating from his Watergate experience, this is a remarkably unbiased and well-reasoned piece of research that sees impeachment as a judicial solution to an essentially political problem. Arguably the best volume on impeachment to appear in the last half-century (Hoffer and Hull notwithstanding).

Note. "The Law of Impeachment." 65 *Albany Law Journal* 223-24 (July 1903). Unremarkable discussion of the definition of impeachable offenses.

Lawrence, William. "The Law of Impeachment." 6 *American Law Register* (N.S.) 641-80 (September 1867). (May also be cited as 15 *American Law Register* 641 (September 1867)). A clear anti-Johnson attack on Dwight, *supra*, which concludes that impeachment will lie for any acts prejudicial to the public interests; like Dwight, an oft-cited and very influential piece.

Lindley, L.G. "Impeachment in the Nineteenth Century." 67 *Current History* 13 (July 1974). A one-page summary of the Chase and Johnson impeachments from the "political process" point of view.

Luchsinger, Daniel, Note. "Committee Impeachment Trials: The Best Solution?." 80 *Georgetown Law Journal* 163-90 (1991). Argues that Senate Impeachment Trial Committee procedures are both unfair and unconstitutional; concludes, however, that the Senate may address these problems adequately by amending the committee's rules, though more extreme measures such as resorting to a full Senate trial are obvious alternatives.

McAdoo, W.G. "Alternative Method to Impeachment for Trial of Inferior Court Judges." 42 *Case and Comment* 9-12 (Summer 1936). Substance of McAdoo's proposal in Congress for vesting the power to remove federal judges in a judicial body.

McConnell, Mitch. "Reflections on the Senate's Role in the Judicial Impeachment Process and Proposals for Change." 76 *Kentucky*

Law Journal 739-61 (Spring 1987-88). An insider's account of the Claiborne impeachment. Argues against the introduction of any new means for judicial removal.

McWhinney, Edward. "Congress and the Presidency and the Impeachment Power." 7 *Indiana Law Review* 833-51 (1974). Adopts a rather strict interpretation of the impeachment power. The article's strongest point is a discussion of the difficulty American researchers encounter in attempting to locate, understand, and apply English precedent to American impeachment.

Maxman, Melissa H., Note. "In Defense of the Constitution's Judicial Impeachment Standard." 86 *Michigan Law Review* 420-63 (November 1987). Opposes, on the basis of original intent interpretation, alternative means of judicial removal; ignores evidence that challenges this conclusion.

Melton, Buckner F., Jr. "Federal Impeachment And Criminal Procedure: The Framers' Intent." 52 *Maryland Law Review* 437-57 (1993). Examines the 1798 Senate debate on the jury trial question and what light the debate sheds on the applicability of Bill of Rights guarantees to the modern impeachment process.

_____. *The First Impeachment: The Constitution's Framers and the Case of Senator William Blount.* Diss. Duke University, 1990. The purpose of this citation is to warn researchers to avoid the dissertation, which this book has superceded in all respects. A much briefer treatment of the subject than the present work; everything that appears in the dissertation appears in this book, with the exception of a few substantive and typographical errors.

Morgan, Charles Jr., Eastman, Hope, Gale, Mary Ellen, & Areen, Judith. "Impeachment: An Historical Overview." 5 *Seton Hall Law Review* 689-719 (Spring 1974). An overview of the subject; heavy reliance on Berger. Argues that impeachment is designed primarily to check political abuses committed by the executive branch.

Note. "Exclusiveness of the Impeachment Power Under the Constitution." 51 *Harvard Law Review* 330-36 (December 1937). Concludes that no alternative to impeachment should be instituted due to controversy and questionable constitutionality.

Nunn, Sam. "Judicial Tenure." 54 *Chicago-Kent Law Review* 29-44 (1977). A defense of the author's Judicial Tenure Bill that makes the case for the necessity of some alternate form of judicial removal in light of the increasing size of the federal judiciary; somewhat at odds with Kurland's views.

_____. "The Judicial Tenure Act." 13 *Trial* 26-31 (November 1977). Another defense of Nunn's bill. Adopts the controversial position that the concept of an independent judiciary does not incorporate the idea of a judiciary independent from its own internal disciplinary measures.

Otis, Merrill E. "A Proposed Tribunal: Is it Constitutional?" 7 *University of Kansas City Law Review* 3-49 (December 1938). An emotional article, authored by a judge, which strongly opposes any idea of an alternative to impeachment for judicial removal.

Potts, C.S. "Impeachment as a Remedy." 12 *St. Louis Law Review* 15-38 (1927). Adopts a broad construction view but also suggests the development of alternative procedures to impeachment. Based almost exclusively on secondary sources and state materials.

Pound, Roscoe. "Justice According to Law." 14 *Columbia Law Review* 1-26 (January 1914). One of a series of articles bearing this name; in this one Pound critiques administration of justice by the legislature (including impeachment) and concludes it to be inefficient, arbitrary, and capricious.

Note. "The Presidential Impeachment." 1 *American Law Review* 388-89 (January 1867). A discussion originating within the context of Reconstruction efforts to impeach Johnson. Concludes that the defendant's presence is not needed if the offense charged is not indictable.

Rankin, Robert S. "Is There a Time Limit for Impeachment?" 28 *American Political Science Review* 866-72 (October 1934). Argues, in light of federal and state impeachment material, that impeachments will lie for acts done in a prior term of office and that resignation does not bar impeachment proceedings. A broad construction interpretation, in chronological terms, of the impeachment power.

Rawle, William. *A View of the Constitution of the United States of America.* Philadelphia: H.C. Carey and Lea, 1825. Chapter 21 comprises a survey of impeachment, finding that it is an appropriate redress for political offenses.

Rehnquist, William H. "The Impeachment Clause: A Wild Card In

The Constitution." 85 *Northwestern University Law Review* 903-18 (1991). Views impeachment as a device that could, and in the impeachments of Samuel Chase and Andrew Johnson nearly did, cause severe damage to the principle of separation of powers; omits discussion of similar potential effects of the broad view of the power that many Federalists took in the Blount impeachment.

Riddell, William Renwick. "Powers of a Colonial Legislature in Impeachment and Contempt." 21 *Proceedings and Transactions of the Royal Society of Canada* (3d Ser.) (Section 2) 83-90 (May 1927). Brief survey of some impeachments in the North American colonies. See also this entry under English impeachments, *supra*.

Rogers, E. Mabry & Young, Stephen B. "Public Office as a Public Trust: A Suggestion that Impeachment for High Crimes and Misdemeanors Implies a Fiduciary Standard." 63 *Georgetown Law Journal* 1025-49 (May 1975). A discussion of the legal concept of trust and its application to public office and impeachment in England and the United States; suggests the standard for impeachment ought to be one of breach of public trust. Relies heavily on secondary sources but research of English law is good.

Ross, G.W.C. "'Good Behavior' of Federal Judges." 12 *University of Kansas City Law Review* 119-27 (April-June 1944). An historical argument that *scire facias*, a writ once used in England to remove judges, not being expressly barred by the U.S. Constitution, is implicitly incorporated into American common law. Very persuasive but based on a secondary source interpretation of English law as well as controversial premises.

Schnapper, Morris Bartel, ed. *Presidential Impeachment: A Documentary Overview*. Washington: Public Affairs Press, 1974. A compilation of government and other documents examining questions of impeachment in general and the Watergate proceedings in particular.

Schneider, Nicole H., Comment. "Senate Impeachment Trials—To Review Or Not To Review, What Would Marshall Do?." 4 *Seton Hall Constitutional Law Journal* 237-78 (1993). Examines *Nixon* and other recent litigation, as well as presenting brief histories of judicial review and the political question doctrine, and concludes that the Supreme Court should find impeachment issues justiciable.

Shartel, Burke. "Federal Judges—Appointment, Supervision, and Removal—Some Possibilities Under the Constitution." 28 *Michigan Law Review* 870-909 (May 1930). Part of a series, this article proposes a system whereby judges would remove their fellow jurists. Contains a critique of impeachment and a partial listing of investigations not reaching the impeachment stage.

Shaw, James Kevin. *The Impact of Politics on United States Senate Voting on Impeachment.* Diss. University of Nevada at Reno, 1980. A superficial quantitative analysis of partisan voting trends in the Senate. Deals only with one or two votes per impeachment, ignoring the numerous votes on procedural matters. Groups parties together in such a way as to fit into an arbitrarily predetermined model for analysis. A poor work but the only available quantitative study of any aspect of impeachment. See entry under Special Finding Aids, *supra.*

Simon, Maria, Note. "Bribery And Other Not So "Good Behavior": Criminal Prosecution as a Supplement To Impeachment Of Federal Judges." 94 *Columbia Law Review* 1617-73 (June 1994). Finds that criminal sanctions, including removal and disqualification, as a supplement to the impeachment process, were an acceptable means of policing the federal judiciary even in the nation's early days.

Simpson, Alexander. "Federal Impeachments." 64 *University of Pennsylvania Law Review* 651-95 (May 1916). See entry below.

_____. "Federal Impeachments." 64 *University of Pennsylvania Law Review* 803-30 (June 1916). See entry below.

_____. *A Treatise on Federal Impeachment.* Philadelphia: The Law Association of Philadelphia, 1916. A reprint of the above two articles, written by one of the counselors in the Archbald case. A general survey that characterizes impeachment as judicial function that will lie for nonindictable offenses. Although Simpson raises almost every major question to be found in subsequent books and articles on impeachment, because of his "advocacy" approach, many of the questions are poorly answered. The leading work on impeachment for decades, it is still well worth reading.

Sloan, Jerome S. & Garr, Ira E. "Treason, Bribery, or Other High Crimes and Misdemeanors—A Study of Impeachment." 47 *Temple Law Quarterly* 413-56 (Spring 1974). A textual analysis of the phrase "high Crimes and Misdemeanors" in light of practice both before and after the Constitutional Convention. Concludes that impeachable offenses are those acts which have a reasonable relation to the administration of the actor's office.

Smith, Alexa J., Note. "Federal Judicial Impeachment: Defining Process Due." 46 *Hastings Law Journal* 639-74 (1995). Examines the application of due process and political question principles to impeachment.

Stoltz, Preble. "Disciplining Federal Judges: Is Impeachment Hopeless?" 57 *California Law Review* 659-70 (May 1969). Asserts that impeachment meets none of the ideal criteria for disciplining of federal judges (apolitical, confidential, procedurally fair), but that it could, through procedural modification, come to meet most or all of them.

Story, Joseph. *Commentaries on the Constitution of the United States*. 3 Vols. Boston: Hilliard, Gray and Company, 1833. Volume 2, chapters 9 and 10 contain a clear, well-written and influential survey of impeachment by one of the most important nineteenth century commentators on early American law. Chapter 12 mentions in passing Blount's impeachment and expulsion.

Sweeney, J.P. "Presidential Impeachment and Judicial Review." 23 *American University Law Review* 959-93 (Summer 1974). Argues that while the Supreme Court has jurisdiction over impeachment, the questions of impeachment with which the court would be faced would be political and thus nonjusticiable, and that judicial review would create more problems that it would solve. Logical structure of arguments as to jurisdiction is unconvincing, yet a correct prediction of *Nixon's* outcome..

"Symposium on Judicial Discipline and Impeachment," 76 *Kentucky Law Journal* 633 (1987-88). A collection of writings on such topics as constitutional parameters of impeachment, judicial discipline, and judicial misconduct; includes the article of McConnell, *supra*.

Taylor, Hannis. "The American Law of Impeachment." 180 *North American Review* 502-12 (April 1905). Opposes the concept of removal of judges for private wrongdoing. Good summary of several English cases, but almost no citations. Apparently a defense of Swayne.

Ten Broeck, Jacobus. "Partisan Politics and Federal Judgeship

Impeachment since 1903." 23 *Minnesota Law Review* 185-204 (January 1939). An examination of impeachments and voting patterns in twentieth century impeachments. Concludes that some evidence exists to indicate partisan motives in impeachment which at the time of this article's writing appear to be declining.

Thomas, David Y. "The Law of Impeachment in the United States." 2 *American Political Science Review* 378-95 (May 1908). Argues that the U.S. Constitution adopted English precedent and practice except where it expressly altered it, and thus that a loose construction regarding all questions not answered by the Constitution is the correct one.

Thompson, Frank Jr. & Pollitt, Daniel H. "Impeachment of Federal Judges: An Historical Overview." 49 *North Carolina Law Review* 87-121 (December 1970). A restrictive reading of the impeachment power. Heavy reliance on secondary sources.

Thomson, Meldrim Jr. "Genesis and Growth of the Federal Judiciary Impeachment Clause." 40 *Law Notes* 24-26 (September 1936). Addresses the question of the applicability of impeachment to inferior court judges. Recommends that another means of removal be found.

Van Hecke, Maurice Taylor. "Pardons in Impeachment Cases." 24 *Michigan Law Review* 657-74 (1926). Although dealing with state impeachment powers, this article is useful for its analysis of the rationale for excluding impeachments from the operation of executive pardons.

Van Nest, G. Willett. "Impeachable Offenses Under the Constitution of the United States." 16 *American Law Review* 798-817 (November 1884). Takes the curious view that American impeachment lies for crimes as measured by general notions of common law, with a different standard of conduct applying to public officials. Wording of argument suggests a desire for a stricter interpretation than is the actual outcome of such an approach.

Van Valkenberg, William E. "Impeachment—God Save the King from Overzealous Subordinates." 1974 *Utah Law Review* 71-91 (Spring 1974). Submits that the president should be liable to impeachment for acts of his personal subordinates who do not hold statutorily defined executive positions.

Volcansek, Mary L. *Judicial Impeachment: None Called for Justice.*

Urbana: University of Illinois Press, 1993. An examination of the Claiborne, Hastings, and Walter Nixon impeachments; denounces impeachment as both clumsy and violative of judicial independence, and calls for a higher standard of judicial behavior and more competent prosecutorial investigation into judges' alleged criminal behavior as means of avoiding future impeachments.

Walthall, Timothy. "Executive Impeachment: Stealing Fire from the Gods." 9 *New England Law Review* 257-91 (Winter 1974). A rather shallow, uncritical article that entreats Congress not to be afraid to use impeachment to control executive abuses. Exemplifies the type of article growing out of Watergate that appeared in such numbers in the mid-1970s.

Wigmore, John H. "Joseph Story on the Impeachment of Public Officials—The Senate's Repudiation of the Constitutional Mode of Impeachment of Executive Officials." 19 *Illinois Law Review* 44-55 (May 1924). Consists mostly of excerpts from Story's commentaries.

Williams, Napoleon B., Jr. "The Historical and Constitutional Bases for the Senate's Power to Use Masters or Committees to Receive Evidence in Impeachment Trials." 50 *New York University Law Review* 512-620 (June 1975). An extended argument for the use of evidentiary committees, to the effect that the House of Lords used such committees and that this knowledge was available to the framers of the American constitution. Following this is an argument, from different principles, in favor of the use of masters to hear evidence. The former is very well argued (and timely in light of recent developments), the latter less so.

Wright, Francis X. "The Trial of Presidential Impeachments: Should the Ghost be Laid to Rest?" 44 *Notre Dame Lawyer* 1089-1103 (1969). Concludes that impeachment is both outmoded and useless for removing a president as well as a dangerous political device subject to partisan abuse; recommends relocating the process (which is judicial) to the Supreme Court, which would exercise it more responsibly. Coming at the end of a long hiatus that saw little impeachment activity, the entire article (in addition to its problem of contradicting the considered opinion of the framers as to the location of the impeachment power) is completely undercut by events since 1973.

Yankwich, Leon. "Impeachment of Civil Officers Under the Federal Constitution." 26 *Georgetown Law Journal* 849-67 (May 1938). A textual analysis of the impeachment provisions which construes the power narrowly, calling for a constitutional amendment to provide for a more efficient process of judicial removal.

E. The Blount Impeachment

Borden, Morton. *The Federalism of James A. Bayard.* New York: Columbia University Press, 1955. Chapter 5 provides a good account that utilizes many of the more accessible sources. Accurate in its assessment of partisan influences. See entry under biographies, *supra.*

Bushnell, Eleanore. *Crimes, Follies, and Misfortunes: The Federal Impeachment Trials. Urbana: University of Illinois Press, 1992.* Chapter 2 consists of a history of the Blount impeachment. Very good for a quick overview of the proceedings, despite one or two erroneous conclusions. See entry under the heading of impeachment in general, *supra.*

Hoffer, Peter C. & Hull, N.E.H. *Impeachment in America, 1635-1805.* New Haven: Yale University Press, 1984. The balance of chapter 8 presents the best summary of the legal aspects of the Blount impeachment heretofore in existence, but it does contain some unwarranted (and unsupported) assertions, such as specific reasons for particular senators' reasons for voting as they did. See entry under United States impeachments, *supra.*

IV. Primary Sources

A. Published

Adams, Abigail. *New Letters of Abigail Adams, 1788-1801.* Edited by Stewart Mitchell. Boston: Houghton Mifflin Company, 1947. In addition to describing the general atmosphere in Philadelphia during the week of Blount's exposure, Abigail Adams also recounts (probably second-hand) the scene in the Senate as the incriminating letter was read.

Adams, John. *The Works of John Adams*. Edited by Charles Francis Adams. 10 vols. Boston: Little, Brown and Company, 1850-56. Has general information on administration activities during the time of the impeachment.

Bayard, James A. *Papers of James A. Bayard*. Edited by Elizabeth Donnan. Washington: The American Historical Association, 1915. Contains a letter from Harper to his constituents describing the conspiracy and Congress's reaction.

Blount, John Gray. *The John Gray Blount Papers*. Edited by Alice B. Keith. 4 vols. Raleigh: State Department of Archives and History, 1952-82. The principal published collection of Blount papers, these volumes consist mainly of the papers of William Blount's brother, also including letters from William Blount on the subject of Tennessee affairs, land speculation and other business dealings, the conspiracy, and the impeachment.

Cappon, Lester J., ed. *The Adams-Jefferson Letters*. 2 vols. Chapel Hill: Published for the Institute of Early American History and Culture at Williamsburg, Virginia by the University of North Carolina Press, 1959. Volume 2 contains an 1812 letter of Adams commenting briefly on the outcome of the conspiracy and impeachment.

The Debates and Interesting Speeches in the Fifth Congress of the U. States at Their First Session: Begun and Held at Philadelphia on the Fifteenth day of May, 1797. Newbergh, New York: David Denniston, 1797. (Evans 32965). Includes accounts of both House and Senate proceedings regarding the impeachment and expulsion; largely a reprint of information to be found in Porcupine's Gazette, *infra*.

Ellicott, Andrew. *The Journal of Andrew Ellicott*. Philadelphia: Budd & Bartram, 1803. Describes reaction on the frontier to news of the conspiracy: also a valuable source of information about conditions in the Mississippi Valley during the late 1700s.

Elliot, Jonathan. *The Debates in the Several State Conventions on the Adoption of the Federal Constitution*. 4 vols. Washington: Printed for the editor, 1836. This group of records (both this edition and the one below) have been the best collective source of ratification debates since their publication; they are in the process of being superseded by the Documentary History, *infra*.

Elliot, Jonathan. *The Debates in the Several State Conventions on the Adoption of the Federal Constitution.* 2d ed. 5 vols. Philadelphia: J.B. Lippincott & Co., 1859. A more complete version of the above work.

Farrand, Max, ed. *The Records of the Federal Convention of 1787.* Revised ed. 4 vols. New Haven: Yale University Press, 1937. The standard source for research on the convention. Incorporates the notes of Madison, Yates, Mason and others. Now supplemented by Hutson, *infra.*

Gallatin, Albert. The Gallatin Papers. New York: New York Historical Society. (Film). Contains a small number of letters from Gallatin to his wife and others describing both the conspiracy and the general temper of Philadelphia in 1797.

Grove, William Barry. "Letters of William Barry Grove." Edited by Henry M. Wagstaff. 9 *James Sprunt Historical Publications* 45-88 (No. 2) 1910. Includes some of the correspondence found in the William Barry Grove Papers at the University of North Carolina (see entry under unpublished primary sources, *infra*).

Hutson, James H., ed. *Supplement to Max Farrand's The Records of the Federal Convention of 1787.* Cambridge: Yale University Press, 1987. Contains some corrections of Farrand regarding the notes on impeachment.

Jefferson, Thomas. *Jefferson's Parliamentary Writings: "Parliamentary Pocket-Book" and A Manual of Parliamentary Practice.* Edited by Wilbur Samuel Howell. Princeton: Princeton University Press, 1988. In addition to the Parliamentary Manual that undoubtedly served as a guide for the Senate during Blount's impeachment, this volume also prints a transcript of the nearly illegible letter from Jefferson to Samuel Livermore of January 29(?) 1798.

_____. *The Papers of Thomas Jefferson.* Washington: Library of Congress. (Film). Reel 34 contains material from the appropriate time period.

_____. *The Writings of Thomas Jefferson.* Memorial edition. Edited by Albert Ellery Bergh. 20 vols. Washington: The Thomas Jefferson Memorial Association, 1903-04. Contains additional letters of Jefferson.

_____. *The Writings of Thomas Jefferson.* Edited by Paul Leicester

Ford. 10 vols. New York: G.P. Putnam's Sons, 1896-99. Volume 7 includes some important material conveying Jefferson's thoughts about substantive and procedural impeachment questions.

Jensen, Merrill, ed. *The Documentary History of the Ratification of the Constitution.* __ Vols. Madison: State Historical Society of Wisconsin, 1976-. An exhaustive (though at times poorly organized) work incorporating ratification convention debates, newspaper accounts, published commentaries, and private correspondence relating to the ratification issue. When completed, it will clearly supercede Elliot.

King, Charles R. *The Life and Correspondence of Rufus King.* 6 vols. New York: G.P. Putnam's Sons, 1894-1900. Volume 2 has several letters from King describing events in England relating to the conspiracy and its discovery.

Madison, James. *The James Madison Papers.* Washington: Library of Congress, 1964. (Film). In addition to a small number of very valuable letters between Madison and Jefferson on various constitutional aspects of the Blount impeachment, this collection also includes several letters to Madison from John Dawson describing the activities of the House investigating committee.

_____. *Letters and Other Writings of James Madison, Fourth President of the United States.* 4 vols. New York: R. Worthington, 1884. Volume 2 reprints some of the letters to be found in the above collection.

Overton, John. *The John Overton Papers.* Chapel Hill, N.C.: University of North Carolina. (Film). Includes a letter from Willie Blount discussing the outcome of the impeachment.

Pickering, Timothy. *The Timothy Pickering Papers.* Boston: The Massachusetts Historical Society, 1966. (Film). Good source of information on the reactions and activities of Pickering, the administration, and the federal government in general regarding the conspiracy, especially in middle and late 1797.

Robertson, James. "Correspondence of Gen. James Robertson." 4 *American Historical Magazine and Tennessee Historical Society Quarterly* 336-81 (October 1899). Letters between Sevier, Robertson, Blount and Cocke regarding the conspiracy. One of a series of articles containing Robertson's correspondence.

Turner, Frederick Jackson. "Documents on the Blount Conspiracy,

1795-97." 10 *American Historical Review* 574-606 (April 1905). Good source for Liston's actions before and during the unveiling of the conspiracy.

Washington, George. *The Writings of George Washington*. Edited by John C. Fitzpatrick. 37 vols. Washington: Government Printing Office, 1931-1941. Includes several letters written during the summer of 1797 describing Washington's reaction to news of the conspiracy.

B. Unpublished

Dartmouth College Library. Letter of William Eaton to John Ripley, November 24 1798. Contains attacks of Eaton upon Ripley on the subject of the latter's testimony before Congress.

_____. Silas Dinsmoor to Levi McKeen, December 24, 1841. Describes the relationship between Blount and Burr.

Duke University Library, Manuscript Department. David Henley Papers. Contains correspondence between Hawkins, Henley, and others regarding the discovery of the conspiracy.

_____. James Iredell Sr. and James Iredell Jr. Papers. Comments of Oliver Wolcott on the impact of the conspiracy are to be found within.

_____. Jared Irwin Papers. Contains letters from Abraham Baldwin relating to the House impeachment committee's investigations.

Historical Society of Pennsylvania. Edward Carey Gardiner Collection. Includes a letter from Blount to Sevier describing Blount's attempted interview with Adams in July 1797.

Library of Congress, Manuscripts Division. Bayard Family Papers. Includes secondary accounts of the impeachment, focusing on Bayard's role therein.

_____. William Blount Papers. A modest collection that includes some information on the impeachment.

_____. Andrew Ellicott Papers. Includes letters between Pickering and Ellicott dealing with frontier issues.

_____. Harry Innes Papers. Includes letters between Innes and Thomas Todd on the Burr trial and on the possibility of Humphrey Marshall's involvement in the Blount Conspiracy.

Massachusetts Historical Society. Theodore Sedgwick Papers. Some items of correspondence in this collection contain Sedgwick's views on the impeachment.

New York Historical Society, Manuscript Room. John Gray Blount and Thomas Blount Letterbook. Fair source of some elements of the Blounts' personal and business lives.

_____. Rufus King Correspondence. Contains correspondence between Sedgwick and King.

New York Public Library, Rare Books and Manuscripts Division. Miscellaneous Papers. Contains some letters written by Blount that reveal his political views circa 1796-97.

_____. Thomas Jefferson Letters. Typescripts of some pertinent letters of Jefferson appearing elsewhere in published form.

University of North Carolina Library, Southern Historical Collection, Chapel Hill. Walter Alves Papers. Contains general political information regarding Congress during the time of the impeachment.

_____. Ernest Haywood Papers. Also general political information— this from North Carolina politicians (including those in Philadelphia).

_____. John Haywood Papers. As above.

_____.William Barry Grove Papers. Contains letters in which Grove describes the conspiracy and his beliefs concerning British involvement. Some of these letters are reprinted in the published collection of Grove's papers; see entry under published primary sources, *supra*.

V. Government Documents

A. Secondary

Butler, Anne M. & Wolff, Wendy. *United States Senate Election, Expulsion, and Censure Cases 1793-1990* Washington: Government Printing Office, 1995. (Serial Set 14216). Contains brief descriptions of such cases, including those of Blount, Humphrey Marshall, and John Smith.

Byrd, Robert C. *The Senate 1789-1989: Historical Statistics 1789-1992*. Washington: Government Printing Office, 1993. (Serial Set 13723-26). Volume 4 contains a list of senators who have faced expulsion charges, together with the nature of those charges and the proceedings' disposition.

Cannon, Clarence. *Cannon's Precedents of the House of Representatives of the United States . . .* 6 vols. Washington: Government Printing Office, 1935-41. A continuation of *Hinds' Precedents, infra*; continues volume numbering, beginning with Volume 6. This volume contains precedents on impeachments occurring after time period covered by *Hinds' Precedents*. Volume 11 includes an index digest of impeachment material found in both works.

"Concerning the Removal of Officers." 30 *Congressional Digest* 40 (February 1951). A superficial, one-page summary of the impeachment power.

Hinds, Asher Crosby. *Hinds' Precedents of the House of Representatives of the United States including References to Provisions of the Constitution, the Laws, and Decisions of the United States Senate.* 5 vols. Washington: Government Printing Office, 1907. A digest of various House precedents. Contains material pertinent to impeachments in general as well as detailed examinations of each particular impeachment through 1907. Continued by Cannon's Precedents, *supra*.

Riddick, Floyd Millard. *Procedure and Guidelines for Impeachment Trials in the United States Senate.* Washington: Government Printing Office, 1986. reprint of a pamphlet that outlines, in historical form, Senate impeachment procedures.

Robison, Norborne T.N. "Trial of Impeachments." 12 *Congressional Digest* 127 (April 1933). One page description of impeachment process that contains some factual errors.

Sumner, Charles. *Expulsion of the President.* Washington: Government Printing Office, 1868. A survey of impeachment obviously written to justify Congress's efforts to remove Johnson. As biased as any work on impeachment.

Swanstrom, Roy. The United States Senate 1787-1801: A Dissertation on the First Fourteen Years of the Upper Legislative Body. Washington: Government Printing Office, 1988. (Serial Set 13846). A reprint of the original work of 1962; a bit uneven in places, but reveals the uncertain relationship of Senate to House and executive during the Federalist period.

U.S. Library of Congress. Congressional Research Service. "Impeachment: An Overview of Constitutional Provisions, Procedure, and Practice" by Elizabeth B. Bazan. Washington: Congressional Research Service, 1988. Addresses the questions of who is impeachable and the definition of impeachable offenses. Essentially a legal memorandum, this article makes heavy use of Hinds' and Cannon's Precedents in an attempt to describe, rather than prescribe, the state of impeachment law.

_____. National Archives and Records Administration. *Guide to the Records of the United States House of Representatives at the National Archives, 1789-1989*. Washington: United States House of Representatives, 1989. Page 353 contains a listing of impeachment investigations conducted by the House (including those not resulting in impeachments).

U.S. Congress. House. Committee on Judiciary. *Constitutional Grounds for Presidential Impeachment*. Washington: Public Affairs Press, 1974. (SuDocs Y4.J89/1:Im7/3). A survey of impeachment—particularly the issue of criminality—that includes all articles of impeachment in preceding federal impeachment episodes.

_____. *Trial of Good Behavior of United States District Judges*. Washington: Government Printing Office, 1937. (SuDocs Y4.J89/1:D63/18). Contains some committee discussion concerning the exclusiveness of the impeachment power.

_____. *Impeachment: Selected Materials*. Washington: Government Printing Office, 1973. (SuDocs Y4.J89/1:Im7/2). Contains debates on various matters of impeachment procedure, articles of impeachment, and some reprints of secondary articles.

_____. *Impeachment: Selected Materials on Procedure*. Washington: Government Printing Office, 1974. (SuDocs Y4.J89/1:Im7/4). Excerpts from Hinds' and Cannon's Precedents on impeachment law. Very handy.

U.S. Congress. House. Committee on Judiciary. Special Subcommittee. *Legal Materials on Impeachment*. Washington: Government Printing Office, 1970. (SuDocs Y4.J89/1:Im7). Contains excerpts from various House proceedings on impeachment.

U.S. Congress. Senate. *Proceedings of the United States Senate in the*

Impeachment Trial of Alcee L. Hastings, a Judge of the United States District Court for the Southern District of Florida. Washington: Government Printing Office, 1989. (SuDocs Y1.1/3:101-18). Contains the record of that portion of Hastings's impeachment proceedings held before the entire Senate, as well as materials relating to *Hastings v. United States Senate* and *Nixon v. United States Senate.*

_____. *Proceedings of the United States Senate in the Impeachment Trial of Harry E. Claiborne, a Judge of the United States District Court for the District of Nevada.* Washington: Government Printing Office, 1987. (SuDocs Y1.1/3:99-48; Serial Set 13670). Contains the record of that portion of Claiborne's impeachment proceedings held before the entire Senate, as well as materials relating to *Claiborne v. United States Senate.*

_____. *Senate Manual.* Washington: Government Printing Office, 1953. (Serial Set 11669). Contains rules of procedure and practice in the senate when sitting on impeachment trials.

U.S. Congress. Senate. Committee on the Judiciary. *Trial of Good Behavior of Certain Federal Judges.* Washington: Government Printing Office, 1941. (SuDocs Y4.J89/2:J89/7). Contains some discussion of the exclusiveness of the impeachment power.

U.S. Congress. Senate. Committee on Rules and Administration. *Impeachment: Miscellaneous Documents.* Washington: Government Printing Office, 1974. (SuDocs Y4.R86/2:Im7). Contains five monographs on issues of procedure, evidence, the effect of adjournment on underway impeachments, and the judicial review question; broad construction of Senate's powers generally prevails throughout.

_____. *Senate Rules and Precedents Applicable to Impeachment Trials.* Washington: Government Printing Office, 1975. (SuDocs Y4.R86/2:Im7/2). Texts of August 1974 Senate debates on questions of modifying existing rules of impeachment procedure.

B. Primary

American State Papers: Miscellaneous. Volume 1 contains information—mostly from the Attorney General's office—on the Turner investigation.

American State Papers: Foreign Relations. In addition to being a very good source of background information on the diplomatic aspects of western activities, Volume 2 also contains several documents relating to the Blount Conspiracy, particularly McHenry's June 1797 report to Adams.

Annals of the Congress of the United States, 1789-1824. 42 vols. Washington, 1834-56. A forerunner of the Congressional Record; the best-known source for the first 35 years of Senate and House minutes. Volumes 7, 8, and 9 together comprise what is by far the most important and copious source both on the conspiracy and the impeachment proceedings. The report of the House committee, along with the journal of the Court of Impeachment (December 1798-January 1799) are to be found at the end of Volume 8. Volume 12 contains some passing references to the Blount affair, and Volumes 5 and 6 have information on the Turner investigation.

National Archives. Journal of Impeachment Proceedings Before the U.S. Senate, 1798-1805. (Film M1253). A rough journal: the account of the proceedings against Blount is the source for the account appearing in *Annals of Congress*, though the latter contains some minor omissions and variations.

_____. Journal of Legislative Proceedings of the U.S. Senate, 1789-1817. (Film). Rough journal; the source for *Annals of Congress*.

U.S. Congress. *Proceedings on the Impeachment of William Blount, a Senator of the United States from the State of Tennessee, for High Crimes and Misdemeanors.* Philadelphia: Joseph Gales, 1799. (OCLC 1170770, 6071795). A summary of impeachment proceedings extracted from the journals of both houses.

U.S. Congress. House. *Deposition of Gen. Elijah Clark, of the State of Georgia, Respecting a Letter . . .* Philadelphia: 1798. (Evans 34786). Interrogatories from the new House impeachment committee to Clark, and his answers.

_____. *Letter from the Chevalier d'Yrujo . . .* Philadelphia: 1798. (Evans 34788). A letter from Yrujo explaining his connections with Ripley.

U.S. Congress. House. Committee on Impeachment of William Blount. *Further Report from the Committee, Appointed on the Eighth of July Last, to Prepare and Report Articles of Impeachment Against William Blount, a Senator of the United*

States, Impeached by the House of Representatives of High Crimes and Misdemeanors. Philadelphia: 1798. (Evans 34793). Additional evidence gathered by the House committee after its main report of November 30, 1797.

_____. *Further Report from the Committee, Appointed on the Eighth of July Last, to Prepare and Report Articles of Impeachment Against William Blount, a Senator of the United States, Impeached by the House of Representatives of High Crimes and Misdemeanors.* Philadelphia: 1798. (Evans 34787; OCLC 11275743). Incorrectly identified in Evans as a "ghost" of the above report (and not actually printed therein), and possessing the same corporate author and title, this report is actually the second supplementary report produced by the house committee, containing two letters—one from Yrujo and one from Ripley.

_____. *Further Report of the Committee, Appointed on the Eighth July Last, to Prepare and Report Articles of Impeachment Against William Blount, a Senator of the United States, Impeached by the House of Representatives of High Crimes and Misdemeanors . . .* Philadelphia: John Fenno, 1798. (Evans 34792). The articles of impeachment.

_____. *Further Report of the Managers Appointed to Conduct the Impeachment Against William Blount.* Philadelphia: 1798. (Evans 34790). Report of the House managers, probably of December 21, 1798, requesting that the House direct them to ask the Senate to compel Blount's attendance before proceeding further with the impeachment.

_____. *Report of the Committee of the House of Representatives of the United States, Appointed to Prepare and Report Articles of Impeachment against William Blount, a Senator of the United States, Impeached of High Crimes and Misdemeanors.* Philadelphia: John Fenno, 1797. (OCLC 4962336). The main report of November 30, 1797.

_____. *Report of the Committee of the House of Representatives of the United States, Appointed to Prepare and Report Articles of Impeachment Against William Blount, a Senator of the United States, Impeached of High Crimes and Misdemeanors.* Philadelphia: John Fenno, 1798. (Evans 34785).The main report of November 30, 1797; a slightly different version from than appearing in Annals of Congress.

U.S. Congress. Senate. *A Bill Regulating Certain Procedures in Cases of Impeachment*. Philadelphia: John Fenno, 1798. (Evans 48698). Heavily debated on the floor during early 1798, and never passed, this bill (submitted by Humphrey Marshall) seeks to regulate such matters as oaths and attendance of witnesses.

_____. *Journal of the Senate of the United States of America: Being the First Session of the Sixth Congress: Begun and Held at the City of Philadelphia, December 2, 1799, and in the Twenty-Fourth Year of the Independence of the Said States*. 5 vols. Washington: Gales and Seaton, 1821. (SuDocs Z3.4:3). Volume 3 contains an account of the Blount, Pickering, and Chase impeachments taken from the Senate Journals as found in the National Archives, *supra*.

_____. *Report of the Committee Appointed to Report the Proper Measures . . . William Blount . . .* (Philadelphia: W. Ross, 1798) (Evans 48714). The report of February 22, 1798, recommending an adversarial process for discussing Read's resolution on the amenability of senators to impeachment.

_____. *Resolved, that the Duty or Trust Imposed by the Constitution . . .* Philadelphia: John Fenno, 1798. (Evans 48715). Read's resolution of February 14, 1798 regarding the amenability of senators to the impeachment process.

U.S. Congress. Senate. Committee on Impeachment of William Blount. *Report, in Part, of the Committee, Appointed on the 18th Instant, to Consider What Rules are Necessary to be Adopted by the Senate in the Trial of William Blount*. Philadelphia: Way and Groff, 1798. (Evans 34789). Sets forth Senate procedures as to pleading, examination of witnesses, and the like.

U.S. Congress. Senate. Committee to Whom was Referred the Bill Regulating Certain Proceedings in Cases of Impeachment. *Report of Amendments*. Philadelphia: John Fenno, 1798[?]. (Evans 48660). Amendments to Evans 48698, *supra*, reported February 1 by the Marshall committee. See 7 *Annals of Congress* 491, 494-96, 506 (1798).

VI. Newspapers

The Aurora. Philadelphia: Benjamin Franklin Bache. Continued by his widow after Bache's death, the Aurora was a Republican organ. In addition to anti-Federalist invective during July 1797, contains singular (and sometimes misdated) accounts of Senate debates during early 1798.

The Boston Gazette. Boston: Benjamin Edes. Contains editorial information on the expulsion and regular court proceedings.

Claypoole's American Daily Advertiser. Philadelphia: David and Septimus Claypoole. Contains good accounts of Senate proceedings, although contemporary readers alleged inaccuracies to exist therein. Reporting seems factual; any bias is well hidden.

The Connecticut Courant. Hartford: Hudson and Goodwin. Editorials and letters discuss questions of bail, trial in *absentia*, and regular court proceedings.

Gazette of the United States. Philadelphia: John Fenno. A Federalist paper containing good accounts of the events of July and August of 1797. Also has alternate accounts of some debates that took place in December 1798.

The Independent Chronicle. Boston: Adams and Larkin. A Republican paper; in addition to anti-Federalist editorials, this publication contains accounts of Senate proceedings in July 1797, December 1798 and January 1799.

The Maryland Gazette. Annapolis: Frederick and Samuel Green. Contains some information on the criminal proceedings against Blount relating to the conspiracy.

The Massachusetts Mercury. Boston: Young and Minns. A Federalist paper that contains good coverage of the expulsion proceedings.

The Newbern Gazette. New Bern, North Carolina: John C. Osborne and Co. Contains mainly reprints from other papers; reveals interest of North Carolinians in the activities of one of their better-known citizens.

The Newport Mercury. Newport, Rhode Island: Henry Barber. Contains some coverage of the oral arguments of January 1799.

North-Carolina Gazette. New Bern, North Carolina: Francois X. Martin. Coverage similar to the Newbern Gazette.

The Philadelphia Gazette. Philadelphia: Andrew Brown. A fairly balanced publication. Has extensive coverage of the events of July 1797; also has alternate accounts of some December 1798 House debates and some coverage of the January 1799 oral arguments.

Porcupine's Gazette. Philadelphia: William Cobbett. A Federalist party organ, source of some of the most scathing political comments to be found among Philadelphia printers.

The Universal Gazette. Philadelphia: Samuel Harrison Smith. Contains accounts of Senate debates in February 1798 on the subject of the use of juries in impeachment trials; some of these accounts also appear in the *Aurora.*

Index

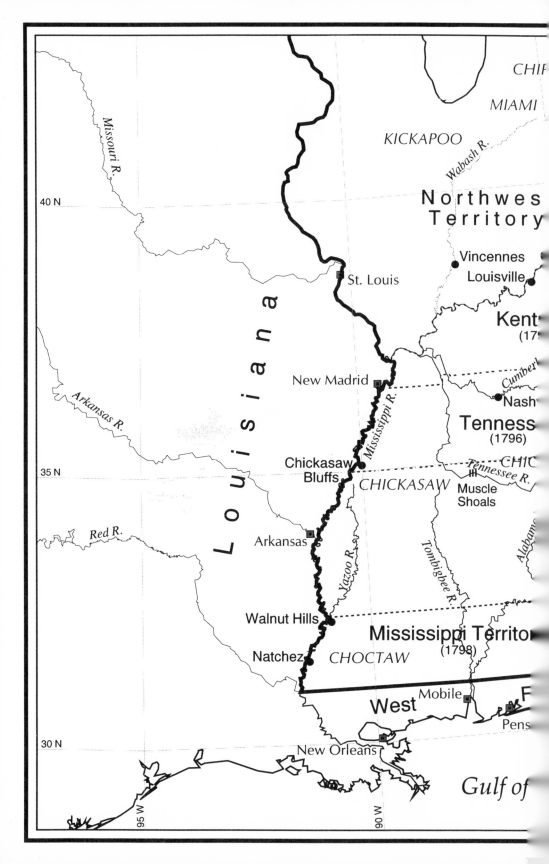